Ki te Whaiao

An Introduction to Māori Culture and Society

Tānia M. Kaʻai
John C. Moorfield
Michael P. J. Reilly
Sharon Mosley (Editors)

PEARSON
Longman

Hei whakamaumaharatanga tēnei pukapuka ki ngā tīpuna, ki ngā tauira me ngā tohunga o te mātauranga nāna nei te huarahi i para mā mātou e whai atu.

www.pearsoned.co.nz

Your comments on this book are welcome at
feedback@pearsoned.co.nz

Pearson Education New Zealand
a division of Pearson New Zealand Ltd
67 Apollo Drive, Rosedale, North Shore 0632, New Zealand

Associated companies throughout the world

© Pearson Education New Zealand 2004
First published 2004
Reprinted 2004, 2005, 2007 (twice)

ISBN 978-0-582-54572-4

All rights reserved. No part of this publication may be reproduced, stored in a retrieval system, or transmitted, in any form or by any means, electronic, mechanical, photocopying, recording, or otherwise, without the prior permission of the publisher.

Produced by Pearson Education New Zealand
Printed in Malaysia, LSP
Typeset in Palatino 10.5/12

We use **paper from sustainable forestry**

Te rārangi ūpoko
Contents

He wāhinga kōrero – Foreword	v
He mihi – Acknowledgements	vi
He kupu whakataki – Preface	vii
He tīmatanga kōrero – Introduction	ix
Ngā iwi o Te Ika-a-Māui – North Island iwi	xii
Ngā iwi o Te Wai Pounamu – South Island iwi	xiii

Te Ao Māori – The Māori World   PART ONE

1. **Te tīmatanga mai o ngā atua** – Creation narratives — 1
   Michael P. J. Reilly

2. **Te ao Māori** – Māori world-view — 13
   Tānia M. Ka'ai and Rawinia Higgins

3. **Ngā hekenga waka** – Canoe migrations — 26
   Jim Williams

4. **Te reo Māori** – Origins and development of the Māori language — 30
   John C. Moorfield and F. Lorraine Johnston

5. **Papa-tūā-nuku** – Attitudes to land — 50
   Jim Williams

6. **Whanaungatanga** – Kinship — 61
   Michael P. J. Reilly

7. **Ngā tikanga o te marae** – Marae practices — 73
   Rawinia Higgins and John C. Moorfield

8. **Tangihanga** – Death customs — 85
   Rawinia Higgins and John C. Moorfield

9. **Rangatiratanga** – Traditional and contemporary leadership — 91
   Tānia M. Ka'ai and Michael P. J. Reilly

10. **Ngā mahi a Tāne-rore me Te Rēhia** – Performing arts — 103
    Nathan W. Matthews and Karyn Paringatai

11. **Ngā mahi toi** – The arts — 116
    Pakaariki Harrison, Kahu Te Kanawa, and Rawinia Higgins

12. **Ngā tuhituhinga reo Māori** – Literature in Māori — 133
    Jane McRae

Ngā Ao e Rua – The Two Worlds

PART TWO

13	**Te tūtakitanga o ngā ao e rua** – Early contacts between two worlds *Erik Olssen and Michael P. J. Reilly*	140
14	**Te Tiriti o Waitangi** – The Treaty of Waitangi *Janine Hayward*	151
15	**Mana Māori motuhake** – Challenges to 'kāwanatanga' 1840-1940 *Lachy Paterson*	163
16	**Ngā poropiti me ngā Hāhi** – Prophets and the churches *John Stenhouse and Lachy Paterson*	171
17	**Te mana o te tangata whenua** – Indigenous assertions of sovereignty *Tānia M. Ka'ai*	181
18	**Te tāminga o te mātauranga Māori** – Colonisation in education *Brendan Hokowhitu*	190
19	**Te mana o te reo me ngā tikanga** – Power and politics of the language *Tānia M. Ka'ai*	201
20	**Ngā tuhituhinga reo Pākehā** – Literature in English *Chris Prentice*	214
21	**Ngā hekenga hou** – Pacific peoples in Aotearoa/New Zealand *Michelle Saisoa'a*	227

He papakupu – Glossary   238
Te rārangi kaituhi – List of contributors   241
Te rārangi pukapuka – Bibliography   244
Ngā kuputohu – Index   253

He wāhinga kōrero
Foreword

Kua ngaro te hunga i mahi, i rongo, i kite i te hōhonutanga o ngā kaupapa e rārangi ake nei i roto i ēnei tuhinga. He mānga kai ngā kōrero nei e toko ake ai pea te hiahia i te kaipānui ki te whai atu i ngā whānuitanga o ngā whakaaro kua rārangitia ki roto i tēnei māra kupu. He whāngai anō hoki i te hinengaro i te ngākau tangata ki ōna kai e pātaritaritia ai ki ngā taonga o te ao Māori.

Otiia, e whakatakoto tūtohu ana ēnei kōrero e taea ai e te tangata te whai atu i ngā hīnātore e mārama ake ai ngā tikanga me ngā āhuatanga o te taru nei o te Māori.

Ahakoa kua takoto kē anō he kōrero pēnei, kātahi anō ka whakahuihuitia kia noho ki te wāhi kotahi e māmā ai ki ngā momo tāngata o tēnā o tēnā ngakinga ki te pānui. Kua rerekē anō te ao e noho nei te Māori nā reira he tirohanga anō a ēnei kōrero hei whakaohooho whakaaro hei ārahi anō i te hunga mā rātau e pānui.

He kete kōrero tēnei pukapuka e nanaohia mai ai ngā whakaaro o roto hei rūnanga kia turakina atu ngā parepare o te kore e mārama, kia tipu ai ko ngā whakaaro kōaro kore.

Ka mihi ki te hunga nā rātau i whakamātau te pae tawhiti kia tata, i whakamaua ai te pae tata kia tina.

'He taonga tuku mai nō tawhiti'

There is a considerable need for a comprehensive volume of this kind for anyone setting out on a serious exploration of the Māori world, its mind-frame, its customs, its history and the circumstances in which it finds itself. While the obvious demand is from tertiary-level students, this text will be valued through all levels of our society. The primary need is for access roads into the network of Māori culture. This book will, at the very least, offer directions to the highways.

It is a huge challenge to present a comprehensive introduction to any culture, to cover its past, its dynamic present and its sense of its own direction. *Ki te Whaiao* confronts this challenge with a rich collection of introductions – a whole series of starting points. These chapters do not attempt to be definitive and necessarily include generalisation. But, taken as a whole they combine to produce a considerable achievement – a broadly based map of a dynamically evolving Māori world.

J. Wharehuia Milroy
Sir Tipene K. t. O'Regan

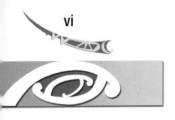

He mihi
Acknowledgements

The editors wish to thank all those who helped in the production of this book, including the following:

- The staff of Te Tumu, the School of Māori, Pacific & Indigenous Studies, University of Otago for their enthusiastic support of this book;
- Pakaariki Harrison, Kahu Te Kanawa, Jane McRae, Erik Olssen, Janine Hayward, Lachy Paterson, John Stenhouse, and Chris Prentice who responded so readily to our requests to write sections and chapters;
- The administration staff of Te Tumu and families of staff for their support and help;
- Professor Alistair Fox, Assistant Vice-Chancellor of the Division of Humanities, University of Otago, for his continuing support and for providing funding for a research assistant to help produce this book; and
- The Stout Research Centre, Victoria University of Wellington for hosting Rawinia Higgins on her RSL to write her chapters.

The authors and publisher would like to thank all those individuals and institutions who supplied images or photographs for use in this book. The source of the photographs has been acknowledged alongside or below each one. Photographs supplied by the Alexander Turnbull Library, Wellington, New Zealand are acknowledged by a file reference and the initials 'ATL'.

Maps by Jonette Surridge; illustrations by Pauline Wimp. Cover photos by Mark Strange (*korowai* woven by Elenora Puketapu-Hetet), Alan Dove (people) and Rawinia Higgins. We would also like to thank the Ngāti Rongo Marae committee for permission to use the image of their meeting house, Rongokārae.

A note on the cover photos
The meeting house is Rongokārae at Ruātoki. It is named after a Ngāti Rongo ancestor and symbolises the inheritance bequeathed by the ancestors. It also represents the importance the *marae* has always played in Māori culture and society. The two people are Rachael Ka'ai-Oldman and Dean Mahuta. These two senior students at Te Tumu, the School of Māori, Pacific & Indigenous Studies at the University of Otago, were chosen because they are examples of the success of Māori-medium education. Together they represent *iwi* of both the North and South Islands. Rachael is from Te Whānau-a-Ruataupare of Ngāti Porou and the Ngāti Wheke *hapū* of Ngāi Tahu, while Dean is from Ngāti Mahuta of the Tainui tribes. His playing of the *pūtātara* and Rachael's traditional costume used for the performing arts symbolise the renaissance of not only Māori music and traditional instruments, but of the whole language and culture. Both Rachael's cloak and the one on the back cover represent a continuous, yet creative art using natural and indigenous materials. Dean wears modern clothing while playing a traditional instrument to represent the relevance of Māori cultural practices in the modern world. Together Rachael, Dean and the meeting house symbolise the link between traditional and modern Māori society and the somewhat arbitrary division of this book into its two parts.

He kupu whakataki
Preface

Most Māori Studies departments in universities and other tertiary institutions in Aotearoa/New Zealand offer introductory courses in Māori culture and society. However, there is no one textbook that can be used for such studies. Often pertinent extracts from a number of sources are collected together by the teachers of these courses to provide suitable background readings. This book has been written in an attempt to fill that gap with a single text, introducing students to Māori society from creation to the twenty-first century.

Ki te Whaiao: An Introduction to Māori Culture and Society is also aimed at several other audiences of readers, including Māori who want to know about their own world, as well as Pākehā and visitors to this country who may wish to know more about the Indigenous people of Aotearoa/New Zealand.

The eighteen authors for the chapters of the book are mainly academic staff of Te Tumu, the School of Māori, Pacific and Indigenous Studies of the University of Otago, but experts from other departments in the Division of Humanities of the University (notably English, History, and Political Studies) and the University of Auckland, have also contributed chapters. Pakaariki Harrison and Kahu Te Kanawa, acknowledged experts in carving and weaving, have made a valuable contribution to the chapter on arts. The authors not only come from a diverse range of intellectual backgrounds, but also include Māori, Pacific and Pākehā scholars, as well as emerging and established scholars in their fields. For some of the authors this is their first published work, for others it distils decades of personal research. The unity we have sought from this diversity of authors gives expression to the bicultural/multicultural vision of Te Tumu, where Māori, Pākehā and Pacific scholars teach and research topics, notably the language and culture of Māori, as well as those of other Pacific peoples, in order to advance an Indigenous understanding of the world and the place of all peoples within it.

The orthographic conventions used in this book follow those advocated by Te Taura Whiri i te Reo Māori, The Māori Language Commission. In general, spellings of Māori words follow those of Williams' *Dictionary of the Maori Language*. As advocated by Te Taura Whiri i te Reo Māori, compound place names and proper names are linked by hyphens with the first letter of the name being capitalised. If there is an initial 'Te', it is capitalised separately. The other parts of the name are lower case, except those parts which are themselves proper names, e.g. Te Ika-a-Māui. Long vowels are marked by the macron, including in proper names and place names, although not in quotations unless these were marked in the original. Vowel lengths of Māori personal names have been marked. The five volumes of *Ngā Taumata Rau* have been used for guidance in determining these.

Where dialectal variations occur, such as *kūmera* and *kūmara*, the most commonly used form is preferred. Some names have several forms. For example, variations of the Māori names for the South Island include: Te Wai Pounamu, Te Waipounamu, Te

Wāhi Pounamu, Te Wāi Pounamu, Te Waka o Māui and Te Waka-o-Aoraki. In such cases the versions used in the *New Zealand Historical Atlas* and the maps produced by Ngā Pou Taunaha o Aotearoa, the New Zealand Geographic Board, *Te Ika a Māui* and *Te Wai Pounamu* are used for guidance. As with the five volumes of *Ngā Taumata Rau*, these authoritative works have had important input from Māori scholars. Furthermore, the editors have made the decision to use Aotearoa/New Zealand when referring to the country as a whole, which not only reflects the bilingual approach used throughout *Ki te Whaiao* but also differentiates Aotearoa as a traditional term used by Māori for the North Island only.

While there is a trend in English-language publications in New Zealand, especially in non-academic writing, not to use italic type for words and expressions from Māori and Pacific Island languages, we have chosen to print Māori in italics throughout the book. This convention helps with the clarity of writing and avoids any confusion when words with the same form in Māori and English are used (e.g. *rite* and 'rite', *pine* and 'pine'). It also helps reduce ambiguity with words that have been adopted from Māori into English with a changed or restricted meaning. If such words are used with italic type it ensures that the reader knows that it is the Māori language meaning that is being used. Translations of these are given when they first appear in the book. The glossary at the back of the book includes all of these words that appear more than once.

Some chapters use a significant number of Māori terms. Many of these are words that Māori would use when they are speaking English. Very often these are terms that are difficult to translate into one word in English, e.g. *atua*. They are also words that students would be expected to know by the end of an introductory course on Māori culture and society.

In Māori, the form of a word is not normally altered to show number, tense, etc. These elements of meaning are carried by separate words. It is now generally accepted that this rule holds for Māori words that appear in English text, e.g. Māori rather than Māoris; *atua* rather than 'atuas'. This convention has also been followed in this book, except where they appear in quotations.

Regional variations form an important part of *te reo Māori*, for example, in the south *ng* often becomes *k*. One important example of this in the present work is illustrated in the use of Ngāi Tahu and Kai Tahu to describe one of the principal *iwi* of Te Wai Pounamu. A further example occurs in the interchangeable usage of Rangi and Raki (for the Sky Father), depending on which *iwi* the oral narrative originates from.

Obviously, a book with such a broad subject area cannot treat separate topics in any depth. At the end of each chapter, the reader is directed to further reading. Not only will these be useful resources should the reader be stimulated to find out more about particular topics, but these books and articles will also be useful references for essay writing.

He tīmatanga kōrero
Introduction

This book describes traditional and contemporary Māori society and its interaction with Pākehā society since first contact. It gives expression to the voices and words of Māori scholars, or to those works informed by their world-view. Emphasis has been placed on the clarification of Māori cultural concepts throughout the work in order to give readers a deeper understanding and to stimulate their interest in the key themes developed by the authors. Some chapters highlight important cultural practices intrinsic to Māori society, and aim to provide a broad knowledge base for the reader. Other chapters are written as comprehensive introductions to particular topics which we consider important dimensions of Māori society either in the past or at present. Some chapters adopt different points of view based on their authors' respective interpretations of historical and contemporary events (e.g. Chapters 15 and 17 on sovereignty).

The book has been arranged in two parts. The first, called *Te Ao Māori* (The Māori World), examines a series of selected topics concerning Māori society from inception to the present day. The first two chapters establish basic themes and concepts of traditional and contemporary Māori society. Chapter 1 narrates some tribal histories about the creation, including Io, the division of Rangi and Papa-tūā-nuku, the first creation of human beings, and concludes with a discussion of important myth-messages. Chapter 2 defines important Māori cultural concepts, such as *whakapapa*, *mana*, and *tapu*, before locating these ideas within a contemporary discussion of Western and Indigenous understandings of the world.

Chapters 3 to 5 place Māori society within the ancestral cultures of the wider Pacific. Chapter 3 describes the migration of the first canoes from the Pacific and their early settlement in Aotearoa/New Zealand. It also addresses common misunderstandings, such as the 'Great Fleet', deliberate or accidental voyaging, the two-wave theory, and the identity of the Moriori. Chapter 4 recounts the Oceanic origins of Māori within the Austronesian language family, its colonial encounters with the English language – including its early orthography – and the subsequent developments of bilingualism as well as the shift to English amongst many speakers of Māori. It ends positively by describing the Māori language today, and the increasing trend toward a bilingual ability in both English and Māori, which New Zealanders generally need to support by affirming the value of Māori as a language for today's society. Chapter 5 discusses Māori attitudes to land and their management of it, beginning with their Polynesian forebears and finishing with the Ture Whenua Māori (Māori Land Law) Act passed in 1993.

Chapters 6 to 9 focus on important features of Māori society and its cultural practices. Chapter 6 analyses the nature of Māori social structure in traditional and contemporary times, as well as associated community values that define the dynamics of Māori society and its kin-based groups. Chapter 7 establishes the form of the modern Māori

marae, and describes the typical order of the well-known *pōhiri/pōwhiri* or ritual of encounter. Chapter 8 concentrates on death rites, notably the *tangihanga*, which is the most important contemporary expression of Māori beliefs and practices. Chapter 9 is concerned with leadership, in both its traditional and contemporary settings, based on Māori understandings of what this role entailed, as well as selected case studies of Maniapoto and his brothers, and the modern educationalist, Kumeroa Ngoingoi Pēwhairangi.

The final three chapters in *Te Ao Māori* turn to the arts. Chapter 10 describes the various performing arts, including categories of song, *haka* and musical instruments. Chapter 11 describes some traditional Māori art forms – carving, weaving and *moko*. Chapter 12 retells the recording of oral literature in writing since the nineteenth century by Māori scholars, a process that continues today.

The second part of this book, *Ngā Ao e Rua* (The Two Worlds), addresses the relationships that have developed between Māori society and Pākehā society in Aotearoa/New Zealand since the early decades of the nineteenth century. Chapter 13 details the years of early contact between diverse groups of Pākehā – such as sealers and whalers – and their Māori hosts, especially in the far north of the North Island and in the southern parts of the South Island. The changing nature of Māori society is described, with attention paid to emerging tribes, such as Ngā Puhi, and their leaders, such as Hongi Hika. Chapter 14 acknowledges the importance of *Te Tiriti o Waitangi*, the Treaty of Waitangi, both for colonial New Zealand society, and Aotearoa/New Zealand today.

The subsequent three chapters develop the themes of the Treaty of Waitangi, notably the varying understandings of that potent European concept of sovereignty, expressed through the Treaty words, *kāwanatanga* and *tino rangatiratanga*. Chapter 15 elaborates on the series of challenges, both violent and non-violent, undertaken by Māori against the Crown's understanding of what *kāwanatanga* allowed it to do. Important challenges came from the Kīngitanga (King Movement); the Taranaki prophets, Te Whiti and Tohu; nineteenth century parliamentary movements; the prophet, Rua Kenana; and the religious leader, Wiremu Rātana. Chapter 16 examines the protest tradition of the prophets and their religions, especially of the Pai Mārire faith, and the Ringatū Church. It ends with a brief consideration of Māori within the mainstream Christian Churches. Chapter 17 presents another view of Māori assertions of *tino rangatiratanga* in defiance of the New Zealand State, especially since World War II. Most of these actions have included some form of non-violent or symbolical protest, sometimes met with force by the Government of the day, which like many Pākehā New Zealanders, resisted any changes to its essentially monocultural vision of modern society. The chapter stresses the vitality and optimism of contemporary Māori society, especially manifested through various forms of cultural renaissance.

The next two chapters explore issues surrounding colonisation, education, and the status of the Māori language. Chapter 18 argues that the constraints of the colonial educational system limited the potential of all Māori children, regarding them as fit only for physical or manual subjects, and thereby consigning them to a working class status in New Zealand society. Despite the apparent changes since the 1970s, efforts to develop a genuinely bicultural educational system for Māori, or to give children's parents a greater role in the management of schools, have ended in tokenistic achievements, which still assume an assimilationist philosophy. Chapter 19 traces the decline of Māori as a medium of communication, and the growth of a truly Māori educational system which teaches the language within a school environment founded on Māori cultural principles. These are examined in some detail. In effect, this is the Māori-initiated counter to the colonialist educational processes criticised in the previous chapter.

The next chapter reflects upon the ways Māori write of themselves. Chapter 20 presents the growing body of writing in English by Māori writers since the 1940s. Across various literary forms, these works frequently weave into their poems and stories important cultural values and depictions of Māori life, while also addressing fundamental human concerns.

The final chapter returns this introduction to Māori society back to its point of beginning, by describing the new migration of Pacific peoples to Aotearoa/New Zealand since World War II, and the ways they have sustained and transformed their societies within the country of their adoption without losing their sense of identity. Like contemporary Māori they have had to sustain their different cultures and languages within a society historically unused to such diversity. Through their churches, schools, media and sporting groups, Pacific peoples continue to assert their distinctive identity in a new land while recognising the *tangata whenua* as the Indigenous people of Aotearoa/New Zealand.

Ngā iwi o Te Ika-a-Māui – North Island iwi

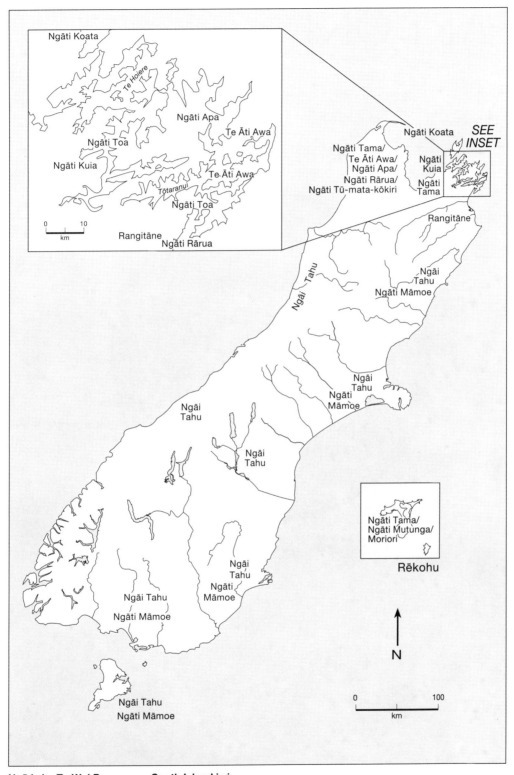

Ngā iwi o Te Wai Pounamu – South Island iwi

PART ONE

Te Ao Māori – The Māori World

Chapter 1

Te tīmatanga mai o ngā atua
Creation narratives

Michael P. J. Reilly

In all human societies mythological narratives about the creation of the world help explain who we are and how we live our lives. For Māori, creation myths form an important part of their world-view, conveying 'myth-messages' that people practise as ideals and norms in their own lives (Walker, 1992). Given the large body of mythological material which has been collected since the nineteenth century, this chapter selects three groups of creation myths that describe important moments in the Māori genesis, and explores some of the mythological messages conveyed to subsequent generations. The first group of myths concerns the supreme being, Io, who initiates the creative process according to certain Māori *iwi* (people/s). The second group, arguably the best known of the three, describes the creation of the world as a consequence of the separation of Rangi and Papa-tūā-nuku. The final group relates the creation of the first human beings by the *atua*.[1] Following the retelling of these myths, the chapter concludes by discussing some of the important messages they convey to subsequent generations. Where possible, the chapter will foreground the original Māori language sources (with translations) so that the ancestral voices are heard at first hand.

 Io

Io, the supreme *atua*, is controversial. A respectable body of scholarship argues that information about this 'god' has been at least influenced by the introduction of Christianity during the first half of the nineteenth century. However, narratives about Io draw deeply from a Māori world-view, complete with *karakia*,[2] suggesting that this being was an *atua* for at least some *iwi* and *hapū* (clan/s) before contact with Europeans introduced new ideas (Shirres, 1997; Schrempp, 1992). The following discussion of Io derives from two tribal traditions, the Ngā Puhi of Northland and Ngāti Kahungunu of Hawke's Bay/Wairarapa, as recorded by the Ngā Puhi *tohunga* (priest, skilled person) and Anglican priest, Māori Marsden, and by the Ngāti Kahungunu scholar, Hoani Te Whatahoro.

According to Marsden (1992), Io existed at the beginning, as 'the foundation of all things' (Io-taketake), in Te Korekore, 'the realm of potential being'. The supreme status of Io was repeatedly emphasised by Whatahoro (1913: 14, 16):

> *Ko Io he ingoa poto tera nona; ko Io-nui, koia te atua nui o nga atua katoa.*
>
> *(Io is the shortened name; Io-the-almighty is the supreme atua of all the other atua.)*

1 Te tīmatanga mai o ngā atua

> *Ko Io-te-wānanga o nga rangi ia, te putake o nga mea katoa; nana te wairua o nga mea katoa, nana te ora o nga mea katoa.*
>
> (Io-the-all-wise of the heavens is the origin of all things; it is the spirit of every thing, it is the life of every thing).

For Marsden, Io encompassed both active (Io-mata-kākā) and passive elements (Io-mata-ane) within the one self. Whatahoro (1913: 17) amplified the totality of Io's being:

> *Kua whaiti nga mea ora, nga mea mate, ki te aroaro o Io-mata-ngaro; kaore he putanga ketanga. Ka whaiti nga atuatanga katoa ki a ia anake te wahi mo ratou, nga atua o te hunga mate, nga atua o te hunga ora.*
>
> (The living and the dead things are gathered together in the presence of Io-the-hidden; there is nothing outside or beyond. All the aspects of atua come together in the place of [Io] alone, the atua of the dead, and the atua of the living.)

According to Marsden, out of the conjunction of active and passive elements, Io initiated creation through a process of genealogical recitation or naming. During a period of 27 nights Io first created a framework of Te Korekore (the void), Te Kōwhao (the abyss), and Te Pō (the night). Then Io caused the state of being to come into existence, first as a seed in Te Kore and Te Kōwhao, and then as a steadily growing plant, which expanded and developed in what Michael Shirres (1997: 115), in his commentary on Marsden's writing, described as 'an insensate movement towards being and self-realization.' This growth was driven by the *mauri* (life principle) which Io had placed in the first seed, and led to the emergence of Te Hihiri (elemental and pure energy).

From this state of pure energy, Io initiated further growth, initially at Te Mahara (the subconscious level), then leading on towards Te Whakaaro (consciousness), Te Wānanga (knowledge and wisdom) and Te Whē (the seed word). Io then breathed Te Hauora (life) into the creation process, producing Atamai (shape) and Āhua (form), then Te Wā (time), and Te Ātea (space). These processes produced the 'material natural world of sense perception' (Shirres, 1997: 116), thereby permitting the emergence of Rangi (the sky) and Papa-tūā-nuku (the earth), and eventually, Te Ao Wairua (the world of spiritual beings). With the emergence of Rangi and Papa, Io then delegated the further process of creation to them and their offspring.

Whatahoro does not describe a genealogical coming into being of the universe, but he does suggest Io's central role in creating everything in the world. For example, he wrote (Whatahoro, 1913: 14, 17, 107):

> *Ko nga mea tenei i tauherea e Io-mata-ngaro ki a ia anake; ko te wairua, ko te ora, ko te ahua o nga mea katoa, na enei e toru nga mea katoa i whai ahua ai, i tona ahua i tona ahua.*
>
> (These are the things that Io-the-hidden retained to [itself]; the spirit and the life and the form; it is by these that all things have form according to their kind.)

Na, nga mea katoa i whakaahuatia e te atua o nga ao, o nga rangi, o nga kapua, o nga Kauwhanga, o nga wai, he mahi katoa ta ratou.

(Now, all things were given form by the atua: the worlds, the heavens, the clouds, the open spaces, the waters, they all had a purpose.)

Creation genealogy

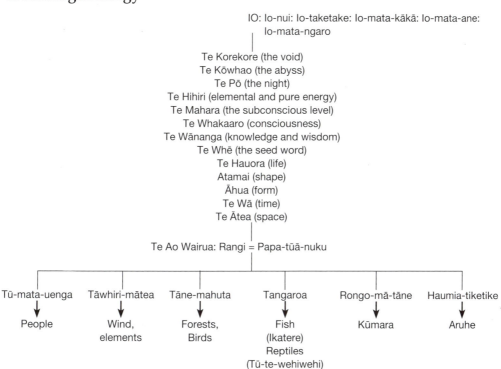

Source: Adapted from Marsden, 1992; and Te Rangikāheke

 ## Rangi and Papa-tūā-nuku

The Ngā Puhi and Ngāti Kahungunu traditions describe a world brought into being out of nothingness by the powers of Io. Having created Rangi and Papa, Io is removed from an active creative role, which is taken over by these primal parents and their offspring. Two tribal traditions about this first family of *atua* were written in 1849 by *tohunga*, Te Rangikāheke of Te Arawa in the Rotorua region, and Matiaha Tiramōrehu of Ngāi Tahu in the South Island. Te Rangikāheke's story focuses on the separation of Rangi and Papa by their offspring (Grey, 1853, 1956, 1971). This is the moment when the physical world starts to take on its present form.

According to Te Rangikāheke, in the beginning Rangi and Papa clung to each other so that their children lived within darkness. Dissatisfied, the children decided to separate their parents. One child, Tū-mata-uenga, wanted to kill them, but Tāne-mahuta, his brother, sought only to separate them, so that one would be beneath them as a parent and the other above them as a stranger.[3] All Tāne's brothers tried to separate their parents, but failed. Finally, Tāne successfully pushed them apart.

One of his brothers, Tāwhiri-mātea, did not agree with this course of action out of his great love for his parents. In association with his father, Rangi, he decided to make war against his brothers. Tāwhiri and his offspring, the elements, attacked Tāne and destroyed his forests. Next Tāwhiri assailed Tangaroa and his descendants. Two of these, Ika-tere, 'father of fish', and his brother, Tū-te-wehiwehi, 'father of reptiles', decided to part, one going to the sea, and the other inland, warning each other of their likely fates, as cooked food. Papa-tūā-nuku took and hid two of her sons, Rongo-mā-tāne and Haumia-tiketike.

Tāwhiri now attacked Tū-mata-uenga. Tū was the only one of the brothers who stood and fought Tāwhiri and Rangi until they were calmed. Tū-mata-uenga now decided to kill his brothers for their failure of strength in stopping Tāwhiri's quest for compensation. Tū-mata-uenga first attacked Tāne, fearing that the latter's numerous progeny might cause him harm; he fashioned traps and caught them. Next, he found Tangaroa's descendants, made nets from flax, and caught them. Then he located the hair of Rongo and Haumia, dug his brothers up, and let them dry in the sun.

The separation of Rangi and Papa – drawing by Russell Clarke

Source: Grey, 1956

At this point in some of his narratives, Te Rangikāheke explained that Tāne-mahuta was the trees and birds; Tangaroa, the fish; Rongo-mā-tāne, the *kūmara*; Haumia-tiketike, the *aruhe*[4], or fernroot; Tāwhiri, the wind; and Tū-mata-uenga, people. Te Rangikāheke added that Tū-mata-uenga ate his *tuākana* (elder brothers) as *utu* (compensation) for leaving him to fight Tāwhiri alone. They became his *tēina* (younger brothers), and fell under his authority. Only Tū's adversary, Tāwhiri, was beyond the former's power. He remained an opponent, his anger equal to that of Tū, his *teina*. Tū-mata-uenga's authority over his fallen *tuākana* was further marked by his series of different personal names, each marking some attribute he had shown in fighting his brothers. He also acquired authority over his kin by using *karakia*. There were distinct *karakia* for each of his defeated *tuākana*, as well as ones for Tāwhiri and Papa-tūā-nuku.

Te Rangikāheke's narratives conclude by describing how the light greatly increased after the separation, as did the generations of people who had been hidden until then, including Tū-mata-uenga and his brothers. Some of his accounts provide lists of ancestors, descended from Tū, who begin to settle the world, down to important semi-divine ancestors such as Tāwhaki, Māui-tikitiki-o-Taranga, and Uenuku. Finally, as a consequence of Tāwhiri's wrath against his brothers, large parts of their mother, Papa-tūā-nuku, disappeared into the sea. The increasing numbers of

Tū-mata-uenga's descendants (down to the Māui brothers) had to subsist on the remaining dry portion.

Like many *tohunga*, Te Rangikāheke left much of the interpretation of the narrative up to the reader. Some of the myth-messages will be discussed in the conclusion of this chapter. However, the link Te Rangikāheke himself made between the restive brothers and aspects of the physical world highlights the key point of the myth. Beginning as an act of the *atua*, the separation initiates a process of differentiation whereby the parents, their various sons, and their descendants, become associated with aspects of the natural world of the Māori. Rangi, so distant that he becomes a stranger, is the sky. Papa is the earth, still nurturing and protecting her young. Tū-mata-uenga, the violent one, is the *atua* of warlike human beings who exploit the world around them. Tāne, the peaceful and creative being, is *atua* of the forests cut down by men, and of the birdlife caught by human hunters. Tangaroa is the *atua* of the oceans, and of sea creatures (some of whom left that domain to find refuge on land). These too are caught (on land and at sea) and consumed by human beings. Tāwhiri, the *atua* of the weather, is, like Tū, filled with violent motions that only humanity can withstand. Rongo and Haumia between them are *atua* for foods which people either cultivate (the *kūmara*), or gather in the wild (the fernroot). In gaining control over his brothers, Tū consumes them, thereby establishing the cultural logic behind acts of cannibalism; namely, to bring the object consumed under one's powers, and render it subordinate to one's authority (the senior *tuākana* becoming junior ranking *tēina*). With the parental separation successfully completed, the world of the *atua* unfolds and expands, and takes on its present form, with subsequent generations continuing a process of differentiation as they carve out their separate lives within it. But the gains, in Te Rangikāheke's view, also involve losses, notably the disappearance of much of mother earth into the sea.

 ## Raki and Papa-tūā-nuku: a South Island narrative

The Ngāi Tahu *tohunga*, Matiaha Tiramōrehu (1987), presented another rendering of the Rangi and Papa story as part of a larger creation narrative. His text opens dramatically, with the *atua* singing creation into being. Like the Io tradition, the world is conceived as a genealogy, beginning with Te Pō, and continuing on through types of Te Ao (Days), to states of Te Kore, to end with Te kore-matua (The Parentless) which produced Te Mākū (The Damp).

According to Tiramōrehu, Te Mākū lived with Mahora-nui-ātea and produced Raki (or Rangi in northern dialects). Raki lived with Pokoharu-a-te-pō, and they produced Te Hā-nui-o-raki, and a series of progeny, all offspring from this first union, including Taputapuātea and Mahere-tū-ki-te-raki, 'ngā Ariki mātāmua tonu tēnei a Raki' ('the first Lords from Raki'). Raki then married Papa-tūā-nuku, and they produced their first son, Rehua, and daughter, Hākina, as well as other spiritual beings, which continue to dwell in the heavens. There were numerous other offspring from this union including such *atua* as Tāne, Paia, Tū, and Roko, down to Uenuku, Ruatapu, and finally, Paikea. Tiramōrehu believed humanity was descended from Paikea. Raki had a series of other wives, including Hekeheke-i-papa, some of whose offspring remained in the heavens, Hotu-papa, Māukuuku, and Tauhare-kiokio.

A significant episode concerns Papa-tūā-nuku, Raki's second wife. She had originally been married to Takaroa (or Tangaroa in northern dialects). Papa had gone to live with Raki when her first husband had gone away with the *popoki* (placenta) of their child. By the time he returned Papa-tūā-nuku and Raki had produced a number of children, notably Rehua and Tāne. The two men went and fought on the beach; Takaroa wounded Raki by piercing him through the buttocks with a spear. Though Raki survived, his subsequent children were sickly and weak.

Raki, who was still clinging on top of Papa-tūā-nuku, now told Tāne and his *tāina* (younger brothers) to kill him so that people might live. When Tāne enquired as to how they would do this, Raki informed them that they must separate him from Papa-tūā-nuku, so that the light might grow for the children. When Tāne suggested his elder brother, Rehua, should undertake the deed, Raki insisted that it had to be done by all the brothers, '*kia rewa ai ahau ki runga, kia tupu ai te whai[a]o i a koutou*' ('so that I float above, so that light may grow up for you'). Tāne then accepted the *tikanga* (plan) to kill his father, '*kia tipu ai te ao hei ao*' ('so that the world can develop to be the world').

Tāne now gave instructions to other of Raki's offspring, to stamp down on Papa, and prop Raki above. According to Tiramōrehu, this was the beginning of the construction of Raki by Tāne. Rehua, Tāne, and their younger brothers helped lift up their father, while Paia prayed to give them strength. As the children separated the parents they bid each other farewell, and Paia continued praying, as Tāne propped his parents apart. At the end, everyone gave a great shout. Tiramōrehu (1987: 5, 27) concluded this separation narrative with these comments:

> *Otirā i te okotahi o Tāne te whakaaro i tana waihakatanga i te raki, nāna anō i poupou kā taha o te raki, i mau katoa anake i a ia. Nāna hoki i purupuru ngā wāhi e hāmama ana, i mau katoa anō i a ia. No te otika a Raki te haka, ka mārama hoki te ao hei ao.*
>
> (But Tāne alone was giving thought to the construction of heaven, he also propped up the sides of the heaven, and it was all made stable by him. He it was also that stopped up the places which were open, and it was all made stable by him. When Raki was finished being constructed, the world was bright as a world.)

At first sight Tiramōrehu's narrative differs considerably from Te Rangikāheke's, with Raki, for example, having numerous wives besides Papa-tūā-nuku, and violent Tū being much less prominent. Nevertheless, a number of important ideas reoccur. The separation is effected by Tāne and his brothers, and transposes the world from one of darkness where the parents cling together, to one where they have been relocated to the sky and earth so that there would be light. Tāne's creative role is reaffirmed, even strengthened, for it is this *atua* who plans and constructs the heavens. Appropriately for an *iwi* with extensive coastal and sea resources, Takaroa – the preeminent oceanic *atua* – is prominent, being Papa's first husband, who subsequently defeats Raki himself in battle.

Kia tupu ai te whaiao (so that the light may grow)

Creation genealogy

```
Te Pō (the night)
Te Ao (the days)
Te Kore (the void)
Te Kore-matua (the parentless)
Te Mākū    =    Mahora-nui-ātea
                    |
            *Raki    =    Pokoharu-a-te-pō
                    |
        ┌───────────┼───────────────┐
Te Hā-nui-o-raki   Taputapuātea   Mahere-tū-ki-te-raki

       *Raki    =    Hekeheke-i-papa
       *Raki    =    Hotu-papa
       *Raki    =    Māukuuku
       *Raki    =    Tauwhare-kiokio
       *Raki (2) =   Papa-tūā-nuku    =   (1) Takaroa
                          |
        ┌────────┬────────┼────────┬────────┐
      Rehua   Hākina    Paia      Tū      Roko
                          |
              Tāne = (1) Io-wahine = (2) Tiki-auaha
                              |
                            People
```

* Denotes the same person

Source: Adapted from Tiramōrehu, 1987

1 Te tīmatanga mai o ngā atua

 The creation of humanity

Having created the natural world, the *atua* turned to considering ways to populate it. Various *tohunga* related stories about the making of the first human beings. Tiramōrehu recounted this event, sustaining Tāne's creative role established in his earlier separation story. Tiramōrehu (1987: 9, 31) described the initial idea:

> *No konei a Tāne i whakaaro ai e tupu anō ia te tangata ki te waihanga, a waihangatia e ia ki te whenua tana mea whakamātautau.*
>
> (Then Tāne thought he would create humankind, and from the earth he created his trial model.)

Tāne carried out the trial in Hawaiki, with Tāne kneading the human body from its earth. Once he had completed the form, he said a prayer, and then named that first human body, Tiki-auaha. Now people would settle the world, and Tāne was pleased with his human creation.

After this trial, Tāne thought he would create a woman to be a partner for Tiki-auaha. He also formed her from Hawaiki's soil. Tāne copulated with her and chanted a prayer. The lengthy text of this *karakia* describes Tāne's sexual experimentation as he sought for the correct location in the woman's body to place his penis (Tiramōrehu, 1987: 9–10, 31–3). The following gives a sense of the text:

> *Tēnei ka tū he uha, he uha pihaea.*
> (Here stands the female, the female pihaea.)
>
> …
>
> *Me paka [or 'panga'] ki whea nei taku ure i aha ki tō upoko,*
> *No te huruhuru tēnā nōhanga waikōpiha, ehara tēnā.*
>
> (Where shall I apply my penis? What about your head?
> That pool is the place of the hair, not that.)

Using similarly worded verses Tāne sought out various parts of the woman's anatomy, from her forehead, to other openings in her face such as nose, eyes, ears and mouth, and on to other parts of her body, from her neck, breasts, navel, and anus down to her feet. In each verse, Tāne verified either: the appropriate activity (such as the mouth being for swallowing food), or the occurrence of the correct excretion associated with that part of the body (such as mucus, tears, wax, sweat, or faeces), or the proper location of a particular body part. The final couplet brings Tāne to the right place:

> *Me panga ki hea nei taku ure i aha ki tō tara nei, e pai ana tēnā tō tara,*
> *Mo te ure tēnā nohoanga, mo torenga makiki mo torenga makaka,*
> *Nga ai, ka nene, ka renga, ka peke.*

(Where shall I apply my penis? What about your vagina, your vagina is a good place. That place is the place for the penis, for the straight erection, for the bent erection. It couples, it sports, it is full, it springs.)

As a result of the strength of this chant, the woman, named Io-wahine, ran forth. As Tiramōrehu explained: '*Ko te tangata tuatahi i hangā ai e ia ko Tiki-Auaha, ki muri iho nei hoki kua waihangatia anō e ia he wahine*' ('The first human being created by him was Tiki-Auaha, and afterwards he created a woman'). Tāne then thought she should become Tiki-auaha's wife, and so they married and lived together. Their issue eventually peopled the world (Tiramōrehu, 1987: 10–11, 33).

Whatahoro (1913) provides an account of the creation of the first woman. After Tāne-matua (Tāne-the-parent, a name given by Io) and his *tuākana* had completed their other tasks, they began asking themselves how they would raise descendants in Te Ao-mārama (the world of light). Their *tuakana*, Uru-te-ngangana, told them to search for a female who could take on their own likeness in order to produce progeny ('*Me kimi te uha hei tango i to tatou ahua, hei whakatipu uri ki te Ao-marama nei*').

The brothers initially sought female *atua* like themselves, but decided that the most appropriate female had to be from Papa-tūā-nuku (the Earth). Therefore, the brothers paired off and went in search of the *uha*, (the female), without success. They then searched for it amongst the creatures living in the world. However, they did not find an appropriate form for the *Iho-tangata* (the form or likeness and attributes of man).

At this point, Rō-iho, Rō-ake, and Hae-puru instructed Tāne-matua to go and heap up the earth at Kura-waka ('the *puke* (mons veneris) of the Earth Mother' (Best, 1976: 121)). There the brothers created the form of the female. Tāne breathed *te manawa ora* (life) into her nostrils, mouth and ears. Once this woman, named Hine-hau-one, had taken human form she was given over to Tāne-matua, '*kia hikaia a Tiki-ahua ki roto i te puta o Hine-hau-one*' (so that the penis personified as Tiki-āhua might have intercourse in the opening of Hine-hau-one). Best (1976: 132) explained that 'Tane represents the male principle … Tiki personifies the male organ'.

Tāne pierced a series of orifices (including the ears, the eyes, the nose, the mouth and the anus), which produced various excretions. His *tuakana* then told him to enter Hine's *awa karihi* (the vagina). The '*takutaku a Tupai i te ure o Tāne-matua*' (the incantation of Tūpai to excite the penis of Tāne-matua) was recited. This was a *karakia whakapiri* (an adhering chant) to join as one the thoughts and bodies of Tāne, the husband and Hine, who became his wife. Their issue included Hine-tītama and a series of other daughters.

Tiramōrehu and Whatahoro developed the theme of differentiation established in the Rangi and Papa separation narratives, and elaborated on the process by which human beings, as distinct from *atua*, were generated. The work of Io in initiating genesis, and the construction of the natural world by *atua* such as Tāne, is completed by the creation of human males and females, whose offspring people the world.

 ## Myth-messages

The first myth-message concerns the importance of genealogy and kinship relations. Elsdon Best (1976: 57) observed that the 'Maori of yore appears to have thought out what he deemed a feasible line of evolution, and decided to explain it in manner genealogical'. J. Prytz Johansen (1954: 9) linked this process with kinship: 'The whole cosmos of the Maori unfolds itself as a gigantic "kin"'. The genealogical recitations of the creation by Io found in Māori Marsden's writings, and again in Tiramōrehu's singing of the world into being, reflect this understanding of the development of the world. It is as if the world were conceived of as a vast and interlinking family tree, from the remotest states of darkness and void, to the teeming descendants of Tū-mata-uenga, Tāne, Tiki, Io-wahine, and Hine-hau-one.

This interconnecting genealogy reflects a Māori view of the universe as 'a two-world system' where the material world proceeds from the spiritual world, and is interpenetrated by it (Marsden, 1992). Shirres (1997: 26) elaborated on what he called a 'Maori model of the universe' where,

> *the world of the atua is not separated absolutely from the world of everyday activities, from the secular world. Rather, the two worlds are closely linked, all activities in the everyday world being seen as coming under the influence of the spiritual powers.*

Just so, Io-matua-kore (Io-the-parentless) created the universe and Te Ao Wairua, and the *atua*, Tāne-matua, established Te Ao Mārama, and populated it through the creation of human beings.

A second myth-message concerns the relations between the sexes. Given the genealogical structuring of evolution, Māori scholars conceptualised the world as proceeding through a series of male and female couples (except for beings such as Io). As Hanson and Hanson (1983: 20) observed: 'The Maoris perceived sexuality in all corners of the world.' Whatahoro (1913: 32, 137) put it this way:

> *Na, he uha ta nga mea katoa i whai tohua ai, ahakoa he aha te mea he hoa tona; kaore he mea i tu noa ko ia anake kaore he hoa; he hoa to nga mea penei.*
>
> *([Now,] each thing has [its] female [counterpart] through which it conceives; whatever there is, it has a wife [female]; there is nothing that stands alone without its female – all things have their female counterparts.)*

Some writers, such as Best, interpreted this sexual division of the world to be an unequal, or at least an ambivalent, one. Discussing Hine-hau-one, Best (1976: 124–5) continued:

> *The wairua (spirit) of the godlike supernatural beings was now transferred in part to the human race ... The seed of life is with the male, with the female is the passive, nurturing haven bed. The seed (or fruit) of the god is with the male, because he is the offspring of gods. The female sprang from the earth, and with her are the nurturing waters.*

If women were less than divine, then Best also stressed a negative aspect of them. Referring to the *whare o aituā*, an allusion to the detumescence of the penis following

intercourse, Best (1976: 121) commented: 'This 'house' of misfortune, of ominous inferiority, is represented by this world, by the earth, by dread powers of destruction and pollution.' The sexual climax was understood as a conflict between Tiki and Karihi (in other words, between the male's penis and the woman's genitals), in which the former was defeated. Johansen (1954: 236) explained the link between this sexual act and creation:

> *In the culmination of sensual delight the man in nuce feels the whole mystery of creation: that woman actualizes man's life, but that, bringing forth life, she imbues it with defeat and death.*

Tiramōrehu's frank and joyful account of Tāne's creation of the first man and woman suggests a more equal relationship between the sexes. Tāne-matua created both from the prestigious earth of Hawaiki, the ancestral homeland, and spiritual gathering place. If Tiki-auaha (a personification of the penis), was the model, then Io-wahine was distinguished by first having intercourse with her creator. So strong was she at her creation that Tiramōrehu described Io-wahine as running outside ('*a oma ana i waho*'). Only after this state of rampant freedom did Tāne think of marrying her to Tiki. Given her activity, and the power of her creation chant, Io-wahine's marriage may not have been as passive an affair as Best had imagined. Papa-tūā-nuku too showed her independence and lack of passivity when changing husbands; or in Te Rangikāheke's account, when saving her children. Johansen (1954: 214, 224, 230–1) described Māori women as being traditionally 'more robust than the man', taking the lead in initiating relationships ('erotically aggressive'), and participating in marriage 'on an equal footing' with their husbands. Was the strength and vitality of the human race inherited only from the men?

A third myth-message explores male forms of behaviour. Relationships between men were frequently filled with martial strife, as evidenced by Te Rangikāheke's narrative concerning the conflict amongst the sons of Rangi and Papa. In this fighting, a significant line of tension existed between *tuakana* and *teina*. For Te Rangikāheke, Tū-mata-uenga embodied violent, decisive action, and was the ancestor of people. He is frequently described with the phrase, '*koia anake i toa ki te whawhai*' (he was the only one brave enough to fight). Tāwhiri, his equal on the field of conflict, was similarly passionate and angry. Tāne represented a more pacific model; a characterisation in keeping with the creative impulses described by Whatahoro and Tiramōrehu, for whom Tāne is the creator of humanity. Significantly, it is Tāne whom both Tāwhiri and Tū attacked and defeated first in Te Rangikāheke's account. In this creation narrative, violent action equates with the warrior mentality, involving acts of retribution, and ritual humiliation and manipulation. Fortunately for humanity, Māori creation narratives suggest that this is not the only model to which a male may aspire.

Another myth-message concerns the philosophical dimension of these creation narratives. According to these stories, the world was generated out of nothingness through the parentless Io who encompassed everything within its own singular existence. Alternatively, a male and female *atua* were so tightly bound as to be one. From this state of unity or completeness, the world was separated out into a series of states and entities. While this enabled the world to come into being, emerging from undifferentiated darkness into Te Ao Mārama, it also left the beings who emerged vulnerable to conflict and further divisions as well as losses. If Io represents unity, then Tū-mata-uenga stands for violent division, which the creativity of Tāne, in conjunction with the vitality of the female form, works to overcome through the birth of new life, with its fresh possibilities. By narrating, reciting or singing these creation accounts, Māori *tohunga* bound together the immanent possibilities found within them, just as a tribal genealogy has the flexibility to allow first one, then another descent line to be emphasised, while still holding the larger web of connections in place as part of the total kinship system.

Notes

1. The *atua* are ancestors of ongoing influence with power over particular domains.
2. *Karakia* are ritual chants that acknowledge *atua*. These are recited before entering, and when leaving their domain. In modern Māori society, *karakia* also refers to Christian worship.
3. Tāne, Tāne-matua, and Tāne-mahuta are variants of the same name, depending on the origin of a myth; the same rule applies to Hine-ahu-one and Hine-hau-one. The particular variant used throughout this chapter depends on the source of the myth.
4. *Aruhe* is the rhizome or underground root-like stem of the *rarauhe* or bracken fern. The *aruhe* was a staple food in many regions, available when other crops such as *kūmara* failed. It was grown in special areas since particular soils produced better quality rhizomes. These were dug up with a *kō* – a stick-like earth working tool – dried and stored for future use. Preparation involved steeping in water and pounding to rid it of excess fibres, before roasting over a fire. The *aruhe* was often presented as a cake, and was a very sustaining meal favoured for manual workers or travellers.

FURTHER READING

Useful introductions are Marsden (1992), and Walker (1990, 1992); and at a more advanced level, Shirres (1997). However, reading the original narratives provides the best way of learning about this topic.

Chapter 2

Te ao Māori
Māori world-view

Tānia M. Ka'ai and Rawinia Higgins

This chapter explains how *tapu*, *noa*, and *mana* (see pages 17 and 18) as the three primary cultural concepts of the Māori world provide a foundation from which all other cultural concepts can be understood. Collectively these concepts frame a Māori world-view. Furthermore, the chapter locates *te reo me ngā tikanga Māori* (Māori language and customs) in the modern world after surviving the impact of colonisation.

The Māori world-view is holistic and cyclic, one in which every person is linked to every living thing and to the *atua*. Māori customary concepts are interconnected through a *whakapapa* (genealogical structure) that links *te taha wairua* (spiritual aspects) and *te taha kikokiko* (physical aspects). The most commonly known definition of *whakapapa* is 'genealogical table' (Williams, 1971: 259), which describes the relationships or connections between groups of people. However, for Māori, this definition extends beyond human relationships into connections between humans and their universe. This intricately woven *whakapapa* has often made defining individual customary concepts extremely difficult, as each concept is defined by its relationship with other concepts and not in isolation. It is this *whakapapa* between *te taha wairua* and *te taha kikokiko* that brings to life different aspects of Māori culture.

Māori primary cultural concepts are layered one on another through *whakapapa*, as are personal relationships. The concepts fall into three broad areas: social institutions, social relationships and spiritual and physical relationships. Language is central to the way Māori view the world; it is the life-blood of Māori culture, and it is related to politics, *mauri* and *mana* (see pages 17 and 18). *Te reo Māori* is the link between knowledge and meaning, and teacher and student. It is the strand that links the concepts through time and to each other.

Māori interpret the landscape differently from Pākehā and bestow importance on places and geographical features in a different way. The Pākehā who came to Aotearoa/New Zealand originally had their traditional ways of viewing the world, as did Māori.

The language of Māori ancestors is woven into the landscape and expresses the *whakapapa* link to the people's origins from the *atua*. The relationship Māori people have with the different *atua* is reflected in the customary concepts that make up *tikanga Māori* (Māori cultural practices). An example of this relationship is the concept of *mana*, one of the most important concepts of Māori society, which Williams (1971: 172) defines as: 'Authority, control'; 'Influence, prestige, power'. *Mana* originates from the *atua*; this concept of *mana atua* is the primary source of *mana* for Māori (Shirres, 1997). The *atua* are manifested in all of the natural world of the Māori:

- Rangi-nui in the sky
- Papa-tūā-nuku in the land
- Tāne in the forest
- Tangaroa in the sea and marine life
- Haumia-tiketike in uncultivated foods such as *aruhe*
- Rongo-mā-tāne in the *kūmara* or cultivated foods
- Tāwhiri-mātea in the winds
- Rū-au-moko in earthquakes and volcanic activity.

Just as the *atua* are part of the *taiao* (natural world), so *tāngata Māori* (Māori people) – who live within the natural world – are connected to the *atua* (Shirres, 1997; Patterson, 1992). The diagram on the right illustrates this connection:

The relationship of mana

The social structure of Māori society is based upon *whakapapa* because people descend from the *atua*, and a person's individual *mana* therefore depends on these descent lines.

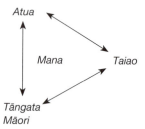

Māori social structure

The *ariki* (paramount chief) was seen as descending from the *tuakana* line (senior line) as opposed to those from the *teina* (junior) birth lines. In Māori society, the *tuakana* line was understood as having a closer relationship to the *atua* by its position in the layout of the whakapapa. Because of their greater mana, the *ariki* were the paramount chiefs of *iwi*. By comparison, *rangatira* (chiefs) could acquire their *mana* through *whakapapa* or achievement (see Mahuika, 1992). However, it should be noted that they were more distant from the senior line in the genealogical table than that of the *ariki* and thus their *mana* usually extended over *hapū*, rather than the larger *iwi*.

Further down the social strata, the amount of *mana* an individual acquired through *whakapapa* was dependent on how far removed the person was from the *tuakana* line, and therefore from the *atua*. At the farthest remove were the *tūtūā* (commoners) and the *taurekareka* (war slaves), the latter possessing no *mana* by virtue of being captured in war. Yet in saying this, Shirres (1997: 53) comments that: 'To be a person is not to stand alone, but to be one with one's people, and the deeper the oneness the more we are truly persons and have that *mana tangata*'.

The above discussion highlights the fact that there is an intricate relationship between *mana, ariki, rangatira, tūtūā, taurekareka, tuakana, teina,* and *atua*. This is without exploring issues surrounding *mana whenua* (mana of the land), *mana moana* (mana of the sea) or *mana motuhake* (separate mana).

All Māori customary concepts such as *mana* have extensive relationships with each other in a similar fashion to a kin group's *whakapapa*. In this sense, *whakapapa* may be defined as networks of relationships, or interconnections, between peoples (genealogy), between peoples and nature (ecology), between people and *atua* (cosmogony), and between people and cultural concepts (kinship and socialisation). These relationships are recorded as a series of layers or strata. The cultural concept of *tapu* can be added as another layer to that of *mana* as part of a *whakapapa* of *te ao Māori* (the Māori world). So close is the relationship between these two concepts, that a number of nineteenth century Māori manuscripts treat the words as interchangeable. Shirres (1997: 37) highlighted the connections:

> *Mana is the power of being [that is alive or active], a power that is realised over time. On the other hand a thing has its full tapu as soon as it begins to exist …. The child who is of chiefly line has not yet the mana, the power, of a chief, but has already the tapu of a chief. Tapu is being with potentiality for power [mana].*

To return to our model of the Māori social structure (page 14), *tapu* will act as another layer placed on top of the *mana* found in the *tuakana* line. However, it should be noted that whilst *rangatira* acquired *mana* and *tapu*, John Patterson (1992: 71) points out: 'The chief, then, for all the *mana* and *tapu* that are associated with the office, is not seen as being some high and distant god-like creature, but rather as a near-at-hand, protective figure.'

The protective characteristic of the chief was closely associated with *tapu* in that it acted as a means of social control. Elsdon Best states that:

> *The system of tapu was a series of prohibitions, and its influence was very far-reaching – so much so that it entered into all activities of native life. The laws of tapu affected all crises of life – birth, marriage, sickness, death, burial, exhumation; all industries; and no person in the community was exempt from its stringent rules. To disregard those rules meant disaster to the individual; but the punishment meted out to the transgressor was not inflicted by his fellow-tribesman – it was imposed by the gods* (Best, 1974: 89–90).

Such a system of prohibitions, restrictions or influences was intended to safeguard the *tapu* of each person, in relation to the community, the *atua* and the natural world (Shirres, 1997). These systems are manifested in the numerous customary concepts of the Māori and are described in the tables on pages 17 to 19. The concept of *tapu* was also connected through this series of controls with all forms of *tikanga Māori*. The relationship between *mana* and *tapu* is closely associated with *noa*. *Noa* is often described as being 'profane, unclean, or unrestricted'; therefore, it is treated as an antonym of *tapu*. However, a deeper understanding of the relationship of *tapu* and *noa* shows that the perceived opposition between the concepts is not *noa* in direct opposition to *tapu* but, to what Shirres (1982, 1997) describes as the 'extensions' of *tapu*.

2 Te ao Māori

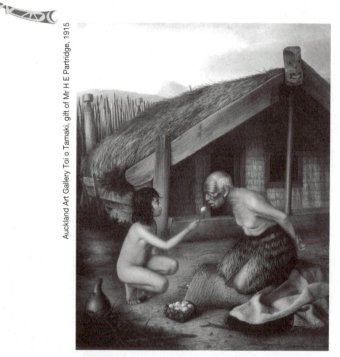

Tohunga were so *tapu* that they could not touch food, shown here in a painting by Gottfried Lindauer

Shirres (1982) describes *tapu* as being analogous with *noa*, and therefore, the intrinsic *tapu* that is prevalent in everything is not affected by *noa*, only the extensions of *tapu* are affected by this concept. This highlights again the interconnectedness of aspects of Māori culture with each other, and the relationships that define these concepts.

The late John Te Rangiāniwaniwa Rangihau, a distinguished Māori scholar who was immersed in *te ao Māori* and Pākehā education, integrated various Māori concepts into a diagrammatic representation of the Māori world-view. In doing this he focussed on common Māori concepts and avoided specific tribal metaphors and terminology. In his diagram (below) Rangihau explains *Māoritanga* (Māori culture) in relation to *Pākehātanga* (Pākehā culture). Such a connection might suggest that Rangihau sought to link Māori with Pākehā, as if in a shared *whakapapa*, in order to articulate a bicultural world-view, reflective of an ideal New Zealand society.

Māoritanga

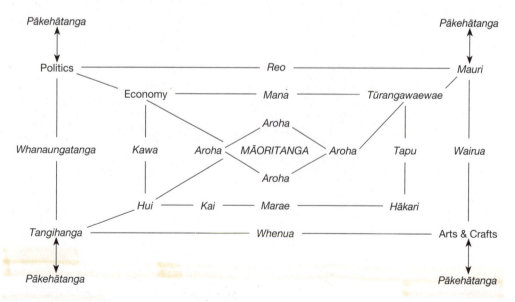

While Rangihau locates Māoritanga at the centre of his Māori world-view, this is

flanked by the concept of *aroha* (love/concern for others) suggesting that contemporary Māori understand *aroha* as their core social concept. Furthermore, Rangihau states:

> *Kinship bound us together in this situation. To me, kinship is the warmth of being together as a family group: what you can draw from being together and the strength of using all the resources of a family. And a strong feeling of kinship or whanaungatanga reaches out to others in hospitality* (Rangihau, 1992: 183).

Rangihau favours a series of interlinking boxes that stresses how every concept is related to the other. He links the core of *aroha* with important areas of Māori culture and society. The following table is an arrangement of some of the key Māori concepts into particular classifications.

Social Institutions	
Hākari	A special feast or banquet, usually at the end of a *hui* where people have gathered for a particular purpose or function, for example, at the end of a *tangihanga* (see Chapter 8). The *hākari* is one of the instruments used to remove *tapu* (*whakanoa*) (see Chapter 7).
Hui	A term used to describe any form of gathering or meeting that follows Māori protocol. For example, *pōhiri*, *tangihanga*, or a *marae* committee meeting (see Chapters 7 and 8).
Marae	A term known throughout the Pacific, where it refers to a ritual site; in contemporary Aotearoa/New Zealand this refers to a complex of buildings and the surrounding land (see Chapter 7).
Tangihanga	A death ritual where the deceased person lies in state for a period from three days to one week depending on circumstances. This usually takes place on the *marae* and takes precedence over other *hui*. The mourning process allows for the open expression of grief, wailing and shedding of tears as a means of healing people after their loss (see Chapter 8).
Wharekura	A traditional institution of higher learning, sometimes referred to as *whare wānanga*. *Kura* refers to something highly prized, as *mātauranga Māori* was in *te ao Māori*. In modern times, this term has been adopted by *kaupapa Māori* educational initiatives (see Chapter 18).

Social Relationships	
Kāinga	A term used to describe a person's home; sometimes called *kāinga tūturu*. *Kāinga* also refers to unfortified settlements in the pre-contact period. The term is linked closely with other cultural concepts such as *tūrangawaewae* and *ahikā* (see Chapter 5).
Mana	A term closely linked to the concept of *tapu* used to refer to authority, power, control, influence and prestige in relation to *atua*, people, land and the environment. *Mana* is linked to other cultural concepts such as *tuakana/teina*, *whakapapa*, and *rangatiratanga* (see Chapter 9).
Noa/Whakanoa	Terms related to the freeing of an entity from *tapu* restrictions. For example, the *hākari* at the end of a *tangihanga* releases participants from the mourning process (see Chapter 8).

Rāhui	The most common forms of *rāhui* are those relating to pollution and conservation. *Tapu* is an essential element in the implementation of *rāhui*. There are numerous tribal examples of areas falling under *rāhui* because of bloodshed in a food resource area. The transgression of combining blood with food creates a profanity which requires the area to be placed under restriction for a certain period of time. Conservation *rāhui* is a form of traditional land and sea tenure. This form of resource management was adopted to preserve food supplies from exploitation and greed.
Tapu	A term describing the influence of *atua* within the universe and over all things animate (people, insects, animals) and inanimate (mountains, rivers, *waka*). It also relates to a system of protective prohibitions or restrictions which control relationships between entities (people, land, environment) and their respective expressions of *tapu*.
Tūrangawaewae	A term used to locate the very source and origins of a person's *whakapapa*, sometimes referred to as one's 'roots' or place of belonging, for example, one's *whānau*, *hapū* and *iwi* histories and aspirations, including genealogy, performing arts, *whakataukī*, *tikanga*, cultural obligations and responsibilities and politics.
Utu	*Utu* is often defined as 'revenge'. However, this is only one aspect of its fuller meaning. As revenge, it is usually applied as a result of an incident where the *mana* and *tapu* of a person was challenged. In this case, retribution is sought to regain and restore a balance with the initial offended party. However, balance is often temporary, as *utu* is continually sought by each party until an agreement is reached between them when the matter is considered *ea* (balanced). More often than not, the initial *hara* (wrong) is so insignificant that it is overshadowed by the later events of *utu*. 'The traditional concept of *utu* pervaded the Māori social, legal, political, and economic order' (Ministry of Justice, 2001: 67).
Whanaungatanga	A term describing a kinship network which links Māori to their *whānau*, *hapū*, *iwi* and *te ao Māori*. It is a cultural framework for Māori identity (see Chapter 6).

Spiritual and Physical Relationships	
Wairua	A term describing a spiritual life principle of a person and the relationship they have with the world around them. *Wairua* crosses between the physical and spiritual dimensions and includes the various levels of consciousness that drive certain behaviour in particular situations. Associated cultural concepts include *mauri* and *tapu*.
Tikanga/Ngā Tikanga	A term used to describe a system of protocols that are observed within *te ao Māori*, based on cultural traditions, practices, values and beliefs. The word *tika* means right or correct, therefore the extension of the word to *tikanga* implies an appropriate or customary way of behaving within Māori contexts.
Hinengaro	A term to describe a person's mind, both the conscious and the unconscious. It relates to the ability of people to intellectualise about themselves and the world around them.
Tinana	A term to describe the physical reality of a person, i.e. the body.
Mauri	A term used to describe a life force or life principle and ethos of all objects both animate and inanimate within the universe. This life force can be focused into a material object. Carved *mauri* stones were buried in tribal lands to maintain the *mauri*, or fruitfulness of crops under Rongo. Like *mana*, *mauri* could be strengthened, diminished or transmitted. It is associated closely with other cultural concepts such as *atua*, *tapu*, *mana* and *wairua*.

Whenua	A term commonly used to refer to land. However, it is linked to the notion of birth in that it also refers to the placenta, which according to *tikanga Māori* is returned to the land. The act of giving birth is referred to as *whānau*. The term *hapū* in this context refers to being pregnant. Therefore, the term *whenua* underpins the kinship structure and the very essence of Māori society (see Chapter 6).
Kai	A term commonly used to describe food. It is closely associated with cultural concepts such as *manaakitanga* (see Chapters 6 and 7).

Just as *whakapapa* connects people with their kin, with the land and with the natural world, so also does *whakapapa* connect people with their cultural concepts. The *tātai* (lines of descent) in a *whakapapa* act like a web with each descent line linked closely, so that the respective *tātai*, representing a cultural concept, work interdependently to make up the Māori world-view.

The Māori world-view

All cultures evolve over time as new technology is introduced and as various ethnic groups are exposed to one another. Furthermore, all cultures in contemporary times have artefacts from the past that serve as cultural indicators of the way in which its people behaved and as reminders of where they came from.

Historically the western world has defined countries using maps and geographical markers that describe landscape and population. New Zealand is no exception. The western conventions are used by tourists to this country and by Pākehā New Zealand in general. However, Māori interpret the same landscape quite differently. This interpretation is part of the Māori world-view.

Places of importance to *hapū* and *iwi* often do not appear on modern maps. These historically significant locations are remembered and referred to by the people, especially in *whaikōrero* (oratory). For example, Whatiwhatihoe, a settlement established in the 1880s by Tāwhiao, the second king of the Kīngitanga movement, no longer exists as a settlement but is still referred to by the people of the Tainui group of tribes.

The cultural imprint of socialisation determines our perspectives on the world in which we live. Each individual is socialised as a member of a specific cultural group. Thus, each person learns to see the world in a particular way. The language learned during this process is important because words are used to describe our view of physical and spiritual reality (Hewitt, 1992). For example, Māori have a range of words and phrases to describe types of *pounamu* (greenstone) (see Chapter 4), its special significance to Māori and its uses, while the tourist would merely see *pounamu* as an attractive semi-precious stone. It follows that a particular world-view is available only to a person brought up to see the world that way. Becoming a Māori involves learning a specific and particular perspective of the world. Language promotes the learning and reflects and often drives cultural practices. Ngoi Pēwhairangi (see Chapter 9) made this point in explaining why Pākehā could not understand the deeper aspects of te ao Māori.

> *I know there are a lot of Pakehas who would love to learn, not only the language, but the Maori heart. And it's a thing one can never teach. Quite a number of Pakehas are sincere about it. This is part of the Maori they want to*

learn: respect nature, respect for anything Maori, how they should come on to a marae, how they should come into a meeting house, and how to learn to speak like an orator. But anyone can speak on a marae once they've been shown the proper procedure. This is just scratching the surface. Maoritanga goes deeper than that and I don't think Pakehas are aware of this. They think that because they've been to university and studied the language and the culture, they've mastered it. To me listening, it sounds as if there is no depth there at all, especially as far as tapu is concerned. There is so much tapu connected with the whole culture and I don't think Pakehas can absorb it (Pewhairangi, 1992: 11).

Another example of the difference between a Māori and a Pākehā world-view is contained in the geographical portrait of the country. Te Ika-a-Māui, known as the North Island, is the fish of Māui. Te Wai Pounamu or Te Wāhi Pounamu, known as the South Island, literally means the waters of greenstone or the place of greenstone.

Te Ika-a-Māui

However, it is also referred to as Māui's canoe (the prow to the north and the stern to the south) from which he fished up the North Island. Rakiura, known as Stewart Island, is sometimes referred to as the anchor to Māui's canoe.

North Island Māori also express geographical locations that challenge Pākehā perceptions of the landscape around us. Pākehā living in the North Island often say they go up (meaning northwards) to Tāmaki-makau-rau and down (meaning southwards) to Te Whanganui-a-Tara. However, North Island Māori express themselves differently, a difference that is attributed to a combination of *runga* (up) and *raro* (down) and the way in which they interpret the physical geography of Te Ika-a-Māui as a landmass based on their traditions and world-view. A map of the North Island with Wellington at the top and Cape Reinga in the Far North at the bottom, while foreign to the tourist and Pākehā population, is to the North Island Māori a reflection of how they see Te Ika-a-Māui (see map opposite). They refer to Te Upoko-o-te-ika (the head of the fish), Wellington, as *kei runga* meaning up but southward and Te Hiku-o-te-ika (the tail of the fish), the Far North, as *kei raro* meaning down but northward. Every culture living in New Zealand views the world differently and valuing that difference is an important step toward understanding the Māori world-view.

Māori have a particular concept of time that differs from that of the Pākehā. Māori describe the past as *ngā rā o mua*, meaning 'the days before'. By contrast, the future is described as *ngā rā kei muri*, meaning 'the days after'. This reflects a world-view where Māori 'move into the future with their eyes on the past' (Metge 1976: 70). This attitude looks to the past as a guide for the present and the future.

It has been proposed that we all carry around our own subconscious and culturally conditional filters for making sense of the world around us (Knudtson and Suzuki, 1992: 3). It is not until we encounter people with a substantially different set of filters that we have to confront the assumptions, predispositions and beliefs that we take for granted and which make us who we are. It is not the intention of this chapter to discuss the difficulties encountered when divergent cultures meet and are forced to interact. What is important is to identify some of the characteristics that distinguish a Māori world-view, characteristics which are shared by many Indigenous societies.

There is a commonality in the evolution of Indigenous people situated in historically subordinated circumstances within the world's industrialised nations. In many ways, Indigenous people in Fourth World situations have originated from the same conditions and are confronting the same struggles for legitimacy that faced Third World countries following independence. In many instances, these initiatives are associated with a broader self-determination and community development agenda. In other instances, they are a response to new opportunities created by changes in government policy or funding sources; and in still other instances, the initiatives originate from an educational view framed by a strong sense of cultural integrity and hegemony (Barnhardt and Harrison, 1992: 7).

One of the most arresting and significant features of a Māori world-view is the over-riding sense of commitment of Māori to the collective interests of the Indigenous community with which they are associated. This is manifested through *iwi* organisations driving initiatives such as treaty claims, to achieve self-sufficiency for the tribe, and the staging of annual events that bring the people together to celebrate their tribal identity, such as *hui-ā-tau* (annual gatherings).

Māori see the land and the landscape as an integral part of *whakapapa* to be taken care of for future generations. This feature of a Māori world-view is significant as it connects to cultural concepts such as *mana, tapu, noa, rāhui* and the relationship women have with the land and, of course, with Papa-tūā-nuku as earth mother.

> *All this stems from the fact that down through the centuries the Maori has been very close to nature. People who live in this way apply to nature and to things around them this feeling of aura. In the case of the Maori, they give everything a mauri and this takes them into the world of conservation and being very much aware of the environment and how much they owe to their environment. So they do not create an imbalance. For Maori generally I believe there is this emotional tie to the land because of their mythology and because of the way they have been taught where they have come from – the whole mythology of creation* (Rangihau, 1992: 187).

Another dimension is that of spirituality, in the sense of attending to the development and well-being of the whole person and the integration and balancing of all aspects of people's lives physically, emotionally, intellectually and spiritually. Connected to this is the critical role of elders who are regarded as the culture-bearers or repositories in relation to the transmission of traditional values, beliefs, knowledge, skills and customary practices. For this reason elders hold a cherished position in Māori society.

Another feature of a Māori world-view is the significance of the Indigenous language, its survival and use. The Māori language is the window to the soul of the people and to sustaining their cultural identity (see Chapters 4 and 19).

As Sir James Henare stated:

> *… The language is the core of our Maori culture and mana. Ko te reo te mauri o te mana Maori (The language is the life force of the mana Maori). If the language dies, as some predict, what do we have left to us? … our Maori language, as far as our people are concerned, is the very soul of the Maori people. What does it profit a man to gain the whole world but suffer the loss of his own soul? What profit to the Maori if we lose our language and lose our soul?* (WAI 11, 1986: 40–41).

The traditional way of constructing, organising and using knowledge is yet another feature of a Māori world-view. The most significant characteristic in this regard is the traditional emphasis on orality over literacy as the means for codifying and transmitting knowledge. Connected to this is the way in which Māori view knowledge in a holistic framework that allows learning to be life-long, rather than age-specific. Of course tribal elders have a significant role to play in this area to ensure that cultural practices and knowledge are handed down.

Another aspect of a Māori world-view is that Māori celebrate difference. This is reflected in the structure of Māori society (*whānau, hapū, iwi*) where order is maintained by specific cultural practices that link the past with the present and future. This means Māori are not homogeneous; that they do not have a 'one size fits all' view of the world, or a 'we are one people' outlook. Māori thrive on celebrating their tribal identity in the first instance and then their collective identity as Māori thereafter. Rangihau emphasised these ideas in his now classic statement:

The late John Te Rangiāniwaniwa Rangihau, of Ngāi Tūhoe, an expert in the art of *whaikōrero* at Whāngārā, East Coast

> *My being Maori is absolutely dependent on my history as a Tuhoe person as against being a Maori person. It seems to me there is no such thing as Maoritanga because Maoritanga is an all-inclusive term which embraces all Maori. And there are so many different aspects about every tribal person. Each tribe has its own history. And it's not a history that can be shared among others. How can I share with the history of Ngati Porou, of Te Arawa, or of Waikato? Because I am not of those people. I am a Tuhoe person and all I can share in is Tuhoe history.*
>
> *To me, Tuhoetanga means that I do the things that are meaningful to Tuhoe … I have a faint suspicion that Maoritanga is a term coined by the Pakeha to bring the tribes together. Because if you cannot divide and rule, then for tribal people all you can do is unite them and rule. Because then they lose everything by losing their own tribal histories and traditions that give them their identity* (Rangihau, 1992: 190).

One final dimension of a Māori world-view is that Māori society is based on a shared power system within social hierarchies, rather than a top-down scheme. This means that the critical mass are included in shaping the future of the iwi. In doing this they are being self-determining.

Key indicators to understanding a Māori world-view	
Tribal identity	The importance of a sense of place and belonging through genealogical ties.
Land and landscape	The recognition by the people of the need for respect for the harmony and balance of the land and the resources it provides.
Spirituality	Based on a spiritual view of and response to the natural world.
Elders	Elders serve as a critical link to the past in the present context to ensure cultural practices and tribal knowledge remain intact for future generations.
Language	The recognition that the language contains so many cultural indicators that enrich one's identity.

Culture	The importance of culturally-determined ways of thinking, behaving, communicating and living as Indigenous people.
Diversity	The celebration of tribal identity and a rejection of non-indigenous labels and definitions that homogenise Māori people.
Kinship structure	Based on a collaborative/shared power system within social hierarchies where cultural concepts manage people's behaviour and their relationships with each other and their environment.
Self-determination	The recognition of the rights of Indigenous peoples to live as Indigenous people. To be healthy, Māori people need access to learning their language; to education and qualifications and quality learning environments; to employment and a high standard of living; to have their culture valued in relation to Te Tiriti o Waitangi; to live as Māori and as global citizens; and to be active participants in determining their own future.
Concept of time	Māori look to the past as a guide for the present and the future.
Cultural knowledge	Cultural knowledge is viewed in a holistic framework with all aspects interrelated. It enables one to function with a degree of comfort in Māori contexts and to understand what is going on within that context. Hence, the connection between cultural concepts and a Māori world-view.
Reciprocity	Based on the view that mutual respect is the cornerstone of human relationships and between humans and their environment.

Conclusion

The positive rediscovery and revival of aspects of traditional culture and learning within contemporary Māori society can be attributed to Māori people critiquing Pākehā definitions and constructions of Māori society, and asserting explicitly the validation and legitimisation of their own culture. Rangihau, amongst others, stressed these points by observing the amazing number of Pākehā who seemed to know more about Māori matters than he did. He argued that it was about time that Māori:

> *were allowed to think for ourselves and to say things for our reasons and not for the reasons set down by Pakeha experts. The Maori is content to stand right where he is, retain his culture and retain his identity, and be himself, not a foreigner, in his own country* (Rangihau, 1992: 189).

Historically, the development of New Zealand society since the signing of the Treaty of Waitangi in 1840, and up to the latter part of the twentieth century, assumed that once Māori people were shown the superiority of the European way, they would reject their own culture and become westernised in outlook, lifestyle and community organisation. Rangihau spoke for many Māori, past and present, when he gently made the following observations:

> *You see, when Pakeha say we are all one people, they seem to mean that you're brown and a unique feature of the indigenous scene. But they want you to act as a European provided you can still retain the ability to poke out your tongue, gesticulate and do your Maori dances. That is Maori culture. The other part says to me, we want you to become part of us and lose all your institutions*

and all those things which are peculiarly Maori like the Department of Maori Affairs and Maori representation in Parliament. We want to give the world the image of all of us being absorbed into European culture or New Zealand culture. I can't go along with this because I can't feel I can be a Pakeha. What's more, I don't want to be a Pakeha. There are a lot of things which I do not like, compared with the things I do like in the Maori world. But I'm being asked to become a Pakeha so that I can then be counted as a New Zealander. Cor blimey, I am a New Zealander and you can't take that away from me. I am a New Zealander, Maori New Zealander and I can't see that it should create such a fuss every time I talk about retention of my culture and setting up Maori institutions like marae and everything else (Rangihau, 1992: 189).

The ethnocentric view which Rangihau objects to is flawed, as it founders on the belief that Māori people would eventually devalue their cultural base, substituting it for another, namely that of Pākehā. Instead, Māori society has rejected absorption. Māori continue to interpret their culture and landscape from the Māori world-view. Furthermore, Rangihau's model of Māoritanga developed in the 1970s as a tool to understand a Māori world-view is thirty years later, in 2003, a robust model which continues to provide a cultural framework for understanding Māori society.

FURTHER READING

Introductions to *te ao Māori* are found in Mahuika (1975), Shirres (1997), and Ministry of Justice (2001).

Chapter 3

Ngā hekenga waka
Canoe migrations
Jim Williams

Traditions of the migration of Māori ancestors from Hawaiki have been handed down through the generations. All *iwi* have canoe traditions but they differ from *iwi* to *iwi* according to their ancestral focus. Even *iwi* from the same *waka* (canoe) can show differences depending upon the role of their own *tūpuna* (ancestors). Anthropologists, over the years, have recorded many versions, academics have long debated the details, in particular, the whereabouts of Hawaiki, and archaeologists have searched for material proof of the varying traditions. It was often assumed that the voyaging ancestors were, themselves, Māori. However, it is now recognised that they were Polynesians who became what is now recognised as Māori, in response to the New Zealand environment.

The traditions of initial migration

Schoolchildren have long been taught that Kupe discovered Aotearoa/New Zealand (usually, it is claimed, about AD 950) and found it unoccupied. However, David Simmons (1976) points out that not all *iwi* had a tradition of Kupe and in fact, some have traditions that seem to be older. He claims that a Kupe tradition was confined to the Hokianga district, the West coast of the North Island and Ngāti Kahungunu area, and that the Arawa people of the Rotorua district, in particular, had no tradition of Kupe. The east coast and Horowhenua traditions of Kupe specify that the land was populated when he arrived, but other versions either state, or strongly imply (for example: 'he saw only birds'), that nobody was here (Simmons, 1976: 42–59).

Arrival traditions of the Māori are not those of a single unified people with a common history, but a collection of differing *iwi* traditions with common links. Some *iwi* say that Māui caught his great fish long before the time of Kupe and that there were already people living here then. Archaeological studies suggest that arrivals were spread over 500–600 years, culminating in 'The Great Fleet'. Archaeologists, however, are divided on the issue of early dates. Some years ago, their consensus agreed with oral tradition. Now, they are not so sure (Prickett, 2001, 2002). So, each of the various traditions can be viewed as the correct version – each for its own people, reflected deeply in the *mauri* and *tikanga* of each *iwi*.

The traditions provide at least three different explanations for initial discovery. The first involves curiosity in Hawaiki over where the *kuaka* (godwits) went to; as they were observed flying through at the same time each year, indicating land somewhere off to the south. Eventually explorers, following the *kuaka*, discovered Aotearoa. The Kupe tradition says that he was chasing a mischievous octopus, Te Wheke-a-Muturangi, which he eventually caught and killed in Cook Strait (Simmons, 1976). The Māui version says that Māui, in his canoe, Mahānui, had been lost at sea for many days before he came in sight of the west coast of Te Wai Pounamu. A number of important South Island place-names date from his arrival, including, of course, the place where Māui caught his great fish at the Kaikōura Peninsula (Te Taumaunu-a-Māui) on the north-east coast of Te Wai Pounamu (Beattie, 1941).

The exact origin of the first settlers, that is, the whereabouts of Hawaiki, has been debated since the arrival of the first Pākehā. Most scholars now agree that Polynesia was settled from the west, from Fiji to Tonga and Samoa and then to East Polynesia. However, the particulars remain unresolved. Certainly, Hawai'i (AD 500), Easter Island (Rapa Nui) (AD 400) and Aotearoa/New Zealand were amongst the last to be settled. For many years, the 'orthodox model' of academics, had Aotearoa/New Zealand first being inhabited around AD 800, which is consistent with the earliest *whakapapa* (Prickett, 2001). However, some recent revisions of academic thinking propose a much more recent first arrival and archaeologists are now divided on this subject. Prickett (2002) and Howe (2003) each summarise the current academic position which varies from a majority view of an initial arrival date of AD 750 to AD 1400, to some extreme views suggesting dates as early as 2000 years ago. Māori, however, continue to use *whakapapa* as the basis to date the arrival of *ngā waka*.

'The Great Fleet'

Many North Island peoples focus on the so called 'Great Fleet' – the seven famous canoes which are said to have arrived around about the middle of the fourteenth century, an average of about 25 generations before 1900. We sing of '*Ngā waka e whitu*', the seven canoes, but in fact the names of the seven can change to suit the singers as there are in fact many more than seven canoes remembered from that period of Māori history. This idea of a great fleet was proposed by the early ethnologist S. Percy Smith, who said that by 'fleet', he did not wish to suggest a single convoy (1910), but these days that disclaimer is often overlooked and 'fleet' is assumed by many to mean 'convoy'.

In the table below, the canoes listed on the left are those most commonly associated with the fleet. Those on the right have more local importance, and are usually considered to have arrived before the fleet.

In Te Wai Pounamu there are *whakapapa* that go back 20 generations earlier, to Rakaihautū and his people who arrived on *Uruao* which landed at Whakatū (now Nelson) (Beattie, 1941). These people, the Waitaha, talk of groups who were even earlier still, but about whom little is remembered. Also, in the Hokianga, Bay of Plenty,

Ngā waka (the canoes)	
Aotea	Māhuhu-ki-te-rangi
Te Arawa	Māmari
Horouta	Ngā-toki-mata-whao-rua
Kurahaupō	Nukutere
Mātaatua	Uruao
Tainui	
Tākitimu	
Tokomaru	

3 Ngā hekenga waka

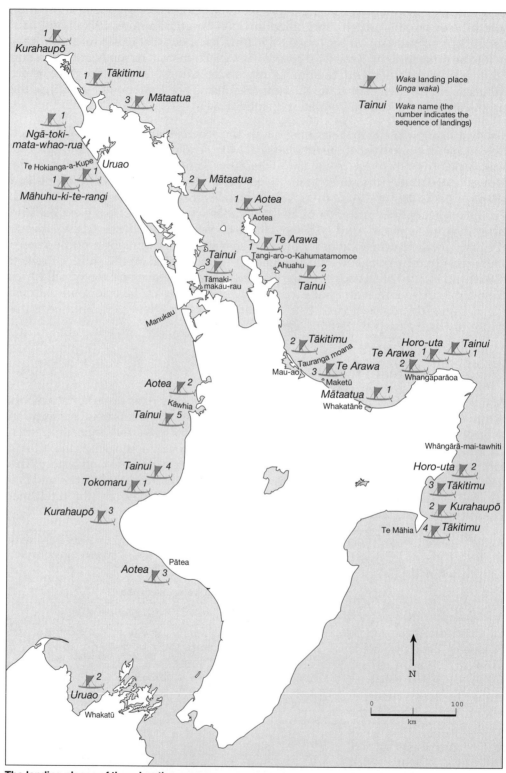

The landing places of the migration canoes

Source: Based on McKinnon, 1997, Plates 17–23

Taranaki, the East Coast, and other areas, *whakapapa* record pre-fleet ancestors. *Whakapapa* is the key, but *whakapapa* is selective, in the sense that choices have to be made about which line to emphasise, as the number of ancestors doubles in each generation. The tendency is to emphasise the line that has the most *mana*.

 ## Waka landing places

The landing places of the canoes – *ngā ūnga waka* – in Aotearoa/New Zealand continue to be of prime importance in Māori histories today. Their significance arises from the *whakapapa* of Māori people which are frequently traced back to the ancestors who came to these shores on board the *waka*. Some of the better known landing places are shown on the map opposite.

 ## Deliberate voyages?

There has been debate in academic circles for many years about whether the discovery of Aotearoa/New Zealand was accidental, and whether two-way voyages took place. Māori traditional belief is very clear on this point and, although the traditions differ from area to area, as we might expect, this gives them strength as each substantially supports the others. Most areas have traditions that refer to return journeys.

The *Hōkūle'a*, a Polynesian ocean-going double canoe built in traditional style, which has been sailed, using traditional navigation methods, on voyages between island groups, including from Hawai'i to Rarotonga and Aotearoa/New Zealand and to Rapa Nui (Easter Island)

Kerry Howe points to the 'initial amazement of European explorers that 'primitive' peoples could have sailed to remote places before they did' (2003: 62). One of the objections to the theory of deliberate voyaging was that, from East Polynesia,

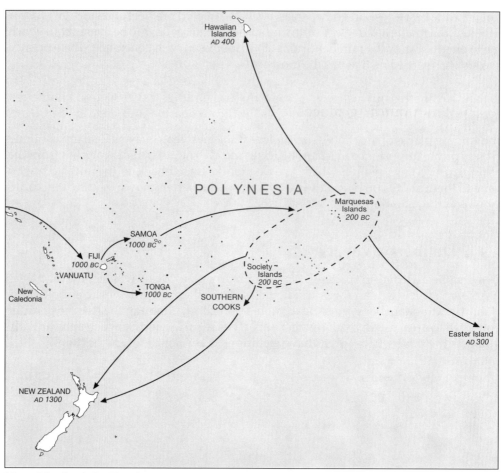

Map of the South Pacific, showing the likely sailing routes of the migration canoes
Source: Based on Howe, 2003, Map 4: 68

voyagers had only a 15 degree arc in which to sail to target landfall exactly between North Cape and East Cape. If they strayed outside of this arc they would sail right on by. 'Too small a margin of error,' said the doubters. Oral history, however, tells us that the sailing instructions for the *Tākitimu waka* were quite specific. The venturers were advised to keep sailing due South until Autahi (Canopus, which is not visible from lower latitudes, but was accurately described) appeared in the evening, three finger widths above the southern horizon. Then, it was time to turn west. By following these instructions, or others like them, a much larger target was available: right from North Cape to Stewart Island! It is important not to overlook the Polynesian expertise at navigation, which was based not only on detailed astronomical knowledge, but included knowledge of currents, changes in sea colour and temperature, prevailing winds and cloud formations. Stars were named and the points on the horizon where they rose and set were well known for each time of year. There was 'a mental construct [of] knowledge of seasonal wind and wave patterns and currents'. Some of these aspects were 'local knowledge', others, including knowledge of bird life, currents and cloud formations, were general indicators of distant land, and involved a system for slowly increasing focus on a target as it approached. 'The tops of higher islands can be seen from a great distance, up to 130 kilometres away'. During the day, certain cloud formations and species of bird signalled the approach of land before voyagers could actually see it. At night changes in water temperature and current could indicate that they were in the lee of a land-mass, and the cries of birds were a guide to distance, as some species venture further from land than others. It was well known which birds were migratory and which returned home. 'Boobies range 50 to 80 kilometres out to sea, whereas terns and noddies travel 30 to 40 kilometres' (Howe, 2003: 102–105). Drift objects also indicate nearby land and, in the case of large landmasses with significant rivers, salinity of the water can decrease well out to sea. A number of traditions refer to canoes being blown off course, yet the expertise was available to navigate them to their destination. Navigational ability was at least equal to that in Europe at the same time, but based on very different criteria.

In a number of cases, the names of all those who travelled on the *waka* are known and each *waka* carried an average of about 60 people, probably from two or three related *whānau*. In the case of the Tainui, four generations of one family is recorded.

What they brought with them

As well as the migrants, most of the *waka* carried dogs, and *kiore* (the Polynesian rat) – whether intentional or not; *kūmara*, *taro*, yams and gourds; and the *aute*, or paper mulberry. Some traditions tell of a variety of cabbage tree, *karaka* and the *pūkeko* also being brought, although it seems that all three were already here. Of course, they also brought a range of tools, weapons, and other equipment that would be necessary for life in a new land, as well as clothing and ornaments and a knowledge of techniques and processes that were important to sustain their culture. It is likely that other flora and fauna were also brought along. As well as dogs and *kiore*, pigs and chickens had accompanied ancestral Polynesians all the way from their origins in Southeast Asia, many centuries earlier, and it seems likely that they would all have been brought to Aotearoa/New Zealand too (Prickett, 2001). However, pigs and chickens either did not survive initial settlement or were eaten. It seems likely that staples such as bananas, breadfruit and coconut would also have been aboard, again not surviving in the new, colder land. Indeed, traditions tell of the difficulties encountered with getting *kūmara* and yams to grow here.

The evidence from oral tradition, archaeology, language, plants and animals, and from human biology all indicate that the migrants came from somewhere in central East Polynesia, more than 3000 km away (Prickett, 2001). Traditions do not accurately identify the various places called Hawaiki or Tawhiti, though the latter is very similar to Tahiti. More specifically, Rangi-ātea, also mentioned in the traditions, is very close to Ra'iatea in the Society Islands group. Patunui-a-Aio, homeland of the much earlier *Uruao* migration, is more problematical because the traditions say that the emigrants came from inland, away from the sea. The traditions also comment on the emigrants' reaction to their first sight of the sea, and say that some went to Hawaiki and others came to Aotearoa/New Zealand (Beattie, 1918).

The most likely homelands are somewhere in the Society group, possibly with a stopover in the Cooks. It is unlikely that all voyages came from a single island and certainly not in one generation. Traditions also suggest Rangitahua, the Kermadecs, as a stopover place, at least for the *waka Kurahaupō* (Broughton, 1983), which was damaged there, and *Aotea*, which picked up some of the passengers from *Kurahaupō*.

This was not generally accepted by academics until recently, when evidence of a human presence was discovered on Raoul Island. The evidence included chips of *pounamu*, which indicate a stopover on a return voyage, just as the traditions tell us (Prickett, 2001). This is, in fact, the strongest material evidence of return voyages.

Whilst it may not be possible to piece together all the details of the story from oral traditions alone, they do provide a valuable framework for investigation. Archaeologists and historians have been trying for a long time to complete the picture of the original migrations. However, it may be that proof of some traditions does not exist, or just has not been found yet. Recent advances in science have resulted in some re-writing of the story, but Māori traditions remain steadfast, while open to some re-interpretation. The suggested dates for original settlement that were generally accepted in the 1970s and 1980s (AD 850–950) are more consistent with *whakapapa* than the revised dates (twelfth and thirteenth centuries) (Prickett, 2002). New techniques in pollen study and DNA analysis may further refine the accepted dates. A major problem with citing first dates is in proving that the very earliest arrival sites have actually been found.

 ## Common misunderstandings

Political agendas, educational theories and research results change and develop over the years. But there are two errors concerning Māori history that were taught in Aotearoa/New Zealand schools at least until the 1980s. These errors are interconnected and therefore are still widely held, especially amongst those who completed their schooling before the 1980s.

 ### Two-wave theory

An early theory held that Aotearoa/New Zealand was populated by two separate waves of immigration, the Māori of the 'Great Fleet' being the second wave (Smith, 1898). This theory has now been thoroughly disproved. The error probably came about because early archaeologists saw from the artefacts they found that the earliest inhabitants and the people here at the time of European contact were culturally different, but they did not yet have evidence that clearly showed a slow transition in cultural characteristics from the earliest inhabitants to those living here in the eighteenth century. However, now, following more recent discoveries, it is possible to see a full range of artefacts showing the gradual development of different regional cultural characteristics.

 ### Moriori

Over the last hundred years or so, early *tangata whenua* (local people) were often referred to as Moriori. Modern research shows that the culturally distinct Moriori people inhabited only the Chatham Islands, where they developed their own unique culture in the same way that Māori did on the mainland (Prickett, 2001). There is no evidence of a similar group on mainland Aotearoa/New Zealand. Many people believe that the development of the early theory that Moriori were the original inhabitants, who were killed and exiled by the Māori, was a way of exonerating colonial intrusion into Aotearoa/New Zealand.

Early peoples

As already stated, several *iwi* recognise the existence of earlier groups, who pre-dated the arrivals of their own ancestral *waka*. Ranginui Walker (1987) argues that among North Island tribes, earlier inhabitants are often remembered. In the Tūhoe area of the Bay of Plenty, the land rights of *tangata whenua* inhabitants are linked by marriage to the aristocratic ancestry of the migrant, eponymous ancestor, Tūhoe Pōtiki. This is confirmed by the *whakataukī* (proverb):

> *Nā Toi rāua ko Pōtiki te whenua, nā Tūhoe te mana me te rangatiratanga.*
> *The land came from Toi and Pōtiki, all forms of chiefly authority from Tūhoe.*

 ## Internal migration

Whilst many territorial adjustments occurred through localised increases and decreases in territory, some major geographic re-adjustments also occurred in the pre-contact era. For example, Te Āti Awa of Taranaki moved in from the Bay of Plenty, via Northland (Simmons, 1976). However, the South Island has been the destination of a series of migrations, from the Pacific and from within Aotearoa/New Zealand. The people who became known as Waitaha arrived on the *Uruao* from Polynesia around AD 850; Kāti Māmoe moved in from the Hawke's Bay in the sixteenth century, and Ngāi Tahu followed them, again from the East Coast, North Island, in the seventeenth century (Tikao, 1939). The *whakapapa* of South Island Māori today show a merging of these ancestral groups, amongst others, bearing witness to the intermarriage that was so important strategically (see Chapter 6) as new groups arrived. In many cases these internal migrations may have involved only a few hundred individuals, mostly men, but they became key ancestors in the *whakapapa* of their descendants.

 ## Phases of occupation

'Settlement'	up to	AD 1200
'Expansion and rapid change'	between	1200 and 1500
'Traditional'	between	1500 and 1769

Source: Based on Davidson, 1984: 223–4

The settlement phase in Aotearoa/New Zealand is characterised by scattered coastal communities that gradually penetrated inland. Initially the resources known to them in the Pacific, such as seafood, predominated. It is instructive to consider the differences that the earliest arrivals would have experienced. Their first impression would have been, undoubtedly, the immense size of the two main islands compared with Polynesia. The trees would have been much bigger, and more prevalent than had previously been seen. Many well-known foods would not have been available and, above all, it would have seemed cold. Food, clothing and housing would have been immediate concerns, and each would have been dealt with rather differently than had been the case in their homeland, due to significant differences in resources and the need to protect themselves from the cold. Thus, there were very early adaptations to the new environment. The freely available timber would have been utilised in varying degrees for building rather more substantial dwellings. By the end of the 'Settlement Period' permanent houses were built. The oldest known, at Moikau, Palliser Bay, has been dated to the twelfth century (Davidson, 1984). It closely resembles the well-known *wharepuni* sleeping houses, with a rectangular shape, a front porch that was enclosed on three sides and a central, internal hearth. Such dwellings were built well before the pallisaded *pā*, or fortified settlements, and were part of a *kāinga*, or permanent settlement. Seasonal camps, or *nohoanga*, had temporary dwellings, of the bivouac type, that would be replenished on successive visits.

New fibres would have been tested and utilised for clothing. *Moa* and seals quickly became major food sources. Palynology, the study of pollen laid down over the centuries, tells us that bracken increased significantly, at the expense of forest trees, from about the time of the first arrivals, strongly suggesting bush clearance by the initial occupants.

By AD 1200 all regions seem to have been discovered and all resources were being exploited. A major change the new arrivals experienced was a significant difference in rock types. In migrating from island Polynesia they crossed 'the Andesite Line', a fault line that divides the older, geologically complex west and south Pacific from the rather young volcanic and coral islands of the north and east. Archaeology tells us that by the end of the settlement phase in Aotearoa/New Zealand all these new rock types were being exploited. Some people have difficulty in accepting that the colder South Island would have been occupied as early as the North. However, just as with the seals and whales of the late eighteenth century and the gold of the nineteenth century, the ready availability of *moa* and *pounamu* would seem to have been sufficient attraction. Considerably larger numbers of *moa* remains have been found in the south (Anderson, 1983). Most were located at river-mouth butchery sites, to which the catches from further inland were floated on rafts of flax or *raupō*, known as *mōkihi*. Anderson suggests that well in excess of 100 000 *moa* must have been killed during the early occupation of southern New Zealand.

Adaptation/growth corresponded with the decline of the *moa*, which was probably extinct by AD 1500 (Anderson, 2002). *Kūmara* were prevalent as far south as Banks Peninsula, and *pā* (fortified villages) were beginning to emerge, especially in the north, mainly to protect crops. *Pā* did not reach Te Wai Pounamu until much later and numbers were small. By AD 1500 all artefacts are recognisably Māori (Mead, 1984).

The term 'classic' is ascribed to the phase that the first Europeans saw, with many complex *pā* and recognisable regional differences. Just as the early arrivals had adjusted to their new environment, so too did the advent of tribalism and the relative isolation that followed lead to local adjustments. These adjustments are reflected in traditions, dialects and especially art. All are Māori, but each *iwi* was (and is) a separate social, cultural and political unit. Māori, at the time of the European contact, were not one homogeneous people.

Becoming Māori

Undoubtedly, the early Polynesian arrivals were not Māori, as such; they became Māori here in Aotearoa/New Zealand, in response to the new environment and in isolation from their relations who stayed behind in the Pacific. New foods required new equipment and different methods of cooking and cultivation, new and larger trees offered new opportunities, as did the new, harder rocks. A cooler, sometimes colder climate and wider expanses of land and forests, rivers and lakes, all rich with their own resources, demanded that the focus be shifted from the sea to the land. All necessitated the acquisition of new knowledge and techniques. As each group became self-sufficient, there was a decrease in dependence upon, and contact with, other groups. Eventually, this trend resulted in the differences in language and *tikanga* (customs) that we associate today with different *iwi*. Similarly, the relative isolation of descent groups from one another resulted in regional customs and tribal differences that were to be a feature of the Classic period, as by then, each group had adapted to a slightly different environment. Population pressures, and the ensuing competition for resources, led to the development of rigid systems of resource allocation and *iwi*-centrism and often inter-tribal conflict. As *iwi* have grown, and ramified, those that descend from a single *waka* are, of course, more closely related than *iwi* descending from different *waka* (see Chapter 6). Accordingly, *waka* has become a term for a loose political association of related *iwi*, sometimes used to describe a confederation of tribes, or region (for example: the Te Arawa confederation, the Mātaatua region).

 ## Conclusion

> *A culture is an adaptation to a specific environment and a change in environment will usually be accompanied by cultural adjustment* (Clarke, 1968: 142).

Prominent anthropologist David Clarke's quotation above can be extended to support the idea that a dramatic change in environment will be followed by a dramatic cultural adjustment. This is exactly what happened when the Polynesian ancestors of Māori arrived from the Pacific. When they arrived they would have been culturally indistinguishable from their relatives who had stayed behind, but over the years they evolved the distinctive Māori culture we know today.

FURTHER READING

Simmons (1976), Best (1924), Smith (1910), and Gudgeon (1895) all discuss early Māori arrivals. Davis (1990), Evans (1997) and (1998), Howe (2003), McKinnon (1997) and Prickett (2001) all provide general information of relevance to this chapter.

Chapter 4

Te reo Māori
Origins and development of the Māori language

John C. Moorfield and E. Lorraine Johnston

This chapter traces the origins of *te reo Māori* (*te reo*) and its relationship with other Polynesian and Oceanic languages. It discusses various aspects of *te reo* after first settlement, including dialectal variation and the state of *te reo* before and after European colonisation. There follow discussions of the impacts of writing and the English language, leading to the current socio-linguistic situation. The chapter finishes with a look at some of the strategies used for revitalisation of *te reo*.

 Origins

Historical linguists have traced the origins of *te reo* back to an original language known as Proto-Austronesian.[1] Scholars believe Proto-Austronesian originated on the island of Taiwan at least 5000 years ago. Austronesian languages occur throughout East Asia and the Pacific, from Madagascar in the west, to Rapa Nui (Easter Island) in the east, and from the Melanesian island chain to Aotearoa/New Zealand.

At some point Proto-Austronesian divided into four major sub-groups, and all but the Taiwanese languages belong to the sub-group known as Malayo-Polynesian. Proto-Malayo-Polynesian underwent a series of two-way splits that ultimately led to Proto-Oceanic, which is the original language that separated into approximately 450 Austronesian languages in Melanesia, Micronesia, and Polynesia. There have been frequent migrations within Oceania from the time at which Proto-Oceanic formed and a great deal of interaction between the language communities, so the linguistic diversions cannot be accurately mapped as two-way splits.

Although there is general agreement amongst historical linguists that there are nine sub-groups of Proto-Oceanic, there is considerable debate about how they fit together. As can be seen in the map opposite and the diagram on page 38, *te reo* descends from the Eastern Polynesian dialect of the sub-group known as Central Pacific. This dialect is known as Proto-Polynesian.

There has been, and still is, considerable speculation about when all these diversions occurred. It seems likely that the spread of the Oceanic languages followed a similar pattern and timeline to the spread of Lapita pottery. If this is the case, the Central Pacific sub-group was probably formed between 1300 and 1000 BC. The diagram on page 38 gives some indication of a possible timeframe.

4 Origins and development of the Māori language

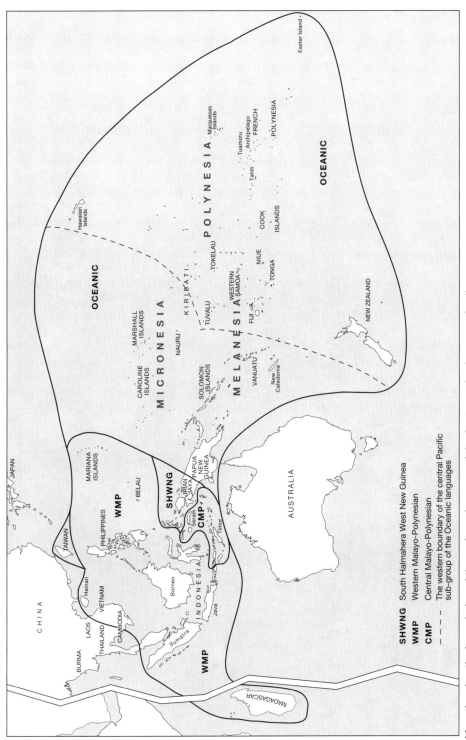

Map showing the boundaries of the major subgroups of the Austronesian language family

Source: Bellwood and Fox, 1995

4 Te reo Māori

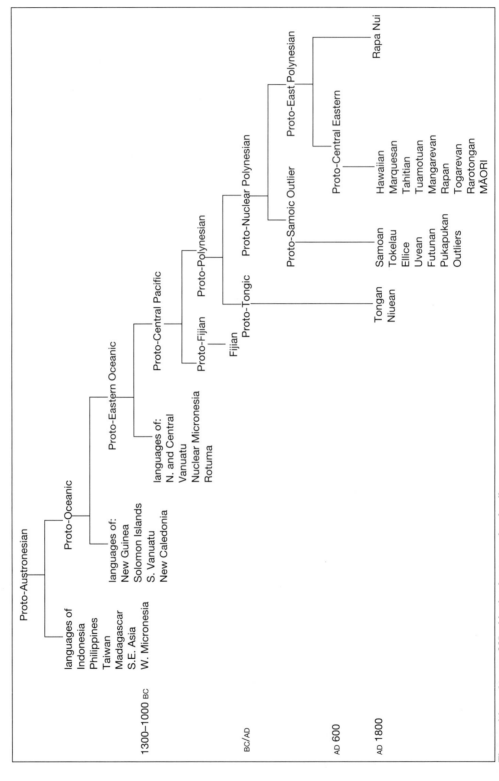

The position of te reo Māori in the Austronesian family
Source: Adapted from Davidson, 1984

Dialect

There are a number of regional dialects of *te reo*, which Bruce Biggs has grouped as South Island, Western, and Eastern. Biggs places Northland, Waikato-Maniapoto, and Taranaki in the Western dialect area, with Bay of Plenty and the East Coast in the Eastern dialect area. He then argues that Central tribes such as Te Arawa and Tūwharetoa share features of east and west (Biggs, 1961, 1968). Ray Harlow (1979: 133) conducted a comparison study of dialect wordlists and concluded that his statistics supported Biggs' proposed dialect areas. Differences are mainly in content words (lexicon) and sounds (phonology). There are, however, a number of quite significant differences within these broad areas.

Although there has been no formal study to date of syntactic variation between dialects, there is considerable anecdotal evidence that there are grammatical differences between dialects. There are also differences in the preferences for one structure over another, where two structures are available to fulfil the same function.

Pre-colonial and early colonial history

Every language is tied closely to the culture of the people who speak it. Before the arrival of the Pākehā, *te reo* was certainly perfectly suited to the world of its speakers. *Te reo*, like all living languages, has adapted to and continues to accommodate developments in technology and changes in the communication needs of its speakers. It had adapted to the changes experienced in living in Aotearoa/New Zealand as opposed to the environment in Hawaiki and it continued to adapt to the new technology and culture brought by the colonists. William Colenso wrote in 1867, almost one hundred years after Captain James Cook's first visit, that he had never known an old Māori '(or a young one who knows his own language), ever to be at a loss accurately and minutely to describe whatever he wished of any new thing or transaction to his countrymen' (Colenso, 1867: 46). Where there are important aspects of a culture in which fine distinctions are required, a language will develop to cope with these.

For example, in Māori society *pounamu* was, and is, a valued resource, which Ngāi Tahu used for trade with northern tribes. Consequently, terms developed to describe the different types of *pounamu*.

He momo pounamu Some varieties of greenstone	
Tangiwai	a translucent variety with streaks of white in the texture of the stone. Found at Piopiotahi (Milford Sound) and Te Wai Pounamu (Greenstone Valley)
Kahurangi	a light-green translucent variety, without flaws or spots; a highly valued variety
Inanga	a whitish or creamy-coloured variety, named after *inanga* (whitebait)
Tōtōweka	a variety with red/brown dots or streaks
Kahotea	dark-green with black spots

Kawakawa	olive-green and semitransparent, resembling the leaves of the *kawakawa* shrub
Kōkopu	a variety like *tōtōweka* but with smaller regular dots like the freshwater fish of the same name
Kokotangiwai	a soft and brittle variety which has streaks of white in the texture of the stone, similar to *tangiwai* but of rougher appearance. Found at Piopiotahi (Milford Sound) and Te Wai Pounamu (Greenstone Valley).
Pīpīwharauroa	a white and green variety like the dappled breast plumage of the bird of the same name (shining cuckoo)
Raukaraka/karaka	very dark-green variety, like the leaves of the *karaka* tree
Aotea	cloudy-white or blue-grey, like *ao tea* (white clouds)
Tongarewa/ tongarerewa	a semitransparent variety
Kutukutu	a speckled variety
Auhunga	a pale variety

Like *pounamu*, *kūmara*,[2] *taro*, and *harakeke* (flax) were extremely important resources in the lives of Māori, and developed multiple synonyms to distinguish the different types.

It is sometimes claimed that indigenous languages are unsuited for scientific purposes. But the following examples will make it obvious that *te reo* was perfectly adequate in aspects of science that were relevant to the culture and economics of the Māori in the early nineteenth century.

In the world of astronomy, there was an extensive body of knowledge of the celestial realm, only some of which survives. There are terms for the types of celestial bodies and the planets. While Māori often grouped the stars into constellations differently from European groupings, there was a thorough understanding of the movements of the stars and planets. Each of the lunar months of the Māori was heralded by the appearance of particular stars.

This astronomical knowledge was important for the division of time and the *maramataka* (the Māori calendar). Each night of the lunar month had its own name, and the *maramataka* contained knowledge about the suitability of a particular night for such things as planting crops, fishing, hunting birds, gathering wild crops, and harvesting resources. The movement of the stars and constellations was also important in the sophisticated navigational system of Polynesians. Of course, the language conveyed all this information.

There are many other aspects of the field of science that could be discussed where the knowledge of Māori was quite profound, resulting from close observation of the environment. Hand in hand with this was the linguistic capability to convey that knowledge. Other examples include the detailed terminology and knowledge about eels, fish and fishing; birds and their behaviour; the weather; and trees and their medicinal uses.

In the pre-European Māori world, communication over distance was by way of messenger or a series of messages relayed over shorter distances, often accompanied by some visual symbol. Communication over time was by way of visual symbols. These occurred in the patterns of *whakairo* (carving), *tukutuku* (woven wall panels), *kōwhaiwhai* (painted rafter patterns) and sometimes in patterns woven into clothing.

Tradition, values, and societal mores were transmitted orally from generation to generation, usually from grandparents to grandchildren. *Waiata* (song), especially *oriori* (an instructional chant), and *kōrero pūrākau* (myth, legend and historical tales) also played a large part in intergenerational transmission of knowledge and values, as did proverbial sayings, known in Māori as *whakataukī* (proverbs about social values), *whakatauāki* (proverbs that urge particular actions or behaviour), and *pepeha* (statements of tribal identity). There are a significant number of these. Here is a popular one relating to the pursuit of excellence and diligence:

> *Whāia e koe te iti kahurangi; ki te tuohu koe, me maunga teitei.*
> (Pursue the small valued treasure; if you stoop, let it be to a lofty mountain.)

Many *whakatauāki* and *whakataukī* encourage hard work, emphasise the importance of learning, and urge the pursuit of perfection. In fact, there were *whakatauāki* and *whakataukī* relevant to all areas of life, whereas *pepeha* regulated the aspects of tribal coherence.

Not only was *te reo* perfectly adapted to the pre-colonial world of the Māori, the Māori people also managed to communicate effectively over distance and time without the need for a phonology-based writing system.

With the advent of colonisation, missionaries came to these shores to convert the native population to Christianity. The foundation of Christian teaching of the time was catechism and scripture, so in the missionaries' view there was an urgent need to develop a writing system for *te reo*.

Orthographic development and print

Missionary scholars attempted to develop an orthography of *te reo*; each contributing to the 'finished product' which is in use today. As with many other languages around the world, scholars transmuted *te reo* to writing using a set of symbols developed for another language and another culture.

One of the earliest attempts at recording *te reo* was by Dr John Savage, in 1807. He included in his book a vocabulary list, which demonstrated major inconsistencies in the way ethnographers reproduced the sounds of *te reo*. Savage, like many others of the time, wrote the sounds as he heard them, and in relation to the sounds of the English language, with the result that often only the writer understood what the symbols were intended to represent. Thomas Kendall, in *He Korao no New Zealand* (1815), also represented the sounds of *te reo* inconsistently.

The first attempt to develop a representational orthography for *te reo* came three years later, when two Māori went to England and met with Professor Samuel Lee,

Professor of Arabic at Cambridge University. Lee was unable to complete the work when the two Māori had to return to New Zealand due to ill health. In 1820, Kendall went to England accompanied by two other Māori, who also met with Professor Lee. Later the same year the Lee/Kendall orthography was used for the first time. This was very close to present-day orthography, with the exception of later refinements by the Reverend William Yates in 1830. Apart from showing no distinction between the w and wh sounds, and no marking of vowel length, Yates' orthography was the same as we use today.

Alongside the development of orthographic conventions, the use of print medium was growing. All printing was carried out in either Sydney or England until William Colenso established the first successful press in the Bay of Islands in 1835. Most of the printing from this press was in *te reo*, but written by missionaries for the purposes of religious instruction. The Wesleyan Reverend Woon established a press on the Hokianga in 1836, again used mainly for religious purposes.

Interest in reading and writing was steadily growing amongst the Māori population during this period (Parr, 1961), with many Māori who had learned to read and write from the missionaries passing the knowledge on once they returned home. Indeed, as Bruce Biggs (1968: 73) speculates, 'It seems possible, indeed likely, that by the middle of the nineteenth century a higher proportion of the Māori than of the settlers were (sic) literate in their own language'. An independent traveller of the time (Jameson, 1842) noted that in nearly every village in the North Island the young Māori could all read and write *te reo*, and often taunted illiterate Pākehā. The books produced by the missionary presses were therefore in great demand, as the only available mass-produced reading material in *te reo*.

In 1858, the Austrian Emperor presented a press and type to the Māori of Ngāruawāhia. This was the first time that the Māori language was printed by Māori, for Māori, and the press was used for political purposes, printing the Kīngitanga newspaper *Te Hokioi*.

Bilingualism and the shift to English

The Education Ordinance Act of 1847 allowed for government subsidy of boarding schools, but to gain the subsidy, schools had to teach in both the English and Māori languages. Many young Māori were keen to learn to read, write and speak in English once the opportunity was there, but learning the English language was a much longer and slower process than the gaining of literacy had been, and most of the teaching continued to be in *te reo*.

The unsettled conditions during and after the land wars of the 1860s led to the death of the mission schools. The Native Schools Act, 1867, which allowed for the establishment of government day schools, also hastened their demise, as it meant the withdrawal of support for the mission school system. Government schools had to teach in English as far as practicable and, in fact, were encouraged to employ teachers who spoke only English. Despite these developments, *te reo* continued to be the main medium of communication for Māori, in all domains, into the early twentieth century, as most Māori were still living in homogeneous rural communities.

By 1920, some Māori, Sir Āpirana Ngata amongst them, had begun advocating the teaching of the English language in Māori schools, as English had become the language of commerce. It is almost certain that these Māori believed that the *marae*, the home, and other Māori domains would ensure continued transmission of the language. The vision was for a bilingual nation, or at least a bilingual Māori population, and they could not have foreseen the disintegrating of Māori communities that arose from the urban migration that followed the end of World War II. Government policy for the urbanisation of Māori was to 'pepperpot' Māori who migrated to the cities amongst the non-Māori population, to aid their integration into the urban environment. However well-intentioned this may have been, in practice it meant the demise of Māori speech communities within the cities.

Wherever two languages are in contact over a period of time it is inevitable that some form of bilingualism will develop to accommodate the inter-group communication needs, and differing forms of societal bilingualism have influenced *te reo* in its post-colonial history. In the early years of contact, most Māori spoke only *te reo*, most Pākehā spoke only English (or French in some cases), and communication between the two groups was by way of a few bilingual individuals. By the early twentieth century many individuals, both Māori and Pākehā, were bilingual, but slowly the situation was moving to a point where the majority of bilingual speakers were Māori. The current situation is that the statistical and political majority are monolingual speakers of English, and speakers of *te reo* are bilingual. Not only that, for the majority of English/Māori bilinguals, English is the first language, and *te reo* the second. The continued survival of the language depends on a very small pool of first language speakers of *te reo* who are also speakers of English, and a moderately larger group of bilingual individuals for whom *te reo* is a second language.

Chapter 19 discusses more fully the various political influences that affected *te reo* and Māori education. Suffice to say here that by the time Richard Benton conducted a survey of speakers of Māori between 1973 and 1978, Māori themselves had already begun to realise that their language was under serious threat, and many had resolved to act. Benton's survey showed that only 20% of Māori were fluent in the language, and the vast majority of those were elderly.

 ## Current socio-linguistic situation

There are very few domains left where *te reo* is the dominant or preferred language (for instance on the *marae* at *hui* and *tangihanga*), and many Māori today do not have ready access to these domains. A great deal of Māori cultural activity takes place on ancestral *marae* in rural areas, but most Māori now live in urban centres. A steady urban drift, particularly since World War II, has led to the disintegration of *te reo* speaking communities, and hence a decline in the number of Māori language speakers. In the 2001 Census, one in four people who identified as Māori reported the ability to speak the language, and nearly half of these are under 25 years of age (Statistics NZ, 2001). While it is encouraging that young people are acquiring the language, it is of concern that the greater percentage of *te reo* speakers continues to be in the over-sixty age group. English is the language of instruction in the vast majority of school classrooms. It is also the overwhelmingly dominant language of the media.

In the last 20 years, there have been some exciting developments in the struggle for *te reo* to return to being an everyday language heard in a wide range of contexts. These developments include:

- Te Kōhanga Reo (Māori language pre-school), Kura Kaupapa Māori (Māori language primary school), Wharekura (Māori language secondary school) and Wānanga (Māori tertiary institutions) using *te reo* as the communication medium;
- parents using *te reo* with their young children;
- Māori-operated radio stations throughout the country, all of which broadcast at least partially in *te reo*;
- some Māori language programmes on television and the prospect of a Māori television channel;
- at least one university degree taught in *te reo*;
- the 1987 Māori Language Act which established Te Taura Whiri i te Reo Māori (the Māori Language Commission) and made *te reo* an official language of this country;
- teacher education programmes for staff in Māori language classes and Māori medium classes and schools;
- Māori Studies departments at all New Zealand universities;
- an increasing number of publications in *te reo*;
- popular music composed and sung in *te reo*.

Māori continues to be the formal language of the *marae*. Here, Professor Wharehuia Milroy of Ngāi Tūhoe delivers a *whaikōrero* at Oparure Marae in the King Country.

The National Māori Language Survey (NML) figures show encouraging signs that these initiatives are having an impact. Seventy-one per cent of adults surveyed listened at least once to *te reo* on the radio or television in a typical week, including 58% of the non-speakers. Seventy-five per cent of those who had school age children in the home enrolled them in either immersion or bilingual classrooms (Te Puni Kōkiri, 1998). Ministry of Education statistics carried in the NML report showed that between 1992 and 1996 the number of children enrolled in Māori medium education, in Kōhanga Reo, Kura Kaupapa Māori, and Māori medium classrooms, rose by 57%.

Lexical expansion in te reo Māori

There are a number of ways in which new vocabulary was, and is, created in *te reo*. As a result of the changes introduced by the colonists, many words were given new shades of meaning, for example, *parareka*, the horse-shoe fern whose large starchy rhizome was cultivated and eaten, is still used by Ngāti Porou of the East Coast as their word for the potato because of its similarity to the traditional food. Likewise, *mōwhiti/mōhiti* (ring/hoop) is used for spectacles, *ngā mōwhiti/ngā mōhiti*. Giving new meanings to existing words is a process used in all languages. Some of the names for varieties of greenstone given earlier are examples of this process in pre-European times.

The lexical bank is also expanded by the translation of concepts, a process known as loan translation or calquing. An example is *pāpara kāuta* for public house or pub. In this particular example, the word *pāpara* is a loanword from the English word 'public', while *kāuta* is from *te reo* meaning cooking shed, house, or shack.

A third way that new words were, and are, created is by joining or juxtaposing two established words. There are many examples of this from *te reo* in the nineteenth century, for example:

- *kī taurangi*   to promise, pledge, from *kī* (to say, saying) and *taurangi* (incomplete/unfulfilled)
- *wahahuka*   boasting, bombastic, from *waha* (mouth) and *huka* (foam, froth)
- *kirikā*   fever (*kiri* skin; *kā* to burn).

The addition of a prefix or suffix in a prescribed way is another common method of generating words in *te reo*, for example:

- by the addition of the causative prefix *whaka-* and its short form *whā-* (to make):
    - *whakamate*   to put to death
    - *whakatū*   to erect, set up
    - *whātoro*   to stretch out, touch
- by the addition of the prefix *kai-* (the person who) to transitive verbs:
    - *kaikōrero*   speaker
- by the addition of one of the nominalising suffixes *-nga*, *-tanga*, etc. (i.e. to turn the verb into a noun):
    - *hokinga*   return
    - *whakaaturanga*   show, exhibition.

Once European visitors began to arrive in Aotearoa/New Zealand, many new words were created by borrowing from the new languages that Māori encountered, most notably, but not exclusively, from English:

- *parau*   plough or to plough
- *tera*   saddle
- *hōiho*   horse.

Examples borrowed from other languages include:

- *mīere*   honey (from the French *miel*);
- *ture*   law (from the Hebrew *torah*);
- *whakawhetai*   to express thanks (from Tahitian).

The illustration opposite shows part of a full-page advertisement for Smith and Caughey in Queen Street, Auckland in the Māori newspaper *Te Korimako* of 15 November 1883. Numerous loanwords are included, mainly for items that would not have existed prior to the arrival of the Pākehā. Examples include: *moni* (money), *Te Mete* (Smith), *Kauwhe* (Caughey), *pauna* (pound), *paraikete* (blanket), *ota moni* (money order), *Kuīni Tiriti* (Queen Street), *Ākarana* (Auckland), *himi* (shimmy/chemise), *kawe* (cover/bedspread), *panikoti* (petticoat/dress), *winihi* (winceyette), *iāri* (yard) and *tōkena wūru* (woollen socks).

Modern *te reo*, both spoken and written, has many words which have been adapted from non-Polynesian sources and, usually, these have been changed to suit the phonological rules and orthographic conventions of Māori. In Aotearoa/New Zealand this process of adopting words from English into Māori and vice-versa has expanded the lexical bank of both languages. Harry Orsman has included about 700 headword entries in *The Dictionary of New Zealand English* that have been borrowed from *te reo*. The most obvious relate to the natural world, for example *kākāpō*, *kauri*, and *tarakihi*.

Borrowing is a normal language process. It is not something unique to *te reo*. In recent years there has been a trend by some speakers and learners of *te reo* to reject borrowing from English, seemingly to keep the language pure, but this is also possibly to reject the language of the colonists and to counter derogatory criticism about the language.

Once English became the language of the school and *te reo* was not required to cope with developments in certain domains of use that belonged to the school and higher learning, its adaptation slowed or ceased to develop in those areas. Mathematics and modern science are examples. However, in the last ten years these subjects have begun to be taught in Māori-medium classes, so the creation of vocabulary to cope with these subjects has taken on a new impetus. Te Taura Whiri i te Reo Māori, the Māori Language Commission, has spearheaded this development in response to requests from schools, speakers and learners of *te reo*, and translators.

The accusation is often made, particularly by people who do not speak the language, that *te reo* is not able to cope with some domains of use in the modern world. It would be more correct to say that for about 120 years it was not required to cope with such areas of language as mathematics and modern science because in that time those subjects, and others, were always taught in English and were not normally part of everyday conversation. Once English became the school medium in the education of Māori children, the future of *te reo* was threatened. Its status declined in the eyes of children. How could a language have status for children if it was not part of school life?

 ## The revival of bilingualism

Some firmly held myths have been propounded about bilingualism, not only in New Zealand but in other parts of the world as well. This is despite evidence that would be obvious to most people travelling in other countries, such as in Europe, where bilingualism and multilingualism are normal.

12   TE KORIMAKO.   [Nowema 15, 1883.

☞ KA RANEA TE MONI ☜
KI TE MEA KA WHAKAAETIA TE TANGO I TE

Takai Taonga Rongo Nuia TE METE raua ko KAUWHE.

He rau noa atu nga reta whakanui, na te Pakeha, na te Maori.

Ko Nui Hare, no Motukaraka, e ki ana "I tae tika mai te Takai-taonga; a nui atu taku pai ki ara hanga katoa. Mehemea i hokona e konei ena taonga, kia rua pauna, ki a koe kotahi ano."

E tuturu ana te pai o ia o ia puweru, e ai Ta Muri, ki te kore e paingia nga takai, me whakahoki mai kia whakahokia atu te moni.

Kahore ano he Takai Taonga i whakahokia mai ka a maua, kahore he kupu whakahe mo te utu.

Nga utu o etahi Taonga. Engari me whakaatu mai i te utu, i te ahua o te puweru.

Ki te mea he £1 te utu o te Takai, kahore te kai hoko e utu i te haringa atu ki nga unga atu o nga wahi katoa e taea tikatia ana i Akarana.

Ekore rawa nga taputapu e tukua atu ki te kore e tae tahi ake te moni me te tono, no te mea ko te take i ngawari ai te utu, he tere mai no nga moni.

He puweru anahe, he Paraikete hoki. Engari koa me peka mai nga Maori kia kite ratou i te ahua o nga Kakahu, i te ngawari hoki o te utu.

☞ MO TE MONI ANAKE. ☜

Ko nga tono katoa me te Taonga me Takai mai ki te Tiaki, ki te Noti ra nei, ki te Ota Moni ra nei, Me tuku ki a

TE METE RAUA KO KAUWHE,
300 me te 302, Kuini Tiriti,
AKARANA.

☞ Mo te Moni anake.]   [Mo te Moni anake. ☜

Himi Wahine, 1/6 ki te 5/6
Kawe Moenga, 2/11 ki te 10/6
Toroiho, 2/6 ki te 7/6
Panikoti, Huruhuru, 2/11 ki te 12/
Arapaka me te Hatini Panikoti kei ana utu ano
Taihi, 2/3 ki te 10/6; 3/6 ki te 5/11
Kakahu Tamariki, 1/11 ki te 5/11
200 Korako, Tiakote, Pihua, 10/ ki te 84/

NAMA 18. – HE TAKAI MO TE KAI-NOHO TAKIWA. – Te Utu, 63/.
1 pea Koata 11, Paraikete Taimaha
10 iari Winihi, 15 iari kaore ra nei
2 pea Tokena Wuru Poto, na te ringi i whatu. Ki paingia, me tokena wahine
6 iari Parene Raununui
12 iari Kareko kaha kerei
6 iari Kareko Ma, kaha rawa
7 iari Winihi, hei hate; 10 iari Mea Muka ra nei
1 Panikoti Mahana, whatu-a-ringa
1 Pouaka-Pupu, nga taonga o roto, he Miro, he Huku, he Ngira, he Pine, me te Temara.

PUWERU TANE, TAMARIKI HOKI.
He Tarau, 5/11 ki te 10/6
He Tarau, he Kouma, 12/6
He Koti 8/6
He Huti, pai atu, 35/
Huiti Tamariki, 7/6 ki te 19/6
Tuiti Kaiapoi, he Huiti, 19/6 ki te 27/6
Huiti Puru Raranga, 21/ ki te 47/6
Koti, 10/6
Huiti Kaiapoi, 45/9 ki te 63/
Potae, 2/6
Toroiho mo nga Wae mo te Uma, 1/6 ki te 2/6
Kara, /6 te pouaka; Rinene, /6 ki te /9

Neketai, /6
Tarau Mohikena, Whai Kara, 4/11
Mohikena Mea Ma, 6/6 ki te 10/6
Tarau Rinene, 3/3 to 4/6
Tarau Taka Puru, 3/11 ki te 4/6
Hate Tane, he muka e ia tuitui e matou, 2/9
Mo etahi, 1/9
Hate Waiti, 2/6 ki te 7/6
Kara pai te Ahua mo te iari, /3¾, /4¾, /5¾
Kakahu Otamira, 1/1 mo te iari
Nga mea Puwheru, Pango me ara atu ahua he Hatini, /6½, 7¼, /7½, /10¼, 1/1½
He Karatia Whakahekeheke, 3¼, /4¾, /6¾, /8¾
Puru Raranga mo te tamariki, mo te Puweru eke Hoiho, /11¾; he Wuru anahe, ¼, 4/6, 1/8, ki te 3/6
He Noni Wera, i nga kara katoa, 1/3½ te iari
He Wuru Anahe, he Kamaraiti, /10 ki te 1/4

Source: *Te Korimako*, November 15, 1883. Auckland City Library, Special Collections

It was a commonly held view for some time by various people, including educators, that maintenance or development programmes for a minority language in schools would retard English language development. Consequently, it was assumed that if minority children had deficiencies in English, then they needed instruction and practice in English, not in their own language. Parents of minority children were fed the advice that they should communicate with their children in English or their children would be confused and their chances of academic success would be reduced.

In fact, this was not only bad advice, but in Aotearoa/New Zealand it has resulted in the steady decline in the number of speakers of *te reo*. Research evidence published in the last thirty years not only supports the idea that being brought up speaking two or more languages is not a disadvantage, but that there are some subtle advantages, as well as the major benefits of being able to speak two languages and being comfortable in two cultures.

Some of these advantages include:
- Proficiency in two languages
- Greater social sensitivity and cultural understanding, i.e. more tolerance of other people and different cultures
- Better first language skills
- Greater adeptness at divergent and creative thinking
- Increased cognitive, social and emotional development
- Greater verbal and non-verbal intelligence
- Better understanding of how languages work. New languages are learned more easily
- Positive self concept and pride in one's background
- Increased probability of employment
- Stronger relationships between home and school
- Maintenance and revitalisation of the Indigenous language and culture.

This is borne out to some degree by the NML, which reported that Māori who had completed post compulsory education training were more likely to speak *te reo* than those whose formal education finished at school (Te Puni Kōkiri, 1996). Māori with university degrees were found to be considerably more likely than others to speak *te reo*. Over three-quarters (76%) of people with university degrees spoke Māori to some extent. Of those adults who were employed at the time of the survey, the people most likely to speak *te reo* were employed in legislative, administrative, managerial and professional occupations, and in technical and associated professional occupations.

Joshua Fishman (1980) has stressed the importance of 'reward systems'. People in a speech community speak the way they do because of the influence of reward systems requiring such speech. Using the language of the family, community and society emphasises a person's membership of that particular group. This social aspect has the greatest influence on the child, but educational, fiscal, political and religious spheres play their part as well – increasingly so as the child grows up and moves out beyond the influence of the home. These most certainly have been significant in determining the changes in the state of *te reo* since early contact with Pākehā.

Any development that adds to the reward system for speaking *te reo* is useful. This is why Māori language programmes on television and the Māori television channel are important. It is also the reason that Māori-medium education is so integral to the maintenance and revival of the language.

Schools, government departments, institutions (like universities), churches and the media can help language maintenance by using and reinforcing the minority language, in our case *te reo*, aiding literacy and fluency in it and giving it status in the eyes of the child and the community – or they can do the opposite and counteract the influence of the minority group child's family and community. As Fishman points out:

> *Stable bilingualism and biculturalism cannot be maintained on the basis of open and unlimited interaction between minorities and majorities ... Open economic access and unrestricted intergroup action ... are destructive of minority ethnolinguistic continuity (1980: 171).*

Notes

1. A proto-language is the hypothetical ancestor of a group of related languages. For example, Proto-Austronesian is the hypothetical ancestor of all the Austronesian family of languages.
2. Colenso lists 47 Māori names of varieties of *kūmara* from northern and eastern tribes, pointing out that the list was not exhaustive (1880: 32–33). His sources were three Māori from Te Tai Tokerau (Northland) and three from Te Tai Rāwhiti (East Coast). Best collected 94 names for varieties of *kūmara*, but notes that these were collected from a number of different districts, so it is possible that some were different names for the same varieties (1925: 55–56).

FURTHER READING

For a discussion of the relationship between the spread of Austronesian languages and Lapita pottery, see Spriggs (1984, 1995). Further discussion on lexical and phonological differences in dialect can be found in Harlow (1991), and for examples of syntactic differences in Māori language dialects, see Biggs (1989). For a study of the grammar of the Māori, see Harlow (2001).

Chapter 5

Papa-tūā-nuku
Attitudes to land

Jim Williams

Land is fundamental to Māori identity. Accordingly, it is much more than a mere resource; it is a large part of Māori *mana* as well as being the primary ancestor; it embodies the past and, at the same time, is the foundation for future generations. Māori are connected to the land by *whakapapa*: on one level, inheriting resource rights (*take*) from certain ancestors; on another level, being linked to specific places because ancestors are there. Through their deeds, ancestors' *mauri* has become the *mauri* of the place where the deed was performed and, accordingly, the ancestor is seen as being part of that place. This ancestral connection is one reason for the spiritual connection that Māori feel with the land and which obliges them to care for it on behalf of all generations yet to come.

The Māori word for land is *whenua*, the same word as for the placenta, which in most *iwi* was buried in the earth, at a place of importance to the *whānau* (often with a tree planted over it). At death, the body was buried in a place sacred to the *whānau*, completing the circle. This symbolises interconnectedness between people and the land, which is the basis of the word for local people: *tangata whenua*.

The Māori view of land is rooted in the creation story featuring Papa-tūā-nuku, Rangi-nui, Tangaroa, Tāne, Tāwhiri-mātea, Tū-mata-uenga, Rongo, Haumia, and others as the *atua* who influence their various domains (see Chapter 1). *Atua* is often translated as 'gods' but it is rather more helpful to remember that present generations are linked to them by *whakapapa* and therefore to think of them as 'ancestors of ongoing influence'. To understand the Māori attitude to resources it is important to appreciate the relationships between these *atua* and the need for humans to take particular care whenever the domains of different *atua* are being affected. *Karakia* are the ritual formulae for expressing the required respect at these times and, especially, when mediating between the domains of different *atua*.

Māori are not just joined to the land, they are an integral part of nature, with a relationship to every other living thing, defined by *whakapapa*. From it comes the requirement for people to be guardians of nature. Māori refer to such stewardship as *kaitiakitanga*. Integral to effective *kaitiakitanga* is the notion that the *mauri* of resources must not be impacted by people's actions. *Mauri* may be enhanced but never weakened as it is the key to the health of both individual species and whole ecosystems.

Polynesian origins

It is important to keep in mind the island origins of ancestral Māori, as land rights in Aotearoa/New Zealand were largely based on the same ideas that had existed in Polynesia. On their arrival in Aotearoa/New Zealand, the culture and many of the attitudes of our *tūpuna* (ancestors) were the same as those they had been familiar with in their Pacific homelands. Slowly, the details were adapted to suit the requirements of the local environment.

Accordingly, let us look at the *whakapapa* of 'Ngāti Mea', the people of a hypothetical island, somewhere in island Polynesia.

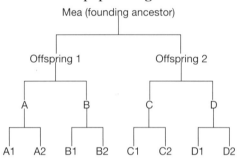

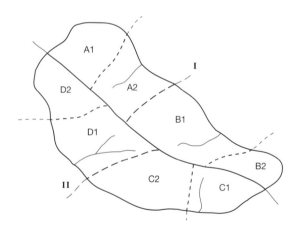

Geographical distribution of clan segments on the hypothetical island

Source: Kirch, 1984: 32

As can be seen in the map (left), there is a correspondence between the *whakapapa* and land ownership on our hypothetical island. The eponymous ancestor, Mea, (the ancestor after whom the group was named) would originally have had rights over the whole island. In the next generation, two children shared the island, their boundary being the solid line along the centre. Then, their families A, B, C, and D brought about a further subdivision where the thick broken line cuts the island into quarters. When descent groups split in this way, they are said to ramify. Eventually, further ramification occurred so that there are now eight segments. In the example each is at the same genealogical distance from 'Mea'. Each should be considered as a family group, or *hapū*, each with its own island territory.

Other points to note in the diagrams are:

- Water rights are identical to land rights in all cases.
- Boundaries extend out to sea so that each territory contains some of each type of terrain:
  - hills,
  - valleys,
  - coastal strip;

  and each type of water:
  - streams,
  - swamps,
  - shallow coastal waters,
  - reefs,
  - deep sea.

  (The parcel of land, water and resources allocated in this fashion is known as an ecotone, which may be thought of as 'a little bit of everything available'.)
- The focus is not really the land as such, or even land and water, but the resources, or *mahinga kai*, that are supported. *Mahinga kai* are local habitats where a particular group of resources are exploited in a sustainable manner.

The ethic involved is not one of land ownership but *kaitiakitanga*, which obliged each generation to pass on to their descendants at least as good a supply of resources as they, themselves, had inherited. This led one Ngāi Tahu *kaumātua* (elder) to emphasise, at a hui in 1997, the responsibility to forthcoming generations: 'We did not inherit the land: we have it on loan from our grandchildren.' Those who exercise *kaitiakitanga* are known as *kaitiaki*. In the physical world, *kaitiaki* are those folk who hold *mana whenua*; in the spiritual dimension, *kaitiaki* are *atua*, usually the spirits of deceased ancestors. Margaret Mutu (2002: 87) writes, 'These spiritual assistants often manifest themselves in physical forms such as fish, animals, trees or reptiles.' Spiritual *kaitiaki* are sometimes referred to as *taniwha*.

The right to hold responsibility for land or resources is *mana whenua*; it is based on *take* and *ahi-kā*. It should be stressed that *mana whenua* operates at various levels and is always local. Tribal *mana whenua* will operate over the wide area that is their *rohe* (territory), whilst that of a single *whānau* will relate to specific resources within the greater tribal *rohe*. *Mana whenua* is linked, inextricably, with *rangatiratanga*, the right to exercise authority. *Rangatiratanga* is usually inherited from the male line. In contrast, *mana whenua* can often come through the female line. For example, Ngāi Te Atawhiua is one of a number of Ngāi Tahu *hapū* that have women as their eponymous ancestor and these are, in the main, Kāti Māmoe women who brought the *mana whenua* to their Ngāi Tahu marriage partners. Herries Beattie (1954) comments that intermarriage between Ngāi Tahu men and Kāti Māmoe women was much more common than the reverse. This was a means of securing access to Kāti Māmoe resources. Emma Stevens (1993) concurs, based on her interviews with a group in South Westland who continue to describe themselves as 'Kaati Mamoe'.

It should be stressed that to a Māori, one does not hold *mana whenua* **over** land, for that would be tantamount to claiming *mana* over Papa-tūā-nuku. *Mana whenua*, drawn from Papa-tūā-nuku, is held in an area and relates to decisions **about** resources. It is the basis for all the responsibilities incumbent in *kaitiakitanga*.

The folk who exercise *kaitiakitanga* over a territory are sometimes known as *tangata whenua*. They hold responsibility for the land. Important to the understanding of this is the fact that it is a form of communal ownership, *rangatira* always representing the wider descent group.

Rights to land were considered to have been obtained by *take*, sometimes referred to as *take whenua*. As George Asher and David Naulls (1987: 5) explain, 'although slight tribal differences existed in the customs associated with Māori land tenure, there was general agreement on the basic principles by which tribal rights to land were established'.

Take	
Taunaha/Whenua kite hou/Tapatapa	These are rights obtained through initial discovery (or naming) and still held by the descendants. All *iwi* have their traditions which, supported by archaeological evidence, suggest that Māori had discovered all areas of New Zealand by the twelfth century.
Take tuku	Rights ceded to an outsider, someone who would not normally be expected to have such rights, for example an incoming migrant, as part of a peace treaty, or in compensation for a serious misdeed. *Utu*, or reciprocity, is the essential notion behind such grants.
Take ōhākī/Take tūpuna	This literally translates to deathbed speech or inheritance. In the normal course of events, for land rights that had been inherited, the *take* that had applied in the previous generation would be passed on. However, sometimes, at death, a special disposition of land could be made. *Take ōhākī/Take tūpuna* refers to the latter.
Take raupatu/Umutāngata	Land obtained through warfare, often supported by marriage. Since contact, *raupatu* is the term that Māori use to refer to confiscation by the Government.

However, in all cases, for land rights to continue there was an important over-riding consideration of *ahi-kā*, or *ahi-kā roa* (continued possession). For example, when land was taken in warfare it was necessary for the conquerors to completely expel or enslave the vanquished in order to establish their own entitlement. Then, the victors must remain in possession (Asher and Naulls, 1987). It is usually believed that at least three generations of absence are required before the 'fires are cold' and the new occupancy fully confirmed.

Although inheritance through the male line was favoured, rights were ambilineal. An individual could claim rights through any one of four grandparents. However, as a claim had to be confirmed by residence, normally only one such set of rights could be claimed (Walker, 1987). The ability to claim through women was particularly important in times of war and internal migration, as strategic marriages could ensure that rights would not be questioned in later generations. A Ngāi Tahu *whakataukī* stresses this combination:

> *Nā te rākau kē i riro ai te whenua.*
>
> *It was through the male appendage (rather than warfare) that land rights were obtained.*

Ancestors in the landscape

Tūpuna not only provide the inherited entitlements, they are the land. At birth, their *whenua* was buried in the ancestral land, at their death they were buried in it. They, and their deeds, are recorded in the place-names, many of which are not entered on official maps. In many cases these are now considered '*wāhi tapu*' (sacred places). All this contributes to folks' connection to the land and reconfirms their *mana whenua*. As Mutu (2002: 78) points out: 'The imposition of an English-based tenure system cannot change that fact.'

In many districts the interests of a number of *hapū*, and sometimes *iwi*, overlapped in the same general area. This was particularly so in the South Island where the focus was on individual resources rather than the land itself. Accordingly, it could be the case that in a single locality the rights to take birds from a forest would belong to the descendants of one *tupuna*, while the rights to the waterways running through that forest would belong to the descendants of another. Moreover, descendants of a third could have the rights to any fernroot that grew under the trees, while the *mana* to cut down specific trees might belong to the descendants of a fourth (Anderson, 1980).

In the event that any group had plenty of a certain resource, e.g. *tītī* (mutton birds) but their neighbour had very little, a limited usage right might be ceded to the neighbour, especially if harvesting of the resource was labour intensive or the season short. This was another form of *tuku* and was an important way of securing boundaries by ensuring the goodwill of one's neighbours. Boundary disputes could often be avoided by allowing neighbours a limited access. Merata Kāwharu (1998) explains that *tuku* was the usual way of ceding a land interest to somebody who was not of the descent group that had *mana whenua*. She explains that it was more akin to a lease than to a sale. In other instances, a similar situation might be achieved through trading the birds for another resource that was rare within the area of the first group. Thus, *kaitiakitanga* was not merely claimed by a group but confirmed by the wider society, with particular emphasis on one's neighbours.

Disputes

As the *mana* of various chiefs increased or decreased and as strategic marriages altered the power balances, certain adjustments would be required, especially as population pressures built up. Usually adjacent *hapū* made their adjustments peacefully, but if these proved unsuccessful, war could break out, often leading to changes in resource access rights and new marriages; each would again bind the groups in a peaceful relationship. Most wars were fought over women and/or resource rights as shown by the *whakataukī*: 'He wahine, he whenua, i ngaro ai te tangata' (for women and for land, men die). Sometimes an excuse, such as an insult to the *mana* of a chief, might be used, but the real focus is likely to have been resources. It must be stressed that in the event of land being captured, the principle of *ahi kā* continued to apply. If the victors could not completely extinguish the fires of the vanquished then they would not gain rights. This was particularly so in parts of Te Ika-a-Māui. The history of warfare in Te Wai Pounamu is much more recent and tended to be over issues of personal *mana* – again that was usually just the excuse; the real objective was the land and its resources. The early nineteenth century wars with Te Rauparaha and his allies were largely to do with access to *pounamu*.

 ## Resource management

An essential concept for management of natural resources is *rāhui*. *Rāhui* worked somewhat like the well-known duck-shooting season, which runs from the first Saturday in May until the end of July. Then a *rāhui* is imposed until the following May. In traditional times, whenever resources were becoming depleted, or were needed for an important, forthcoming occasion, a *rangatira* would impose a *rāhui*, or 'closed season'. Strong social controls ensured that the *rāhui* was not broken, as to do so was to trample on the *mana* of the *rangatira* who had imposed it, whereupon he would use all the force at his disposal to punish an offender. The *tītī* (muttonbird) islands in Foveaux Strait continue to be managed in this manner – nobody may set foot on the islands during the breeding season.

By contrast, *wāhi tapu* are permanently set aside and the resources not harvested. It was believed that sanctions of a spiritual nature would ensue if a break of *tapu* occurred. Other areas were deemed *owheo* and harvesting of any resources was forbidden, not for reasons of *tapu* but to facilitate the good stewardship of resources. Only when the people were under considerable threat could *tikanga* be broken, and a harvest permitted and it would take *karakia* by the most important *tohunga* to effect such a relaxation of the rules.

 ## Boundaries

Boundaries of geo-political districts, i.e. areas controlled by different groups, were usually the barriers that were most easily defended. Following the Polynesian model, this was usually the top of a ridge, but occasionally – particularly in Te Wai Pounamu – rivers could be boundaries. But as it was normal in Māori society for both sides of a river to be in the same ownership, whereas Pākehā regard the river itself as the boundary, this became a major issue between the two cultures.

 ## Alienation

Land that was transferred to Pākehā ownership, by lease or freehold, at any time since the signing of The Treaty of Waitangi in 1840, is said to have been 'alienated'. Alienation has had a major effect upon Māori attitudes to land (Ward, 1986).

In the decades immediately after the signing of The Treaty of Waitangi, Māori were confirmed in the possession of their land, but by the beginning of the 1860s pressure on the settler Government for more land was becoming overwhelming. The Native Land Act 1862 and The Land Settlement Act 1863 marked the beginning of a series of laws designed to implement the changing Government philosophy. They legalised the confiscation of millions of acres, mainly in the Waikato, Bay of Plenty and Taranaki and enabled the settler-dominated Māori Land Court to determine ownership of Māori land, with a view to facilitating its sale. Further legislation with a similar objective followed and it was not until The Maori Affairs Act 1953 that Māori concerns for their land were reflected in legislation that focused on promoting Māori use of their land. But, of course, by then most of it had gone. Of Aotearoa/New Zealand's approximately 66 million acres, less than four million is still in Māori title, and only about 40 000 acres of that is in Te Wai Pounamu (Walsh, 1971; Ward, 1999:

The Ngāti Kahungunu tribe signing over ownership of Lake Wairarapa to the Crown at Papawai Pā. At the centre of the table sits Judge Butler. To his left is James Carroll. Tamahau Mahupuku sits on the ground to the left of the table. Many other prominent Wairarapa Māori leaders are also shown in the photograph. Papawai Pā was the seat of the Māori Parliament in the 1890s.

5   Attitudes to land

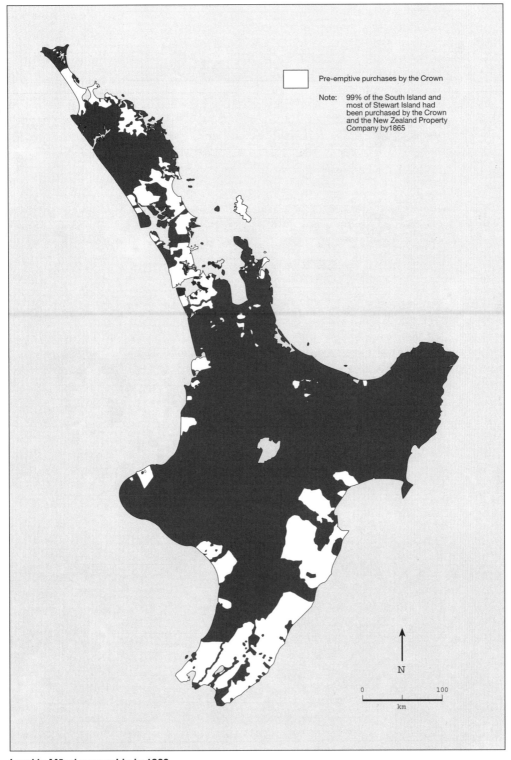

Land in Māori ownership in 1860

Source: Redrawn from maps produced by Max Oulton for Alan Ward, *National Overview* (Wellington: Legislation Direct, 1997)

58   5   Papa-tūā-nuku

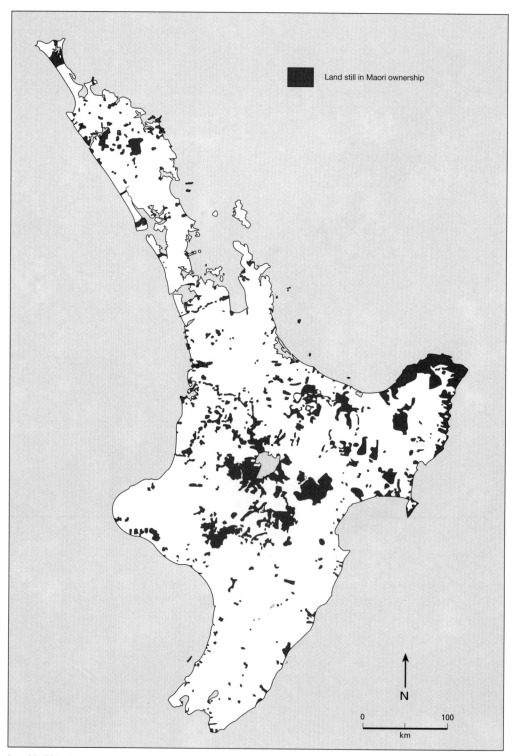

Land in Māori ownership in 1939

Source: Redrawn from maps produced by Max Oulton for Alan Ward, *National Overview* (Wellington: Legislation Direct, 1997)

maps 162–166). Land which has never been freeholded is termed Customary Title (previously, Native Title). Freehold land, or land that has come within the European land registration system, even if owned by Māori, is not, legally, Māori Land.

Land loss, and geographic dislocation from ancestral land, usually due to internal migration for economic reasons, are major causes of the marginalisation of Māori in contemporary Aotearoa/New Zealand society.

 ## Contemporary concerns

Despite losing much of their land, many Māori have persisted in holding traditional attitudes. However, this is by no means universal. When the new Māori land bill (which eventually became law as Te Ture Whenua Māori 1993) was being discussed in the early 1990s, there was vigorous debate about whether the new act should provide for the sale of Customary Land or whether the defining principle of permanent retention should prevail (Durie, 1998).

Te Ture Whenua Māori 1993 was the result of extensive consultation between Government and Māori and is built on traditional Māori philosophies, including such concepts as:
- Land is a *taonga tuku iho* to be held in trust for future generations.
- Accordingly, the act restricts alienation by:
  - giving new powers to Māori landowners to facilitate the retention, development and management of their land, including the opportunity to bring land previously freeholded back into customary title;
  - clarifying the Māori Land Court's role in such ways as to facilitate the desires of Māori owners.

In particular, Te Ture Whenua Māori 1993 provides for a series of new types of trust which allow Māori land to be managed on behalf of various classes of beneficiary, in particular those whose interests have become fragmented over the generations.

Many Māori, who continue to recognise a spiritual attachment and a sense of ongoing responsibility, both to the land and to future generations, are opposed to the prevailing European perspective in which land is regarded as a commodity, to be bought, used and sold to the financial advantage of the owner. In turn, neither do all Pākehā owners understand the more spiritual Māori perspective. This is an ongoing source of tension, made worse by the power-sharing that Māori are being offered as part of Treaty settlements. Power-sharing can be difficult at any time, but is especially hard when the parties fail to appreciate one anothers' outlook.

Dr Ranginui Walker (1990) confirms that for many Māori, traditional attitudes toward land persist, though some younger, urban Māori do see ancestral land only in terms of its economic worth. During the 1980s, this contributed to the debate over the new Māori Land Act, as mentioned above. Nevertheless, it is probably fair to say that for the majority, links to ancestral land (and waterways) remain powerful, even where that land has long been alienated. Folk continue to bury their *whenua* on the land, and to identify with it in their *mihi* (greeting).

> *Ko Aoraki te mauka,*
> *Ko Ōpihi te awa,*
> *Ko Kai Tahu te iwi.*
>
> *Aoraki/Mount Cook is the mountain*
> *Ōpihi is the river*
> *Ngāi Tahu are the people.*

FURTHER READING

Asher and Naulls (1987), Davis (1990), Sinclair (1992), and Smith (1960) all provide valuable information for this chapter.

Chapter 6

Whanaungatanga
Kinship

Michael P. J. Reilly

Māori creation narratives (see Chapter 1) stressed the important place of genealogies and kinship relations in Māori society. Kinship has been described as one of 'the fundamental categories of knowledge' for Māori. Not surprisingly, Māori take care to establish their kinship ties with both the natural world, and with other human beings. Indeed, kinship became a special study of 'high-born Māori'. Some in the nineteenth century were able to recite genealogies of up to 1400 people (Johansen, 1954). A person's various relationships, generated through marriage, kin ties and living arrangements, established the social structures of classical Māori society (in the eighteenth and early nineteenth centuries) and of the Māori society which emerged as a result of New Zealand's colonisation. Standard descriptions of Māori social structure have in the past simplified the more complex historical reality by establishing a four-tier hierarchy comprising the *whānau*, the *hapū*, the *iwi* and the *waka*. Each level supposedly progressed automatically up to the next tier once their population had grown to a sufficient size and genealogical depth. This chapter will critically review the standard descriptions of this hierarchy, incorporating newer research that stresses the complex dynamism of this social system. Other issues to be covered include the importance of rank, class, and the cultural concept of *manaaki*. The chapter will end by describing the changes wrought upon Māori social structures by colonisation.

Whānau

In classical Māori society, the *whānau* (literally, 'be born') formed a person's 'inner circle' of kinship. The *whānau* was that 'part of the kinship group which lives intimately together' (Johansen, 1954). More specifically, *whānau* was the 'joint and extended family', which 'comprised the most intimate circle of social relationships' (Winiata, 1956). Usually such a group comprised some three generations, such as an older married couple and a number of their descendants as well as their partners; or a group of siblings, partners and their children, possibly extending to grandchildren, and great-grandchildren (Metge, 1995).

Several distinctive but overlapping usages of *whānau* can be identified in classical Māori society (Metge, 1995). The first was the *whānau* defined as a group of siblings born from the same parents, for

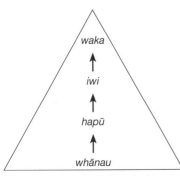

Simplified, standard description of Māori social structure

example, Te Whānau-a-Apanui. Other usages, still found in traditional twentieth century communities, included the following: first, *whānau* as a descent category – containing all the descendants from a fairly recent common ancestor; second, *whānau* as a descent group – incorporating only those descendants who lived and worked together; and finally, *whānau* as an extended family – comprising descendants, their outside spouses and adopted children, all of whom lived and worked together. All these *whānau* forms named themselves after the common parent or ancestor. These usages highlight the distinction maintained between *whānau* members who descended from the same ancestor, and *whānau* members, such as marriage partners, who did not. Both were important to a *whānau* in order to produce further generations of *whānau* members, complete work projects and maintain relations with other kin groups.

According to some scholars, classical *whānau* were not only descent groups and families, but also 'the household unit' in a Māori village, with its own separate quarters. In short, it formed 'the basic social group within Māori society'. Not only did members of a *whānau* live together, but they also worked together as a group ('the most convenient work unit'). Thus men, women, and children undertook their respective labour tasks, such as food gathering, building, cooking and the making of goods, such as tools, weapons and garments. Grandparents would care for and educate their *mokopuna* (grandchildren), a particularly close and warm relationship, and one that was often more generous than that between parent and child (Winiata, 1956). Usually female marriage partners went to live with their husband's *whānau*, but men would reside with their wife's people if she were of higher rank. This arrangement

Members of The University of Waikato *whānau* and Te Whānau-a-Ruataupare at a graduation, Pākirikiri Marae, Tokomaru Bay, East Coast in 1995

would mean that any children would gain access to the property rights of the more prestigious of the two *whānau*. Aside from high-ranking marriages, most unions were endogamous, that is, between relations, though never with closest kin, such as first cross-parallel cousins, as this amounted to marriage with classificatory brothers or sisters (Johansen, 1954; Winiata, 1956).

Individual Māori lived their everyday lives within the *whānau*. As a *whānau* expanded in membership, so the intimacy and warmth became harder to sustain. More junior offspring, perhaps two, three, or four generations down from the founder parents, would begin to move away and establish their own separate home. Related *whānau* would be created by such a process of fission. This disintegration of the original family was countered by a process of fusion, whereby members from the different *whānau* would marry (*moe*, literally, 'to sleep with') and produce children who, as descendants from the two *whānau*, revived the intimacy of the original kinship bonds. Such offspring could also enhance peaceful relations where inter-*whānau* conflict had taken place. Similarly, relationships were sustained through the process of adoption (*whāngai*, literally, 'to feed'), when a child would be given to a relative to raise as their own in order to strengthen the kinship ties between the biological parents and the adoptive one (Johansen, 1954; Winiata, 1956).

Recently, some research suggests that this classical *whānau* may not have been as prominent or may have taken other forms, at least in some regions. According to this information, the *kāinga* were too small to be subdivided into accommodation for separate *whānau*. Where *pā* were divided up, unrelated groups were separated off. References to *whānau* could describe other forms of groupings, such as a chief, his warrior followers and their dependents. When the records did describe 'families', they referred not so much to *whānau* (in the sense of an extended family unit) but to some other grouping of kin, probably a minor *hapū*. The likeliest unit to conform to the familial sense of *whānau* was that of the chief (comprising his various wives and younger children). Other adult relatives generally resided in separate *kāinga*, including daughters married to chiefs who lived elsewhere (Ballara, 1991).

Hapū

Beyond the intimate circle of a person's *whānau* was the *hapū*. Commonly called a 'sub-tribe' or, more accurately, a 'clan', *hapū* literally means 'to be pregnant'. Textbook definitions describe a *hapū* as comprising a number of *whānau* who all traced themselves back to the *hapū*'s eponymous ancestor (the *tupuna* whose name was taken by the kin group). However, such a process was not a given:

> Whether or not these new *whānau* combined to establish themselves as a *hapū* depended on their having not merely the numbers but also effective leadership, adequate resources and the fighting capacity to defend their independence (Metge, 1995: 37).

Most endogamous marriages took place amongst the *whānau*, which comprised a *hapū*. The one *hapū* of closely related *whānau*, however, did not always equate to a person's *kāinga* or *pā*. Village communities might comprise more than one *hapū*, living in different quarters, under the common leadership of a chief (*ariki* or *rangatira*). The various *whānau* of a *hapū* would come together for major building projects and for military purposes (Johansen, 1954; Winiata, 1956).

 ## Iwi

At an even farther remove from the daily life of an individual Māori stood the *iwi*, which literally means 'bones' (of one's kin). Traditionally, *iwi* is equated with 'tribe', though other translations include 'people/s' or 'nation'. The *iwi* was also named after a *tupuna* from whom the ancestors of different *hapū* descended. This was the largest unit of 'social-political organisation' in classical Māori society, but in reality it was a rather 'loose federation of smaller constituent groups related by common descent and ties of affinity' (Winiata, 1956). Each constituent group, the *hapū*, was in fact quite autonomous. However, the *iwi* became important when war threatened the survival of the various *hapū*. The *iwi*, under its chiefly leadership, would then cooperate in battle. The kin ties amongst the autonomous *hapū* were further sustained by marriages amongst the higher-ranking families which descended from the *iwi*'s eponymous ancestor (Johansen, 1954; Winiata, 1956).

 ## Waka

Beyond these various kin groups, descended from particular male and female *tūpuna*, lay the *waka*. In Māori traditional histories these *waka* had brought the people from islands in the Pacific to landfall in different parts of New Zealand, including the Chatham Islands (or as its Indigenous people, the Moriori, call it, Rekohu). The historical narratives of different kin groups always begin their stories about the deeds of their ancestors, with the actions of those *tūpuna* who formed the crews of the different *waka*. Ultimately, certain *iwi* would affiliate themselves to one or other of these canoes, and trace their descent from individual crew members. Historically, the landfall sites formed the original homelands in New Zealand of the kin groups that descended from those *waka* (see Chapter 3). However, in classical Māori society the *waka* were no more than a focus of sentimental regard in the songs and stories of descendants, and did not have any reality as a political or social grouping (Winiata, 1956).

 ## An alternative view: hapū and iwi

Recent historical research, notably into the nineteenth century records of New Zealand's Māori Land Court, has modified these standard descriptions of the classical Māori *iwi* and *hapū* (see Ballara, 1991, 1995, 1998). According to this view, older textbook descriptions of these kin groups have been influenced by the effects of colonisation, and a European tendency to find or invent indigenous social hierarchies with which they could negotiate for political and economic control. Instead of a static structure of *waka*, *iwi*, *hapū*, and *whānau*, a more organic understanding of Māori kin groups is put in its place, where the fortunes and existence of individual groups waxed and waned with the generations.

Iwi before colonisation did not operate as corporate groups, but rather as conceptual categories serving to link various dispersed *hapū* to a common ancestor. Originally, an *iwi* had been a single *hapū* living in a particular district. In time the *hapū* grew to a point that sections of it split off from what became the *tūturu* (core) *hapū*, and went and lived in different localities as 'colonies' of one or more *hapū* '(conceived) from that original group' (Ballara, 1998: 127). These *hapū* either lived nearby or amongst neighbouring groups descended from other *iwi*, with whom they eventually intermarried. In time these *hapū* would usually adopt as tribal designations the names of particular male or female descendants from the eponymous *iwi* ancestor. The shared *iwi* ancestral ties would normally motivate related *hapū* – or at least some of them – to combine in the event of a larger external threat. Besides war, high-ranking marriage ties also reaffirmed the connections and alliances between the scattered *hapū* (Ballara, 1998).

According to this alternative view, the *hapū* functioned as the principal political and social entity that acted together as a corporate body in war and in peace. Such *hapū* could vary greatly in size, with some verging on becoming an *iwi*, with ramifying 'sub-*hapū*', some of which lived in different communities from the others (Ballara, 1998). The reasons for *hapū* splitting off from the original kin group varied, but included the need to give lands to each offspring from a powerful chiefly marriage. Conflict over such lands, over women, the pressures upon a group's resource base from a growing population, or a chiefly person's loss of *mana* were also common reasons for one or other section to migrate away from the homeland to another location. Intermarriage with neighbouring non-kin groups meant that such migrant *hapū* could eventually develop multiple-*iwi* or *hapū* affiliations. Such groups opted to support one or other group depending on the particular circumstances, thereby enhancing their independence (Ballara, 1998).

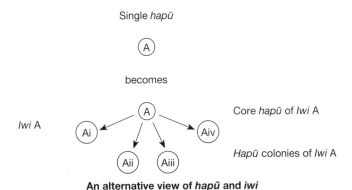

An alternative view of *hapū* and *iwi*

The independent-mindedness of individual *hapū* (and their chiefs) was a major feature of classical Māori social life. With no larger and coercive social institutions, each *hapū* could decide for itself what it should do. As a general rule, *hapū* from the same *iwi* would fight together when all of them were threatened by war. However, even in battle, each *hapū* was commanded by its chief who could decide to opt in or out of the fight. It was also not unknown for different *hapū* to opt to support opposing sides in a war, or for one *hapū* in dispute with another related *hapū* to call on non-kin allies. Whereas fights between close relatives of different *hapū* were normally controlled by considerations of kin ties, fighting was more ruthless between groups unrelated or only distantly related to each other (Ballara, 1998). Even so, relations frequently sought to protect or assist kin on the other side. Such actions by these 'taharua' ('doubly related persons') were respected practices in war (Johansen, 1954).

6 Whanaungatanga

Classical Māori *hapū* adopted varying styles of living, with some residing and working in separate locations from others. More commonly, *hapū*, especially the smaller ones, or parts of larger *hapū*, combined together in communities ruled by a leading chief from their senior *hapū* (see Chapter 9). The *hapū* were not always closely related, and some were in a subservient relationship to the chief, living on allocated pieces of land. These communities, lasting sometimes several generations, formed the centre of people's lives, with most ordinary community dwellers aware only of those kin relationships they shared with others residing in that particular community. The *hapū*, or smaller groups, such as a *whānau*, or certain individuals in the community, would have inherited use-rights to particular food resources and pieces of land scattered across the surrounding area. These lands and resources were typically interspersed amongst those of related *hapū* or non-kin neighbours. Varying sized groups of kin would move about these resources on a seasonal basis, living in small *kāinga*, and returning to a larger settlement (often associated with a *pā*) for winter (Ballara, 1991, 1995, 1998).

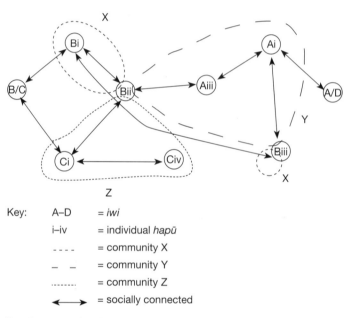

Development of multi-*iwi* and *hapū/whānau* communities

 ## Rank

Birth order within a classical Māori kin group was of central importance, with individuals being classified as *tuakana* or as *teina* (see Chapters 1 and 2). These referred to relationships between siblings or cousins of the same sex, so that there were male and female *tuakana* and *teina* within a kin group, such as a *hapū*, or the *whānau*. As offspring married and produced children, so certain genealogical lines proceeding from *tuakana* or *teina* ancestors would become senior or junior in terms of status and rank to another. Naturally, chiefly lines would be *tuakana* to others. The essential distinction between *tuakana* and *teina* continues to be made by many today.

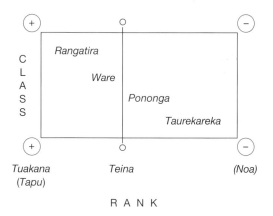

Social rank and class

 ## Class

Not only was classical Māori society genealogically ranked, but organised into social classes, with the key distinction being between those of chiefly or commoner status. Individuals who traced their ancestry back through various high-ranking lines were of *rangatira* rank, whereas those with weaker or non-existent connections to the ruling lines of their kin group were regarded as *ware* or *tūtūā* (Winiata, 1956). Not surprisingly, these classes took on positive and negative connotations, with *rangatira* implying someone noble or well bred, whereas a *ware* was ignorant, careless, and lacking in thoughtfulness (Williams, 1971). As a mark of their position, chiefs were served by *pononga* (servants) selected from amongst their kin. The worst social position was occupied by *taurekareka*. Having been captured in war, and come under the power of their captor (thereby becoming *noa*), a *taurekareka* was 'hardly considered a real human being' (Johansen, 1954: 24). They carried out various menial tasks including the *noa* function of cooking. Such a person was treated with contempt, and was considered to be possessed with the *hau otaota*, the 'spirit making him to become rubbish' (Shirres, 1997; Winiata, 1956).

Manaaki

In Māori oral traditions, a person without kin, such as a person living apart; a slave; a person with no children close by; or a wandering stranger, were considered aberrations, existing outside the norm of human life. The norm was 'that the Maori must be surrounded by relatives in order to be a real human being'. Otherwise, such a person as the wanderer was proverbially like the dog, a being without *tikanga* (law or custom) ('*He kuri, he tangata haere, kaore ona tikanga, ona aha*') (Johansen, 1954: 24, 25).

The importance of kin ties was highlighted by a story about conflict between close relations. Hoani Te Whatahoro (1915: 256, 270) commented on this lamentable situation:

> *he tohu kino te tahuri mai o te whakitoka ki te tuarongo ka patu. Ki te tukitukia te whare kei whea he whakaruru mo te hau, mo te marangai. Ma te whare e ora*

6 Whanaungatanga

> *ai te tangata i te tupuhi, ma te kai e ora ai te tangata o roto o te pa tuwatawata; ma te manaaki i te tangata e tu ai te mana– e wehi ai te tangata ki a koe.*
>
> *it is a very bad thing for the door to turn upon the back of the house. If a house is destroyed, where is there a shelter from the winds and the storms? The house gives shelter from the storm; food supports men within the palisaded pa; by respect to other men is mana acquired, and men will fear you [i.e., respect you].*

This statement is an important one. Its key phrase, '*ma te manaaki ... te mana*', has also been translated as, '[b]y solidarity (*manaaki*) between human beings their power (*mana*) is maintained' (Johansen, 1954: 27). *Manaaki* (derived from the word *mana*) is an important cultural concept expressing kinship solidarity through the mutual support of relatives:

> *The real sign of a person's mana and tapu is not that person's power to destroy other people, but that person's power to manaaki, to protect and look after other people* (Shirres, 1997: 47).

Manaaki stands for a sense of reciprocity, of giving and receiving. In classical Māori society, this could only be achieved by residing together, and hence *manaaki* in effect created a sense of kinship. Important expressions of *manaaki* within the kin group included the *manaaki* shown by the people to its *rangatira*. Such support enhanced the *mana* of the leaders and, as a consequence, of the group itself. Conversely, the *rangatira* showed *manaaki* for the people, and thereby secured their loyalty and love. Such double-sided *manaaki* strengthened the kin group itself, both internally and in relation to other groups. This idea is found in Whatahoro's key phrase '*ma te manaaki i te tangata e tu ai te mana*' ('By loving and honouring people a communal life is created and a community in strength' (Johansen, 1954: 30, 91). The importance of *manaaki* continues in Māori society today, being evidenced in *marae* protocols, and kin group relationships (see Chapter 7).

The solidarity of the group showed itself especially in situations of war, or where there was a need for *utu*. In the latter circumstances, 'it is not a question of person confronted with person, but of kinship group confronted with kinship group' (Johansen, 1954: 35). In attacking one individual, their kin group had to become involved:

> *Kin ties meant that there were no non-combatants in Māori society; individuals, males and female, young and old, were part of an interlocking network of social obligations. Their 'private' quarrels automatically involved the wider group* (Ballara, 1991: 380).

The sense of unity found in the kin group has been famously characterised as the 'kinship I' (Johansen, 1954). The perfect embodiment of this identification of the individual-as-kin group was of course its chief. Many famous chiefly utterances can be found where leaders identified themselves with the tribe's achievements; an identification which extended across generations back into the group's ancestral past, and into the future of its yet unborn children.

Modern Māori social organisation

The colonisation of Aotearoa/New Zealand did not abruptly alter the old ways of living and social organisation. The most recent research demonstrates clearly that *hapū* 'remained the primary political, economic and social unit of Māori society into the 20th century' (Ballara, 1998: 227). However, the membership of such *hapū* was increasingly based purely on descent from a common ancestor, rather than on shared residence within a community.

Alongside this continuity of social structure, a number of historical changes can be discerned prompted by internal and external forces acting on Māori society (see Ballara, 1998). Amongst the internal factors faced by Māori society in the late eighteenth century were the consequences of an increasing population. The resulting pressure on resources appears to have contributed to an increasing level of violence as competing groups more often involved non-kin in their tribal wars in an effort to achieve decisive gains in resources. This led to large groups either migrating away from the scene of their defeat, or moving into an area in order to assist a local party in a war against their neighbours. The introduction of European technologies, such as muskets, only aggravated these existing conflicts. In response, previously scattered *hapū* united, living side by side in fortified refuges, from whence they were able to war collectively against incoming groups. Conflicts between residents and migrants also more sharply defined the lines of difference between kin and non-kin groups. Not surprisingly, the embattled *hapū*, while retaining their operational independence, became more conscious of their ties with other kin in related *hapū* through their shared *iwi* affiliations.

The external pressures on Māori society exerted by the process of colonisation were very damaging to the integrity of Māori social structures and kin ties. Even so, a strong thread of resistance, and Indigenous efforts to overcome these external forces, was sustained, and continues to this day. European strategies to obtain Māori lands and resources, especially through the nineteenth and early twentieth century Māori Land Court, seriously undermined existing tribal structures by changing tenure from a community base to individual holdings more vulnerable to outside purchase. Many *rangatira* were compromised by their dealings with the Government and the Land Court. Kin groups became divided between land sellers and non-sellers, with disputes sometimes leading to civil war, encouraged by local Europeans interested only in destroying any resistance to their insatiable land hunger. Social disruption also occurred when Māori individuals or groups took up opportunities to participate in the emerging colonial society and its economy. This included internal migrations to new, separate Christian communities, movements away from ancestral lands, and participation in larger groupings of kin (for instance, in a government road gang), or non-kin (in itinerant shearing gangs), or as individuals (in the churches or Public Service).

As a response to such changes, smaller *hapū* disappeared, and Māori increasingly identified themselves as members of larger *hapū*, the even larger *iwi* structures, or sometimes the *waka*, all of which, with their greater range and depth of genealogical connections, could better withstand these external pressures. Through the course of the later nineteenth century these enhanced kin groups developed various strategies of resistance, such as collegial chiefly government and tribal *rūnanga* (councils), in order to better deal with the Government and its agents of colonisation such as the Land Court. Ironically many Pākehā, looking in from the outside, simplified the Indigenous identification with larger descent groupings by interpreting Māori as simply forming a discrete number of super-tribes. They overlooked the subtle internal politics of these larger descent groups where various-sized *hapū* continue to this day to assert their right to be heard in the counsels of their modern *iwi* structures.

In addition, Māori supported pan-tribal or non-kin based organisations, such as the Kōtahitanga (Unity) movement, the Kīngitanga (King Movement), Māori religious groups (Pai Mārire, Ringatū), and more recent twentieth century formations, such as the Rātana Church, the Māori Women's Welfare League (Te Rōpū Wāhine Māori Toko i te Ora), and the Mana Motuhake Party (see Chapters 15, 16, 17). There is also a range of Māori organisational groupings that owe their origin to government legislation or are based on Pākehā organisational structures. These may be loosely kin-based or not. Many tend to follow Pākehā protocols. Examples of these include tribal *rūnanga*, *marae* committees, Māori Trust Boards, church groups, and *kapa haka* (Maori performing groups). Other groups focusing on promoting the use of *te reo Māori* and *tikanga Māori* are those supporting particular Te Kōhanga Reo, Kura Kaupapa Māori, Wharekura, and gatherings of people involved in the Te Ataarangi Movement. All of these bodies aim in some way to resist assimilation to European ways, and to sustain the spiritual and physical wellbeing of the Māori people.

The *whānau* kin group that existed within the *hapū* and *iwi* also changed as a consequence of colonisation. The *whānau* in the twentieth century was much larger than its classical counterpart, often comprising more than one household. Such *whānau* did not always live closely together, and were inclined to work together on a more occasional basis. In response to modern economic conditions, they had often given away their function as a productive unit. 'In these respects they were more like the 18th-century *hapū* than the 18th-century *whānau*' (Metge, 1995: 40). In addition to the classical usages as a descent group and an extended family, the modern *whānau* has developed new meanings. *Whānau* can now refer to a nuclear family of parents (or single parents) and their offspring. It can also include a more informal grouping of kin, or friends and family, or work colleagues, or sporting associations, which act as if they were a kin group of *whānau* in pursuit of some common purpose (Metge, 1995).

Cross-cultural partnerships (Māori to Pākehā) and marriages have become a feature of contemporary Māori society. The enculturation of children into Māori society from cross-cultural relationships is largely dependent upon the willingness of the parents to successfully negotiate the demands of both Māori and Pākehā society, and commit to a bicultural relationship in the fullest sense. However, if this does not occur, the inevitable fate of the children is to be disconnected from the *whānau*, *hapū*, *iwi* structure and the Māori world. This is even more poignant for children from estranged parental relationships where the children are raised solely by the Pākehā parent or where the Māori parent has died.

 ## Conclusion

Past descriptions of Māori social structures have suffered to varying degrees from the Eurocentric preference for model making *in abstracto* (in the abstract), devoid of

any acknowledgement of the local and historical circumstances which formed and transformed Māori society through time. Various kinship terms, notably *iwi*, *hapū*, and *whānau* overlap in their usages, with *whānau* being metaphorically extended to groups of *hapū* and *iwi* size, in both classical and contemporary societies, and vice versa. Conversely, a large modern *whānau* is, to all intents and purposes, a *hapū* in all but name (Metge, 1995; Webster, 1998). Rather than focusing on a static and sequential kinship model where a growing kin group moves automatically through the stages of *whānau*, *hapū* and *iwi*, it is probably safer to begin with the common cultural values, such as *manaaki*, which all groups of Māori share in an ideal world. These shared values create the group's sense of community and not the particular name (such as *whānau* or *hapū* or *iwi*) chosen to describe it. In this respect, a recent observation about modern *whānau* has a broader application:

> *Real life whānau do not and should not be expected to conform too closely to the constructed model. Each has its own character, its own degree of integration and effectiveness, created and recreated out of the interaction between the personalities of its members and the circumstances of time and place. Members' right to work out their own identity and tikanga must always be respected* (Metge, 1995: 78).

The evidence from classical Māori society suggests that a *whānau* might become an autonomous *hapū* provided it had not only sufficient numbers, but also appropriate leadership, access to resources, and sound relations with other kin and non-kin neighbours. Many *whānau* clearly remained very small and intimate groupings of kin, or mixtures of kin and non-kin, who worked or fought together, as dependent parts within the predominant *hapū* communities. The prominence of larger kin groups in Aotearoa/New Zealand, particularly as a political response to internal economic and demographic stresses and to colonisation, appears to have enabled *whānau* to grow in significance, and to effectively replace the smaller *hapū* of classical Māori society. The independent-minded larger *hapū* of earlier times continue to exist today, but within the stronger, and more binding, *iwi* structures which emerged from late in the eighteenth century as a result of changes brought on by changing internal and external circumstances.

Just as Māori society was never static in classical times or during colonisation, present economic and political challenges call forth differing forms of social organisation. In the wake of Crown settlements of Waitangi Tribunal cases and the like, various developments seem to be taking place simultaneously. Some of the larger kin groups, such as *iwi* and *waka*, are moving from corporate groups to legal corporations within the modern global economy. Some *iwi*, *hapū* or *whānau* appear to be waxing in strength, sometimes rediscovering older kin group identities, and asserting a degree of autonomy in their relations with other related groups. Some emerging *whānau*, *hapū* and *iwi* work to achieve some common purpose, with or without kinship or marriage ties existing amongst its members, but based instead upon shared residence, or other uniting issues such as work, politics, sport, health or education. These groupings may terminate once the purpose uniting them is achieved. Interestingly, such groups echo examples of non-familial *whānau* and temporary communities of related and unrelated *hapū* in classical Māori society. Despite the changes, these varying forms of social organisation (including the many national Māori bodies intentionally not based on kinship relations) continue to share common cultural values, thus distinguishing them as *tangata whenua* from others living in Aotearoa/New Zealand.

FURTHER READING

Walker (1990) gives a basic definition of the key terms. Metge (1995) provides a contemporary anthropological interpretation based on her fieldwork. Ballara (1998) locates the subject historically, incorporating new archival research, especially for the nineteenth century. Whereas Metge focuses on *whānau*, Ballara concentrates on *hapū*. Neither author describes the whole of Aotearoa/New Zealand. The reader can only hope that a definitive overview of this subject will be forthcoming.

Chapter 7

Ngā tikanga o te marae
Marae practices
Rawinia Higgins and John C. Moorfield

What is a *marae*? What happens on a *marae*? How are visitors welcomed? What are some of the important formal procedures that happen on a *marae*? These are questions that will be answered in this chapter.

The *marae* is the place where *hui* and most important events of a Māori kinship group take place. Welcoming and hosting visitors, weddings, birthday celebrations, political meetings, *kapa haka* practices, religious services, educational conferences and *tangihanga* are examples of events that are likely to be held on the *marae*.

The term *marae* is found in many of the islands of Polynesia. Elsewhere in the Pacific, the *marae* takes the form of stone-stepped pyramid-style structures used to perform religious rites. These steps or platforms are called *pae* or *paepae*, though in some islands this term also encompasses the altar or courtyard of the *marae*. To the Māori, the *marae* of its Pacific relations is best described as *tūāhu* (ritual sites) as opposed to a Māori view of *marae* that emphasises it as a focal point for culturally important activities. Nevertheless, Māori, like other Pacific peoples, understand the *marae* as being a space with images of *atua* and *tīpuna* (ancestors) accommodated in buildings and spaces within which leaders sit and discuss important matters of the day. As this brief comparison suggests, the *marae* is an important feature in the lives of both Māori and their *whanaunga* (relations) of the Pacific.

In contemporary Aotearoa/New Zealand, the term *marae* is used to refer to a complex that includes a *whare tipuna* (ancestral house), *wharekai* (dining hall), *wharepaku* (ablution block) and surrounding lands. Some *marae* may also have a *whare karakia* (church), sports grounds and housing for *kaumātua* and families. However, the *marae* was originally the term for the space in front of the *whare tipuna*, which is now referred to as the *marae ātea* (courtyard). The *marae ātea* is the domain of Tū-mata-uenga, the *atua* of war, and conversely the *whare tipuna* belongs to the *atua* of peace, Rongo-mā-tāne. The *tikanga* of these respective spaces is determined by the particular characteristics of these *atua*. For example, the *marae ātea* may be described as *te umu pokapoka a Tū-mata-uenga* or 'the fiery ovens of Tū-mata-uenga' (Pou Temara, personal communication, 1990) where matters of violence and war are conducted.

Traditionally all *marae* belonged to kinship groups, either a *whānau*, *hapū* or *iwi*. This remains the same today with the exception of some newer urban *marae*. A *marae* is built on the kinship group's land. The kinship group looks after the *marae* and each person has a role to play in the smooth running of the facility. A *marae* committee also takes the lead in the upkeep of the facility, handles the financial aspects, and takes bookings for groups wishing to use the marae.

The physical elements of the modern marae

Whare tipuna

Many of the traditional *whare tipuna* are named in honour of an ancestor from that people's *hapū*, hence the name *whare tipuna*. However, some *whare tipuna* or *marae* are named in honour of an historical event, such as Te Whai-a-Te-Motu in Ruatāhuna that was named after the great pursuit around the island of the prophet Te Kooti Arikirangi Te Tūruki. Today some urban Māori name their *marae* complex, or *whare tipuna*, after symbolic meanings of unification, such as Te Herenga Waka (the mooring of the canoes) at Victoria University in Wellington. Such names do not refer to a specific ancestor so that all Māori can feel part of that *marae*.

Other names for the main house on the *marae* are *wharenui* (large house), *whare rūnanga* (council house), *wharepuni* (sleeping house), *wharehui* (meeting house), and *whare whakairo* (carved house). Apart from the naming of the house after an ancestor, the *whare tipuna* is likened to the body of the ancestor. Starting from the apex of the house is the *kōruru* (carved face) with the *maihi* (bargeboard) stretching out like welcoming arms to the *amo* (upright supporting posts at the lower end of the *maihi*). At the ends of the *maihi* are the fingers of the ancestor that are represented in the *raparapa* (ends of the bargeboards of the house). The *tāhuhu* (ridgepole) that runs the length of the inside of the house is regarded as the spine, or backbone, of the ancestor, with its

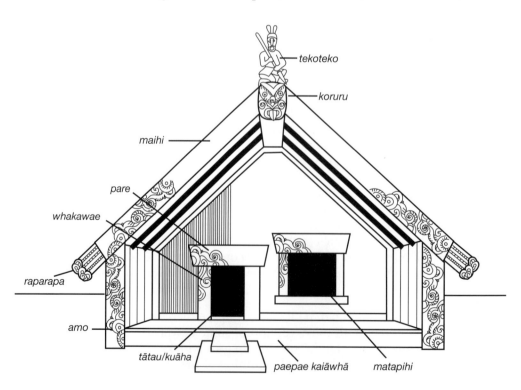

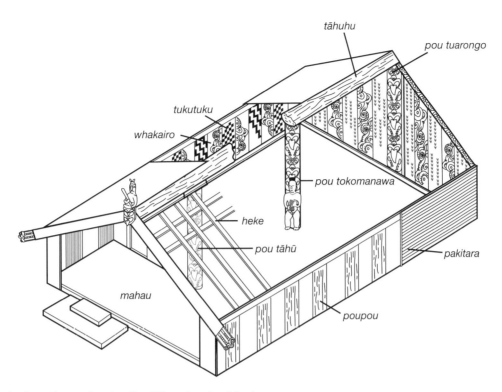

A *whare tipuna* showing the different parts of the house

ribs in the form of *heke* (rafters) descending from the *tāhuhu* to the *poupou* (carved wall figures). The *pou tāhū* (front post), the *pou tokomanawa* (centre post) and the *pou tuarongo* (back wall post) support the *tāhuhu* and represent the connection between Rangi-nui, the Sky Father, and Papa-tūā-nuku, the Earth Mother. The inside of the house is known as the belly or bosom of the ancestor, and in some areas this is acknowledged by naming the *whare tipuna* after this fact, for example, Te Poho-o-Rāwiri (Rāwiri's belly) in Gisborne.

The interior of the house is often decorated with *kōwhaiwhai* that are found on the *heke*. *Tukutuku* is usually located on the walls between each *poupou*, and represent many symbols such as *roimata toroa* (albatross tears), *niho taniwha* (monsters' teeth), *pātiki* (flounder), or *poutama* (ascending steps), to name a few. The *poupou* are usually carved with stylised figures representing ancestors of the *whānau*, *hapū* or *iwi* of the *marae*.

The *whare tipuna* has a verandah area (*mahau*) with a door into the main part of the building on the right-hand side (looking out to the *marae*) and a window on the left side. The house is divided into two main areas, the *tara whānui* (wide side) and the *tara whāiti* (narrow side). The *tara whānui* is located to the left of the door (looking out), with the *tara whāiti* being located on the right-hand side. This unique design caters to the philosophy of *manaakitanga* (hospitality) of the *manuhiri* (visitors), as it allows the greater space to be dedicated to the comfort of the visitors. The *kokonga* (corners) at the front of the house are reserved for the *kaumātua* of each respective group.

Wharekai

Traditionally the *marae ātea* was surrounded by *whare puni* (sleeping houses) and *kāuta* (family cooking shelters). The largest house was that of the *rangatira*, which was where *manuhiri* (visitors) were usually accommodated. *Manuhiri* were fed on the *marae*, with each family providing food prepared and cooked in their *kāuta*. The meal was laid out in the open on the *marae*. Large *wharekai* (dining halls) which are now prominent on most *marae* are a modern development.

In traditional *marae* the communal meal was laid out on the ground

The *wharekai* in many rural *marae* are named after a spouse, close associate, or relative of the *tipuna* who is represented by the *whare tipuna*. As with the *whare tipuna*, the *wharekai* may also be named to honour an event rather than a person. For example, the *whare tipuna* at Tauarau Marae in Ruātoki is named Rongokārae after the ancestor from whom the *hapū* of that marae acquired their name, Ngāti Rongo, and the *wharekai* is called Rangimāhanga after his wife.

In Māori terms, food serves as a means of *whakanoa*. This relationship of *noa* as the 'free from *tapu*' state means that things that are *tapu* should not be placed where food is used. Because the head is considered very *tapu*, food should not make direct contact with this area of the body, or with associated items, such as hats. Items of headwear should not be placed on tables where food is found. For the same reason, one should not sit on tables.

The *ringawera* (kitchen workers) are important people on the *marae*. There are *whakataukī* that highlight their importance, such as: *Mā muri a mua ka tika* (Only if the back is working well, will the front function). This *whakataukī* reminds people that they must ensure that they *manaaki* their *manuhiri* by providing plenty of the best *kai* (food). The proverb also stresses that without people at both the front and back of the *marae* functioning well together, the hospitality of *manuhiri* will be adversely affected; a fact which the visitors will be quick to note.

Rongokārae meeting house at Tauarau Marae, Ruātoki, Bay of Plenty

 ## Wharemate

In some areas, notably those of the Mātaatua (Eastern Bay of Plenty) region, a structure called a *wharemate* is built for use during *tangihanga*. These buildings have replaced more temporary structures that were put up during the *tangihanga* to provide some protection from the weather for the people who sit by the *tūpāpaku* (corpse). When there is no *tangihanga* happening on the *marae* the *wharemate* doubles as the storage space for mattresses and pillows. Because *tangihanga* are the most important type of gathering on *marae* this is the subject of the next chapter.

 ## Pōhiri

The *pōhiri*, or in western dialects *pōwhiri*, is the ritual welcome ceremony that occurs when visitors arrive at a *marae*. In pre-European times it was not always known if the *manuhiri* were coming in peace or with warlike intent. One of the purposes of this ritual of encounter was to determine this.

For most *iwi* the *pōhiri* takes place outside on the *marae ātea* although, for practical reasons, there are significant exceptions to this. Inclement weather may also mean that the *manuhiri* are taken into the *wharenui* for the main part of the *pōhiri*.

When the *manuhiri* arrive at the *marae* they may perform a *waerea* before entering. The *waerea* is a *karakia* that is performed by some *manuhiri* before entering a strange *marae*. It originates from the time when people believed in the risk of being affected by *mākutu*. *Mākutu* is the ability to inflict physical and psychological harm and even death through spiritual powers. Few *iwi* perform *waerea* now.

Whakaeke

When all the *manuhiri* are ready to be welcomed, they gather outside the gate of the *marae*. Traditionally a *wero* was performed as the *manuhiri* moved onto the *marae ātea*. The *wero* is a challenge that is delivered by the *tangata whenua* to the *manuhiri* to determine the nature of the encounter. An armed warrior (or warriors) is sent out to the *manuhiri* at the entranceway of the *marae* to perform this ritual. The execution of this process is considered important in the maintenance of the *mana* of the *tangata whenua*. The warrior places a *taki* (dart), sprig of leaves, or some other token on the ground, and displays his proficiency in the use of his weapon to encourage the leader of the *manuhiri* to pick it up. Picking up the *taki* indicates to the *tangata whenua* that their visitors' intentions are peaceful. The warrior then returns to the *tangata whenua*. In today's society this part of the process is reserved for important visitors to the *marae*, particularly for someone who has not visited the *marae* before. People who have not been formally welcomed on a particular *marae* are said to be *waewae tapu*.

Once the male leader of the *manuhiri* has picked up the *taki* a woman will *karanga*. The *karanga* are the calls made by women, which in many instances today start the *pōhiri*. The initial *karanga* is by one or more women from the *tangata whenua*, and women from the *manuhiri* will respond with their calls as they move onto the *marae*. The *karanga* between the two groups provides the men with information about the visiting group to include in their *whaikōrero*. In many ways, the form of the *karanga* is not dissimilar to that of the *whaikōrero*, as the *karanga* makes acknowledgements to the *manuhiri*, the dead, and the object of the visit.

The *whakaeke*. A group from The University of Waikato moving on to Tūrangawaewae Marae, Ngāruawāhia. Te Rita Papesch (Tainui and Ngāti Porou) is responding to the *karanga* from the *tangata whenua*. She is flanked by Mīria Simpson of Ngāti Awa on her left and Ngāhuia Te Awekōtuku of Te Arawa on her right.

The *whakaeke* is the term to describe the movement of the *manuhiri* onto the *marae ātea*. The *karanga* takes place during this time. Sometimes the *tangata whenua* may perform a *haka pōhiri* to welcome the *manuhiri* during the *whakaeke*. This is the time when the *manuhiri* may choose to respond with their own *haka* (posture dance) in recognition of the *tangata whenua*. During the *haka pōhiri*, it is also common to see women using *rau* (green leaves) with their actions.

The *manuhiri* advance slowly onto the *marae* as a group and stop a little distance from the *wharenui*. At this stage the *karanga* and *haka pōhiri* will end and people will remember the dead and may *tangi* (weep). Once this is over, the *manuhiri* will move to the seating provided for them and the *whaikōrero* will begin.

A *haka pōhiri* being performed to welcome the *manuhiri* at Tūrangawaewae Marae. Leaves are used in performing the *haka pōhiri* as a symbol for the dead.

Whaikōrero

The *paepae* is a term used for both the place where the speakers of the *tangata whenua* sit and for the speakers of *pōhiri*. The usual pattern for seating during the *pōhiri* is to have the men sitting on the *paepae* with the women seated behind them.

The form of the *whaikōrero* does not differ significantly from that of the *karanga*. However, the *whaikōrero* expands on the information shared during the *karanga*. In some areas on the East Coast of the North Island women have speaking rights on the *marae*, but in the majority of the *iwi* only men are allowed to *whaikōrero*. Women are not permitted by some *iwi* to speak on the *marae* because of the association of this speaking space, the *marae ātea*, with the realm of Tū-mata-uenga. When the *pōhiri* is taking place, the *marae* is exposed to all types of warfare, including those that pertain to *mākutu*. Women were revered in Māori society for their ability to give life and to take it away as the following *whakataukī* notes, 'He wahine, he whenua, i ngaro ai te tangata,' (It is because of women and land that men perish). Therefore, Māori were conscious not to expose women to curses or threats that might be made on the *marae ātea*, lest these affect subsequent generations.

In most instances, *whaikōrero* will begin with a *whakaaraara* (warning call) a *tau* or *tauparapara* (a form of *karakia*) before making acknowledgements to the *marae* and *whare tipuna*, the *mate* (dead) and eventually taking into account the *take* (purpose) of the *hui*. The structure of the individual *whaikōrero* is determined by the speaker. However, the process of *whaikōrero* itself is ordained by the *kawa* (protocols) of the particular *marae*. The following are explanations of the two types of *kawa*: *pāeke* and *tauutuutu*, also known as *tū atu, tū mai*.

Pāeke is the most commonly practised form of *kawa* among *iwi Māori*. *Pāeke* refers to the situation where all the speech-making is first performed by the *tangata whenua*, after which the *mauri o te kōrero* (speaking right) is passed over to the *manuhiri*, who then make their speeches. The arrangement of the people on the *marae* usually dictates the flow of the *mauri o te kōrero*. This will start from the first speaker, who is positioned closest to the *whare tipuna*, and move along in sequence to the farthest person on the *paepae*. When the *mauri o te kōrero* is passed to the other side, it first goes to the speaker for the *manuhiri* located farthest from the house, and then moves to the last speaker, who is closest to the house. Thus, the *mauri o te kōrero* is returned back to the *tangata whenua* who are symbolically represented in the *whare tipuna*.

The *tauutuutu*, or *tū atu, tū mai* system differs from the *pāeke* system in that the speakers alternate from the *tangata whenua* to the *manuhiri*. In this form of *kawa* the *tangata whenua* make the final speech, which returns the *mauri o te kōrero* to them. In instances when the speakers for the *manuhiri* outnumber those of the *tangata whenua*, the latter will wait until all of the *manuhiri* have completed their speeches before closing this part of the process with their final speaker, thus ensuring the *mauri* is returned to the *tangata whenua*. This alternating system of *whaikōrero* is used by tribes who claim descent from the people who migrated to Aotearoa on the *Tainui* and *Te Arawa* canoes, notably those of Waikato, the King Country, the Volcanic Plateau, and parts of the Bay of Plenty.

On the completion of each *whaikōrero*, a *mōteatea* (traditional chant) or *waiata* is usually performed. Often the performance of the *waiata* by the many supporters of the speaker is used to *kīnaki* (embellish) the *whaikōrero*. There are many accounts where support is not always automatic, thus ensuring that there is an element of control over what the speaker says during the *whaikōrero*. When this occurs it would be noted by all present that the speaker talked without the *mana* of the people in mind and the people have spoken with their silence. Strictly speaking, the speaker should select his own *waiata*, the words of which should support the content of his speech. However, in reality in the modern situation particular people often have the role of choosing and leading the *waiata*.

The art of *whaikōrero* is a highly developed skill. Good speakers gain *mana* for themselves and the people they represent. A skilled orator will incorporate appropriate *whakataukī*, *pepeha* and *kupu whakaari* (prophetic sayings of charismatic leaders) and references to important geographical and historical places of the *manuhiri* and *tangata whenua*; he will use metaphor and simile; recite appropriate *whakapapa*; make reference to things appropriate to the occasion; and have the skill of keeping the attention of the audience, including by the use of humour. The *whaikōrero* will be delivered in classical language calling on the clever use of words and a depth of knowledge of language and culture. All this will be delivered in dramatic style with timing designed to give the best effect to what is being said.

The following diagram summarises the format of many *whaikōrero*.

whakaaraara
↓
tauparapara/tau
↓
mihi ki te marae and *whare tipuna*
↓
mihi mate
↓
mihi ora
↓
take
↓
mōteatea, waiata and/or *haka*
↓
conclusion

A *koha* (gift or token of appreciation) is given by the *manuhiri* to the *tangata whenua*, usually at the end of the last *whaikōrero*. In traditional Māori society this was in the form of food, especially delicacies from the local area of the *manuhiri*, and/or *taonga* (treasured items), which could range from weapons to finely woven cloaks. Food is taken directly to the kitchen and not laid on the *marae*. Today the most common form of *koha* is a sum of money. *Koha* laid formally on the *marae* is intended to defray costs of the *marae*, but *koha* given quietly to the organiser of the *hui* is intended to help cover the expenses of the *hui*. *Koha* laid formally on the *marae* is taken note of by the *tangata whenua* to ensure that when an exchange occurs between groups the *tangata whenua* can reciprocate in kind.

Hongi

Once the speeches and *waiata* have concluded and the *koha* has been collected by the *tangata whenua*, the *manuhiri* speakers lead their group to *harirū* (shake hands) and *hongi* (greeting by pressing of noses) with the speakers of the *tangata whenua*, who will have stood and lined up with the rest of their people to greet everybody in turn. The *hongi* is a gentle pressing of the noses. In some areas, like Waikato, it is a single press of the noses, but in other areas it is a short press followed by a longer one. The eyes should be closed when the *hongi* is done. It is a more formal greeting but often hugs and kisses between women and between men and women may follow.

The *hongi* represents the passing of breath between the two people. This reflects the story of Tāne (ancestral power of the forests and birds) and the creation of Hine-ahu-one, the first woman who was made from the clay of Hawaiki. In his creation of Hine-ahu-one, Tāne brought life to her by breathing into her nose and mouth, upon which she sneezed, exclaiming, '*Tihei mauri ora*' (the sneeze of life). This phrase is used to indicate the beginning of a *whaikōrero*; therefore, this narrative of the creation of the first human is not only significant to the *hongi* but to the *whaikōrero* as well.

The *hongi* completes the formalities of the *pōhiri*. The whole process of the *pōhiri* is a gradual coming together of the *manuhiri* and the *tangata whenua*, concluding with the physical contact of the *hongi*. However, the rituals of encounter are only fully completed by the sharing of *kai*.

Kai

Once the greetings have been completed on the *marae ātea* the *manuhiri* are invited to partake in *kai*. *Kai* is important because it serves to *whakanoa* the *manuhiri* from the whole process of the *pōhiri*. However, the sharing of *kai* is also significant in the practising of *manaakitanga*. *Manaakitanga* is one of the most important concepts in relation to the *marae*. The word *marae* when used as an adjective denotes 'generosity'. The role of the *tangata whenua* is to provide all that they can for their *manuhiri*, as this reflects on the *mana* of the *tangata whenua*. There are many proverbs that express the importance of *manaaki* as well as tribal *pepeha*, which are articulated to describe the *mana* of a people in their display of *manaakitanga*.

The following diagram illustrates the main features of the ritual of encounter on the marae. Parentheses indicate that that particular part of the *pōhiri* does not always happen.

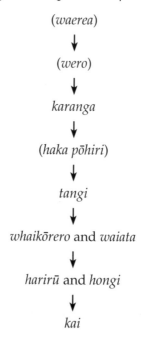

Karakia and mihimihi

Depending on the religion of the *tangata whenua*, they may choose to conduct *karakia* as part of their hospitality. At the end of the evening meal, a bell is struck to indicate that the *karakia* will be undertaken, usually inside the *whare tipuna*.

In accordance with the *atua* of peace, Rongo-mā-tāne, the *mihimihi* (informal speech-making) follows the evening *karakia*. This will start with the *tangata whenua* speakers, who will be seated, from the corner of the *tara whāiti*, and move around the house until it reaches the speaker in the opposite corner of the *tara whānui* of the house. The speakers during the *mihimihi* will stand against the wall to draw inspiration from the carvings, which are a representation of the ancestors of the *tangata whenua*. The *kōrero* (speech) that is delivered is less formal than that on the *marae*, and it is rare to hear *tau* or *tauparapara* being performed inside the house. It is also a forum for more informal speech-making and discussions related to the living rather than the dead, and includes humour, which facilitates connections between the respective groups.

 Poroporoaki

At the end of a *hui* formal farewell speeches take place. These are called *poroporoaki*. The *manuhiri* usually begin the *poroporoaki*, followed by the *tangata whenua*. The *manuhiri* acknowledge the hospitality of the *tangata whenua* and *ringawera* who have provided the visitors with sustenance throughout the *hui*. The *poroporoaki* are sometimes done on the *marae ātea* but more commonly now they are delivered in the *wharekai* after the final meal, or *hākari* (feast).

The formal procedures of the *pōhiri* on the *marae* are adapted for welcome ceremonies in a variety of other contexts. For some *iwi*, *pōhiri* is the term used only for these procedures on a *marae*. For welcomes held elsewhere, the term used is *mihi whakatau*. The procedures of the *pōhiri* act as a template for welcome ceremonies held in other types of venues. Depending on the importance of the occasion, some elements of the *pōhiri* discussed above may be omitted. For example, it is quite common these days for interviews of Māori candidates for jobs to incorporate elements of the *pōhiri* and *poroporoaki*. The applicants and their *whānau* support will be welcomed by the person conducting the selection process, or by someone on the panel who is fluent in Māori and is appropriate for this task. In most cases the *mihi* will be returned. *Waiata* may be sung after the speakers, but time constraints may mean that in practice the *waiata* will not be performed. If the applicant and the *whānau* have not shaken hands and greeted the panel with the *hongi* on arrival, this is done after the speeches. The panel will then interview the applicant asking questions of direct relevance to performance in the advertised position. At the end of the interview, *whānau* members will be invited to speak about the applicant, giving reasons why the applicant is suitable for the position. When the interview is complete, the speaker for the applicant may formally close the meeting with a short *poroporoaki* and *karakia*.

The *marae* is the focal point for all Māori activities. However, more recently the *marae* has taken on new faces in many areas. The building of urban *marae* is the result of the rural-urban drift, which occurred after World War II. These new *marae* accommodate those who have either severed ties with their own tribal *marae* or have joined a different community that is not linked by *whakapapa*, e.g. church groups. Some urban *marae* have been established within Pākehā organisations, such as universities, in order to provide a Māori space for students who find the surrounding institution unsympathetic to Māori cultural values and practices, or antithetical to *mātauranga Māori* (Māori knowledge). In many instances these university *marae* also serve as a learning space for students of Māori Studies.

Other urban *marae* have been built in the tribal territory of a different *iwi*. For example, Mātaatua Marae in Rotorua is a Tūhoe *marae* built on land gifted to them by the Te Arawa people. In Hamilton, there are two *marae* that are not kinship based. Hui-te-Rangiora Marae is run by the Catholic Church, while Kirikiriroa Marae is a pan-tribal *marae* for all Māori living in the city. Such pan-tribal *marae* raise important issues about what protocols are to be followed. Usually the *tikanga* of the *iwi* of the area holds sway. Yet in all these descriptions of *marae*, this distinctly Māori institution continues to rely on the local people to maintain it. For many Māori these *marae* become their life.

FURTHER READING

Salmond (1975) is the most thorough study of this topic, but the books by Harawira (1997) and Tauroa (1986) provide useful practical guides to *marae* practices. Walker (1975) and Kāretu's (1975 and 1978) essays discuss some of the issues related to modern practices on the *marae*.

Chapter 8

Tangihanga
Death customs

Rawinia Higgins and John C. Moorfield

In the last chapter the important formalities held at *hui* on the *marae* were discussed. Probably the most important type of *hui* is the *tangihanga*. This chapter will begin by looking at the mythological origins of death customs and then discuss the *tangihanga* in traditional and contemporary society in order to develop an understanding of the customs pertaining to the dead. Other traditional practices related to the dead such as *takahi whare*, *hari mate*, the *hahunga* ceremony and *hura kōhatu* will also be explained.

Remembering ancestors is important to Māori. Regardless of the nature of a gathering, Māori will acknowledge their ancestors and the recently deceased kin of those present. Like other Māori customary practices, the ceremonies connected with death have evolved over time with the social changes resulting from developing technology and contact with Pākehā culture. Despite these changes, of all Māori customary practices today, the rituals pertaining to the dead are probably the closest to the form practised before the arrival of the Pākehā.

Rituals associated with death and mourning have their foundations in the mythological beginnings of the *atua*. The most common narrative of the first occurrence of death is the fleeing of Hine-tītama down to Rarohenga, the place where the spirits of the dead reside, after learning that her husband was also her father. Tāne pleaded for her to return, but she was so ashamed that she refused, telling him to return to their children – but that when the time came, she would draw them to her. She said:

> *Hei konā, e Tāne, hei kukume ake i ā tāua hua ki te ao; kia haere au ki raro hei kukume iho i ā tāua hua ki te Pō.*
>
> *Remain, O Tāne, to bring forth progeny to the world of life; I go below to draw them down to the world of darkness* (Mead and Groves, 2001: 74).

Tāne eventually acceded to her wishes and from that time on she was referred to as Hine-nui-i-te-pō (the great woman of the place of departed spirits).

Another character that features with Hine-nui-i-te-pō is Māui-tikitiki-o-Taranga. Māui sought to destroy Hine-nui-i-te-pō in order to bring eternal life to humankind. This he attempted by changing into a *mokomoko* (lizard), and entering Hine-nui-i-te-pō through her vagina and coming out through her mouth. Māui had brought along his friends in the form of birds, and the fantail was so amused by Māui wriggling around in an attempt to enter Hine-nui-i-te-pō it started laughing and thus woke Hine-nui-i-te-pō, who crushed Māui between her legs. The killing of Māui in this manner brought mortality to humankind. Before his quest to conquer her, Māui discussed the issue of immortality with Hine-nui-i-te-pō, telling her, 'Let man die as the moon dies', meaning that human beings would wane or die like the moon and then arise again, hence attaining a form of immortality. Her response was, 'Let him die forever and be buried in the earth, and so be greeted and mourned' (Best, 1995: 377).

In today's society, much of that philosophy still applies. In all Māori rituals of encounter, tributes to the dead are often the first mentioned and, more often than not, are referred to again at the very end, as with this common example from the conclusion to a *whaikōrero*:

> *Ka āpiti hono tātai hono, te hunga mate ki te hunga mate. Ka āpiti hono tātai hono, te hunga ora ki te hunga ora.*
>
> Let the ties that bind the dead be joined with the ties that bind the living.

The continual reference to the dead in Māori rituals highlights their importance in cultural paradigms. Many Māori believe that if they were to discontinue their practices of mourning and remembering the dead then the essence of Māori culture would be lost. For it is within these practices that many aspects of Māori culture are displayed. Some of the mysteries surrounding the rituals pertaining to the dead can be unlocked by an understanding of the terminology used, their origins, and their traditional usage. The following will examine the customary practices for the dead commencing before death and finishing after final burial.

Traditionally, when a *rangatira* sensed that death was near he would summon his people for his final instructions to them. These final wishes and farewells were called *ōhākī*. The *ōhākī* usually contained both political and legal elements; the former were embodied in some form of advice to the tribe, and the latter in the distribution of his goods. The political nature of the *ōhākī*, in many instances, would be an instruction about *utu* that needed to be undertaken by certain members of the tribe for injustices served on the tribe. Many *ōhākī* are not recorded in literature, as often they would direct where the remains were to be buried. In traditional society, *rangatira* were buried in secrecy lest their enemy discover the remains and later desecrate them. The public gathering of people to listen to the final instructions would ensure that all wishes were acted upon.

Because death is associated with a powerful *tapu*, a *whare tūroro* was built in a place apart from other buildings and the living. The *whare tūroro* was a temporary structure where the dying person was placed. After the person died the *whare tūroro* was burnt down to remove *tapu*, or to *whakanoa* the area. The moving of the dying person to a temporary shelter avoided the need to destroy larger, more valuable buildings.

The way in which people who had not yet reached *kaumātua* status died determined how they were mourned. Some deaths were considered honourable, and others were considered ignoble. *Mate tauā* was death as a result of warfare, and for a young adult to die in this manner was considered a *mate rangatira* (noble death), as he had given his life for the cause of the people. That this type of death was highly esteemed is suggested by the kind of references to it recorded in the numerous *mōteatea*. *Mate aitu* or *mate tara-ā-whare*, death by sickness or natural causes, *mate aituā*, death by accident or *mate whaiwhaiā*, death by means of *mākutu* were considered dishonourable forms of death for those who had not yet reached *kaumātua* status. Numerous *mōteatea* also describe the wasteful nature of these types of death.

Upon one's death in traditional society close female relatives would remove the *tūpāpaku* and prepare it for display. This entailed washing the corpse and rubbing oil, and sometimes *kōkōwai* (red ochre), onto it and finally dressing the hair with feathers. The corpse would then be placed with the knees to the chin and the arms wrapped around the legs. Eventually, the *tūpāpaku* would be wrapped in fine mats and cloaks. Once this was completed, the corpse was usually transported to the *marae* in a dugout canoe, known as a *waka tūpāpaku*.

Tangihanga

The body was either placed in the verandah of the *whare* or in a separate temporary *wharemate* upon an *atamira* (stage or platform). The *tūpāpaku* would remain on display for the duration of the *tangihanga*. This sitting posture of the *tūpāpaku* was important because when it was placed on the *marae* it gave the illusion that the corpse was able to acknowledge people who would arrive to pay their last respects. All forms of *karanga* and *whaikōrero* that are delivered at *tangihanga* speak to the *tūpāpaku* in person as if they were still alive. This is because the *wairua* (spirit) of the deceased is believed to remain with the body for a time.

Contact with Pākehā introduced an influx of new diseases. Hygiene became an issue for the Māori Council and Māori heath professionals such as Te Rangi Hīroa (Sir Peter Buck). They pushed for a law change to the way in which *tangihanga* were to be conducted. This required the displaying of the corpse in a coffin, thus having the *tūpāpaku* lying in state rather than sitting up to acknowledge the speeches. In contemporary society the final farewells that are made to the corpse are still practised and are an important part of Māori customs pertaining to the dead. Normally the coffin is open while it lies on the *marae*.

The *kawa* of the *marae* determines the location of the *wharemate*. Other names for *wharemate* are *whare taua* and *whare pōtae*. Today these locations of the *tūpāpaku* include: inside the house on the centre back wall under the *pou tuarongo*; under the third *poupou* on the *tara whānui* of the house; under the window on the verandah of the house; or a make-shift separate house is built to the side of the house to act as a *wharemate*.

The immediate family of the deceased are called the *whānau pani*, the *kiri mate* or the *kura tūohu*. Their role during the whole process of mourning is purely to mourn and to remain beside the *tūpāpaku*. The rest of the *whānau* or *hapū* take on the roles of organising and preparing the *marae*, representing the *whānau pani* on the *paepae*, doing the *karanga*, and preparing the food. Traditionally the *whānau pani* fasted throughout the whole period of mourning, but in modern times this restriction has been relaxed, although the *whānau pani* usually eat when the flag has been pulled down, which indicates that the *marae* is closed off for the night. This period gives the *ringawera* an opportunity to be by the *tūpāpaku*, as it is the custom that the deceased are never left on their own. In traditional society the female members of the *whānau pani*, especially the *pouaru* (widow), would often cut their hair as a *koha* to the *tūpāpaku* and lacerate their face and bodies using shells or obsidian flints as a way of expressing their grief.

Women wear *pare kawakawa* during the *tangihanga*. These are wreaths of *kawakawa* leaves, or other greenery, worn around the head. The *kawakawa* plant is an important plant for Māori. It is used for medicine and for opening houses and was used for the *tohi* (dedication) ceremony for newborn babies. In earlier times, the purpose of the wreath was to disguise the stench of the decomposing corpse, as the *kawakawa* leaves have a strong scent. Today, many *iwi* continue to use *pare kawakawa* and greenery as a symbol of death. The wearing of black, especially by women, is an added symbol of death that has been adopted from Pākehā culture by many *iwi*.

The *tangihanga* takes precedence over all other *hui*. If a *hui* is being held on the *marae* of the deceased at the time of death, the *tangihanga* is likely to cause the postponement or cancellation of the rest of the *hui*. People at the *hui* are expected to remain at the *marae* to pay their respects and to take part in the *tangihanga*. A *tangihanga* usually lasts three days. In the past, *tangihanga* could last for longer periods of time as determined by the rank of the deceased and the distance mourners had to travel to the *tangihanga*. The *tangihanga* process allows for the open expression of grief, wailing and tears as a means of healing the person who has suffered the loss. Māori discourage people from concealing their emotions. It is regarded as therapeutic for all who participate to feel comfortable expressing their grief openly.

Tangihanga are conducted in a similar manner to other *hui*, using the rituals of encounter. During *karanga* and *whaikōrero*, tributes and farewells to the *tūpāpaku* are made as if the person is still alive. This reflects the belief that the *wairua* of the deceased remains with the *tūpāpaku* during the *tangihanga*. During the tributes to the deceased *tono mate* may be made. *Tono mate* occur when other *hapū*, or *iwi*, request permission for the body to lie at their *marae*. This is common for people who may originate from more than one *hapū* or *iwi*. When the deceased is of high rank, there are instances where this has caused heated debate amongst people over where the body will eventually rest. In other instances, groups may *tono* for a *kawe mate/hari mate*, which is the process of taking the memory of the deceased to a different area so that people who were unable to attend the *tangihanga* can mourn the deceased in a similar way. In this case, a photograph of the deceased replaces the *tūpāpaku*.

At the conclusion of the *pōhiri* each group of visitors will file round to *hongi* with the *tangata whenua* and especially with the *kiri mate*. In the North Auckland tribes people will also *hongi* the *tūpāpaku*, but this is unusual among other *iwi*. Because the *manuhiri* have been in close proximity to the *tūpāpaku* many will still *whakanoa* (remove the *tapu*) themselves by washing their hands and sprinkling water over themselves.

On the last night before the final committal, *poroaki*, or final farewells, are encouraged. This last night before the burial is a celebration of the life of the deceased. It is sometimes called the *pō mihimihi*. These farewells are more informal than those performed on the *marae* during the rituals of encounter. The *pō mihimihi* also allows

8 Death customs

the *whānau pani* to have an opportunity to speak and make acknowledgements to those who are present.

During the time that the *tūpāpaku* lies in state on the *marae*, groups of visitors arrive to pay their respects. Locals are expected to come to pay their respects on the first day in order to accommodate later groups coming from further afield.

On the last day of the *tangihanga* the coffin is closed and a church service is held on the *marae* before the body is carried from the *marae* to the *urupā* (burial ground). As the pallbearers carry the *tūpāpaku* off the *marae*, *kuia* (elderly women) will call *poroporoaki* to the *tūpāpaku*.

The *nehu* (burial), today, involves a church service at the graveside, but often, men will make brief farewells to the deceased at the graveside and *kuia* may call *poroporoaki* as the grave is covered. On leaving the *urupā* people sprinkle water over themselves from a tap or container of water at the gate to *whakanoa* themselves.

Committal to the ground, or *nehu*, is the norm today. However, in earlier times the *tūpāpaku* were buried in either shallow graves, in caves or placed in trees in secret places. These temporary measures were eventually followed by the ceremony of *hahunga*, or exhumation. The location of temporary and permanent burial sites was kept secret so that enemies would not desecrate the remains of the dead.

At the end of the *tangihanga* a *tohunga* or church minister, along with the *whānau pani* and others, go through each room of the house of the deceased to *takahi whare* (trample the house) to dispel any spirits that may still be dwelling there, and also to allow the living to feel safe inside it. *Karakia* are recited and water is sprinkled in each room. This is a *whakanoa* process to remove the *tapu* associated with the *tūpāpaku*. As described earlier, in traditional times the dying were often kept apart from the rest of the *hapū* and placed in a *whare tūroro* which was eventually burnt to the ground as a means of *whakanoa* upon that person's death. The *takahi whare* has a similar purpose, but uses water and *karakia* as a means of *whakanoa*.

After the burial service and the *takahi whare* everybody returns to the *marae* for a *hākari*. This is an important part of the process of the rituals associated with the dead. The *hākari* at the *tangihanga* brings the *whānau pani* back into the world of the living, as they are perceived to have been in the world of the dead during their mourning. It is a means of *whakanoa* for not only the *whānau pani*, but for all of those who have attended the *tangihanga* and *hura kōhatu*.

Traditionally the *hahunga* (exhumation) ceremony was the final part of the grieving process. The *hahunga* would take place after a year or so, once the flesh had fully decomposed from the corpse. The *kaitiaki* (guardians of the dead) would collect the bones from their temporary graves so that they could remove any remaining flesh and wash the bones for the ceremony. The ceremony would consist of the bones being displayed on the *marae*, to be mourned over again by the *whānau pani* and all who had come to pay their respects. Te Rangi Hīroa states that the weeping and expressions of emotion were more intense at a *hahunga* as it would be the final time that the *whānau pani* would physically see the deceased (Buck, 1949). After the ceremony, the bones were committed to their final resting-place by the *kaitiaki*. Today the *hura kōhatu* replaces the practice of *hahunga*.

Hura kōhatu

The *hura kōhatu* is a memorial ceremony at the grave and is commonly known as an unveiling, or the unveiling of the headstone. Like the *hahunga* ceremony, this happens at least a year after the burial. *Manuhiri* are welcomed onto the *marae* with the *whānau pani* sitting around a photograph of their loved one and other photographs of deceased relatives. The mourning process starts again during this period. From the *marae*, the people go to the grave to undertake the task of unveiling the stone with a church service. Today this symbolises the final part of the process of mourning, as it allows closure for the *whānau*. As with the *hahunga* ceremony, it is seen as an important part of the grieving process, to provide an end, but also a remembrance of one's loss. It also serves to unify *whānau* who may have lost contact since the *tangihanga*.

The process of mourning is a long one, beginning at the time of death and continuing until the *hura kōhatu*. These practices display many aspects of Māori culture. Despite the evolution of new forms, all the basic elements remain. Even the *hahunga* custom is present in the new form, the *hura kōhatu*. The dead are always acknowledged in *karanga* and *whaikōrero* regardless of the purpose for the gathering. The recollection of the dead reminds us all of our past. The importance of the *tangihanga* and its central place in *marae* custom is reflected in the fact that it takes precedence over any other gathering on the *marae*.

FURTHER READING

For the best discussion of traditional custom related to death in the early period of contact with Pākehā, see Oppenheim (1973). For the modern context see Dansey (1975), Mead (1997), and Salmond (1976).

Chapter 9

Rangatiratanga
Traditional and contemporary leadership

Tānia M. Ka'ai and Michael P. J. Reilly

'Māori' as a term to describe all of the individual *iwi* of Aotearoa/New Zealand is a relatively new concept. Before colonisation, Māori society was based on *iwi*, *hapū*, and *whānau* groupings each led by chiefs of varying ranks. Leadership was not necessarily hereditary – rather, the best person for the position was chosen; sometimes by the existing leader, sometimes by group consensus, and at other times by marriage or conquest. However, leadership was also based on *mana* and this was usually inherited, although it was possible to gain *mana* by achievement. Leadership was also not gender orientated, although the circumstances of existence in pre-European Aotearoa/New Zealand tended to require an active style of leadership that favoured men. This chapter will begin with a discussion of leadership in traditional times, followed by a look at how colonisation and new styles of society have affected the qualities required in a leader and the way in which Māori of today lead their people. What constitutes a leader in Māori society is best understood through the knowledge recorded by Māori people, and through particular case studies of traditional and contemporary leaders.

 ## Chiefly qualities

During the second half of the nineteenth century, two chiefs, Wiremu Maihi Te Rangikāheke from Ngāti Kererū, a *hapū* of Ngāti Rangi-wewehi, and Himiona or Rua Tikitū of Ngāti Awa, wrote about leadership qualities. Above all else, chiefs needed economic skills in *mahi kai* (food activities) which included the production and supply of both wild and domesticated food resources. Second to this was knowledge of war, which included training *toa* (warriors), planning strategies, evaluating enemy

Wiremu Maihi Te Rangikāheke, also known as William Marsh, of Ngāti Rangiwewehi (died 1896)

capabilities as well as displaying personal courage on the battlefield. A chief also had to be proficient in more pacific arts, showing notable *atawhai tangata*, kindness and liberality, and *manaaki*. These traits were best displayed in the welcoming and feasting of guests. Other peaceful skills included an ability to organise and lead followers, in building and other large projects; in the arts of persuasion, notably oratory but also song composition; in traditional knowledge of the past, especially genealogy; and in diplomacy, particularly in the mediation of land boundary disputes between neighbours. Ability in these several areas enhanced the *mana* of the chief and their people while also attracting more followers to them (Grove, 1985).

The New Zealand historian, Angela Ballara (1991, 1998), has extensively analysed the remarks made about chiefs by Māori witnesses in the nineteenth century Native Land Court. Chiefs were drawn from a small group of genealogically qualified men and women who were the senior kin of a chief. They frequently possessed *mana tangata* (power and authority over their people) as well as *mana whenua* (authority over the land itself). For a conquering male chief the latter power could only be obtained through a union with a chiefly woman of the *tangata whenua*, the people of the land. These witnesses stressed that *mana* was both inherited from a chief's ancestors and achieved through a proficiency in war leadership, oratory and song composition. Such achieved power was also open to non-chiefly classes. *Mana* could be enhanced through a chief's successes as host, leader, or manager of lands and people. Conversely, failure in such areas led to a loss of *mana* and, as a consequence, to a weakening of authority over others.

Chiefs in tribal society

Ballara depicts a tribal society in which several *hapū* or even parts of different *hapū* – the principal Māori corporate and social group before colonisation – would cluster together into communities which lived under the *mana* of a ruling high chief (see Chapter 6). The chiefly leader had the right to dispose of parts of their land and even some of their people, especially those in a client or protective relationship. The chief inherited his or her *mana* from a predecessor in the senior *hapū* at the centre of that community. Beneath him or her were lesser chiefs, usually the leaders of the individual *hapū* making up the community, who acted as *kaitiaki* (caretakers) for parts of the community's lands and resources. Ballara (1998: 206) emphasises the reciprocal nature of the relationship between a chief and the people despite the apparently awesome power of the high chief: 'allegiance was given and received as part of a mutually accepted compact of protection in return for support in terms of tribute and service in war'. Parts of a community might even refuse assistance, an act that usually led to the migration of the various parties and the eventual break-up of the community, followed by the formation of new ones under different leaders.

This Land Court testimony complements Maharaia Winiata's classical description of the chief's position in tribal society (Winiata, 1956, 1967). Winiata separated out the different aspects of Māori pre-European chiefly leadership, identifying the all-encompassing authority over the largest Māori social units, the *iwi* and the *waka*, with the *ariki*. Beneath this leader was a series of lesser *rangatira* chiefs who descended from the more junior family lines and who stood at the head of the smaller, autonomous social units, the *hapū*, which made up the *iwi* and ultimately, the *waka* (see Chapter 6). All these leaders remained connected to each other and to all the members of the *iwi* and *hapū* through 'the web of kinship', which prompted a sense of mutual respect between classes. The chief looked upon members of the tribe as younger brothers or sisters and they looked up to the chief as their elder.

 ## Wahine rangatira

According to Winiata, chiefly first-born women – variously titled, *ariki tapairu*, *kahurangi* or *tuhi mareikura* – retained the status accorded to their birth rank, but 'active political leadership' was devolved to the male. Where the first born male proved incapable of leadership, Winiata argued that selection was made from eligible chiefly men on the basis of their warrior skills, their administrative competence and their interest in the tribe's welfare. Ballara's most recent discussion of female *ariki* inclined to support Winiata's position. While pointing out their *mana whenua* over a community, she placed the active political leadership more firmly in the hands of their husbands, who acted as executive chiefs. Yet, women did play a more political role. Elsewhere, Ballara (1991: 307) commented that 'women who combined high rank with force of character, whatever their age, could play important roles in the affairs of their people.' Winiata, along with other scholars (e.g. Mahuika, 1992), noted women who could participate as chiefs in the highest political deliberations of their tribe. Winiata also noted that leadership of the smallest social unit, the *whānau*, or extended family, was shared between the oldest male and female couple.

 ## Chiefly roles

Winiata emphasised the roles any chief – male or female – would typically carry out. Any chief, through primogeniture, possessed supernaturally ordained powers of *mana* and *tapu* from the gods. As a consequence, *ariki* carried out specific rites and rituals, such as exhumations, imposing *rāhui*, and courage-giving ceremonies before battle. Many of the tribe's religious activities were performed on the *ariki*'s behalf by *tohunga*, the 'ritual leader', who was of chiefly standing. Winiata described the *tohunga* as 'the philosopher, the guide and friend of the chief' who, from that position, could exert much indirect political power. The *ariki*, in association with the *rangatira*, would decide on matters of foreign policy, such as the declaration of hostilities against other *iwi*. The *ariki* was also responsible for the effective management of the tribe's internal administration, working 'as arbitrator, persuader, adviser and supervisor' of the lesser leaders and the people. To this end, oratory was an important part of a chief's repertoire, for he acted, in Winiata's words, as 'the master of arts and letters' in the *iwi* (1967: 30–38).

 ## Rereahu and his sons

A case study of the chiefly sons of Rereahu from the Tainui *waka* highlights many of the chiefly qualities described in these commentaries. Rereahu had first married Rangi-ānewa, from which union came Te Ihinga-a-rangi. A second marriage to the higher-ranking Hine-au-pounamu produced Maniapoto, and his *teina*, Matakore; by this later marriage, Rereahu had succeeded in securing a woman from a more senior line, thereby guaranteeing higher status for their offspring. Marriages and their resulting descent lines formed as much a part of chiefly power games as wars, feasts or oratory.

Rereahu had long been observing his children for leadership abilities and, as death approached, he announced Maniapoto as his successor. Recognising the importance of his first-born son, the *mātāmua*, Te Ihinga-a-rangi, Rereahu first bid his eldest child go away and attend to the *tūāhu*, before making the succession announcement. Rereahu anointed Maniapoto and had him bite the crown of his head, thereby inheriting the father's chiefly *mana*, or *rangatiratanga*. Upon his return, Te Ihinga sought to contest Maniapoto's elevation to tribal leadership. The soundness of Rereahu's decision and Te Ihinga-a-rangi's lack of chiefly acumen were demonstrated by subsequent events.

One day Te Ihinga-a-rangi entertained Maniapoto's uncle. Te Ihinga ate the best pieces and gave his guest the poorer parts of the food. Te Ihinga-a-rangi then talked of his hatred for Maniapoto and his desire to kill him. Such miserliness and indiscretion were soon exposed to Maniapoto when the uncle warned him of his brother's designs. Significantly, Maniapoto had been a far more generous host. Maniapoto demonstrated his own chiefly and warrior abilities when he gave instructions for his uncle to pass on to Te Ihinga-a-rangi the message that Maniapoto and his people would be leaving their lands and moving elsewhere. The covetous older brother and his warriors soon settled into the abandoned village, only to be caught out by his *teina*'s sudden and surprise attack. After slaying many of his brother's tribe, Maniapoto had Te Ihinga-a-rangi brought before him. There he spat upon the *tuakana*'s head, so lowering his status. As a mark of his shame, Te Ihinga-a-rangi left for more remote and inland places. In the histories of the Tainui *waka* he became far less well known than his *teina*.

The correctness of Rereahu's choice of a younger son, Maniapoto, as leader of his tribe, was confirmed by these events. The latter was a generous host, exemplifying qualities of *atawhai tangata* and *manaaki*. This presumed great skills in *mahi kai*. He was also a better war leader, outfoxing his older brother, who suffered a loss of *mana* and was forced into exile. Despite Te Ihinga's failings, his father had consistently respected his son's status as *mātāmua*, shown by the latter's responsibility for the tribe's *tapu* ritual sites where the chiefs and *tohunga* communicated with the *atua*. If Te Ihinga-a-rangi had not been consumed by hatred at his *teina*'s elevation he would doubtless have retained his important sacerdotal role while Maniapoto took responsibility for the executive leadership of the tribe in matters of peace or war.

Maniapoto's later chiefly career brings together other distinctive chiefly traits. He is notable for having contracted a series of marriages with the youthful grandchildren of his defeated *tuakana*. This suggests that there must have been great age disparities between Rereahu and Te Ihinga-a-rangi, and Maniapoto. These marriages marked the encompassment of the defeated *tuakana*'s line by the dominant *teina*. As the principal chief of his community, Maniapoto succeeded in controlling the senior descent lines from which future leaders would be drawn.

During this period, Maniapoto allowed some new migrants to use part of his lands. They were clearly in a client relationship. However, they sought to challenge Maniapoto's authority by insulting the bones of Rereahu. Rather than precipitately attack them, Maniapoto sent a *teina* to test the migrants and so discern their intentions towards him. The migrants decided to attack. At the moment of their assault upon his village, Maniapoto was embracing his new wife. His warriors were arrayed under the leadership of his *tēina*. When Maniapoto emerged from his house, he knelt down in front of his people, his *taiaha* (spear-like striking weapon) lying in front of him. The migrant's chief approached right up to him, challenging him to a duel. At that precise moment, as his opponent stood close to him, Maniapoto snatched up some sand and gravel and threw it into his enemy's eyes. Blinded, the migrant's chief was easily thrown to the ground. Maniapoto bit his head and so lowered his *mana*. One of Maniapoto's nephews then sought permission to kill the defeated chief, which was granted. The migrants, seeing the death of their leader, lost heart and fled. All of them were slain by Maniapoto's pursuing warriors.

In his later career Maniapoto was the ruling high chief of his community, comprising several *hapū*. He ritually diminished a client chief and destroyed his *mana*, before having him executed. The importance of chiefly leadership in war is suggested by the way that the defeated side gave way as soon as their leader was dead. By marrying offspring from the senior lines, Maniapoto ensured his political dominance. His fertility was further demonstrated by his embracing of a new wife. That he did so in the midst of an attack only showed his chiefly composure. He demonstrated his military abilities by his careful observation of his rebellious clients, and his success in single combat. Use of tricks and ruses, such as blinding an opponent, were acceptable acts under the warrior code. As custom also dictated, Maniapoto was supported in all his actions by his *tēina*, junior male kinsmen, who willingly carried out his instructions (Jones, 1995).

The mutually satisfying relationship between *tuakana* and *teina* is exemplified in the life of Maniapoto's younger brother, Matakore. The latter had always supported his *tuakana* and, as a result, he was bequeathed large amounts of land, and married well into another powerful *iwi*, Te Arawa. Because of these military and marital alliances, Matakore and his people were able to live in a land without warfare or rancour. He has been described as a peace-loving chief. He was not like other chiefs who desired meat or fish from their people. Since he treated the people so well he was venerated and given the first fruits of the land. According to a favourite story retold by his descendants, Matakore's most preferred occupations were the pleasures of sexual intercourse and the blissful inactivity of sleep (Jones, 1995). The tranquillity of Matakore's life was made possible with the support of his elder brother, and an important marriage into another powerful *iwi*. Rather than acting as a warrior, Matakore's career stresses the productive and fertile qualities of a leader whose mild demands upon his community earned him a reciprocal respect from the people.

Contemporary leadership

Te Rangikāheke and Tikitū and the case study of Rereahu's chiefly sons stress the qualities required by a traditional Māori leader. The second half of this chapter will describe the appropriate attributes of leaders in Māori society today.

Attributes of a leader

- Ability to strategise and plan for the future to ensure the wellbeing and survival of the people they are managing – politically, socially, economically, spiritually and intellectually.

9 Rangatiratanga

- Ability to make sound judgements.
- Ability in *te reo me ngā tikanga Māori*.
- Ability to communicate effectively (orally and aurally).
- Ability to represent the people in all forums, in an effective and efficient manner.
- To be a role model for the people they are representing.
- To have excellent organisational skills.
- Ability to motivate, inspire and mobilise the people.
- Ability to critically reflect and evaluate their own performance as a leader.
- Ability to manage conflict amongst the people, seek resolution and make difficult decisions.
- Well developed negotiation and facilitation skills.
- Sophisticated knowledge of, and experience in *te ao Māori*.
- Ability to be multi-tasked.
- Active participation in Māori cultural activities at a grass-roots level such as attending *tangihanga* and tribal *hui*.

Ascribed and inherited leadership as evident in traditional Māori society is still relevant in contemporary Māori society. The impact of colonisation upon Māori society (such as the 1847 Education Ordinance Act, and the 1907 Tohunga Suppression Act) has for 130 years forced the declining Māori population to prioritise individual needs such as education and employment, often ahead of the needs of their *iwi*. Therefore, Māori leadership has evolved in contemporary Māori society to embrace this demographic change. While ascribed and inherited leadership are still very relevant in contemporary Māori society, combinations of these two categories also apply. For example, one might have ascribed leadership, another might have inherited leadership, and others may have a combination of the two.

It is against this background that the following list of Māori people is proposed as examples of leaders in the contemporary Māori world:

Māori leaders, past and present	
Māori Leader	**Most known field[s] of leadership**
Sir Āpirana Ngata (1874–1950)	Politician and scholar
Sir Peter Buck (Te Rangi Hīroa) (1877?–1951)	Anthropologist and scholar
Te Puea Hērangi (1883–1952)	Kīngitanga and the development of the Tainui people
Dame Whina Cooper (1895–1994)	Led the Māori Land March (1975) and first President of the Māori Women's Welfare League (1951)
Kumeroa Ngoingoi Pēwhairangi (1921–1985)	Composer, teacher and co-founder of Te Ātaarangi, exponent of Māori performing arts, Māori and South Pacific Arts Council
John Te Rangiāniwaniwa Rangihau (1919–1987)	Philosopher, orator and scholar of *te ao Māori*
Sir Hepi Te Heuheu (1919–1997)	Paramount Chief of Ngāti Tūwharetoa

Mīria Simpson (1922–2002)	Advocate of Māori language revitalisation, librarian
Hirini Melbourne (1950–2003)	Composer, musician and pioneer of the revitalisation of traditional Māori instruments
Dame Mira Szasy (1921–2001)	President of Māori Women's Welfare League (1973)
Sir James Henare (1911–1989)	Philosopher, orator, and scholar of *te ao Māori*
Whaia te rangi McClutchie (1922–1992)	Female orator known to assume the *paepae* inside Ngāti Porou and beyond
Wiremu Kerekere (1923–2001)	Composer, musician, exponent of Māori performing arts, Māori broadcasting
Pei Te Hurinui Jones (1898–1976)	Playwright, scholar
Tuīni Ngāwai (1910–1965)	Composer, musician, exponent of Māori performing arts
Sir Kīngi Ihaka (1921–1993)	Composer, expert in Māori performing arts, Anglican Minister, Māori and South Pacific Arts Council
Eruera Manuera (1895–1990)	Paramount Chief of Ngāti Awa
Hamuera Mitchell (?–1995)	Orator and scholar of *te ao Māori*
Canon Wī Huata (1917–1991)	Exponent of Māori performing arts, Anglican Minister, composer
Patariki Rei (1915–1995)	Scholar of *te ao Māori*
Dame Erihāpeti Rehu-Murchie (1924–1997)	President of Māori Women's Welfare League (1977)
Sir Monita Delamere (1921–1993)	Leader of Ringatū faith, Waitangi Tribunal
Ruka Broughton (1940–1986)	Scholar in *te ao Māori*, academic
Wiremu Parker (1914–1986)	First Māori language broadcaster, academic
Maka Jones (1927–?)	Advocate of Te Ātaarangi, Ringatū minister
Te Reo Hura (1904–1991)	Leader of Rātana faith
Maharaia Winiata (1912–1960)	Anthropologist, educationalist
Māori Marsden (?–1993)	Philosopher, Anglican Minister, *tohunga*
Hoani Waititi (1926–1965)	Teacher, author, advocate of Māori language revitalisation, scholar of *te ao Māori*
Hepora Young (1926–1997)	Member of the Waitangi Tribunal; crusader of the Māori language
Matiu Te Hau (1912–1978)	Adult education and community leader
Dr Eru Pōmare (1942–1995)	Māori health professional; Academic leader in Māori health and research
Hana Te Hēmara (1940–1999)	Crusader for the Māori language and foundation member of Ngā Tamatoa
Matiu Rata (1934–1997)	Politician, founder of the Mana Motuhake Party
Dame Rangimārie Hetet (1892–1995)	*Tohunga raranga*

9 Rangatiratanga

Irihāpeti Ramsden (1945–2003)	Cultural safety in nursing
Iranui Haig (1913–2003)	Scholar of te ao Māori
Iritana Tawhiwhirangi	Founder of Te Kōhanga Reo movement
Wharehuia Milroy	Advocate of Māori language revitalisation, Waitangi Tribunal, academic, scholar of te ao Māori
Tīmoti Kāretu	Advocate of Māori language revitalisation, expert in Māori performing arts, first Chief Executive Officer: Māori Language Commission
Sir Tīpene O'Regan	Historian, led the Ngāi Tahu Claim
Dame Te Arikinui Te Atairangikaahu	Paramount Chief of Tainui
Pita Sharples	A founder of Te Kura Kaupapa Māori movement, exponent of Māori performing arts, composer, academic
Judge Eddie Durie	Former Chief Judge of the Māori Land Court, Chair of the Waitangi Tribunal, Justice of the High Court of New Zealand
Sir Hugh Kāwharu	Anthropologist, academic leader
Roka Paora	Teacher and advocate for the Māori language
Huirangi Waikerepūru	Led the WAI 11 Māori language claim, crusader for the Māori language
Pakaariki Harrison	Tohunga whakairo

The following case study has been provided to illustrate the various qualities of contemporary Māori leadership which can be found in the career of a woman nationally known for her work of championing the preservation and survival of Māori culture and society into the twenty-first century.

Kumeroa Ngoingoi Pēwhairangi, 1922–1985

Kumeroa Ngoingoi Pēwhairangi (Ngoi) was born in 1922 at Tokomaru Bay. Her father, Hōri Ngāwai, came from the local *hapū*, Te Whānau-a-Ruataupare, while Ngoi's mother, Wikitōria, came from the Ngāti Koi in the Hauraki region. Ngoi's father was a Ringatū minister (see Chapter 16), and an advocate for the Kōtahitanga political movement seeking political autonomy for Māori people. From her earliest years, Ngoi was reared within a strong Māori world and surrounded by religious and political ideas and beliefs that emphasised the autonomy of Māori people, a cause that she spent her life promoting.

Ngoi attended the native school at Tokomaru Bay between 1928 and 1935. While her first language was Māori she quickly showed her intellectual abilities by acquiring English literacy, and winning a scholarship to attend Hukarere Māori Girls College in 1938. During her school years she played in hockey tournaments and performed in *kapa haka* competitions. Both these experiences formed an important dimension of her later leadership. After leaving school, Ngoi remained committed to the Māori performing arts, as a member and leader of Te Hokowhitu-a-Tū Māori Culture Group, founded by her aunt, Tuīni Ngāwai, in 1931. They travelled around Aotearoa/New Zealand performing and raising funds for the war effort in the early 1940s. This was initiated by Sir Āpirana Ngata, himself a renowned leader from Ngāti Porou, who had a skill for recognising and supporting Māori community leaders.

During these years Tuīni Ngāwai groomed Ngoi in the arts of performance, composition, and leadership, encouraging her to become the tutor and leader for Te Hokowhitu-a-Tū. As a tribute to Tuīni, Ngoi compiled her many songs and published them in a collection, *Tuini: Her Life and Her Songs*. Ngoi emulated her aunt, and became well known for her numerous compositions, among them *Kia Kaha Ngā Iwi*, *Ka Noho Au*, and *Whakarongo*. She composed many of these songs for specific events, including the first Royal Visit to Gisborne in 1969. In 1981, the Royal Visit of Prince Charles and Princess Diana offered Ngoi an opportunity to demonstrate her leadership skills when she was responsible for the organisation of the official *pōhiri*.

Kumeroa Ngoingoi Pēwhairangi of Te Whānau-a-Ruataupare, Ngāti Porou and Ngāti Koi (1922–1985)

During the 1970s, Ngoi became a teacher, first at Saint Mary's Convent Girls' School in Gisborne, then at Gisborne Girls' High School. There she taught the Māori language and tutored the Māori Culture Club. In 1973 Ngoi was also appointed as a part-time lecturer for the Department of Māori at Waikato University to teach their Certificate of Māori programme administered through Distance Education.

Ngoi's demonstration of skill in mobilising people irrespective of age, gender, ethnicity or occupation was quickly recognised within Māori educational circles. Therefore, it is not surprising that in 1975, Kara Puketapu, the then Secretary of the Department of Māori Affairs, contracted her to assist the Department in the implementation of the Tū Tangata Programme. This programme focused on rescuing urban Māori youth and connecting them to *iwi*. This involvement lead to Ngoi's appointment in 1977 as an Advisor to the Department of Māori Affairs. In this position she was instrumental in assisting the development of the *Tangata Whenua* Television Series with Barry Barclay and Dr Michael King, who later included a commentary written by Ngoi as part of the foreword to the book, *Te Ao Hurihuri*. The focus of this commentary was a discussion of the notions of *tapu*, *wairua* and the psychology of the Māori child.

Kara Puketapu also consulted her in the preliminary discussions which led to the emergence of the first Te Kōhanga Reo in Wellington, along with the design of the symbol which is now used by the Te Kōhanga Reo National Trust as their official national symbol.

This experience quickly gave rise to another opportunity in tertiary education. In 1977, while still working as a part-time lecturer for the University of Waikato, the National Council of Adult Education employed Ngoi as an Advisor. Commuting between her home at Tokomaru Bay and Wellington, she travelled to many places all over New Zealand promoting adult education, particularly in rural areas, with a special focus on the Māori community. Activities included the advancement of cottage industry crafts such as pottery and weaving, and the learning of *te reo Māori* and culture.

While Ngoi was in this position with the Council of Adult Education, she developed several programmes that mobilised Māori women in particular. In 1979 she co-developed, with Kāterina Mataira, the Te Ātaarangi programme. They piloted this programme with a small group of Māori people in Wellington. Te Ātaarangi can be described as a method of learning and teaching the Māori language in an interactive context using cuisenaire rods. It was the basis of a television programme in 1980 called *Te Reo*; the programme had a series of books with the same name. Ngoi also published her own teacher's manual, *He Paku Āwhina*, in 1982. Te Ātaarangi became so successful that its membership formed a national association at the first national *hui* convened by Ngoi in 1981 at Te Ngāwai Marae, Mangatū. The establishment of the National Weavers Association in 1984 shared a similar history. It too was formed as a result of a national *hui* convened by Ngoi, bringing skilled Māori and Pacific weavers together from all over the country and the Pacific for a week at Pākirikiri Marae, Tokomaru Bay.

Ngoi was also a foundation member of the Māori and South Pacific Arts Council (Te Waka Toi, Creative New Zealand), which was part of the Queen Elizabeth the Second Arts Council established in 1972, alongside people such as Kuru Wāka, Kingi Ihaka and Johnnie Frisbee. She served on this Council until her death in 1985.

Ngoi was considered a *tohunga* (expert) at adjudicating *kapa haka* competitions alongside people like the late John Rangihau. She was constantly called upon to be an adjudicator for Māori Cultural Competitions in both Aotearoa/New Zealand and Australia from 1969 until her death. She adjudicated at festivals such as the Tamararo Competition held annually in Gisborne, the Regional Festivals in New Zealand and Australia, and the Aotearoa National Māori Festival of Arts held every two years.

Throughout her life, Ngoi transformed many people's lives in various ethnic groups, such as Māori, Pacific Island and Pākehā. She had an influence on university staff and students, artists and writers, school children, public servants, broadcasters, tribal leaders, politicians and educators. Her contribution to the wider national community was recognised by the award of a Queen's Service Medal in 1978. Her greatest legacy, however, are the generations of people who have been influenced by her leadership qualities, her personal philosophy and her pedagogical principles of learning and teaching. For these reasons, Ngoi can be likened to world-renowned educational gurus and theorists such as Paulo Freire.

Ngoi's death on January 29 1985 in her home at Tokomaru Bay after a long illness left generations of New Zealanders with memories of a charismatic woman who was revered, loved, respected, admired and cherished for her unrelenting belief and work in the advancement of *te reo me ngā tikanga Māori* and *te ao Māori* and the development of her ideal of a bicultural nation and a dual heritage as espoused in Te Tiriti o Waitangi.

He taonga, he koha, he kura pounamu
A prized possession, a gift, a treasure

Mahuika (1992) discusses 'ascribed' leadership through *whakapapa* and 'achieved' leadership through the display of outstanding personal qualities fitting for leadership. For Ngāti Porou, this included both men and women, as reflected in their tribal histories and in the naming of their *marae*, in the main, after women. It is particularly important to consider leadership origins when considering Ngoi as a leader – one who displayed outstanding leadership qualities throughout her lifetime.

Ngoi descends from Ruataupare, who married Tūwhakairiora. They were both of equal chiefly rank, but over time Ruataupare grew tired of Tūwhakairiora not acknowledging her rank. So she left him and moved from Wharekāhika to Tokomaru Bay. She established her genealogical links with the Ngāti Ira and Wahine-iti people in the area, who accepted her on this basis. Once Ruataupare's *mana tangata* was recognised, it was only a matter of time before she acquired *mana whenua* (Mahuika, 1992), such was the quality of her leadership. This she passed on to her daughters and Te Whānau-a-Ruataupare still hold it today.

Ngoi in her own right possessed the qualities of leadership. She represented the educated leader providing the bridge between traditional society and the new Pākehā one. She held on to old Māori values while taking up the tools offered her by Pākehā knowledge and technology. She stood in two worlds; representing the Māori to the Pākehā while at the same time speaking to the Māori for the Pākehā.

Some of the political and social issues affecting Māori people between 1922 and 1985, Ngoi's lifetime, help demonstrate the intellectual motivation behind Ngoi's leadership. She had experienced World War II and seen part of a generation of Māori men wiped out, thus depleting the pool of *te reo* speakers and teachers. Her concern at this decline led her to spend a number of years teaching the Māori language at all levels, co-developing Te Ataarangi and using television as a medium to reach Māori in their homes – all to advance the status of the language. Ngoi experienced the downturn in the rural sector and the ensuing decline in Māori morale that contributed to the urban drift of the 1950s, resulting in a loss of community vitality and a decline in Māori traditional arts. Her response to this was to foster a revival of weaving as a Māori art form in communities. She composed and taught the performing arts. Ngoi discerned a lack of understanding by Pākehā of Māori values and the Māori worldview and saw a need for this divide to be bridged. Her answer was to convene a *hui* on her home *marae* for specific groups wishing to understand Māori culture, including Ngā Tamatoa, television reporters, directors and broadcasters, artists and writers, to name a few. Ngoi also witnessed urban Māori youth experiencing an identity crisis. She worked hard to influence the policymakers in the Department of Māori Affairs to focus on revitalisation of the culture amongst Māori youth in the cities by taking them to rural *marae* through programmes such as Tū Tangata.

The loss of a leader of the calibre of Ngoi leaves a huge gap in the Māori world. It is unlikely that any one person can ever hope to fill this gap, as the impact of colonisation has eroded many aspects of the Māori culture and made access to specific knowledge more difficult. This creates a new challenge for younger generations. Tīmoti Kāretu composed the following *waiata tangi* (lament) to express the loss he felt about the passing of Ngoi. The imagery in this composition is compelling and indicative of the depth of the loss.

Whakaipuipu mai rā te moana kei waho e
E āki kau ana ki Te Toka-namu-a-Mihi-marino
Ki uta rā, ki Pākirikiri e
Ko te rite o te wai kei aku kamo!
Tīneia mai te whetū mārama o te ao Māori
Kia pōuri, kia tūohu noa, kia mamae au e
Kei hea rā tōu ritenga hei whakamau atu mā te iwi e
E koe, e te ngākau māhaki, e te ngākau aroha,
Te tohunga whakairo kupu, te manu tīoriori o te motu
Mū ana i te rā nei e
Ngaro atu koe i te kitenga kanohi e
Ō taonga ia, ka mahue mai
Anō he toka whatiwhati ngaru
E kore e ngaro, e kore e wareware e
Kāti, e hika, haere i tō tira mokemoke e
Ko au e kapo atu ki te rehu o te tai
E pā mai nei ki ahau e.
(cited in Moorfield, 1996: 84)

The sea off shore is overcast with clouds
As it pounds against Te Toka-namu-a-Mihi-Marino
To the shore at Pākirikiri
It is like tears in my eyes
The bright star of the Māori world is extinguished
I am in sadness, I bow down and I am in pain
Where is your likeness as a focus for the people (to follow)
You the generous heart, the loving heart
The expert in crafting words, the singing bird of the land
Is now silent this day
You have disappeared from view
But your gifts remain
Like a rock where the waves break
Which will never be lost and never forgotten
Well, my friend, go with your lonely travelling party
And I will snatch at the sea spray
Which strikes me.

FURTHER READING

Grove (1985) provides a comprehensive work on traditional leadership. More accessible sources include Mahuika (1992), Mead (1997) and Winiata (1967). Examples of chiefly leadership can be found in any tribal history. *The Dictionary of New Zealand Biography* (available in *te reo Māori* and English) provides biographies of the people mentioned in this chapter, especially Ngoi Pēwhairangi.

The authors would like to thank: Piripi Aspinall, Teripowai Higgins, Nūnū Kīngi, Wikitōria Matahiki, April Waipara, and Karen Wateress for their personal memories of Ngoi Pēwhairangi.

Chapter 10

Ngā mahi a Tāne-rore me Te Rēhia
Performing arts

Nathan W. Matthews and Karyn Paringatai

The performing arts have many important functions in Māori society; they are present in almost all ritual and ceremony associated with Māori culture. This chapter will outline the purpose, form and function of the various types of *waiata*, *haka*, *poi* and *taonga pūoro* and the performance related concepts of *ihi*, *wehi* and *wana*. The various terms related to performance will also be briefly explained to provide an introductory overview of the Māori performing arts.

Waiata tangi

Waiata tangi as the name suggests, are commonly referred to as laments. They are often composed in remembrance of those who have died. The type of death that the person suffered would determine the content of the *waiata tangi*. For example, if someone was murdered, the *waiata tangi* would contain references to the murderer and it would express the hate the composer felt towards that person/people. It would also speak of the composer's intention of revenge and it would be sung often to the *hapū* or *iwi* that the deceased belonged to, to keep the memory of the murder alive. In this way, *waiata tangi* could be likened to a *kaioraora*, which will be explained later in this chapter.

However, the content of a *waiata tangi* written for a person who died a natural death would be vastly different. It would include references to the deceased's lineage, especially if the person was a chief, to the character and personality of the deceased, and it would often recall significant events that occurred in that person's life. Hatred would not be present in this type of composition. The most vivid expressions of Māori language are present in *waiata tangi* for people who die a natural death. One form of these is *apakura*. Women in the *wharemate* compose *apakura* during the *tangihanga*, and they are the women's form of farewell as part of the grieving process.

Waiata tangi written for natural death and unnatural death have a common level of Māori language and expression. Highly specialised, archaic expressions combined with complex metaphors and vivid imagery make it very difficult for even the most able of Māori speakers to comprehend them. People such as Sir George Grey, Sir Āpirana Ngata, and Margaret Orbell have recorded a large number of *waiata tangi*, and usually these authors have provided translations. These translations, despite the dramatic images and feelings they invoke, do not always do the original words justice.

Waiata tangi were not always composed for people who had died. They were written also for a variety of purposes such as loss of crops, loss or death of animals and pets, for land left behind and other such events. People experiencing a loss of any sort could compose a *waiata tangi*. An example of a classic *waiata tangi* written for the loss of land, and perhaps one of the most famous compositions belonging to the *waiata tangi* genre is *E pā tō hau*, written by Rangiāmoa (Ngata, 1974: 236–237).

After nine months of fighting against Government troops, tribes of the Māori King movement were finally defeated and were forced from their homes and lands. A section of one of those tribes fighting, Ngāti Apakura, was forced to take refuge in the Taupō area. On the journey to safety, they reached a mountain called Tītī-rau-penga. One of the men, Te Wano, along with some of his people, climbed the mountain so he could look back on the tribal lands they were forced to leave. Te Wano died whilst looking back at his home and was buried by his people on the top of the mountain. Later his cousin, Rangiāmoa, composed *E pā tō hau* to remember Te Wano, their homeland, and the suffering her people had endured.

 ## Waiata aroha

Waiata aroha are love songs, often focusing on a lost or distant lover. Traditionally they were mainly composed by women (Ngata and Te Hurinui, 1974). Although their tunes are similar, *waiata aroha* and *waiata tangi* differ in the language used. The language used in *waiata aroha* is simple in comparison with the more developed and complex language of *waiata tangi*.

The most frequent themes of *waiata aroha* describe feelings and might recount:
- complaints about an unrequited love;
- the resentment of women who were forcibly parted from a lover;
- anger from women deserted by their husbands because of infatuation for another;
- the loneliness felt by women left at home by their husbands who had gone off to war;
- envy from a woman sharing a husband with a co-wife; and
- regret by a virgin set apart who had transgressed.

One of the most famous *waiata aroha*, which illustrates the second theme, is *Ka eke ki Wairaka*, composed by Rihi Puhiwahine some time between the late 1830s and the mid 1840s (see Ngata, 1974: 150–151). She composed this *waiata* for her cousin lover, Te Mahutu Te Toko, whom her brothers had forbidden her to marry because he was already married and she would have had to accept the status of second wife. She mourned this forbidden love until her death in 1906.

 ## Waiata whaiāipo

Waiata whaiāipo are a type of *waiata aroha*; however, they are bolder in the language used. Literally, they are sweetheart songs, flirtatious and very witty (Orbell, 1991). Early *waiata whaiāipo* were a blend of witty flirtation and provocative performance, often using quite explicit language as the composer spoke of attraction and sexual encounters, past and future; it was this explicitness that made them unique. *Waiata whaiāipo* are sung primarily for entertainment, though they often convey messages to some of the men addressed.

An example of a *waiata whaiāipo* is *Kāore hoki koia te rangi nei*, composed by Rihi Puhiwahine in which she recounts several of her love affairs and flirtations (Orbell, 1991: 78–82). This composition contains little of the explicitness and forthrightness associated with early examples of this type of *waiata*. This is attributed to the changing beliefs and associated moral values following the introduction and spread of Christianity during the nineteenth century. Many aspects of Māori society changed as Māori incorporated the new western religions and their views on morality and decency. The more explicit and descriptive language used in the performing arts reduced.

Waiata tohutohu

Waiata tohutohu are message-bearing songs (McLean and Orbell, 1975). They were composed mainly in the nineteenth century as Māori strove to cope with the arrival of European settlers to Aotearoa/New Zealand and the huge social and political change that this created. Mainly prophets or *rangatira*, such as Tāwhiao, the second Māori King, and Te Kooti Arikirangi Te Tūruki, a Māori prophet and religious leader, composed *waiata tohutohu* as a means of instructing and guiding their followers. This is the main function of *waiata tohutohu*. The prophets who composed these *waiata* often included their prophecies in their compositions.

An example of *waiata tohutohu* is *Kāore te pō nei mōrikarika noa*, which was composed by Te Kooti (McLean and Orbell, 1975: 38). In this song, Te Kooti urges Tūhoe to assert control over their destiny by not allowing the Government to survey or sell their land. Te Kooti would often use existing *waiata* as the basis for his own compositions, but he would change selected words and lines to suit his message or to include his thoughts and prophecies.

Oriori

Oriori are lullabies. These lullabies differ from Pākehā lullabies in that they contain important information for the infant. *Oriori* were composed prior to the birth of the child and sung throughout the antenatal period and early childhood. These compositions were unique to that particular child. Within *oriori* are references to many important facts relating to the child, including *whakapapa* and important events that have taken place prior to the birth of the child. They were used to arouse the interest of the child in tribal mythology and the traditions that mythology contained (Ngata and Te Hurinui, 1974).

Sir Āpirana Ngata describes the composition of *oriori*:

> *The beginning of a lullaby is always couched in terms of praise for the child for whom the lullaby has been composed, or is a recital of its aristocratic lineage; or laments the death of a parent or of a tribesman, or a time of famine, or a period of bitter cold; and in this way establishes the theme of the song* (Ngata, 1974: xiii).

Pō Pō, composed by Enoka Te Pakaru of Te Aitanga-a-Māhaki on the East Coast is a well-known example of an *oriori* (Ngata and Te Hurinui, 1974: 152–161).

Haka

Traditionally there were many types of *haka*, each with its own form, function and importance. Each fulfilled its own social function, e.g.

- use in the rituals of encounter;
- as a psychological weapon on the battlefield;
- to transmit social and political messages (Awatere, 1975: 513).

Although *haka* as a whole are often erroneously cited as war-dances, it is the *peruperu* that is the true 'war-dance'. It was performed on the battlefield when the war party came face to face with the enemy. The *peruperu* is described as the fiercest *haka* due to where and when it was performed and the physical and mental conditioning of the performers.

> *Hard conditioning makes the warriors physically and mentally fit to perform this dance which has the psychological purpose of demoralising the enemy by*

Members of Ngāti Tūwharetoa performing the *peruperu*, with *tewhatewha*, at Waitangi on February 6, 1934

> *gestures, by posture, by controlled chanting, by conditioning to look ugly, furious to roll the fiery eye, to glare the light of battle therein, to spew the defiant tongue, to control, to distort, to snort, to fart the thunder of the war god upon the enemy, to stamp furiously, to yell raucous, hideous, blood-curdling sounds, to carry the anger, the peru, of Tuumatauenga, the ugly-faced war-god, throughout the heat of battle* (Awatere, 1975: 514).

Warriors performed the *peruperu* with weapons and the outstanding physical feature was the high leap off the ground with the legs folded under. It was one of the main psychological weapons used by warriors and because of this, they prided themselves on its performance (Kāretu, 1993).

A *puha* is similar to a *peruperu* except a *puha* is not used on the battlefield; instead, it is performed in the village to send an alarm and call kinsmen to arms (Awatere, 1975). In this role, it is similar to a *tiwha* that was also used to send alarm and appeal for assistance in war. This was either by song (as above) or by a token, such as a *poi* (see page 108), being sent to potential allies.

Tūtū ngārahu, also known as *ngārahu*, *tū ngārahu*, and *whakarewarewa*, and by some tribes as *whakatū waewae*, were performed by the young warriors in front of the elders and experienced warriors before embarking on war (Kāretu, 1993). This type of *haka* was used to test the young warriors' readiness for battle through their ability to perform the *haka*. This *haka* was performed with weapons and the main physical characteristic was the side-to-side jump with the legs held together. Northern tribes also use this particular type of *haka* in their rituals of welcome. An example of a *tūtū ngārahu* is *Ka eke i te wīwī* from Te Tai Tokerau (Kāretu, 1993: 39).

Armed dancers perform *whakatū waewae*, but unlike the *peruperu* and *tūtū ngārahu*, they do not include jumping. Tūhoe uses this type of *haka* as part of their welcoming rituals – an example of a *whakatū waewae* is the Tūhoe haka, *Te Puru* (Kāretu, 1993: 40).

Haka taparahi are the most common *haka* performed, always without weapons, and at some stage the performers will lower themselves to the ground. They are used as ceremonial *haka*, as opposed to a war dance, often for *marae*-based ritual (Kāretu, 1993). Māori increasingly use this type of *haka* to address the social and political issues of the day. An example of this type of *haka* is *Poropeihana* from the East Coast tribe, Ngāti Porou. This *haka* addresses the issue of prohibition and Māori reaction to this law. Dancers perform this *haka* using uniform actions, without weapons, and usually in straight, evenly spaced rows, all of which are characteristics of the *haka taparahi* classification.

Ngeri are short *haka* usually performed without weapons and set actions. This allows the performers to use actions that they deem appropriate to accompany and emphasise the words. They are primarily used as an exhortation to urge the group on towards communal or set goals (Kāretu, 1993).

Both *manawa wera* and *pōkeka* are similar to *ngeri* in that they do not have set actions (Kāretu, 1993). Where they differ is that Tūhoe perform *manawa wera* at *tangihanga* or *hura kōhatu*. *Maemae*, *ngākau maemae*, and *kiriwera* are other common names for various tribal equivalents of *manawa wera*. *Pōkeka*, which are peculiar to the *iwi* of Te

Arawa, are physically similar to the *manawa wera* and *maemae*, but are performed at a variety of occasions.

Kaioraora are chants used to vent hatred and are often described as abusive, defamatory or derisive *haka*. *Kaioraora* means 'to eat alive', which illustrates the depth of feeling involved in these compositions. Traditionally, many composers of this type of *haka* were women. *Pātere* are similar to *kaioraora* in physical presentation but differ in content. *Pātere* were used to restore self-respect or reply to insults or slander. Performers achieved this by reciting the kinship connections of the composer as rebuttal to the slander. *Pātere* generally contain information on principal chiefs, important events, and genealogy. *Poia atu taku poi*, composed by Erenora Taratoa of Ngāti Raukawa to rebut slanderous remarks made about her by Rihi Puhiwahine, is a well-known example of *pātere* (Ngata, 1974: 142).

Haka pōhiri are the haka performed during the rituals of encounter to welcome visitors onto the *marae*. This type of *haka* varies from tribe to tribe, but often includes performances by male and female, both individually and together. It can also include the performance of other types of *haka* such as *haka taparahi*, *whakatū waewae* or *tūtū ngārahu*.

 ## Poi

The *poi* has its own *whakapapa*. This *whakapapa* stems back to Rangi, Papa and the birth of Tāne-mahuta (the ancestral god of forests and all things living in it). While Tāne-mahuta was on his quest to find the human essence, he mated with many animals and plants in order to produce a child in human form. He mated with Hine-i-te-repo, the swamp maiden, and they produced *raupō* (bullrush). He mated with Pakoti, a form of flax, and they produced *harakeke*, a superior form of flax. Tāne also mated with Hine-rauāmoa and they produced Hine-te-iwaiwa, who is the god of anything pertaining to women such as childbirth and weaving. Hine-te-iwaiwa reinforces the link *poi* has with women (Huata, 2000). *Raupō* and *harakeke* are the main traditional sources for making *poi*. The ball part of the *poi* was usually made from the soft fibres of *raupō* and wound up with its dried leaves, while the handle was usually made from either plaited *raupō* or *muka* (flax fibre).

The more ornate type of *poi*, called *poi awe*, were created from *muka* woven into *tāniko*, a knotting and twisting form of weaving, and were much softer than *poi* made of *raupō*. These types of *poi* were often decorated with tufts of dog skin, or feathers. Because these *poi* were softer than those of *raupō*, they were mainly used for swinging, as they did not make the crisp sound of those of *raupō* when they were hit against parts of the body (Best, 1925).

With the arrival of Europeans to Aotearoa/New Zealand and the introduction of new materials, *poi* began to take different forms. Corn *poi* is a form of *poi* that was commonly made from an introduced food source. When corn was husked the husks were pulled down but not broken off. The hairs on the corn were also removed and dried, to make up the stuffing. When everything had dried, a ball was formed by stuffing the hairs and one end of the cord (*muka*) into the husks of the corn. Modern manufacturers of *poi* use Dacron, foam, plastic bags, wool, cotton and other materials, but the method remains the same (Huata, 2000).

The role *poi* played in traditional Māori society varied from region to region. According to early explorer accounts, *poi* were traditionally used only as a game accompanied by a chant and do not feature in any accounts as being anything more than just that.

One traditional account suggests that *poi* was a male dominated sport and used in preparation for war to aid in the agility of the wrist, which was ideal for using *patu* (clubs) effectively in battle. Women also trained in the art of warfare and it would seem that this led to a natural extension into the performing arts area. *Poi* were also sent from one village to another as a symbol of gathering, to enlist the help of neighbouring people in times of battle (Huata, 2000).

Traditionally, *poi* were used to the tune of a chant, similar to a *pātere*. Often, these were termed *haka poi* (*poi* dances); for example, *Poia atu taku poi* by Erenora Taratoa was commonly accompanied by *poi*. Often a journey would be taken in these *waiata* and the *poi* was symbolic of leading the listeners on this journey.

Many *waiata poi* (*poi* songs) today reflect women and their beauty. Their themes are as vast as the themes of *haka*, although the message of the song is not as ferociously displayed. *Poi* can be flirtatious songs composed for attracting a partner, they can be about birds and their movements, about exploring under the sea, a celebration of women, or recollections of historic events and many other equally diverse subjects.

As recently as the 1980s the *poi* was a basic art form. The focus was on swinging the *poi* as an extension of the performer's body. The actions today have moved away from this style and performers have pushed the traditional boundaries of *poi*, to far more intricate actions. There is now more emphasis on the beating of the *poi* as opposed to the simple swinging styles previously used.

Waiata-ā-ringa

All cultures change and the advent of *waiata-ā-ringa* in the Māori performing arts arena was just a natural part of such a change. The arrival of Europeans introduced a sung style of song different to the chanted, melodic rhyme that characterised traditional Māori songs. While *waiata-ā-ringa* are distinctly European in their sound, they are Māori in essence and spirit, and are a modern development of traditional forms of Māori dance and song.

It is difficult to locate a particular point in the history of performing arts when the first *waiata-ā-ringa* was composed, but it is believed that Sir Āpirana Ngata was instrumental in this, so much so that he has often been called the 'father of the action song'. This would mean that the first *waiata-ā-ringa* most likely appeared in the early 1900s when Ngata first entered Parliament (McLean, 1996). At first, Ngata simply translated popular European songs of the day into *te reo Māori*. Later, he borrowed the tunes of the songs and added Māori words of a different theme, a dimension of the Māori performing arts which became extremely popular. Songs such as *E Pari Rā* to the tune of the 'Blue Eyes Waltz', and *Hine e hine* to the tune of 'Home Sweet Home' are among the classics of this period. This characteristic of borrowing tunes has continued into modern Māori society, although it is less common today. From there, it was a short step to add actions that helped to emphasise the words.

Te Rita Papesch (1990), among others, argues that Ngata cannot take all the credit for the development of *waiata-ā-ringa*. Within the Pacific groupings there are close similarities in terms of language, culture and performing arts. According to Papesch, while Ngata was on an overseas trip to Samoa and Rarotonga, he witnessed people standing in rows singing and performing actions to help explain the words. He then brought this aspect of Polynesian performing arts back to New Zealand and began to introduce this in action songs.

During World War I, Ngata's contribution to the war effort was to recruit Māori troops. It was during this time that Ngata popularised action songs by featuring them in concerts he organised all over the country to raise money for the Māori Soldiers' Fund. Situations like this created a perfect opportunity for Māori composers to write songs to farewell and welcome back Māori soldiers, to write about love, grief and loss.

Another person who contributed to the popularising of the Māori performing arts was Te Puea Hērangi of the Tainui confederation of tribes. She organised concert parties to raise funds for the building of Tūrangawaewae Marae, which has become a very important focal point for Māori people all over the country.

Tuīni Ngāwai and her niece Ngoi Pēwhairangi, who also came from the East Coast region, were also prolific songwriters. Their songs have somehow encapsulated every possible mixture of emotions running through their community of Tokomaru Bay at the time. The outbreak of World War II saw the composition of Tuīni's most famous song, *Arohaina mai*, set to the tune of 'Love Walked In'. The song became the unofficial anthem of the C Company of the 28th Māori Battalion and remains today an outstanding example of modern Māori song writing (Pēwhairangi, 1985: 14).

After World War II there were large numbers of Māori people leaving their rural lifestyle behind and moving to urban centres, primarily for job opportunities, and many were to be found in areas where no, or very little, formal school education was required. Many Māori clubs and culture groups were started as a way to promote *whanaungatanga* amongst its members and to celebrate the members' *Māoritanga*. Groups such as:

- Ngāti Pōneke in Wellington, 1936;
- Te Hokowhitu-a-Tū in Tokomaru Bay, 1939;
- Waihīrere in Gisborne, 1951; and
- Te Roopū Manutaki in Auckland, 1969 (Mclean 1996: 342)

soon became adept at implementing *waiata-ā-ringa* in their performances. The language in *waiata-ā-ringa* became very simple. They no longer contained archaic phrases and the vivid imagery often found in traditional chants. The use of these chants, such as *waiata tangi* and *waiata aroha*, was fast becoming redundant in terms of language revival and maintenance. The tunes of *waiata-ā-ringa* were from popular songs of the time and they were tunes that young Māori people instantly recognised.

The themes of early *waiata-ā-ringa* focused primarily but not exclusively on war; they often portrayed expressions of sorrow, loss and love that people felt when their family and friends were killed. The themes of *waiata-ā-ringa* are now broader. They range from tributes to people, places and events, historical events, milestones in Māori history, environmental causes, political agendas and myths and legends. Anything of importance to the composer or Māori at the time of composition was, and still is, incorporated into a *waiata-ā-ringa*.

Like *haka*, aspects of *waiata-ā-ringa* are specific to certain tribes. The most flamboyant performers of *waiata-ā-ringa* are the Ngāti Porou people. Their signature move is the high lifting of the right leg. Another feature, specific to Ngāti Porou, is that actions are contained close to the body and the actions begin a beat before the singing. For western tribes of Waikato, Whanganui and Taranaki, the foot is either not lifted or only slightly lifted, but the whole foot never leaves the ground. Tūhoe lift their feet slightly and the actions are quite large and freer from the body than those of other tribes. The actions are more to the front and are quite soft and gentle (Kāretu, 1996).

The most important thing in relation to *waiata-ā-ringa*, and in performing arts as a whole, are the words. The words are the expression of the group – they must be accurate, fluent and precise. The actions are there only to help emphasise the words and portray the message of the song. Performers, once they have learnt the words and their meaning, can then become adept at knowing when to *pūkana* (dilate the eyes), when to smile or not smile, and all of the other gestures associated with *waiata-ā-ringa* (Kāretu, 1991).

Te hari

Apart from the *marae* the most common place to see Māori performing arts is at competitions, at national, regional and school level. At these competitions the Māori performing arts are largely performed by *kapa haka* groups. There are many specialised terms and conventions for the parts of a *kapa haka* group and their functions. The body of the *kapa haka* group is called the *matua*. In modern times the *matua* is made up of equal rows of performers, generally in separate rows of men and women. The leaders of the group, or of individual items, are known as the *kaea*, of non-specific gender, or *kaitātaki tāne*, the male leader, and *kaitātaki wahine*, the female leader (Armstrong, 1964). An important role fulfilled by women in performance is that of *manu ngangahu*. These are armed women who flank the *matua* to protect the flank of the group and urge the performers on (Kāretu, 1993).

There are many physical ways that the performer can enhance their performance. Perhaps one of the most common physical features of Māori performing arts is the *wiri*, the shaking of the performers' hands as they perform. The *wiri* is symbolic of *te haka a Tāne-rore*, the dance of Tāne-rore for his mother Hine-raumati (Kāretu, 1993).

One of the key physical elements used by performers is facial expression. The eyes are used by the performer to punctuate the words and actions and there are many different types of eye movement. *Whakatautau* is when the women bend their knees and *pōtētē* (close the eyes) during the *haka*. When the eyes are opened wide and the pupils dilated this is called *pūkana*. Both the *pōtētē* and *pūkana* are used to emphasise and highlight a particular action, word or phrase (Kāretu, 1993).

The tongue also has an important role to play in the performance of *haka*. The tongue represents the penis. For this reason it is only the men who *whātero/whētero* (poke out the tongue) during the *haka* and various types of *waiata*. When the tongue is repeatedly protruded it is called *whēterotero* or *whāterotero*. As with *pūkana* and *pōtētē*, *whētero* and *whēterotero* are often used to emphasise a particular phrase, word or action (Kāretu, 1993).

The use of the feet is also important in the performance of *haka*. Apart from the specific types of jumping that are fundamental to certain types of *haka* and *waiata* there are other forms that can be employed by the performer. The most common foot action is the *takahi*, which means to stamp with one foot, and is used commonly in *haka* and *waiata* to keep the beat (Kāretu, 1993).

 ## Ngā taonga pūoro

In recent years there has been a renaissance in *taonga pūoro* (Māori musical instruments), spearheaded by Hirini Melbourne and Richard Nunns, supported by Brian Flintoff, Clem Mellish and others who have become skilled makers of the instruments. They are all members of a group, called Te Haumanu, dedicated to the revival of Māori instrument making and playing. There has been a notable increase in their use in performance, particularly by *kapa haka* groups. *Taonga pūoro* each have their own *whakapapa*, form and function, although there may be tribal variations in these.

The *hue* (gourd) is an important resource for the production of *taonga pūoro*. The *hue puruhau* is made from a large *hue* that has been dried out and had the seeds removed and the top cut off. It is played by blowing across the hole at the top. The *hue puruwai* is a *hue* that has been dried with the seeds left inside. By slowly turning the *hue puruwai*, the sound of running water is created. The *poi āwhiowhio* is made from smaller dried-out *hue*, with two holes drilled into opposite sides and a cord attached so that it can be swung above the head. This creates a sound that is similar to that made by the

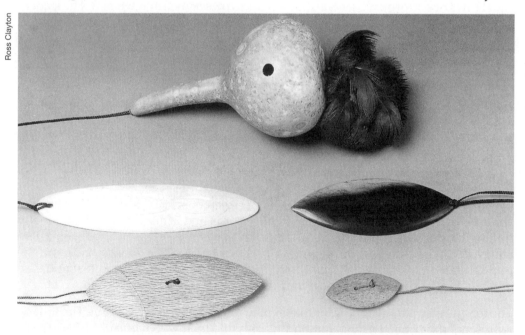

Three types of traditional Māori musical instruments. At the top is a *poi āwhiowhio*, in the centre are two *pūrerehua* and at the bottom are two *porotiti*.

kererū (native pigeon), *riroriro* (grey warbler), and *mātātā* (fern bird). The *poi āwhiowhio* is used in ceremonies before setting out on bird catching expeditions (Melbourne, 1994). The *kōauau pongaihu* is a nose flute made from a small *hue* with the top cut off and two fingerholes drilled into the side. The sound is created by blowing across the hole in the top with one nostril while keeping the other nostril closed with the finger (Melbourne, 1993).

Kōauau is the generic name for the Māori flute instruments. *Kōauau* can be made from bone, wood and stone. They usually have between two and five fingerholes and are played by blowing with the mouth. Exceptions to this definition are the *kōauau pongaihu* and the *kōauau pūpū harakeke*. The *kōauau pūpū harakeke* is made from the shell of the flax snail. It has no fingerholes, and the sound is produced by blowing across the opening of the shell (Melbourne, 1993).

The *nguru*, made from wood, stone or teeth, is similar to the *kōauau* but is curved with a small snout. It can be played either with the mouth, like the *kōauau*, or with the nose. The shape is thought to come from either the neck of the *hue* or the tooth of the sperm whale (Melbourne, 1993).

The *pūrerehua*, or *rangorango*, is made from wood, bone or stone. It is flat and oval in shape and, like the *poi āwhiowhio*, it is swung from a piece of cord producing its sound as it travels through the air. The *pūrerehua* has a variety of functions. In Ngāti Porou it is used to summon rain, in Taranaki it was played at *tangihanga* and in Waitaha it was used to lure lizards (Melbourne, 1993).

The *pūtātara* is a trumpet-like instrument made from the shell of the conch, with a carved mouthpiece attached. It was used to summon, to warn, to announce births and the arrival of canoes (Melbourne, 1993). The *pūkaea* is also a trumpet-like instrument made from wood, with a long hollow body with a carved mouth hole at the end. The *pūkaea*, like the *pūtātara*, was also used to summon and to warn (Melbourne, 1994).

Perhaps the most significant *taonga pūoro* is the *pūtōrino*, as it is unique to the Māori. The *pūtōrino* is made from either two pieces of wood or bone that have been hollowed out and bound together. The shape is that of the *raukatauri*, the bag moth, which is also the name of the goddess of flute music (Hine-raukatauri). The *pūtōrino* produces two distinct sounds, the trumpet call, *te kōkiri a te tāne* (the male voice) and the flute sound, te *waiata a te wahine* (the female voice) (Melbourne, 1993).

Hirini Melbourne (1950–2003) of Ngāi Tūhoe and Ngāti Kahungunu, playing the *pūtōrino*

The musical instruments were not merely played for entertainment, but were important for a variety of purposes, including being used as a way of connecting with the spiritual world.

 ## Ihi, wehi, wana

When examining the performance of any of the Māori performing arts, whether it is *haka, whaikōrero, taonga pūoro* or *waiata*, three key concepts need to be understood. These are *ihi, wehi* and *wana*. These terms are used for performances that are considered excellent, and they symbolise Māori beliefs in what is a good performance. They are the highest forms of recognition or praise that a performance can receive. Outstanding performers are considered to be mediums for their ancestors and the *ihi, wehi* and *wana* of the performers represent the presence of their ancestors within them (Kruger, 1984).

Ihi is often defined as a combination of authority, charisma, essential force, excitement, pride, nobility and awesomeness. It is the embodiment of Māori values and the ultimate in human qualities (Kruger, 1984). The performance of oratory, *haka* or *waiata* allows this force to manifest itself in the performer.

> *When Ihi is present in an artistic event, it is the achievement of perfection. An awe-inspiring occasion that commands the respect, attention and empathy of the audience* (Kruger, 1984: 230).

The projection of *ihi* from the performer elicits a positive response from the audience and arouses their own *ihi* and *wehi*, often described as a spine-tingling sensation (Kruger 1984).

Wehi is described as a strong spiritual and emotional response, often a response of 'reverential fear, respect and awe effected by Ihi' (Kruger, 1984: 231). In relation to *haka* and *waiata, wehi* is the response of awe to the manifestation of *ihi* in the performer or performance.

Wana is a thrilling feeling. It describes the aura surrounding the performance. A performer or member of the audience can feel *wana* only during the performance; whereas *ihi* and *wehi* may be felt long after the completion of the performance. *Wana* is directly linked to an active performance; a carved object or painting cannot have *wana*. A *haka* performance can have *wana* if it is charged with *ihi* and *wehi* (Kruger 1984).

 ## Conclusion

This chapter has given a brief overview of selected areas of Māori performing arts, their function, form and purpose in traditional and contemporary Māori society. Traditional Māori performing arts contained a vivid history of the battles, the sorrow,

Te Kapa haka o Te Tumu, performing a *kaioraora* at the University of Hawai'i, Mānoa campus in 2002

the love, the empathy, the joy, the hate and the beauty of a world far removed from this one. This mixture of emotions is also prevalent in contemporary society, but the issues being addressed are those that are relevant to Māori today. Māori performing arts provide an avenue for people to express their feelings in a way that is uniquely Māori.

It is important to note that the performing arts are not divorced from everyday life or used for entertainment only. They are a dynamic and integral part of Māori life. On the *marae* the performing arts have many functions, from the rituals of encounter, to the debate of political and social issue, to the public declaration of opinion and the entertaining of guests. Māori performance is directly linked to the concepts of *mana*, *tapu*, *ihi* and *wehi* that underpin the structure and operation of Māori society.

FURTHER READING

Huata (2000) provides further details on *poi*, while Kāretu (1993) is an excellent introduction to *haka*, highlighting the characteristics of various types and the role of *haka* in myths and legends. McLean (1996) provides an overview of all the different aspects of Māori music. Melbourne (1993 and 1994) introduces traditional instruments.

Chapter 11

Ngā mahi toi
The arts   *Pakaariki Harrison, Kahu Te Kanawa and Rawinia Higgins*

Māori lived surrounded by their art; their houses were carved monuments to the art of *whakairo*, their clothes were woven tributes to the art of *raranga* (weaving and plaiting) and their bodies were adorned with *moko* (Māori tattooing). The arrival of the Pākehā in Aotearoa/New Zealand introduced new tools and materials to all three of the arts discussed in this chapter. Colonisation also brought about a decline in the traditional art forms for nearly a century. During this period, the knowledge of the *tikanga* of *ngā mahi toi* was held by a few tribal elders. From the middle of the twentieth century, there was a revival of interest in Māori art forms and today they are a vibrant part of *te ao Māori* that has benefited from an amalgamation of old and new techniques and tools.

Whakairo

The word *whakairo* means to decorate or embellish. Its main function is to create understandings that exist and operate within Māori culture, and to help organise social behaviour and promote civil discipline. Most traditions attribute the major developments in carving to the descendants of Toi, an Indigenous family of Aotearoa/New Zealand. Toi was also known as Toi kai rākau (Toi the wood eater), so named because of his great ability with the adze. His son, Rauru, established the art of Māori carving, as enshrined in the aphorism *Ngā mahi a Rauru kī tahi* (The work of Rauru of the singular word). The forest people of Toi were blessed with an abundance of softwoods and adzes made of argyllite or greenstone, enabling them to achieve highly developed skills in carving.

According to some tribal traditions, Rua-te-pupuke can be credited with the discovery of carving. Rua visited the oceanic domain of Tangaroa to rescue his child, Te Manu-hau-turuki, and returned with carvings from Tangaroa's house. These were the original models for all other carvings in the human world (Orbell, 1995). One myth tells how Rua-te-pupuke offended Tangaroa, who sought *utu* by turning Rua's son, Manu, into a *koruru* (Mead, 1986). Rua rescued the carving of his son as well as the others in the house and brought them to Te Rāwheoro, a *whare wānanga* (school of higher learning) at Uawa, Tolaga Bay.

The myth's rationale is that carving is a gift from the *atua*, hence its connotations of sanctity. As an art, it needed to become an activity of mortals, hence its adaptation and desacralisation by the various *whare wānanga*.

The cultural concepts of *mauri*, *mana* and *tapu* are essential components of *whakairo*. The nature of *tapu* in the crafts is now a matter of personal choice rather than an imposition because no one believes that it is enforceable, either spiritually or physically, as it once was. Carvers involve themselves in ritual behaviour because it gives them a spiritual link to forebears who acted in the same way, using virtually the same processes.

The carver's chisel and adze as well as the highly skilled and innovative artisan are celebrated in song, poetry and tribal lore. *Whakapapa*, literary compositions and tribal *kōrero*, as well as expressions of kinship, are deeply imbued in the artwork. The *waka*, the *pātaka* (storehouses raised on poles), and the *wharenui* are objects that are revered throughout Māoridom because they reflect tribal pride and wealth. Both the *wharenui* and the *waka* are metaphors for the bodies of revered and illustrious ancestors. The *tāhuhu*, the *paepae*, and the *pare* (door lintel) of a meeting house are all part of the overall human ancestral symbol that unites all *hapū* and *whānau* in a tribal entity based around a common ancestor. Māori lived inside the metaphorical body of their *tūpuna* (see Chapter 7).

This human metaphor was also part of their *waka*. The symbolism contains the mythical origins of the Māori world-view and the origins of custom and tradition as reflected in the Tāwhaki, Tāne and Māui myths.
For example:

- The *tauihu* (prow) is the position of Tū-mata-uenga, the *atua* who seeks revenge on all those who separated his parents.

- The *parata* (the front portion of a canoe upon which the carved figurehead rests) below the prow is the ancestor connected with the *takere* (keel), which is the equivalent of the *tāhuhu* in the *wharenui*.

- The *taumanu* (thwarts or seats for paddlers) are the equivalent of the *heke* in a *wharenui* and connect the paddlers to the keel.

- The *tapuwae* (footprint, or pathway) is the stern area, from which all *karakia* are uttered, to ensure speed and success.

- The *taurapa* (stern post) illustrates Tāne's upward journey to obtain knowledge and truth. The swirling spirals indicate the winds and storms invoked by Whiro-te-tupua in a vain attempt to stop him. Stern posts also invoke the pathways of Tāwhiri-mātea, Whiro-te-tupua, Hine-nui-te-pō, Māui-tikitiki-o-Taranga, Tāwhaki and various other deities, to ensure success wherever appropriate.

- *Puhi* are the streamers of feathers attached to the *taurapa*. The lower streamer, *puhi-moana-ariki*, and the one above, *puhi-ariki*, were always in contact with Tangaroa, whereas the third streamer, *puhi-maroke*, was not allowed to touch the water. It floated in the wind and was dedicated to Tāwhiri.

- Birds were the intermediaries of humans and the *atua*. The bat and the *kiwi*, the *tūī* and the *korimako*, the *taiko* and the *karae* were all birds of high ritual significance for house and *waka*. The feathers gave a *waka* or *whare* life.

Elements of whakairo

The principal element of design in *whakairo* is the human figure, sometimes called Tiki, after Tāne's first-born. The carver also fully exploits the natural world of the children of Rangi and Papa, creating patterns and designs to meet every need. The *manaia* (the stylised side view of a face used in carving) and other secondary supportive figures inspired by this generative element, are testimony to the depth of a carver's passion and creative urge. The lush lines of *pikopiko* (young fern shoots), the regular patterns of the waves, the symmetry of reflection, and the mystery of the heavens, come under close scrutiny.

Te moko tukupū wānanga

Te moko tukupū wānanga are those carved patterns which were devised by carvers to give added meaning and strength to their work. Patterns were devised from elements of earth, sea and sky in order to achieve this end, taking into cognisance the beauty, balance and symmetry of the works of the supreme creator. These are the designs invented by the Hakuturi (mysterious forest dwellers) and gifted to the people. It is said that their origin is a metaphoric reference to the first noises made by a falling tree (*whēke*) and that they are manifestations of the first messages from Rangi and Tāne to carvers of the *wānanga*. The designs are symbolic of the first *kōrero* and reflect the way carvings are created to speak or pass on messages.

No carver was allowed to achieve perfection – only *atua* could do this. Any new images and messages had to come by way of their instruction and inspiration, hence the mystical beliefs surrounding origin myths and the need for ritual practice.

Pūwerewere

The *pūwerewere* (spider-like designs), *rauponga* (bold spirals like fern leaves), *koru* (a curled design like the emerging fern leaf), *tete* (a curled leaf design) and *pītau* (perforated spiral design) are a few of the design elements derived from the forest environment and brought to life as part of a heritage obtained from Tāne. Similar links are made to Tāwhiri-mātea and Tangaroa in the swirls and spirals of sea, sky and winds, not forgetting the austere and forbidding lines of Tū-mata-uenga as seen in the various forms of *pākati* (fine dog's tooth pattern), *tuarā kurī* (dog's spine bristles) and *nihoniho* (dragon's teeth). These lines and patterns were also designed to create a sense of movement, for example by using spirals.

These patterns, created by carvers, are gouged, etched and incised into the forms of their *poupou* and are visible reminders of a common heritage. No pattern is created without thought to the environment that provides both the materials and inspiration. Accordingly, all carvings provide a cryptic account of the evolution of the universe and other important cultural information.

Pākati

Perhaps the most celebrated and difficult pattern to master is the angled *pākati* pattern. This often runs between parallel grooves (*haehae*). Ngāti Porou carvers of the Waiapu

Valley developed the style known as *ponga* in which *rauponga* (fern leaf) featured as a major element of design. Examples of this design include those by Te Arawa carvers. Some practitioners developed their own types of *pākati*. Te Arawa and Ngāti Porou were renowned for the excellence of their *pākati* and *haehae* designs. The introduction of steel tools, especially the V parting chisel, resulted in an efflorescence of *pākati* patterns.

Rectilinear influence

The three major weaving art forms of *raranga* (plaiting), *whatu* (weaving) and *tukutuku* (lattice work) use vertical and lateral components which result in geometric patterns. Although not widely copied by carvers, they nevertheless provided an added element to design. Such patterns as *pākati*, *taratara a Kae* (Kae's sharp teeth), *tuarā kurī* and multiple compositions such as *rauponga*, *whakatara* (making peaks), *waharua* (double mouth) and *nihoniho* became part of the rectilinear repertoire. The geometric influence, which undoubtedly has its origins in Polynesia, extended into the painted art of *kōwhaiwhai* on rafters, canoes and textile decoration.

Poupou

Poupou, the carved wall pillars of famous ancestors of the *hapū* or *whānau*, are the most well-known elements of *whakairo*. These *poupou* must have a direct *whakapapa* relationship to the *tāhuhu*, the ridgepole and main *whakapapa* line. Living descendants find their places in the house by identifying with this *whakapapa*. Tribal carving styles have developed in representing these ancestors.

The head

This is the most important part and, as such, is carved disproportionately large. Because the hair was regarded as the link between the *ariki* and their *atua* it was sacred and therefore is an important part of the carving. The carved *moko* on the face has the same significance as *moko* has in reality, symbolising rank, responsibilities and rights.

The tongue

This is the vehicle of the oral tradition. Song, poetry, *whakapapa*, *wānanga* (higher learning), *kōrero*, *whakataukī* and all the associated oral modes were transmitted by this vital organ. The retracted tongue implies secrecy; the held tongue, discipline; the thrust-out tongue, challenge. The tongue to the left or to the right, and even the double tongue, all have special symbolism. The exposure of the teeth denotes total domination. This warlike expression goes back to the time when Tū-mata-uenga was making war on his brothers and eating their progeny (see Chapter 1).

The limbs

The size of the limbs may be disproportionate, and might appear to be almost comical in appearance and proportion. However, the symbols carved on them can elicit much information. The sexual organs were similarly large for male and female *tūpuna*, indicating their potency during their lifetimes as parents and leaders, and after death as the powerful ancestors of numerous people. Nevertheless, what at first sight appears incongruous, is actually symbolic of a deeper, mythical interpretation and may give clues to the nature of the ancestor.

The fingers

Many carvings show hands with only three fingers. Some people assert that the number of fingers has little or no meaning. However, the spatial distribution is related to sculptural considerations and also to the artist's perception of the spiritual state of the ancestor concerned.

Manaia

Where there is a space you will find *manaia*. The carved patterning of artistically devised figures can be twisted and contorted in an infinite variety of ways to fill an equally infinite variety of spaces. This versatile element represents the aura of the chiefly person illustrated in the carving and reflects the energies and power of his or her divine descent.

A mixture of grooves, spirals and notches is used as surface decoration on carvings. These add strength and unique qualities to shallow sculpture and lustre to three-dimensional works, though much of the original meaning and interpretation has been lost and will probably elude definition.

This open perforated spiral was carved as part of a burial chest and is called *takarangi* and represents *te ao mārama*.

In the above illustration, the open perforated spiral (*takarangi*) represents the third state of existence (*te ao mārama*). These open spirals are found on *pare*, on *tauihu*, and on *taurapa*. Their appearance on carved bone chests has a connotation of rebirth. On the *tauihu* these spirals are known as *whare pūngāwerewere* (spider houses) and are symbols obtained from the mysterious forest dwellers known as Hakuturi. *Whare pūngāwerewere* is a metaphor for the 'house' of carving, which is the forest.

A Tāne te wheke rangi

The illustration on page 121, showing a detail of a *paepae*, is a good example from which to interpret Māori iconography. The central figure is the *Ahorangi* (teacher of high standing) receiving various mystical *tātai* (recital lists) from the divine sources of the *manaia*, which represent the muted voices of Tāne and Rangi. Each *manaia* has an extended foot which represents the well known past, and a short foot situated

Illustration of a carving from the centre of the *paepae kaiāwhā* of the Te Oha *pātaka* (c 1820–22) which originally stood at Waerenga near Mourea, Rotorua. It was reputedly carved by Manawa and Tahuriorangi of Ngāti Pikiao with greenstone tools. On either side of the central figure are *manaia*.

mid-riff, representing the unpredictable future. The hooked thumb on the left denotes governorship.

 ## He taonga tuku iho – a gift handed down

Whakairo is a gift from the ancestors. It reminds us of their constant presence and of the deep respect that they had for the natural world and the sustenance it provided. *Whakairo* is commemorative, aesthetically and artistically pleasing and functional in its decorative context. It serves to inform its communities, enhance and project their culture and instil pride in their own, as well as the achievements of their forebears.

Tribal *wharenui*, *waka*, *pātaka* and a number of utilitarian objects are a constant reminder of the pride taken in artistic innovation, quality workmanship and adherence to a long tradition of myths, legends, narratives and the multiplicity of themes handed down by the earlier masters. In the decoration of tools, utensils, weapons and other small articles,

Tohunga whakairo and carving instructor, Pakaariki Harrison of Ngāti Porou

the unimpeded function of the object took precedence. Carving as an embellishment was not meant to interfere with function. Small carvings were both decorative and symbolic. Articles requiring little or no physical movement were more likely to have elaborate overall decoration. Decoration traditionally related to fertility, production, success, ancestry or genealogy (as in *tātai kōrero*). It also enhanced the social value of mundane articles such as canoe bailers and digging sticks.

Objects such as weapons, tools, paddles, bailers and bowls were also intended to be aesthetically pleasing works of art in their own right, and were fashioned accordingly. The motifs and symbols on small articles were essentially the same as on larger works such as *pātaka*, *wharenui* and *waka*. The *toki-poutangata* (a greenstone adze, traditionally used as a weapon of war) was a visible symbol of seniority. Aspiring carvers learnt their craft under the careful supervision of their elders who advised them on technique, style, subject matter and the inclusion of tribal narrative. Utilitarian objects such as *matau* (fish-hooks), *kūmete* (bowls), personal ornaments such as *hei tiki* (neck ornaments), and weapons such as *taiaha* and *wahaika* all warranted special instruction. Among the small items were the *waka huia* and *papa hou*, boxes for storing small personal objects such as prized *huia* feathers, amulets, necklaces and pendants. They were well carved and treasured heirlooms. An aura of *tapu* surrounded them because of the *taonga* they contained, especially the *heru* (combs and pins) for the *tapu* hair and head. Attention was paid to the detail of the carvings. Because they were hung from the rafters of their houses, greater emphasis was placed on the bottom of the boxes.

The main images carved in miniature were those which predominated in carvings for *waka tauā* (war canoes) and *wharenui*. Creation narratives, legends and history were the principal topics. *Papa hou* and *waka huia* with no carved figures, but which have intensive spiral designs, may represent *te kore*, the first state of existence. Those which depict an intertwining of a number of figures are in *te pō*, the second state, while those which show a pair copulating are from the creation narrative. There are a number of other themes which can be seen in more recent examples. *Te ao mārama*, the third state, is more obvious in doorway lintels and canoe carvings.

Any work which expresses Māori sentiment, or invokes elements and concepts that use ancient and modern components together to create new work is modern Māori art. Modern Māori art stems from the ancient forms. It has created new images and messages from the mother craft and has divested itself of ritual and ancient cultural practice. The elitism and secrecy inherent within the priesthood and the constraints imposed by the law of *tapu* have largely been removed from Māori art.

Today of course, there is a great interest from all sectors of the community now that many of the traditional constraints have been lifted. Contemporary artists have put in place the groundwork and inspiration for widening participation.

Colonisation brought about a decline in traditional Māori arts. However, the advent of steel tools and an insistent demand in the tourist market created a change in artistic emphasis. Much more elaborate and ornate feather boxes began to appear and compositional aspects became purely aesthetic. This had a carry-over effect with canoe paddles and bailers becoming beautifully shaped and lightly carved to cater for the tourist market. The *waka tūpāpaku* (box for the bones of the dead), *maripi* (a knife of shark's teeth with a wooden handle) and *pūtōrino* also became objects of aesthetic appeal. *Moko* chisels, *kūmete* (wooden bowl), *teka* (projecting foot of a *kō*, a digging implement) and *pōito* (float for a net) did not escape the attentions of the artist. Until the establishment of the Institute of Māori Arts and Crafts in Rotorua in the 1920s, the traditional aspects of carving were kept alive only by a small remnant of surviving masters. Initiatives by Sir Āpirana Ngata and a compelling urge by the Māori people for a renaissance of culture halted the decline of traditional arts. Unfortunately, however, most of the literature written during colonisation was not by Māori authors which meant that many religious and philosophical aspects of traditional arts were not studied in depth or recorded.

Modern Māori art is influenced by a number of components which are not obvious at first glance. Together, these components reflect tribal *kōrero* and various *whakapapa*, the strands of which need to be recited in a proper environment and circumstance. Carvers at the Institute of Māori Arts and Crafts learned technical excellence and rigid compliance in copying specially selected works. Only then were they allowed to become involved in major meeting house projects. During the inter-war era many *wharenui* were built and carved, initially under the Pākehā directorship of the Institute, and later under Sir Āpirana Ngata and John and Pine Taiapa. Ngata included innovations in his designs, such as stage and side doors. A concerted and fruitful movement saw the emergence of the modern carver: Pine and John Taiapa, Piri Poutapu, Waka Graham, Billy Mokaraka, Henare Toka, Joe King, the Ruru brothers and many others. World War II brought a lapse in development until the 1950s, when Māori art was introduced into the school syllabus. A minimal number of schools took part, but a new phenomenon was becoming apparent. A small team of young Māori artists from the Department of Education's Art Department under the direction of Gordon Tovey emerged to become the leaders of what is now known as the Contemporary Māori Arts group. Their inspiration has served to give Māori art a new perspective for the new millennium. Para Matchitt, Cliff Whiting, Fred Graham, Arnold Wilson, Cathy Brown and Robyn Kahukiwa are greatly respected artists of this generation of accomplishment and endeavour. They, with a number of others, have contributed to a developing awareness of the integrity of the Māori art tradition and its place in the modern art world. World-wide recognition of Te Māori and its exposure through exhibitions arranged by Te Waka Toi has added international lustre. This has probably exceeded the wildest imaginings of Ngata and those who helped and believed in the revival of *whakairo*.

 ## Raranga

The art of Māori weaving is a traditional skill, passed down through many generations of Māori society. Weaving and plaiting can be found throughout Polynesian, Melanesian and Micronesian societies, where styles and techniques differ depending on climatic conditions and available materials. When Māori arrived in Aotearoa, they found different materials for weaving. The blades of the *harakeke* could be woven diagonally to form a selvage edge, thus requiring only a single weave, as opposed to the doubling of overlay and underlay strips required when using coconut fibre from the Pacific Islands. As this new technique of weaving emerged, Māori realised the potential of the *muka/whītau* (fibre) that lay between a thin and thick epidermis of the *harakeke* blades. Various methods of processing the fibre brought about new forms of weaving such as 'off loom finger weaving'. Mussel shells were used to scrape the *harakeke* strip, which was then rolled on the knee into a *miro/whenu* (warp thread). Following this, the fibre was soaked in water and beaten with *patu muka* (stone implements) and flat greywacke stones to soften the fibre. Finally the dressed fibre was used to fashion garments.

Māori knowledge of weaving was integral to the day to day functions of their lives. Te Rangi Hīroa (Buck, 1950: 211) noted that 'The early settlers brought established techniques with them and with the methods such widely distributed terms as *kupenga* (net), *aho* (line), *matira* (fishing rod), *matau* (hook), *hīnaki* (trap), and *pā* (fish weir). Differences in raw material led to changes and new developments.' The binding and intricate lattice weave techniques used in the construction of *whare whakairo*, adzes, tools and *waka* were processed and practised with accurate precision, thus ensuring strength and balance. Aesthetic beauty in the lined walls inside the *whare whakairo* was encapsulated in elaborate *tukutuku* and *kōwhaiwhai*. These panels were a significant part of the construction of the *whare whakairo*. The *tukutuku* panels often had patterns relating to historical events, *whakapapa*, *atua* and elements of stories pertaining to particular *iwi* or *hapū*. Māori is a culture of oratory which, through the arts, is enshrined in encoded narratives, giving life to rituals, customs and genealogy.

The origin of weaving

Many *atua* are associated with weaving, including Hine-te-iwaiwa, Rukutia and Huna. Hine-te-iwaiwa, daughter of Tāne-mahuta and Hine-rauamoa, presided over childbirth and the art of weaving. Being responsible for ocean tides, she was linked to Tangaroa and Tinirau, and to Māui (Huata, 2000; Best, 1975). Huna is the principal *atua* for *pā harakeke* (flax bush). The word *huna* means to hide, and because some of the processes associated with weaving were *tapu* and secretive, Huna became significant in the art of weaving. Rukutia is believed to be an originator of weaving and plaiting. Her name means 'bound together' or 'bind together', alluding to the process of twisting flax fibre, sometimes known as *te miri o Rukutia*, (Rukutia's thread making), as mentioned in the following *waiata*. One of the finest varieties of *harakeke* bears her name.

He waiata no te Aroha koingo

Tenei to tohu
Ka mau ki a au
Miria mai, e,
Te miri o Rukutia;
Hiia mai, e,
Te hi o Tonganui.
Ka mana, e Rangi!
To whitiki mai;
Makatitia iho
Ki te tara whaiapu,
Whano mauru noa
Te aroha i au.

*Henceforward your landmarks
Are firmly imprinted within me.
Come with your caress,
The caress of Rukutia;
Lure me on
With the lure of Tonganui.
I will secure, O Rangi!
The tie which binds us.
Only a piercing thrust
From a spear-pointed whaiapu,
Might otherwise bring surcease
For the longing within me.*
(Ngata, 1974: 220–221)

Materials

Harakeke and *wharariki* (mountain flax) are the principle resources for weaving in Aotearoa/New Zealand as they are abundant and versatile. However they were not the only raw materials used. Early Māori brought *aute* with them to beat into a form of tapa cloth, but it did not grow well, as the climate was too cold.

There are over 67 known varieties of native *harakeke*. Some are coarser than others. They are distinguished one from another by varying growth characteristics, fibre content and colour. Weavers harvested the *harakeke* according to their usage, which gave them resource control and management over their conservation practices. The *harakeke* plant is known for its medicinal properties from the rhizomes to the tip of the leaf.

15 varieties of harakeke		
Name	**Area**	**Description**
Aonga	–	Variegated
Arotata	Waikanae	Yellowish-green leaves, dark brown edge
Atewheke	Hauraki	Suitable for stripping
Atiraukawa	East Coast, Taranaki, Opunake	Has high quality fibre
Kohunga	Maniapoto, Mangatautari	Fine fibre, easily extracted
Taeore, Taiore	Opunake, Maniapoto	A fine fibre variety, tall droopy. Pale blue-green leaves.
Tapamangu	Waiomatatini, East Coast	Suitable for *piupiu* (a waist garment popular with *kapa haka* groups). Very fibrous. Black margin and keel. Medium height.
Hūhiroa	West coast, Wanganui, Taranaki	Bluish green leaf. Very tall, narrows gradually to a point. Fibre content, good
Paretaniwha	Rotorua	Very tall, erect up to 3 metres. Straight, wide and used for strong *kete* (kit or basket).
Māeneene	Urewera	A favourite *whāriki* (floor mat) flax. Medium green with red margins and keel.

11 Ngā mahi toi

Oue	Tairāwhiti, East Coast, Waikato, Taranaki, Maungatautari	Male has longer fibre. Female has short leaves and fibre. Narrow leaf, margin and keel brownish orange.
Ngutunui	Maniapoto, Taranaki	Erect leaf, short and bendy, blunt point and reddish shadings. Produces a strong fibre.
Ngaro	Taranaki, Waikato	Used for rough garments. Bronze-shaded leaf. Black edge. All purpose variety.
Tāpoto	Hawke's Bay	Strong, straight and short narrow blades. Pale yellow green leaves with bright orange keel and margins. Used for *kete*, *kaitaka* (fine cloaks made of *muka* and having a wide *tāniko* border) and *whāriki*.

Source: Adapted from Orchiston, 1994 and Mead, 1969

Due to different weather patterns and soil conditions, some *harakeke* cultivars in particular tribal areas may not produce the same quality of flax leaf and fibre as they do in other areas. The growth structure and fibre density may vary.

Kiekie and *pīngao* are two other materials often used in the art of weaving. *Kiekie* is an epiphyte that grows in native bush, anchoring its roots and attaching itself to native trees, growing up the trunk, and along branches. The *kiekie* is harvested during warmer months, stripped, boiled, and dried. It is commonly used in the *tukutuku* or *turapa* panels of the *whare whakairo*. *Kete whakairo* (patterned baskets) and *whāriki* are also woven from this material. *Pīngao*, the golden sand sedge, grows in sand dunes. When dried, it turns a golden yellow. This plant has an elevated status amongst Māori weavers, as it is the only natural fibre of colour that cannot be improved upon. There has been a resurgence of *pīngao* planting in many regions of Aotearoa/New Zealand that has been supported by weavers, the Department of Conservation and local interest groups.

Kahu Te Kanawa

Tohunga raranga, and weaving instructor, Kahu Te Kanawa of Ngāti Kinohaku *hapū* of Ngāti Maniapoto wearing a *kahu kiwi* (kiwi feather cloak) and holding a *kete*, standing in front of *harakeke*, the main raw material for such artworks

One of the legends associated with *pīngao* is of the rift between Tangaroa and Tāne-mahuta. Tangaroa became jealous of Tāne's success in separating their parents Ranginui and Papa-tūā-nuku. Tāne-mahuta wanted to end the warring between them and offered his eyebrows to Tangaroa as a gesture of peace. Tangaroa could not forgive his brother and threw the eyebrows back onto the shore, where they remain today – the eyebrows of Tangaroa, the *pīngao*.

The following materials are also used in the art of Māori weaving;

Kākaho	These cylinders are used on the back of a *tukutuku/turapa* panel, and also help to brace objects such as the *manu-tukutuku* (kite).
Houhere or Whauwhi	The lacebark was used for making *kete* and headbands.
Tōī	Traditionally used to make rain capes.
Tī kōuka	Commonly used for cooking baskets. The fibre content is very coarse and strong.
Kuta	A rush that grows in lakes and swamps. It is cylindrical, and a very spongy material when dried out. Used commonly in the northern districts to make *whāriki*.

Kahu Te Kanawa of Ngāti Maniapoto weaving a *korowai*. This is a cloak with black tassels called *hukahuka*. Notice the *tāniko* border at the base of the *korowai*.

Ngā tae – the dyes

The dyes used in weaving are all natural.
The barks of various trees are collected and boiled to produce the required colour in a liquid dye form. Two examples are:

Raurēkau which produces a rich golden yellow colour and which does not require a mordant to set the colour.

Tānekaha which produces a dark rich red. The fibre is rubbed into hot ashes to help set the colour and turn the fibre a darker tan.

Natural dyes are scarce as the felling of native forests is now regulated.

Changes from the classical to modern period

Changes which have occurred can be classified into three time periods:
- Classical period – pre European;
- Transitional period – contact with Europeans;
- Modern period – early 1900s to the present.

The classical period: 1650–1800s

The classical period can be described as the sovereignty and independence period for Māori, a time when Māori exploited the environment and resources, maximising functionality and utilisation to sustain their livelihood. *Raranga* were skills applied to new fibres to produce *kete*, *whāriki*, fishing lines, nets and snares to maintain a food source.

The most prominent feature of Māori weaving, that distinguishes it from Pacific Island weaving, is the development process of turning *muka/whītau* into cloth. *Harakeke* and *muka/whītau* were used in the production of *kākahu* (cloaks), *kaitaka, korowai* and *paepaeroa* (cloaks with ornamental borders of *tāniko* at the bottom and sides). Those trained in the skills and techniques required in the intricate art of weaving were highly respected.

The transitional period: 1800–1900s

Change was inevitable in this period of first contact with Pākehā, with the introduction of new tools, blankets, animals, plant life, food and a new language. Clothes and blankets made of wool were attractive to Māori and stimulated a desire to incorporate wool into *tāniko* (coloured cord woven into patterns) borders of *kaitaka, korowai* and *paepaeroa*. Māori traded their fine cloaks and land for European tools, garments and, of course, blankets. Once the Pākehā established themselves in Aotearoa/New Zealand, diseases such as influenza, tuberculosis and measles became prevalent. The Māori population decreased dramatically, as did the numbers of expert weavers and *tohunga*. They were the ones who carried the *tikanga* (knowledge and intrinsic values) associated with weaving, so many of the old styles and techniques were lost. The signing of the Treaty of Waitangi also brought changes in Māori lifestyles which put negative pressure on many traditional arts. The introduction of new materials for nets, lines, traps and garments meant Māori weaving became a less important skill. Only those who doggedly held on to old values and knowledge retained the weaving techniques and skills necessary for the basketry used in the harvesting of crops and gathering of shellfish.

The modern period: 1900–2000

Groups of weavers remained, even despite the dominance of Pākehā values and laws, and their adoption by Māori. Fortunately, they maintained the traditions, customs and weaving techniques that had been handed down to them from their *tūpuna*.

However, by the mid 1950s, as most weavers were reaching old age, it became evident that part of Aotearoa/New Zealand's cultural heritage would be lost if there was not a resurgence of Māori weaving skills. As a result, the Māori Women's Welfare League approached Rangimārie Hetet, who was well-known for her weaving expertise, to teach other women how to weave – in particular, cloak weaving techniques. In 1983 a weavers' *hui* was called to bring weavers together to form a weavers' *roopū* (group) and to share skills, techniques and new ideas. The weavers committee, now called Te Roopu Raranga/Whatu o Aotearoa, still exists and meets bi-annually in the quest to expand weaving techniques, share new and contemporary weaving ideas, and pass on their knowledge of traditional Māori weaving. As the interest in weaving revived, people asked whether Māori weaving was an art or a craft. Today it is acknowledged as an art form, and is still practised in accordance with our *tūpuna*'s customs and traditions.

Private training establishments and educational institutions have set up weaving courses and students can gain units of qualification through the New Zealand Qualifications Authority, although the unit standards remain a controversial issue. A *hui* held on Papakura Marae in 1993, called the Pacific Rim, brought together Indigenous weavers from Pacific-rim countries. More people are being attracted to the art of weaving, recognising the complexity of skills, techniques and knowledge involved in the art form. University graduates in fine arts programmes are now specifically majoring in Māori weaving. Young artists are incorporating weaving techniques and styles using synthetic materials in sculptures and installations which are exhibited nationally and internationally. Early weavers such as the late Emily Schuster, Ngoi Pēwhairangi, Rangimārie Hetet, Eva Anderson, Ruia Oketopa were all instrumental in keeping Māori weaving arts and skills alive. Modern weavers such as Diggeress Te Kanawa, daughter of Rangimārie Hetet, Cath Brown, Bana Paul, Te Aue Davis, Erenora Puketapu-Hetet, Kath Waiari, Saana Murray, Mate Lawless, Tina Wirihana, Lydia Smith, Florrie Berghan, Rānui Ngārimu, Whero Bailey and many more are maintaining traditions and developing new art forms.

Moko

Moko is the generic term used to describe various types of Māori tattoos. Traditionally *moko* was used to describe male facial tattooing, however, 'with the passing of male facial tattooing, the term *moko* came increasingly to refer to the female tattoo and it retains this meaning in contemporary Maori idiom' (King, 1992: 5) as well as body tattooing.

 Mythological beginnings

Like other Māori rituals, *tā moko* locates its foundations in the mythological world of the gods. Mark Kōpua sources the origin of the word '*moko*' to Rūaumoko's name, 'The Trembling current that Scars the Earth.'

> *Rūaumoko, was responsible for the deep uneven grooves left within the surface terrain of their primal parent, Papa-tūā-nuku. In short, they witnessed, a natural form of moko.*

Mataora brought the practice of *tā moko* to Te Ao Tūroa (the natural world) from Rarohenga. Mataora was a *rangatira* from this upper world who married Niwareka, a *tūrehu* (fairy person) from Rarohenga (the underworld), but after a domestic dispute, Niwareka returned to her father in the underworld. Mataora followed to beg her forgiveness and, on his arrival, encountered Uetonga, Niwareka's father, tattooing a person. Intrigued by the process of *tā moko*, Mataora questioned the validity of Uetonga's work, as the equivalent art form in Te Ao Tūroa was temporarily painted on the face and known as *whakairo tuhi* or *hōpara makaurangi* (Whatahoro, 1913). Uetonga wiped the temporary design off Mataora's face, showing his son-in-law the worthlessness of his adornment. Uetonga explained that *tā moko* was permanent and therefore *mana* was associated with it. Mataora asked Uetonga if he could receive a *moko*, which his father-in-law agreed to provide. The pain Mataora endured during the process was almost unbearable and this led him to chant to Niwareka who came to his side. After the *moko* healed, Mataora and Niwareka returned to Te Ao Tūroa with the arts of *tā moko* and *raranga*.

Evolution in the art of *tā moko* can be attributed to development in technology, politics and the culture of Māori society.

11 Ngā mahi toi

Īhaka Whaanga, rangatira of Ngāti Rākai-pākā and Ngāti Kahungunu who died in 1875. Painted by Gottfried Lindauer.

Technology

Pigments used in the process of *tā moko* were valued highly and manufactured in a sophisticated manner. The most commonly used ingredient in the production of *wai ngārahu* (pigment) was the charcoal produced from resinous trees. Another interesting source of pigment was the *āwheto hōtete* or vegetable caterpillar, which was burnt, ground and mixed with oil.

The indigenous instruments used by *tohunga tā moko* (tattooing experts) were a range of *uhi* (chisels) which produced the deep grooved lines that made *moko* unique. These designs were literally carved into the skin as if it were a piece of wood, hence the relationship between *tā moko* and *whakairo*. Other cultures prefer to use a skin puncturing system of tattooing. When the *tohunga* applied the *moko* he would dip his *uhi* into the pigment and then make the incisions by tapping the chisel with a mallet or fern stalk. In his description of *uhi*, Buck (1950: 298) states:

> *With such implements, the tattooer, on tapping with the mallet, cut through the skin instead of puncturing it and by the continued application of the narrow cutting blade, he had more control in forming his incised design than if he had tried to use a primitive scalpel. The toothed implements were used for filling in and for subsidiary motifs.*

These *uhi* were primarily made from the bone of sea birds. However, with the introduction of metal by Europeans, Māori changed to metal chisels. The use of metal *uhi* continued up until World War I and eventually needles, which were readily available, replaced the chisels.

Tohunga tā moko

In the instances where a *hapū* did not have *tohunga tā moko*, one was invited from another *hapū* to perform *moko* tasks. The *hapū* would commission the *tohunga* with *taonga*, weapons, cloaks, and greenstone and food payments. Like Western art masters, *tohunga tā moko* could gain fame from their work and therefore demand a high commission. The undertaking of *moko* is regarded as an extremely *tapu* process. The shedding of blood is considered very *tapu* and therefore the operation of *tā moko* was executed under strict laws and more often than not held in an area separated from communal living.

Moko has been referred to as a mark of status. However, evidence suggests that this is due to *rangatira* being able to afford the price of the *tohunga tā moko*. Nevertheless, *moko* was a symbol of a person's *mana*, and it was used by *rangatira* as their signature; the designs being particular to the individual, as seen in images of the signatories to the Treaty of Waitangi in 1840 and other early documents.

The adverse effects of colonisation not only affected Māori structures and belief systems, but it extended into the art of *tā moko*. Cowan (1992) notes that there were no records of full facial male *moko* being undertaken after 1865. However, *moko* survived into the mid twentieth century through the *moko kauae* (chin tattoo) of women.

It was more prolific in the Waikato, East Coast and Te Urewera during this time, promoted by Māori religious groups such as Pai Marire and Ringatū (King 1992: 81). Essentially *moko kauae* had become a means of political expression of identity.

Ākenihi Pātoka Hape Rātima, wife of Henare Tomoana leader of Ngāti Kahungunu and Ngāti Te Whatuiāpiti. She has the typical women's *moko* on the lips and chin.

> *The practice of [Pre-European] tattooing was part of an expression of a unified view of life. Post-European tattooing, however, grew out of a new awareness of the Maori as a threatened minority group that needed to assert its identity* (King 1993: 80).

Cultural renaissance

The art of *tā moko* is in resurgence in the twenty-first century with more and more Māori people acquiring some form of *moko*. This cultural renaissance has revived the facial *moko* of both men and women as a symbol of identity amongst Māori, reflecting the feelings of the women of the earlier *moko kauae* period. Many Māori link their *moko* to their identity through their *whakapapa*. It is *whakapapa* that clearly distinguishes the art of *tā moko* from tattooing in general, as Māori designs placed on non-Māori people are considered *kiri tuhi* (skin drawings) rather than *moko*.

In the original *moko* legend, Uetonga explained to Mataora, that *tā moko* has *mana*. This belief continues today. The renaissance culture of *tā moko*, regardless of the type of *moko*, is an expression of a person's *mana tangata* (individual *mana*), their *mana* Māori (Māori *mana*) and of *mana motuhake* (separate identity).

Conclusion

Ngā mahi toi, like the performing arts, are functional and part of everyday Māori life, enjoyed by all Māori. European art, by contrast, often fulfils a more elitist position and tends to be used for entertainment only. The artists of the Māori world range from those who can be regarded as *tohunga* to the person who weaves together a few *harakeke* blades to carry home the day's catch. These arts were created to develop and enhance functional items without detriment to their purpose.

FURTHER READING

See Buck (1952) for more information on *whakairo*, *raranga* and *moko*; Mead (1986 & 1984) for *whakairo*, Te Kanawa (1992), Puketapu-Hetet (2000) and Mead (1968) for *raranga*; and King (1992) for *moko*.

Chapter 12

Ngā tuhituhinga reo Māori
Literature in Māori

Jane McRae

Reading literature in Māori is one way to the heart of Māori culture, to the language, history and traditions. This is a small literature because it developed with colonisation and as spoken Māori diminished; much of it comes with English translation. Publications after the first writing of the language in the early 1800s and up to the twenty-first century group broadly as: grammars, dictionaries and language tutors; social, political and religious literature, including newspapers and translations from English; reproduction of the oral tradition; and literary genres.

 ## Māori oral literature

The printed reproduction of the oral tradition is the richest literature. What Agathe Thornton wrote in *Maori Oral Literature as Seen by a Classicist* about one narrative, could be said of it all: '… on careful interpretation, it turns out to be laden with meaning, deeply rooted in Maori values, and very choice in its construction' (1987: 22). It offers insight into pre-European society, the lives of Māori and Pākehā in the nineteenth century and contemporary Māori philosophy. It allows a reader to join the audience of the once oral society and 'listen' to the Māori ancestors tell, for example, how they snared birds; married; captured a *pā*; recorded their history and wisdom; commented on the topical and expressed feelings; and contemplated the new world with Europeans. It is also resonant in the present – in the orators and singers on *marae*, elders' teachings, and casual speech. As Te Kapunga Dewes has written of this '*taonga tuku iho nā ngā tīpuna*' (cultural heritage from the ancestors): 'Our literary tradition is a creative one because it draws on the indigenous past, and borrows, changes and continues to comment on and adapt to contemporary situations' (1977: 53).

The term oral literature seems contradictory but advises distinctiveness. The genres are not typical of literary studies. They are *waiata, kōrero, whakapapa*, and *whakataukī*. They may be 'literary' in the sense of being of fine quality, but they cannot be categorised as the fiction or non-fiction of literature, for fact and the fabulous often interweave. This literature must be read with a Māori world-view in mind. It asks attention to performance, the sound of texts, and, their subjectivity. Although the oral tradition is generically Māori, it began as the personal recollections of tribal groups and is linked with genealogical relationships and a geographical landscape.

Poetic songs

The outstanding stylistic features of the oral genres are: concision, poetry, set expressions, allusiveness, and rhetoric. These features are very apparent in the *waiata* or sung and recited poetry. Māori used speech and song to 'publish' for everyday life and posterity: instruction in art or manufacture; news; opinion or feeling; appeals to the *atua*; historical chronicle. Singing and listening to *waiata* were essential to learning about, and participation in society; performance of them asked response – sympathy, forgiveness, laughter or divine assistance. Some idea of the vast repertoire, and wealth of information they hold, can be gained from *Nga Moteatea*. For each song, commentary interprets poetics and allusions, and, importantly, documents the circumstance of composition and names of composer and *iwi*. *Waiata* are a tribal archive. They recall the tribal past by references to ancestors, historical incidents, and the landscape. For this reason the compilers, Āpirana Ngata and Pei Te Hurinui Jones, provided *whakapapa* to reveal unstated connections, accounts of significant events and meanings of place names.

The range of songs is evident in the many labels that define form and function, for example, *waiata aroha* or *waiata whakautu* (a song of reply) – as is discussed in Chapter 10. Music and performance also distinguish them (McLean and Orbell, 1990). Amongst the recited songs are rapidly intoned chants to the *atua*, or *karakia*. Hope for a sturdy home is felt in the driving repetitions in this example: '*Rukutia, rukutia ngā pou tāuhu o te whare nei, rukutia ngā poupou o te whare nei, rukutia te tāuhu o te whare nei …*' (Bind, bind the ridgepole posts of this house, bind the wall posts of this house, bind the ridgepole of this house …) (Orbell, 1978: 72–73). *Karakia* are often cryptic but the complexity and power of all the sung and recited poetry is aptly put in Orbell's comparison of it with the 'fierce intricacy' of Māori wood carving (Wedde and McQueen, 1985: 60). It is made explicit in Thornton's uncovering of meaning in Te Uamairangi's Lament for His House, which is both grief over theft of tools to build a house and an avenging spell. A traditional audience had the requisite knowledge of mythology and local circumstance to understand ornate allusions in poetry, allowing the oral composer to be so brief.

The great number of published *waiata* raises the question of how it was possible for the Māori ancestors to remember these, and the other oral genres. Studies demonstrate that for each kind of song there were more or less set structures, imagery and expressions (see Prefaces in Ngata and Hurinui; Mead, 1969; Orbell, 1978). Yet, artful innovation allowed the songs to be pertinent to the time. As illustrated in *Waiata: Maori Songs in History*, in the nineteenth century Māori sang of their encounter with Europeans, particularly of the political but also of the social. In an *oriori* a child is instructed: '… *kia tohutohungia ki te rata pukapuka/Te upoko tuatahi, te upoko i a Kēnehi* … (… and be taught the letters in the book/The first chapter, the chapter of Genesis …) (Orbell, 1991: 28–29). Twentieth-century composers are as apposite. Tīmoti Kāretu writes: 'Haka have always reflected the cares, concerns and issues of the time. The haka of today are no different …' (1993: 49). In *The Penguin Book of New Zealand Verse*, where ancient and modern composers can be compared, Hirini Melbourne contrasts the romantic Tāmaki-makau-rau (Tāmaki of a hundred lovers) with rough changes wrought on it by European settlement (Wedde and McQueen, 1985: 498–500).

 ## Narratives

As a record of the past the oral genres work together to fill the gaps in the spare texts. A song and saying about a chief, his genealogy, a narrative of his prowess in battle and the prayers that divined victory, round out – and preserve by reiteration, his and the tribe's reputation. However, *kōrero* or narratives provide explanation and connection. They have the same features of concision, poetry, formulaic usage, allusion, and rhetoric. They achieve brevity by a lack of detail and by focus on an episode, that is, a significant incident involving one or two named characters. In the nineteenth century, Wiremu Maihi Te Rangikāheke of Te Arawa wrote out his memory of Māui as tightly-constructed vignettes in which that wily hero snares the sun, fishes up the land, finds his parents, gains fire for humans and, finally, succumbs to the greater power of his ancestress, Hine-nui-i-te-pō (see Thornton, 1992).

Māori narrators used poetic devices in their prose. Rhythm and repetition bring musical qualities to the texts. In the narrative about Kahukura (Orbell, 1992: 15), who learns the art of netting from the spirit people, *patupaiarehe*, the word '*kupenga*' (net) rings out repeatedly, anticipating the discovery. An audience hearing about Rona (the woman captured by the moon) feels the futility of her children's search for her in the rhythmical: '*Aa, rapu noa, rapu noa, tee kitea …*' (And, sought in vain, sought in vain, not found …) (Biggs, 1997: 23). There was allusiveness in pithiness: one word, '*pokokohua*' (cooked head), used by Rona to the moon for failing to light her way to get water, indicated the great insult in comparing his sacred head with common cooking.

Like singers, oral narrators worked within a well-defined tradition that assisted memory and performance. There was formulaic phraseology, such as prosaic openings – '*Tērā tētahi tangata ko …*' (There was a man named …) and figurative expressions – '*he urukehu, he kiritea*' (fair-haired and fair-skinned) for the beauty of an aristocratic woman. There were also conventions of structure – beginnings and endings, dialogue, type scenes, and recurring themes and motifs – sons in search of fathers, characters meeting at springs.

The narratives are rhetorical, for each telling is a chance to preserve moral or historical messages. But they also carry the narrator's, and tribe's, advocacy. There is a high degree of similarity in structure, phraseology and subject matter in narratives, but the individuality of each rendering is evident when reading within and across tribal collections, such as *Nga Iwi o Tainui* (Biggs and Jones 1995), Mohi Ruatapu's traditions of Ngāti Porou (Reedy, 1993), or Wiremu Wi Hongi's Ngā Puhi history (Sissons, Wi Hongi, and Hohepa, 2001). This also reveals a key characteristic of narratives – and all the oral genres – the many versions of one text. Oral narrators did not claim the ownership of a composition in the way the literate author does; as the *whakataukī* explains, '*Ehara i te mea he kotahi tangata nāna i whakaara te pō*' (It is not the case that only one man kept people awake at night). They composed for the audience – a lively story about Māui's capture of the sun for entertainment, a long version with genealogy and *karakia* for students.

Unlike the well-labelled *waiata*, narratives are not clearly distinguished. However, three classes based on content can be proposed. Myths relate of ancient times – of the *atua*, life in Hawaiki, canoe voyages to Aotearoa – and are instructive of morality, religion and origins. Those about the sky father and earth mother, Ranginui and Papa-tūā-nuku, and their offspring, the *atua*, and about heroes such as Māui and

Tāwhaki, appealed to compilers of the earliest literature in Māori, such as Sir George Grey in his *Ko nga Mahinga a nga Tupuna* (1854; in English as *Polynesian Mythology*, 1855). Tribal histories of life in Aotearoa, which have been referred to above, form another class, and tales of extraordinary encounters between humans and the supernatural are another, as read in *Traditional Māori Stories* (Orbell, 1992).

Oral narrators achieved dramatic effect by including songs or chants, or by quoting genealogy and sayings. Readers of literature rarely study genealogy and sayings, but in Māori oral tradition they are of prime importance. *Whakapapa*, or explanation by listing, was an effective verbal technique for describing relationships. Matiaha Tiramōrehu's South Island version of the evolution of the universe gives an example when it begins: '*Na Te Pō, ko Te Ao./ Na Te Ao, ko Te Aomārama, ko Te Aotūroa …*' (From the Night, The Day./ From The Bright Day, The Long-standing Day …) (van Ballekom and Harlow, 1987: 1, 23). The literature of genealogy is small, but Māori writers publish it with their traditions because it clarifies and justifies relationships and behaviour. The bare bones of such lists might also be embellished by a relevant saying, for instance, about a descendant's obligation or the nature of a place.

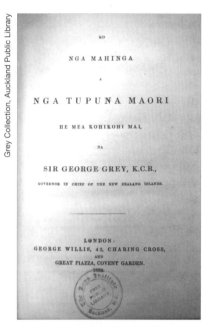

The title page to Sir George Grey's edited collection of oral traditions, which were written down or told to him by Māori in the nineteenth century. This was the first book in Māori of the traditions and, together with his English version of it, *Polynesian Mythology*, it remains a classic.

Sayings in the oral literature are encyclopaedic of Māori life, as *Ngā Pēpeha a ngā Tīpuna* attests. Some espouse morality: '*Nāu te rourou, nāku te rourou, ka ora te manuhiri*' (By your food basket and mine the guests will do well). Some allude to mythology: '*Ko Māui tinihanga koe*' (You are Māui of many devices) approves or disapproves by reference to that hero's exploits. Many are personal to tribal or individual lives: '*Pokopoko-whiti-te-rā*'(Pokopoko causes the sun to shine) lauds the peace-making by this Ngāti Whātua chief. Sayings add a *kīnaki* or relish to song, narrative, genealogy and everyday speech. Variants are common and new ones fit the times: '*E kore e piri te uku te rino*' (Clay will not stick to iron), was a perceptive remark about the meeting between Māori and Pākehā (Mead and Grove, 2001: 319, 235, 345, 33).

Following Māori language and oral tradition into print

The origin and development of a literature in *te reo Māori*, or the Māori language, reflects the early history of New Zealand (McRae, 1998). As H. W. Williams's *A Bibliography of Printed Maori to 1900* records, missionaries and government officials were the first to publish in Māori. Amongst their first publications were language tutors, grammars and dictionaries; religious tracts, hymn books and the Bible;

government documents and literature to inform Māori of European life – translations of *The Pilgrim's Progress* and *Robinson Crusoe*, instruction on how to keep bees and grow hops, histories of Rome and Russia; and newspapers. Māori-language newspapers make up more than 40 titles produced from the 1840s into the twentieth century (see http://www.nzdl.org/niupepa). Government produced some, such as the very first *Ko te Karere o Nui Tireni* (1842–46); churches others, such as *Te Pipiwharauroa* (1899–1913); Māori their own, for instance, the very political *Te Wananga* (1874–78); and philanthropists some, for example, *Te Korimako* (1882–88). They are remarkable for the writing by Māori about political and social issues and for exemplifying their adaptation of the oral arts for the press – by quotation of songs to close letters, articles on tribal history, traditional eulogies and farewells in obituaries.

The history of the transition of the oral tradition to book form begins with Europeans (McRae, 2000). Sir George Grey published collections of songs, sayings and narratives in the 1850s, and John White the six-volume, bilingual *The Ancient History of the Maori*. Both authors gained their material from Māori and edited it for publication. Wiremu Maihi Te Rangikāheke is renowned for his contribution to Grey and for a large manuscript legacy, only a little of which has been published (Curnow, 1985). But he was not alone. Extant manuscripts attest that Māori wrote prolifically in the nineteenth century, recording genealogies, songs, tribal histories and religious and customary practices. From the early 1890s some submitted writing to the *Journal of the Polynesian Society*, with the result that it is a valuable source of Māori oral literature.

The twentieth century accumulated a different literature. There were many reasons for it remaining small, especially the reduction in speakers of the language. There was ethnographic interest, such as S. Percy Smith's *Lore of the Whare-wānanga* about the evolution of the world and gods, and canoe migrations to Aotearoa; and translation, as in Pei Te Hurinui Jones's *Te Tangata Whai-rawa o Weniti* (The Merchant of Venice). Oral texts and translations appeared in journals – *Te Ao Hou*, for instance, and, from the 1970s, were the subject of the scholarly work of Bruce Biggs, Hirini Mead, Margaret Orbell, and Agathe Thornton. In the 1980s Māori began to contribute to this literature, and to make it tribal, by reproducing their ancestors' manuscripts, for example, Anaru Reedy's editing of Pita Kāpiti's teachings about ritual and practice in cultivation and hunting, and Ngāti Porou ancestors (1997).

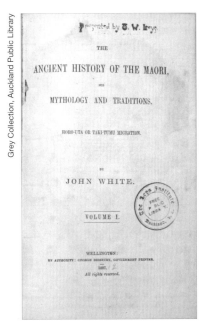

 ## New literature in Māori and the future

The late twentieth century brought new genres to the literature in Māori and an exchange of oral and literary styles. In fiction there were short stories,

The title page to the first of six volumes of oral traditions collected by John White in the nineteenth century. In this extraordinarily large recording of the oral heritage, White arranged his Māori texts, with English translation, according to canoe or tribal groups.

poetry and children's stories; in non-fiction, collected writings and biographies. Little of this new work comes with translation to English, a testament to the desire for survival of the language – also evident in an abundant children's literature in Māori, which rewrites classics of the oral tradition, and writes anew of contemporary life within and outside Māori settings.

Creative writing emerged in translation, for example, Witi Ihimaera's *Te Kaieke Tohorā* (The Whale Rider) and Shakespearean sonnets by Merimeri Penfold (2000), and in original work such as the short stories of *Nga Pakiwaitara* (1995, 1997, 1999), which blend themes from tradition with modern social realism.

A literature of non-fiction has arisen. Collections of articles on social, political and religious matters and letters to newspapers, collated for publication by tribal kin, such as Wiremu and Te Ohorere Kaa's editing of Āpirana Ngata's writing (1996). Biographies recall the focus on a single character in the oral narratives, not only the very many in *Ngā Tāngata Taumata Rau* (the Māori editions of the Dictionary of New Zealand Biography), but those by individuals. Ruka Broughton combines oral and written history in his life of the famous Ngāti Ruanui leader, Tītokowaru (1993); Te Onehou Phillis writes familiarly of her father Eruera Manuera (2001). Hēmi Pōtatau charts a new course with an autobiography, *He Hokinga Mahara* (1991). Autobiographical parallels are recognisable in the oral tradition in the expression of self in genealogy and songs, but in the nineteenth century Māori kept diaries, as illustrated in Renata Kawepō's journal of travel in the 1840s (Hogan, 1994).

What might become of literature in Māori in the future is as uncertain as, and dependent on, survival of the language. Hirini Melbourne envisages an independence, which will maintain the heart and spirit of Māori people and pay tribute to oral and written heritages (1991). This has happened already to some extent. Māori writers in English, as novelist Patricia Grace has put it, compose 'Stories that tell us who we are'. As a result, the predominant themes of the oral tradition: attachment to the land; a concern with human relations; continuity between the gods, ancestors and living; metaphysical and moral reflection, are retained in the modern works in Māori in the twenty-first century and in writings in English by, for instance, Patricia Grace, Witi Ihimaera and Robert Sullivan.

Māori use the phrase '*Kimihia te mea ngaro*' (Seek what is lost) to refer to the loss, or loss from sight, of their cultural knowledge. Literature in Māori (and its translation to English) goes some way to assuage that sense of loss. It retains much information about the culture as it was described and recorded by the ancestors in the nineteenth century. In the twentieth and twenty-first centuries it reproduces that legacy and re-employs it in modern genres and settings for new generations of speakers of Māori, and for those with a curiosity about this literature which is so little known but eminently worthy of study.

FURTHER READING

Read about the history and different types of literature in Māori in Williams (1924) and McRae (1998). Bilingual editions of oral narratives can be found in Orbell (1992) and Biggs and Jones (1995), and of the songs in Ngata (1974) and McLean and Orbell (1990).

PART TWO

Ngā Ao e Rua – The Two Worlds

Chapter 13

Te tūtakitanga o ngā ao e rua
Early contacts between two worlds

Erik Olssen and Michael P. J. Reilly

In the 1790s Europeans used Captain James Cook's charts and instructions to establish semi-permanent contact with the *tangata whenua* in Te Ika-a-Māui's Bay of Islands, and around Te Ara-a-Kiwa (Foveaux Strait) separating Te Wai Pounamu and Rakiura (Stewart Island). These two points of on-going contact helped shape the history of early contact between Māori and the world of the European intruders. These intruders – known as Pākehā in the north and *takata pora* (ship people) in the south – were unlikely emissaries from Eurasia, the world's largest continent, to the inhabitants of the world's last-settled islands in the southwest corner of the Pacific ocean. Those who began visiting the Bay of Islands mainly came from Britain, Eurasia's dominant maritime power, and the newly established United States of America. British sailors, rough and illiterate, were recruited from such seaports as Bristol and Portsmouth. The Americans haled from the ports of New England, a society dominated by Puritans, whose sailors and merchants were, generally, both pious and literate. The sailors who began visiting Te Ara-a-Kiwa were mainly transported convicts from Britain's penal settlements in Australia. Mostly the new Australians were attracted by Cook's accounts of rich seal rookeries.

 ## Sealers and whalers

The dream of gain prompted these early contacts and the sailors and officers of this motley fleet brought Aotearoa/New Zealand into on-going contact with the 'complex, changing and far-flung world system created by the enterprise of West European capitalistic imperialism which by then was dominated by Britain' (Grey, 1994: 5). In 1760 most of the Pacific was beyond the reach of Europe's most capable navigators and sailors. Thanks largely to Cook, by the 1790s that had changed. Prompted by Cook's glowing account of his stay, a small handful of whalers from New South Wales hunted the sperm whale off the North Island and went to the Bay of Islands for repairs and supplies. Because the English Navigation Acts made it illegal to construct ships in any British colony that were large enough for deep-sea whaling, others capitalised on the knowledge. In the early 1800s part of the New England whaling fleet began hunting the giant sperm whales in the waters to the north of Cape Reinga, although it was only in the 1830s that the American whaling fleet became the most important market for provisions and recruits. Some British ships also joined the hunt. In 1807, the *Ferret* of London 'unknowingly distinguished itself by carrying the surgeon John Savage to New Zealand' (Morton, 1982: 130). Savage's *Some Account of New Zealand* (1807) attracted considerable notice off-shore. In 1805, the Sydney papers also reported that several British whaling captains had praised the Bay of Islands as a supply base,

Hunting sperm whales off the coast of New Zealand in the early nineteenth century

with its sizeable resources including timber and potatoes. Some ships were showing up for a second time by 1807. In that year nine ships worked out of the Bay of Islands. The New Zealand whale fishery was established, but not for long. The attack by Whangaroa Māori in quest of *utu* against the *Boyd* in 1809 ended the occasional visits from New South Wales. The War of 1812–14, between Britain and the United States, then virtually wiped out the New Zealand industry. The existence of shore traders and the Church Missionary Society, which established its first outpost at Rangihoua in the Bay of Islands in 1814–15, helped secure the New Zealand whaling industry during the 1820s (Morton, 1982).

In the same period sealers from Sydney began their annual visits to the shores of Murihiku (Southland). There may have been no more than 200 men involved in the Sydney sealing fleet, most of them ex-convicts. (Sealing did not require ships large enough to run foul of the Navigation Acts.) Having largely exhausted the Bass Strait rookeries in the 1790s, the ship owners of New South Wales began venturing across the Tasman, lured by reports of an abundance of fur seals and hair seals (sea lions). In 1792, William Raven left a sealing gang at Tamatea (Dusky Sound), but this venture was a disappointment. By the early 1800s American sealers jostled with Australians. In March 1806, for instance, the *Favorite*, hailing from Nantucket, landed 60 000 pelts in Sydney. In 1809, Captain Mason left eight men on the 'Isle of Wight', just off Dunedin's St Clair beach, and in 20 weeks they took more than 2000 skins. In one week in 1810 some £100 000 worth of skins were landed in Sydney, allegedly from Te Wai Pounamu's southern shores (such secrecy surrounded this industry that reports of locations have to be treated with suspicion) (Hainsworth, 1967; Morton, 1982; Little, 1969).

13 Te tūtakitanga o ngā ao e rua

At this time the sealers established relationships with the *tangata whenua* around Te Ara-a-Kiwa. The dominant chief, Te Whakataupuka, allocated the intruders Whenua Hou (Codfish Island) off Rakiura (Evison, 1993). Local Māori developed extensive cultivations of potatoes to trade for nails, chisels, fishhooks and other items. As Murihiku's seal population fell rapidly, the little ships from Sydney began plundering the sub-Antarctic Islands and developed alternative trades with Ngāi Tahu, picking up such products as timber, salted fish, potatoes and *mokamokai* (dried human heads). The little band of trading ships also acquired knowledge of the right whale's migrations up Murihiku's east coast. In 1829, the first shore whaling station commenced operations. Within a decade some 20 shore whaling stations dotted New Zealand's coast, clustered at both ends of Te Wai Pounamu and the lower North Island, including Te Matau-a-Māui (Hawke's Bay). Some of the stations were owned and operated under the authority of chiefs such as the Ngāi Tahu leaders, Tūhawaiki and Taiaroa (Morton, 1982).

Forming relationships

The presence of Europeans off the coasts and in the bays and inlets had a major impact on Māori living in and nearby the contact areas, an impact that widened as time passed. Europeans meant access to trade and a new range of goods. Māori society – like Polynesian society generally – exchanged goods on a regular and usually reciprocal basis. Māori keenly sought metal products from the very start of contact, especially nails and hooks. Kororāreka in the Bay of Islands became the largest and best known point of contact, a 'town' of some 200 huts by 1831 (Wilson, 1990). The leading Ngā Puhi chief, Hongi Hika, and the northern Bay *hapū* (including Te Uri-o-Hua, Ngāti Tautahi, Ngāi Tawake, Ngāti Rēhia, Te Hikutū, Ngāti Rua and Ngāti Rāhiri) established an early dominance in relations with Pākehā when they convinced

Joel Samuel Polack's drawing of Kororāreka, Bay of Islands in 1835/36

13 Early contacts between two worlds

Ōtākou whaling station at Wellers Point, Otago Peninsula, circa 1832

Samuel Marsden to establish Anglican missions in their territory, first at Rangihoua, and subsequently at Kerikeri in 1819, close by Hongi Hika's *pā* at Kororipo. These moves annoyed the *hapū* on the southern side of the Bay (Ngāre Hauata, Ngāti Hineira, Ngāti Manu, and Ngāti Rangi) who complained of being marginalised. For a while these rival southern *hapū* led by Te Morenga established trading links through Kororāreka, but relations between these two groups remained tense – war broke out in 1819 – with both sides continually vying for greater access to Europeans. In 1830 the northern *hapū* took control of Kororāreka and its trade (Sissons, Wi Hongi and Hohepa, 1987). Edward Shortland, who first visited the South Island Ngāi Tahu in 1842–43, noted how contact with Pākehā promoted extensive re-settlement. In 1823 at Otago, Captain Kent reported two villages just inside the Heads; by 1826, there were five and several others nearby. In the mid-1820s local chiefs such as Karetai sought to attract Pākehā, like the sealer, John Boultbee, to live in their communities by marrying them to kinswomen. This successful chiefly strategy led to the opening of the Ōtākou whaling station in 1832, and the rapid growth in the number of *kaika* (settlements) around the harbour and at nearby beaches (Anderson, 1998).

Many Māori quickly showed an interest in knowing more about the Europeans and the world they had come from. Not all did so. Two Māori kidnapped to instruct the convicts in the arts of weaving flax on Norfolk Island responded differently. Tuki-tahua was very curious but Huru-kokoti was not, thinking 'there is no Country, People, or Customs, to equal his own' (Salmond, 1997: 217). Yet within a decade the Ngā Puhi chief, Te Pahi, and his sons travelled from the Bay of Islands to Sydney to meet the Governor. Others were quick to follow suit. Māori curiosity about the customs and manners of the intruders quickened with an appreciation of their potential value. At the same time so did a concern to modify any of their own customs that might threaten the on-going relationship. In the Bay of Islands most of the *hapū* with a beach frontage understood the key elements in this informal transaction very well as early as 1800. The destructive consequences for local Māori arising from the death of the French explorer Marion du Fresne in 1772 was the sharpest learning curve, although the virtual cessation of contact after the *Boyd* in 1809 reinforced the lesson. Visiting Europeans who wanted to return, also learned to respect local customs, not to take advantage of their greater firepower or to kidnap locals, and to pay for services and goods that had been given (Salmond, 1997). A sizeable number of Pākehā-Māori (Pākehā who lived in Māori communities) helped translate the two cultures to each other, being employed for this purpose by chiefs who frequently married the Pākehā-Māori into their own families (Wilson, 1985).

From the earliest days of contact many Māori crossed into the European world, sometimes drawn by curiosity, but most often with the intention of learning about Pākehā knowledge and technologies in order to benefit their people and enhance their status. Following Te Pahi's success, others, who later became well-known, went to visit the Governor in Sydney, Samuel Marsden at his Paramatta farm or the King in London. Despite Governor Philip King's attempt in 1805 to ban the hiring of Islanders without his permission, hundreds more shipped on whaling vessels and mastered new ways of living, new concepts and new skills. Māori men won an excellent reputation as whalers, with some becoming harpooners, a skill readily adaptable from Māori spear-throwing. A few, such as Ruatara, *teina* to Hongi Hika, went to London, arguably the capital of the Eurasian world. He came home dreaming of creating a town, with English-style houses and paved streets, and farms, to grow crops for export. His uncle, Hongi Hika, also travelled to Australia and England, acquiring valuable knowledge of Pākehā farming practices, and visiting King George IV (Salmond, 1997).

Māori seafarers

In the 1830s and 1840s hundreds of young Māori men shipped aboard the whaling fleet. Māori served on whale ships of all the nations that worked New Zealand waters. Their high reputation made them popular recruits among whaling captains throughout the era of large-scale deep-sea whaling. In the late 1840s Johann Wohlers, the dedicated missionary based at Ruapuke Island in Te Ara-a-Kiwa, believed that 'far too many young Maori men were lost at sea through their passion for boating and whaling' (Morton, 1982: 166–167). Most Māori shipped for a lay of oil or sealskins, the normal form of payment in both industries, although American whalers often signed them for wages. This was usually a matter of convenience, Morton concluded, as they could be left at home rather than taken back to New England. While some Māori seafarers felt cheated of their money when their ship got no oil or sealskins, some of them were abused and not paid appropriately by unscrupulous shipowners (Morton, 1982: 167). Some young Māori men spent years on the Pacific fleets, moving into other trades and places. Even in the 1790s, one or two Māori ended up in the Bass Strait seal fishery in Australia – and one or two Aborigines, notably Thomas Chaseland, ended up in New Zealand (Hall-Jones, 1990). A handful of Māori made successful careers for themselves, winning promotion to first and second mate. In Sydney and Hobart Town (in Tasmania), from the 1820s to the 1850s, Māori seafarers were a common sight.

These Māori sailors did as much to bring back knowledge of the other world as the missionaries. Service on the world's whaling fleets also changed them. They mastered European technologies and methods of work, including rowing rather than paddling (a major advantage being such leverage that smaller crews were possible). Ngāi Tahu achieved complete mastery of the whaleboat – indeed, by 1840 it had completely supplanted the *waka*. It was not just that whaleboats were quicker, and more versatile, but they were much easier (and cheaper) to make. Consequently, the land trails became less important, coastal trade increased and the foundations were laid for Māori dominance in coastal and inter-colonial commerce during the 1840s and 1850s (Morton, 1982).

Māori women participated fully in the new world of the European intruders. Some sailed on board ships, such as the woman who arrived in Sydney in the *Perseverance* and reported on the *Boyd* attack. Others accompanied their European husbands, either working their passage or travelling as passengers, such as Mary Bruce, née Atahoe, daughter of Te Pahi, who visited the Pacific and Bengal before dying in Sydney in 1810 (Salmond, 1997).

 ## Intimate relationships

European writing has stereotyped Polynesian women as exotic and erotic females, and described their sexual transactions with male seafarers as prostitution. In reality, these connections were more complex and ambiguous. Customarily unmarried Māori youth could have any number of sexual partners, but as Ormond Wilson (1985: 65, 69) observed, the 'European innovation' 'was to make [Māori] women marketable and thus provide opportunity for large scale prostitution.' The most common image is of sailors exchanging the ship's nails for sex with local women, and introducing the horrors of venereal disease. However, these early transactions were not always uncontrolled, with some captains such as Cook making efforts to stop the sailors. More successfully perhaps, local chiefs allowed only certain kinds of women on board, notably unmarried or commoner girls. Some women initiated sexual relations with sailors in exchange for trade goods. As contact with Europeans increased, chiefs and male heads of family took control, with reports that some women were forced to visit the ships in order to obtain valued material items for their families. In the Bay of Islands the bilingual Ngāre Raumati chief, Tuai (or Tui) who had visited England, organised ships' visits by groups of young women instructed to ask for gunpowder. Higher ranking unmarried women might live with ships' captains in exchange for European goods (Belich, 1996; Wilson, 1985).

Māori women and their families incorporated some of these male intruders into their kinship structures through marriage. During Cook's sojourn at Tōtara-nui (Queen Charlotte Sound) the parents of a young woman married her to a crewmember with whom she had formed a relationship. Other sailors jumped ship to live with their Māori partners, often with the support and protection of her family. Te Pahi's son-in-law helped interpret and advise the Māori people about Europeans. James Caddell, who survived an attack on his sealing gang at Rakiura in 1810, became the husband of Purerehu, niece of the important chief, Honekai. In later years Caddell was described as having assimilated totally to his wife's people, and had difficulty speaking English (Salmond, 1997). In the north, around the Bay of Islands, marriages between sailors and Māori women lasted only the length of the ship's visit. Until modern times European sailors often took a wife for any extended period ashore. While the women took these relationships seriously, and considered themselves bound to the men even in their absence at sea, many European observers mocked these marriages. By contrast, in the south, the more settled shore whaling operations encouraged long-term marriages, with owners and managers marrying chiefly women, and employees lesser-ranking wives. Such marriages were important preconditions for the men to live and work with the women's communities. The women were well regarded as household managers, learning many skills, including the ability to speak English and to cook new dishes with foods such as potato and pork, while protecting their husbands and children, with help from their extensive kin networks. In exchange, the men participated in the lives of their wives' families, for better or for worse, including participation in tribal wars. Many of these Māori marriages were formalised when missionaries arrived in the locality (Morton, 1982).

Whether the women were involved in fleeting or sustained relationships, they were critical in mediating cross-cultural difference and forging a new and common set of understandings. From many of these customary marriages – and most marriages in large parts of Britain were still customary and were effected without church involvement – elaborate families descended. Atholl Anderson has estimated that whereas the birthrate for Ngāi Tahu female partners of Europeans remained low (2.2), that for their 'mixed-race' offspring was far higher (7.9). As a result, by the 1860s about a quarter of Ngāi Tahu had European ancestry, while 20 years later that figure had topped 60% (Anderson, 1991). Because Māori descent, like British, can be traced ambilineally these children were free to adopt either society as their own. In the north most remained Māori, matrilocality predominating; in the south a lot became Pākehā, patrilocality dominating, with the resulting assimilation in language and many cultural practices (Anderson, 1991).

Māori leaders

A series of confident and capable Māori tribal leaders emerged during the contact period who used their access to European technologies to advance their people. One of these was the Ngā Puhi leader, Hongi Hika. His trip to London in 1820, accompanied by Thomas Kendall, one of the first Anglican missionaries, remains one of the defining episodes in post-contact history. Hongi's dazzling success in obtaining European weaponry armed his *tauā* with the firepower to exact *utu* in full and terrorise much of the northern half of Te Ika-a-Māui. The massive disruptions to traditional *hapū* and *iwi* boundaries permanently re-drew the political map of the north, and contributed to forging Ngā Puhi as a coherent *iwi* (Ballara, 1990). Hongi's campaigns also precipitated even greater upheavals when Ngāti Toa, led by Te Rauparaha, migrated southwards from Kāwhia following their defeat by Waikato forces, with the intention of trading with Europeans, notably for guns. As he journeyed south, Te Rauparaha forged a coalition of *hapū* and *iwi*, which settled on the coastal plains south of the Manawatū and the key offshore islands, Kapiti and Mana, displacing many of its

Hongi Hika (1772–1828), chief of Ngā Puhi

former inhabitants. Kapiti became the key to Te Rauparaha's 'empire', one of those small islands, like Ruapuke in Te Ara-a-Kiwa, that enjoyed a strategic location with Europeans in the days when wind controlled movement at sea (Oliver, 1990). At the unforeseen end of this process, when the victorious coalition had fallen to squabbling, Ngāti Toa's old ally, Ngāti Mutunga, conquered the Moriori of Rēkohu (Chatham Islands) (King, 1989).

Like his northern chiefly counterparts, the Ngāi Tahu *upoko ariki* (head of chiefs), Te Maihara-nui (Tama-i-hara-nui), established a trading post at Takapuneke in Akaroa harbour in the 1820s to take advantage of ships that called there for supplies (Evison, 1993). Muskets also began to be used in war, notably in the disastrous series of intra-tribal killings given the name *kai·huānga* (eat relations). These killings began around 1824 when Murihaka wore Te Maihara-nui's *tapu* dogskin cloak. A spiralling series of killings for *utu* by kin on all sides began to involve increasing numbers of Ngāi Tahu. *Tauā* (war party) from the south, led by Te Whakataupuka and others, armed with muskets, attacked kin in the north, sometimes inflicting heavy casualties. Eventually equilibrium was restored but only after a number of chiefs from the various *hapū* of Ngāi Tahu and their followers had been slain (Anderson, 1998).

Iwi such as Ngāi Tahu and those who followed Te Rauparaha came increasingly into conflict, aggravated by the consequences of their relationships with Europeans. The restless Te Rauparaha first struck southwards in 1828, attacking and defeating *iwi* in the northern end of Te Wai Pounamu, such as Rangitāne. Subsequently he sought *utu* for insults, which brought him into conflict with a Ngāi Tahu *hapū* at Kaikōura, then sheltering refugees from Te Rauparaha's wrath. Ngāti Toa's chiefs later visited Kaiapoi to trade for the highly desired *pounamu*. Initially hospitable relations were soured by various insulting acts, which eventually resulted in the killings of high ranking chiefs on both sides, notably Te Pēhi Kupe, *tuakana* of Te Rauparaha. More notoriously, in 1830 Te Rauparaha made use of an all too willing ship's captain – Stewart of the *Elizabeth* – in search of flax, to seize Te Maihara-nui and his family, who were killed as compensation for the deaths of Te Pēhi and other chiefs. In 1832, Ngāti Toa and its allies laid siege to major Ngāi Tahu settlements, such as Kaiapoi, which were captured, and the occupants killed or forced to flee southwards. Their southern kin, better armed with muskets, led a successful fightback during the early 1830s, nearly capturing Te Rauparaha himself on one occasion. By the early 1840s peace had been restored between the two *iwi* with the release of remaining chiefly captives on both sides (Anderson, 1998).

 ## Social change

As a result of its longer engagement with the Eurasian world, Ngāi Tahu was one of the first *iwi* to experience the consequences of such a relationship. The invasions by the musket-armed northern *iwi* under Te Rauparaha and others from their Manawatū-Kapiti base resulted in upwards of 25% of the Ngāi Tahu population being killed or enslaved, including many chiefs. Ngāi Tahu temporarily abandoned their northern regions, and the existing southwards migration to Ruapuke and Te Ara-a-Kiwa to take advantage of European trade intensified. New settlements were founded at Arowhenua, Kakaunui, Moeraki, around Otago harbour, Henley and Ruapuke. The shorewhaling stations helped the southern Ngāi Tahu absorb the influx. Ngāti Rārua, allies of Te Rauparaha, controlled the Westland *pounamu* until relinquishing control to Ngāi Tahu following the latter's killing of the Ngāti Tama chief, Te Pūoho, another long-time ally of Te Rauparaha's, in 1837. A series of European-introduced diseases, especially between 1834 and 1838, including measles, influenza, tuberculosis and venereal diseases afflicted Ngāi Tahu, although immunity to influenza was reported by 1848. The marriage of so many Ngāi Tahu women to Pākehā men was, according to Atholl Anderson (1998: 194), 'probably a more important cause of population decline by 1840 than any other'. Ngāi Tahu's estimated total population of 5000 had declined by half over the 15 years to 1844. Finally, Christianity began to be introduced at the behest of Ngāi Tahu's chiefs, such as Taiaroa and Karetai, in the late 1830s. James Watkin founded the first mission in Waikouaiti in 1840. In 1844, Tūhawaiki established the Ruapuke mission of Johann Wohlers. The new religion was disseminated through the work of Ngāi Tahu 'native teachers', that is, indigenous missionaries. Amongst the earliest converts were many younger chiefs who became important leaders for Ngāi Tahu during the later nineteenth century (Anderson, 1998). If Ngāi Tahu had suffered unintended consequences from its early engagement with Europeans, its leaders and their people were already preparing themselves for the changing future of Aotearoa/New Zealand.

The situation in the Bay of Islands differed from that in the south. Whereas contact had contributed to the fragmentation of Ngāi Tahu as a polity, the situation in the north was the exact opposite. Starting in the 1770s, a number of related *hapū* based around the Hokianga and Kaikohe regions began to conquer parts of the Bay of Islands, expelling the previous occupants of its coastlines and hinterlands, though the last of them, notably Ngāre Raumati, were not finally defeated until as late as 1826. By the late eighteenth century these conquering *hapū* had formed themselves into the mutually antagonistic northern and southern alliances who competed for Pākehā trade and Anglican missionaries in the Bay of Islands. From 1818 Hongi Hika, more than any other chief, was able to temporarily unite these *hapū*, in alliance with other powerful leaders such as Te Morenga, and fight a series of North Island *iwi*, notably their long-time enemies Ngāti Whātua, as well as Ngāti Paoa, Ngāti Maru, Te Arawa and Waikato. These *tauā* journeyed as far south as Wellington and won a string of victories based on their superior number of muskets. After Hongi Hika's death in 1828, other chiefs led expeditions southwards until the late 1830s. By that time Ngā Puhi had assumed its present form incorporating the related *hapū* in the Hokianga, around the northern and southern parts of the Bay of Islands, and covering an area extending as far south as Whāngārei (Sissons, Wi Hongi and Hohepa, 1987; Ballara, 1990).

As in Te Wai Pounamu, Māori throughout Te Ika-a-Māui, and especially around the Bay of Islands, suffered from the invasion of new diseases. From the 1820s whooping cough and respiratory diseases such as influenza were reported in such localities, with high death rates, though survivors in the former case acquired immunity. The introduction of venereal diseases by ships' crews was a significant problem, with Māori women unwittingly infecting their subsequent Māori partners. Infections may have spread to areas not visited by Europeans through the agency of slaves captured by Ngā Puhi during their southern campaigns and released in later years. Consequently, many of the infected women became sterile, contributing to a population decline. Unlike the south, in the North, intermarriage does not seem to have been a factor, presumably as a result of the larger Māori population in relation to the small and more transient Pākehā community (Pool, 1977). An increasing number of Pākehā in the Bay of Islands during the 1830s meant chiefs desirous of purchasing European goods were selling ever larger amounts of land. By 1836 Anglican missionaries owned a significant amount. Some chiefs began to worry that the foreign goods received as payment for land could not match the permanent value of what was being lost (Wilson, 1985).

The introduction of literacy in the Māori language held more promising possibilities for the emergent Ngā Puhi. During Hongi Hika's epoch-making 1820 visit to England with Kendall and the chief, Waikato, the three men collaborated with the Cambridge University orientalist, Samuel Lee, to compile *A Grammar and Vocabulary of the Language of New Zealand*. According to Kendall's biographer, the work 'laid the orthographic foundations of written Maori' (see Chapter 4). The ability to read and write in *te reo Māori* long interested Māori, with a strong surge of interest in the 1830s coinciding with the availability of reading material, particularly translations of the Bible, printed on the mission press from 1834. Perhaps not surprisingly, conversion to Christianity and literacy went hand in hand, with increasing numbers of young converts spreading their interpretation of Christianity throughout the country. Itinerant missionaries reported a constant demand for books from Māori throughout the country. With literacy, Māori began writing letters to each other, revelling in their ability to communicate ideas across large distances. With colonisation, Māori also addressed their many concerns to Government by letter, and through the many Māori language newspapers that sprang up from the early 1840s. In doing so, they developed styles of writing based upon *whaikōrero*, incorporating oral literature such as song and proverbs, as well as biblical references. Māori scholars wrote much of their traditional knowledge in manuscript books and in publications issued in association with Pākehā scholars (see Chapter 12).

The utilisation of literacy for Māori ends was reflected also in the Māori engagement with Christianity. While large numbers of Māori followed the various Protestant denominations, notably the Anglicans and Wesleyans, others chose Catholicism following Bishop Pompallier's arrival in the Hokianga in 1838, in part to reflect their opposition to the English missionaries and the Protestant *hapū*. Papahurihia or Te Atua Wera, a Ngā Puhi *tohunga* from Te Hikutū *hapū*, was schooled in the Anglican faith at Rangihoua and elsewhere. He developed a syncretist belief system, a striking fusion of Old Testament and traditional belief in which the Nākahi (serpent) became his personal *atua* and Māori were portrayed as the chosen people, the Hūrai or Jews, of the modern world. This faith had supporters in various parts of Te Ika-a-Māui. Opposed to the European missionaries, Te Atua Wera and his adherents supported resistance to Pākehā, with Te Atua Wera becoming Hone Heke's *tohunga* during the latter's campaign against the English in 1845 (Binney, 1990).

 Conclusion

As a result of this half century of both positive and negative contacts between the intruders from Eurasia and the *tangata whenua*, the islands of Aotearoa/New Zealand, the last sizeable group on the planet to be peopled, became part of the emerging capitalist world system as a colony of the British empire. New foods had improved diet and life expectancy at first, although by the 1820s, especially in more densely settled areas, diseases had begun to have a severe impact. New tools, products and ideas had altered the balance of power between individuals and between different *hapū* and *iwi*. In the Bay of Islands Taiwhanga, the first convert and later the first dairy farmer, may mark one end of a complex spectrum of adaptation and learning (Orange and Wilson, 1990). In the south, literacy came later and most of the learning was done within the context of marriage and shore whaling. Nor was the traffic one-way. Europeans who lived in Aotearoa/New Zealand had to adapt. Those who married locals invariably entered into the wider kinship obligations of Māori society and began to grasp the importance of such concepts as *tapu* and *mana*, even as their spouses came to understand the emotional importance of a house being 'ship-shape'. In this period, in short, an almost self-conscious process of hybridisation went on at both ends of the country, only to be swamped when the influx of the Victorian era arrived. The process of accommodation was always selective, especially on the Māori side, a self-conscious process designed to enhance strength and wealth but not destroy identity. In the present era of recognition of Treaty claims and of bicultural identity, such themes of hybridisation and accommodation are resuming their central place in Aotearoa/New Zealand.

FURTHER READING

Salmond (1997) is a comprehensive study of early contacts until 1815. Belich (1996) and Walker (1990) provide overviews and provocative analyses of the period in the context of New Zealand history. For the South Island, Evison (1993) is comprehensive, while Wilson (1985) makes astute observations regarding the north. *The Dictionary of New Zealand Biography* provides a starting point for research on the people mentioned in this chapter.

Chapter 14

Te Tiriti o Waitangi
The Treaty of Waitangi

Janine Hayward

The Treaty of Waitangi is often called Aotearoa/New Zealand's 'founding document'. Exactly what that means provokes intense debate in Parliament, in classrooms, in workplaces, in pubs and in living rooms right across the country. By way of introduction to the Treaty of Waitangi, this chapter reflects on the social and political climate in Aotearoa/New Zealand at the time the Treaty was signed. It gives a brief insight into the colourful and intriguing story of how the British drafted the Treaty and why Māori signed it (particularly as recounted by Claudia Orange, 1987; Ranginui Walker, 1990; and Alan Ward, 1995). It considers the Treaty texts, and the various interpretations given to the texts over the years, and it asks, what should have happened after the Treaty was signed?

 ## The social and political climate

Perhaps the greatest challenge to understanding the Treaty in a contemporary context is the need to understand Aotearoa/New Zealand 'society' around the time the Treaty was signed. It is difficult, if not impossible, to set aside our own understanding of the world as it is today and our values and attitudes as they have been shaped by history, in order to see the world as Māori and the traders and settlers would have seen it in the nineteenth century. But it is very important to try to do so, in order to understand what was motivating and guiding peoples' actions at the time the Treaty was signed. It is tempting also, in contemporary contexts, to simplify these historical events and to label those involved as 'goodies' or 'baddies'; to portray the Crown Treaty partner as a malevolent force and Māori as the unfortunate 'victim'. Such a perspective does not acknowledge the amazing complexity of the human actors involved, or do justice to such a colourful and multifaceted history. This chapter can only briefly sketch the story of the Treaty, and hope to spark an interest in learning more about the personalities and events involved.

Although Māori and British had had about 70 years of contact by 1840, this account of the Treaty begins in 1835, by which time semipermanent settlements of traders were established along the coastlines. These settler-traders knew a good deal about Māori society by this stage. Claudia Orange describes Māori society in the mid-1830s as 'both homogenous, with a shared belief system, culture and language, and varied, with strong tribal identity based on kinship' (Orange, 1987: 7). Alan Ward describes the years between Captain James Cook's landfall in 1769 and the Treaty in 1840 as originally tense, and prone to violent outbursts as the increasing flow of traders and missionaries arrived on the coast. He explains, however, that:

> *The more extreme aggressions and retaliations declined as Europeans learned to respect Maori warrior capacities and numerical superiority, and the Maori to respect naval broadsides and landing parties. Both sides, moreover, increasingly appreciated the advantages of co-operation, and from the early 1800s chiefs sought to locate European whaling or timber cutting stations in their territory and give them protection* (Ward, 1995: 13).

Orange agrees that relations between Māori and the settler-traders were mutually beneficial; Māori were advantaged by trade with Europeans, who in turn needed the local knowledge and assistance Māori offered to access resources. Māori could see advantage in accepting the visitors who arrived on their shores. As Alan Ward muses, 'once [Māori] had experience of the wider world, the intellectual curiosity, boldness and willingness to innovate of many Maori was such that they did not want to cling to an unmodified traditionalism. Perhaps this is only another way of saying that the traditional Maori social structure and value system were open and adaptive, not rigid or inflexible …' (Ward, 1995: 18).

Officially, however, the British were reluctant to intervene formally in the ad hoc settlement of Aotearoa/New Zealand, despite Māori appeals for British intervention as French interest in Aotearoa/New Zealand mounted (Orange, 1987: 7, 11). As this tenuous relationship came under increasing strain, however, the question of law and order was the major preoccupation for Māori who wished to protect their own authority, and for the British who were reluctant to formalise their position in Aotearoa/New Zealand. Relentless pressure from missionaries and humanitarians eventually pressed the British to officially intervene (Ward, 1995: 23). The British conceded somewhat in 1832 and appointed James Busby as 'Resident'. Busby was later to play an important role in the cast of characters at Waitangi. Long before this, however, he exerted his influence over the developing society in other significant ways. Perhaps most importantly, he is credited with encouraging a confederation of northern chiefs to sign a Declaration of Independence in response to increasing French interest in claiming sovereignty over parts of Aotearoa/New Zealand. The meeting of thirty-four northern chiefs, known subsequently as the United Tribes of New Zealand, on 28 October 1835 asked the British Sovereign to protect Māori from any threats to the independence of their 'infant state' (Orange, 1987: 21). This recognition would play an important part in the British decision to sign a treaty with Māori.

By the late 1830s, the British were no less reluctant to formalise their position, but there was an increasing inevitability about colonisation. In early 1839, William Hobson was appointed 'consul', and joined Busby in a growing cast of characters that would be instrumental in determining the upcoming events. Hobson, motivated by his own understanding of circumstances in Aotearoa/New Zealand at the time, recommended to the colonial office that British sovereignty be established over the country. There was some resistance to this approach, however, as an expensive option that would invade Māori rights. Instead, Hobson was instructed to acquire sovereignty over 'the whole or any parts' of the country that Māori wished to cede, and to make provision for Māori welfare (Orange, 1987: 29–30). As Orange notes, the instructions Normanby (of the Colonial Office) gave Hobson, reflect the intractable tensions within colonisation between Māori, the foreign powers, humanitarians and missionaries, which would be played out after 1840. She says:

> [The instructions reflect] Colonial Office difficulty in reconciling conflicting principles and in accommodating the interests of opposing pressure groups. Normanby had to recognise Maori independence, even a sovereignty of sorts, but he also had to negate it; he had to allow for British colonisation and investment in New Zealand, yet regret its inevitability; and he had to show that justice was being done the Maori people by British intervention, even while admitting that such intervention was nevertheless unjust (Orange, 1987: 30).

The instructions were notable in their omissions, particularly their failure to incorporate Māori into the developing colonial administrative structure and to allow for the development of Māori government of any sort, as discussed later. As treaty-making drew closer, two factors would have been foremost in the minds of officials. First, Britain's recognition of Aotearoa/New Zealand's independence meant that treaty-making was preferred over less peaceful means, although this required Māori agreement to a treaty, which made the presentation of a treaty to Māori all the more important. A second concern was for Māori welfare, and the need to protect Māori interests, which would also help secure Māori agreement to a treaty. It must have been evident to officials that it would be in their interests to emphasise Māori protection and to play down the transfer of authority to the Crown in order to facilitate treaty-making.

Formulating the Treaty document

Busby organised a meeting of chiefs for early February 1840 at Waitangi (Busby's home) to discuss treaty-making. Those chiefs who had signed the Declaration in 1835, as well as other chiefs who had not, were invited to attend. While Busby sent out the invitations, Hobson turned his attention to drawing up a document to present at the meeting. Ill health intervened, however, and the task of completing the draft document also fell to Busby, who appears to have prepared his own version of an agreement, which was submitted to Hobson on 3 February. The final document contained a preamble by Hobson, three short articles, and a post-script by Busby (as discussed below). Perhaps the most significant amendment Busby made was to include a land guarantee, which he considered essential in securing Māori agreement.

Although many aspects of the events at Waitangi in early February have been pieced together through tireless historical research, there are still gaps in our understanding of events. We do know, however, that the task of translating the English text into the Māori language fell to missionary Henry Williams (who sought the assistance of his son Edward) on 4 February. Far from experienced translators, the pair nevertheless seemed aware of the significance of their task, announcing (somewhat prophetically) the intention to avoid English expressions which would not translate easily into the Māori language (Orange, 1987: 40).

The signing of the Treaty

Orange gives a vivid and colourful description of the events at Waitangi (Orange, 1987: 43–55). An enormous marquee made of sails was erected on the lush green front

14 Te Tiriti o Waitangi

The surviving portion of the Treaty of Waitangi, signed February 6, 1840

lawn at Busby's residence at Waitangi. Wednesday 5 February was a glorious day, and there must have been a sense of anticipation and excitement as food and other supplies arrived for the gathering, and those attending the meeting began to arrive by canoe. A Union Jack flew at half-mast. As the expectant buzz increased, Hobson, Busby, and Williams were making final adjustments to the Treaty text. When these were completed, they moved to the marquee, which was filling rapidly with Māori seated on the ground and Pākehā standing around the sides of the tent. The officials sat on a platform at a table draped with the Union Jack. Busby explained the purpose of the meeting to those gathered, and Williams read the Māori text of the Treaty. Orange is critical that at no time were the implications of the transfer of power to the Crown made evident to Māori; officials instead emphasised the protection of Māori.

After the Treaty had been read, the chiefs questioned the Treaty and debated its terms for many hours. Some chiefs were outspoken critics of the terms, especially in relation to land. Many other issues were raised by the Māori gathered, including concern that Māori retain authority and that Pākehā officials have the ability to control the Europeans, most importantly in their trade practices. Some Māori, particularly those with close associations with the missionaries, spoke in support of the British and the Treaty. In particular, Tāmati Wāka Nene gave a dramatic speech in support of the terms offered under the Treaty. This was not enough to dampen Hobson's concern when the debate was concluded that the chiefs would not sign the Treaty. The chiefs retired to their camps nearby, and no doubt continued to debate the terms and intent of the Treaty presented to them that day. Unfortunately, little is known of what was said that night amongst the chiefs, but early next morning on 6 February they seemed keen to conclude the Treaty business and return home (particularly as food was running low). This prompted a spontaneous second meeting earlier than originally planned. A few hundred Māori were gathered on Busby's lawn as attention turned towards the act of gathering signatures on the Treaty. Williams read the Māori version of the Treaty, which would have been the first time some chiefs, who had arrived late, had heard the terms. With no time for further explanation of the Treaty, Hobson began to call the chiefs forward one by one. As the first chief approached the table, Hobson was asked by William Colenso, who had played a pivotal role in proceedings, whether he thought Māori really understood the Treaty they were about to sign. Hobson was obviously unhappy to have this matter raised at this late and crucial stage in the proceedings, and brushed the matter aside without a satisfactory response. As Hobson and the other officials shook hands with each signatory, Hobson repeated the now infamous phrase '*he iwi tahi tātou*' (we are now one people). The ceremony finished with three thunderous cheers from the Māori gathered, and the official party departed, leaving the chiefs to accept the gifts distributed to each of them – two blankets and a small quantity of tobacco.

14 The Treaty of Waitangi

Marcus King's impression of the signing of the Treaty of Waitangi, painted in 1938

Māori understanding of the Treaty, according to Orange:

> *left much to be desired. As well as those who had not heard or grasped explanations, there were signatories who had not been fully aware of the nature of the agreement. Williams's Maori text failed to convey the full meaning of the national sovereignty being conceded. Adequate explanations could have overcome this, but failed to do so. Couched in terms designed to convince chiefs to sign, explanations skirted the problem of sovereignty ... and presented an ideal picture of the workings of sovereignty within New Zealand* (Orange, 1987: 56).

She notes also that the Waitangi decision required a remarkable degree of trust on the part of the Māori chiefs (Orange, 1987: 58).

Why did Māori choose to sign the Treaty? Many motivations may have come into play. First, Māori would have been anxious to assert their own authority in the face of increasing numbers of settlers and pressure for land and other resources. Article Two of the Treaty, the land guarantee which Busby considered essential to the bargain to ensure Māori support, was an extension of the 1835 Declaration which recognised Māori independence and sovereignty. It would have appealed to Māori as recognition of their resources, culture and authority within Māori society. The fact that British sovereignty was played down when the Treaty was presented to Māori was an important attempt not to detract from the chiefs' focus on the guarantees of Article Two. Furthermore, land sales had already taken place prior to 1840; Māori must have been anxious to review the legitimacy of those sales and put in place mechanisms to control future sales. British authority would have appealed in this regard.

Māori must also have sought protection in the Treaty. Māori appeals to King George IV had begun many years before the Treaty was signed, particularly during the 1830s when the threat of French colonisation of Aotearoa/New Zealand loomed large. It may also be that a Treaty with the British monarch had an appeal in itself; the strong missionary influence in Aotearoa/New Zealand was anxious to stress the Treaty as a 'compact' between peoples, akin to the sort of covenants Māori were increasingly familiar with in the Bible. But even more so, British officials traded heavily on the idea of Queen Victoria taking a personal interest in the protection of Māori. The reality that elected representatives actually held the authority in Britain was played down; the image of the Queen as a British *rangatira* in whom Māori could place their trust was promoted in the text of the Treaty, in discussions at Waitangi, and for many years after the Treaty was signed. Māori appeals to the Queen after 1840 are evidence enough of the significance of their relationship to the Māori decision to sign the Treaty.

The texts and interpretations

The Treaty of Waitangi is a short and deceptively simple document. As already noted, the Treaty was first drafted in English and then translated into Māori (in a matter of hours). Nevertheless, almost all chiefs who signed the treaty would sign the translated version. The overall purpose of the Treaty was the cession of chiefly authority to Queen Victoria, but Williams' Māori translation of the Treaty did not make this clear.

The Treaty consists of a preamble and three short articles. Article One and Two of the Treaty are usually emphasised, but it is important to consider all parts of the Treaty in turn, as well as their sum total. The preamble to the Treaty in the English text is a lengthy expression of the Queen's desire to protect the Māori people. It states:

> *Her Majesty Victoria Queen of the United Kingdom of Great Britain and Ireland regarding with Her Royal Favour the Native Chiefs and Tribes of New Zealand and anxious to protect their just Rights and Property and to secure to them the enjoyment of Peace and Good Order has deemed it necessary in consequence of the great number of Her Majesty's Subjects who have already settled in New Zealand and the rapid extension of Emigration both from Europe and Australia which is still in progress to constitute and appoint a functionary properly authorised to treat with the Aborigines of New Zealand for the recognition of Her Majesty's sovereign authority over the whole or any part of those islands – Her Majesty therefore being desirous to establish a settled form of Civil Government with a view to avert the evil consequences which must result from the absence of the necessary Laws and Institutions alike to the native population and to Her subjects has been graciously pleased to empower and to authorise me William Hobson a Captain in Her Majesty's Royal Navy Consul and Lieutenant Governor of such parts of New Zealand as may be or hereafter shall be ceded to Her Majesty to invite the confederated and independent Chiefs of New Zealand to concur in the following Articles and Conditions* (Orange, 1987: 258).

The English preamble refers to 'Civil Government' to protect Māori 'Rights and Property'; the Māori translation of the preamble is more brief, and refers to government as *kāwanatanga* under Queen Victoria, which would preserve to Māori their 'chieftainship and their land.'

> *Ko Wikitoria te Kuini o Ingarani i tana mahara atawai ki nga Rangatira me nga Hapu o Nu Tirani i tana hiahia hoki kia tohungia ki a ratou o ratou rangatiratanga me to ratou wenua, a kia mau tonu hoki te Rongo ki a ratou me te Atanoho hoki kua wakaaro ia he mea tika kia tukua mai tetahi Rangatira – hei kai wakarite ki nga Tangata maori o Nu Tirani kia wakaaetia e nga Rangatira maori te Kawanatanga o te Kuini ki nga wahikatoa o te wenua nei me nga motu – na te mea hoki he tokomaha ke nga tangata o tona Iwi Kua noho ki tenei wenua, a e haere mai nei.*
>
> *Na ko te Kuini e hiahia ana kia wakaritea te Kawanatanga kia kaua ai nga kino e puta mai ki te tangata maori ki te Pakeha e noho ture kore ana.*
>
> *Na kua pai te Kuini kia tukua a hau a Wiremu Hopihona he Kapitana i te Roiara Nawi hei Kawana mo nga wahi katoa o Nu Tirani e tukua aianei amua atu ki te Kuini, e mea atu ana ia ki nga Rangatira o te wakaminenga o nga hapu o Nu Tirani me era Rangatira atu enei ture ka korerotia nei* (Orange, 1987: 257).

The first Article of the English version of the Treaty reads:

> *The Chiefs of the Confederation of the United Tribes of New Zealand and the separate and independent Chiefs who have not become members of the Confederation cede to Her Majesty the Queen of England absolutely and without reservation all the rights and powers of Sovereignty which the said Confederation or Individual Chiefs respectively exercise or possess, or may be supposed to exercise or to possess over their respective Territories as the sole sovereigns thereof* (Orange, 1987: 258).

The principal purpose of the first article, therefore, was to establish legitimate British rule in New Zealand. The translation of this concept into Māori, however, was problematic. According to Claudia Orange, 'the choice of *'kawanatanga'* for 'sovereignty' is not such a happy one'. She points out that the preamble had already used the term *kāwanatanga* in requesting Māori to recognise the Queen's authority in New Zealand, and was 'not likely to convey to Maori a precise definition of sovereignty' (Orange, 1987: 40). In fact, *kāwanatanga* was derived from *kāwana* (governor) and had associations with Pontius Pilate, Roman governor in the Bible, and with the governors in New South Wales at the time. (Orange, 1987: 41). The complexities in the meaning of *kāwanatanga* in the first article are compounded by the second article of the Treaty, which states in English:

> *Her Majesty the Queen of England confirms and guaranties to the Chiefs and Tribes of New Zealand and to the respective families and individuals thereof the full exclusive and undisturbed possession of their Lands and*

> Estates Forests Fisheries and other properties which they may collectively or Individually possess so long as it is their wish and desire to retain the same in their possession; but the Chiefs of the United Tribes and the individual Chiefs yield to Her Majesty the exclusive right of Preemption over such lands as the proprietors thereof may be disposed to alienate at such prices as may be agreed upon between the respective Proprietors and persons appointed by Her Majesty to treat with them in that behalf (Orange, 1987: 258).

In the Māori translation, collective and individual possession was omitted altogether and the term *tino rangatiratanga* was used for possession. This would lead to confusion, as Māori understood the term to mean far more than 'possession'. 'In fact,' Orange states (1987: 41), 'it was a better approximation to sovereignty than kawanatanga.' The 1835 Declaration uses *rangatiratanga* to refer to New Zealand's 'independence'. Therefore, the chiefs were likely to have understood the second clause of the Treaty as a confirmation of their own sovereign rights for a limited concession of power in *kāwanatanga* (Walker, 1990: 93). In considering the implications of articles one and two, read together, Orange says (1987: 42), 'Whatever Williams intended, it is clear that the Treaty text, in using kawanatanga and rangatiratanga, did not spell out the implications of British annexation.'

> *Ko te Kuini o Ingarani ka wakarite ka wakaae ki nga Rangatira ki nga hapu – ki nga tangata katoa o Nu Tirani te tino rangatiratanga o o ratou wenua o ratou kainga me o ratou taonga katoa. Otiia ko nga Rangatira o te wakaminenga me nga Rangatira katoa atu ka tuku ki te Kuini te hokonga o era wahi wenua e pai ai te tangata nona te wenua – ki te ritenga o te utu e wakaritea ai e ratou ko te kai hoko e meatia nei e te Kuini hei kai hoko mona* (Orange, 1987: 257).

The significance of the third article of the Treaty is often overlooked. The English version says: 'In consideration thereof Her Majesty the Queen of England extends to the Natives of New Zealand Her royal protection and imparts to them all the Rights and Privileges of British Subjects' (Orange, 1987: 258).

> *Hei wakaritenga mai hoki tenei mo te wakaaetanga ki te Kawanatanga o te Kuini – Ka tiakina e te Kuini o Ingarani nga tangata maori katoa o Nu Tirani ka tukua ki a ratou nga tikanga katoa rite tahi ki ana mea ki nga tangata o Ingarani* (Orange, 1987: 257).

Although the translation of the third article is understood to be the least problematic, its implications should not be underestimated. Through it, Māori were granted the status of British subjects, which in itself was remarkable, as this was uncommon in other British colonies at the time. Akin to modern-day 'citizenship', this meant Māori were considered wards of the state, and were to be fully integrated into settler society.

Finally, the Treaty states:

> Now therefore We the Chiefs of the Confederation of the United Tribes of New Zealand being assembled in Congress at Victoria in Waitangi and We the Separate and Independent Chiefs of New Zealand claiming authority over the Tribes and Territories which are specified after our respective names, having been made fully to understand the Provisions of the foregoing Treaty, accept and enter into the same in the full spirit and meaning thereof in witness of which we have attached our signatures or marks at the places and the dates respectively specified (Orange, 1987: 259).

Serious and important debates over the words and phrases in the Treaty have arisen since 1840. They centre on a tension between the two versions of the Treaty – British signatories, reading the English version of the Treaty, and Māori reading Williams' translation. Both believed (and rightly so, given the differences in the texts) that they had sovereignty over Aotearoa/New Zealand; the British thought it had been ceded to them, the Māori thought they had retained it. As Ranginui Walker notes, 'subsequent to the signing of the Treaty, the Pakeha behaved towards Maori on the assumption they [the settlers] held sovereignty, while Maori responded in the belief that they [Māori] had never surrendered it' (Walker, 1990: 93). Alan Ward qualifies this, however, saying that *rangatiratanga* certainly implied some continuing authority for chiefs and *hapū*, but that the authority of the Crown is clearly (in both versions) superior to that of the tribes (Ward, 1999: 15).

The tensions between the Treaty texts present serious challenges to modern society. It is important, however, not to lose sight of the tremendous and exciting potential the Māori version of the Treaty, particularly when read in isolation, brought to the young colony in 1840. As Alan Ward notes (1999: 7), 'The Treaty of Waitangi was a solemn compact between Maori chiefs (rangatira) and the British Crown to build a nation by their joint endeavours.' With daring and ingenious simplicity, the Treaty conceives of a nation where resources such as land, fisheries, forests and waters are possessed by Māori (as they see fit), while the British have the authority to make the laws, including the laws to guarantee Māori interests. In reality, the tension that existed between Māori rights of possession and the right of the British to make laws was short-lived; it was resolved as British *kāwanatanga* (as law-making authority) undermined Māori *rangatiratanga* (as undisturbed possession).

By 1860, as tensions began to mount, relations between Māori and British were deteriorating, particularly in Taranaki. The Governor called for a conference to discuss the Treaty of Waitangi. The conference was at Kohimarama, near Auckland, in July and August 1860. It was the most representative gathering associated with government since the Treaty was signed, with some 200 chiefs from the North Island in attendance, a great number of whom had signed the Treaty. As Orange notes (1987: 145), 'The conference revealed the nature of Maori comprehension of the agreement entered into twenty years earlier.' Government officials at the meeting used the opportunity to repeat the Treaty's pledges at some length, and emphasised the Queen's love for her subjects. This reassurance was accompanied by a stern warning, however, that Māori would forfeit their rights if they contravened their allegiance to the Queen. Many Māori at the conference expressed concern that the King movement, which was effective at the time in resisting encroachments by land sales, might be interpreted as challenging Māori allegiance to the Queen, and therefore undermine their Treaty rights. This caused great debate amongst Māori gathered at Kohimarama. As Orange explains, the words of Government officials at the conference did little to expose or reconcile the growing tension between the settler government's desire to 'assert undisputed authority throughout the country' and Māori desire to retain '*tino rangatiratanga*'. She concludes:

> *The Kohimarama conference came to serve quite different functions for the officials and for the Maori people. From the government point of view, the conference was just one more attempt to deal with the Maori problem. While it sounded out Maori opinion more comprehensively than before, the gathering was not fully representative in that it excluded chiefs in open opposition to the government .... As a response to the Waitangi treaty, however, the 1860 conference was undoubtedly one of the most influential Maori gatherings ever held. This became apparent when Maori treaty rights, understood to be confirmed by the Kohimarama conference, became a point of reference for the expression of organised Māori protest later in the century .... The most important idea retained by Maori from the 1860 conference was that Maori mana had been guaranteed* (Orange, 1987:148–149).

 ## The Treaty today

Despite the guarantees made in the Treaty of Waitangi, by 1939 Māori retained only about four per cent of the land they had originally controlled, or approximately 2 700 000 acres. The events following the Treaty in 1840 are covered in Chapter 15, and will not be repeated here. Instead, the question 'what went wrong after the Treaty?' will be turned on its head to 'what should have happened after the Treaty was signed?' Furthermore, what did the terms of the Māori text require of the British and Māori partners, if a society were to develop which honoured the Treaty? As Alan Ward (1999: 8) has said, 'Beyond some of the narrow or strained interpretations of particular words and phrases in the Treaty in recent years, there is a good deal of practical common sense in the general terms and principles agreed upon at Waitangi in 1840.' But how might the Crown have acted to honour the Treaty?

First, the Crown might have considered ways to protect Māori from the tide of European settlement and the resulting pressure to amalgamate into the developing European society. In fact, a few years after the Treaty was signed, the establishment of Native Districts was proposed. These districts would be regarded as British territory, and the Crown would be in a position to disallow settler claims to land in the district, and punish settlers who committed offences in the districts. Most importantly, the districts would recognise and accept Māori social systems and allow 'Maori people to adapt to the Western world, at a pace and manner more of their choosing. Nor would [the districts have] condemned them to backwardness as humanitarian critics feared ....' Ward concludes that the result 'would have been a very different New

Zealand, an essentially Maori New Zealand'. Native Districts would also have been an expression of Māori *tino rangatiratanga* and an example of how Crown *kāwanatanga* could protect Māori rights. As it transpired, however, humanitarian attitudes that Māori were British subjects who should be persuaded to abandon 'barbarous' customs, coincided with the settler pressure for land, and undermined any discussion of Native districts (Ward, 1995).

In reflecting further on the Crown's actions, it was certainly inappropriate for the British to establish colonial government in a manner that excluded Māori from the evolving decision-making institutions and processes. Māori made many attempts, some successful, and others less so, to access the courts, and replicate the monarchy and the Parliament (with the King Movement and the Māori Parliament) in order to actualise the society envisaged in the Treaty: Māori and Pākehā together under the British Crown.

Māori insistence that the Treaty be honoured did not abate over the years, but had little impact on the wider society until the 1970s, when unprecedented levels of protest by urban Māori attracted national attention. The establishment of the Waitangi Tribunal, a forum to hear Māori grievances, resulted, and the legal, social and political process of addressing and resolving Treaty breaches has been unfolding since that time. The transactions and processes by which Māori lost control of their resources are judged against the principles of the Treaty of Waitangi. The principles flow from the Treaty's words and the evidence of the surrounding sentiments, including the parties' purposes and goals in 1840. Two key principles are 'partnership' and 'active Crown protection of Māori interests'. Partnership, although not explicitly stated in the Treaty, is a recognition of the exchange made between British and Māori in Articles One and Two of the Treaty; both parties required the concession of the other. Active protection, again words not found in the Treaty, is recognition that the Crown's authority under the Treaty was the result of an exchange with Māori, and that exchange required the Crown actively to protect the interests of Māori with the authority ceded to it.

Many challenges confront the Treaty settlement process currently underway, including funding, time, questions of justice, and the complexities of providing redress for historic grievances. Amidst these challenges, however, it is important not to lose sight of the ingenious

Protests calling for government to honour the Treaty of Waitangi have been held over a number of years. The flag is frequently used to symbolise *tino rangatiratanga*, Māori sovereignty.

simplicity of the Māori version of the Treaty. Contrary to popular belief, there is very little that is complex or unworkable about Te Tiriti; it is the politics of redress and the implications if Te Tiriti were now honoured in full, which cause the conflict surrounding the Treaty today.

FURTHER READING

Ranginui Walker (1990), Alan Ward (1995), and Orange (1987) all provide further reading on this topic.

Chapter 15

Mana Māori motuhake
Challenges to 'kāwanatanga' 1840–1940

Lachy Paterson

(↑ government)

Sovereignty is a concept that evolved from European kingdoms, in which all power, in theory, devolves from the sovereign. In more modern times, even when a king or queen is reigning, the term has developed to mean a society of individuals who collectively constitute a *de facto* sovereign authority. Through the Treaty of Waitangi, Māori ceded sovereignty to the British Crown (see Chapter 14). At least, that was how the British saw it. Māori, however, were guaranteed their *tino rangatiratanga*, their chiefly rights, which reflected the status quo of their close, collective, tribal society. The treaty does not mention the term *mana*; a cultural concept that is embodied in the people and their lands through the agency of chiefly people. By retaining *tino rangatiratanga*, Māori also retain *mana*. As Māori chiefs quite reasonably interpreted the Māori text, they retained an authority amounting to sovereignty over their own affairs.

From the 1840s, Māori have contested the Crown's concept of *kāwanatanga*, particularly where it has affected their *mana* and *rangatiratanga*, using various forms of challenge, depending on historical circumstances. Some strategies, such as land occupations, have been consistently employed over time – reflecting the continuity of Māori cultural tradition.

When looking at an overview such as this, we must remember several points. Firstly, despite the relentless pressure of colonisation, some periods appear 'hotter' than others, such as the land wars of the 1860s. This is not because issues went away at other times, but because the Pākehā mainstream often ignored Māori issues. Māori were also preoccupied with their own survival as a people – Māori suffered poor health due to a lack of immunity to imported diseases, cultural assimilation, and economic and political marginalisation due to land loss. Therefore, they often had little strength to mount challenges against Pākehā institutions.

Secondly, in the century following the signing of the Treaty of Waitangi in 1840, the nature of 'sovereignty' in New Zealand changed. Governors, representing the British Crown, initially ruled the country. However, by 1854, the Pākehā settlers had already managed to establish their own political structures, that is, a central parliament and provincial assemblies. The Governor retained responsibility for defence and Māori affairs and did not relinquish these to the settler government until the mid 1860s. The ability of the *kāwanatanga* (Government), whether that of governors or settlers, to actually impose their will on Māori was not a sudden phenomenon brought about by the signing of a document, it was a gradual process that unfolded throughout the nineteenth and early twentieth centuries.

Thirdly, Māori society revolves around *hapū* and *iwi* concerns. At various times from the 1850s to the present, some Māori have endeavoured to mobilise collectively to challenge the sovereignty of the Crown. However, the paramountcy of tribal interests has often worked against wider Māori unity. This has seen some groups within Māoridom, such as the government's Māori allies in the 1860s war period, co-operating with the Crown to the detriment of other Māori interests. It was not that such tribes did not seek to maintain their *mana* and *tino rangatiratanga*: rather, they considered that they were more likely to be successful within the framework of *kāwanatanga*. Therefore, the *iwi*-centric world-view that dominates Māori political thinking, as well as changing historical and political circumstances, has meant that there are as many differences in this historical struggle as there are continuities.

The term 'challenge' covers a multitude of tactics and practices. It includes open warfare, separation from Pākehā influences, the establishment of pan-Māori bodies, legal manoeuvres, land occupation, protest marches, setting up Māori educational institutions, even speaking *te reo Māori*. Māori have discarded some methods, such as warfare; introduced new methods, such as schools run by Māori themselves; and retained some strategies, such as land occupations, into the present. These challenges are not just reactive responses to the sovereignty of the Crown, but can be seen as an assertion of *tino rangatiratanga* and Māori identity.

The first phase: 1840s to 1870s

In the years immediately after the signing of the Treaty of Waitangi, interaction between Māori and Pākehā was often limited, and the government had virtually no authority over Māori, except what Māori were prepared to accept themselves. Generally, Māori society continued to develop in an autonomous manner. When the demands of *kāwanatanga* did clash with the rights of *rangatiratanga* (see Chapter 14), disputes sometimes culminated in armed conflict. For example in 1843, an armed posse of Nelson settlers, authorised by the local judge, headed to Wairau, near Blenheim, to arrest Te Rauparaha and Te Rangi-haeata in order to take their land. Although these Ngāti Toa chiefs were prepared to await the decision of the Government's Land Commissioner, they were not prepared to accept this show of force. The impetuosity of its leader, Captain Wakefield, ended in ignominious defeat for his squad, after Te Rauparaha was obliged to defend his people. Governor Fitzroy subsequently exonerated Te Rauparaha, although Governor Grey would later kidnap and illegally hold him.

Te Rauparaha, warrior leader of Ngāti Toa and Ngāti Raukawa who died in 1849

The first determined challenge to the Government's sovereignty occurred the following year in the Bay of Islands. Hone Heke, a Ngā Puhi chief, who was the first to sign the Treaty of Waitangi, chopped down the flagpole above Kororāreka (modern Russell). Both the Government and Heke saw the flagpole, and the British flag it sported, as a symbol of government authority. Heke was prepared to challenge that authority, partly because government actions had caused a slump in the local economy but also because they interfered with his rights as a chief. Heke cut the pole down four times, the last co-ordinated with an attack by his ally, Kawiti, which destroyed Kororāreka. Hostilities continued between these chiefs and the Government, backed by Wāka Nene and other Ngā Puhi. After several battles, the conflict ended with a truce in 1846 and it was Ngā Puhi who raised the flagpole again but not until well after the deaths of Heke and Kawiti.

From the late 1840s and into the 1850s Pākehā continued to pour into New Zealand. Many Māori welcomed this influx in the interests of commerce, but how close they wanted settlers living to them depended on how easy trade actually was. Waikato, for instance, had easy access to Auckland markets and so had no compelling desire for Pākehā towns among them, whereas tribes that were more distant sometimes asked the Governor to send Pākehā to them. However, this tide of immigrants put pressure on Māori to sell their land. With complex layers of Māori land ownership (see Chapter 5) and many areas of disputed land, arguments arose in various places in the North Island between *hoko whenua* (land-selling) and *pupuri whenua* (land-retaining) groups, often resulting in murders and feuding. The Government was both unwilling and unable to introduce effective law and order, but generally favoured the *hoko whenua* groups.

Many Māori could see that the loss of their ancestral lands would mean a loss of *mana* and *rangatiratanga*. In an effort to stem these land sales and to maintain order within Māori society, a movement arose during the 1850s to establish a Māori King, who would become the repository of Māori *mana* over their land. Although there was no precedent for kingship within traditional Māori society, Māori not only had European models to observe, but also the example of the biblical Israelites, who had been told 'one from among thy brethren shalt thou set king over thee: thou mayest not set a stranger over thee, which is not thy brother' (Deuteronomy 17:15).

Pōtatau Te Wherowhero, a chief descended through senior lines from the *rangatira* of all the major canoes (see Chapter 3), whose Waikato base was strategically located between Auckland and the Tūwharetoa lands around Lake Taupō, was chosen as King in 1858, and was succeeded by his son Tāwhiao in 1860. While there were varying degrees of hostility towards the Government from factions within the Kīngitanga (the Māori King Movement), their general aim was to establish the King Country under *mana motuhake* (separate power). The King would govern on his 'piece', the Governor on his 'piece', but both would remain under the protection of Queen Victoria. Approval of the Kīngitanga varied from *iwi* to *iwi*, with most support coming from the central North Island tribes. Some tribes were not prepared to place their *mana* under the chief of another tribe and preferred to maintain their *mana* under the aegis of *kāwanatanga*. However, the Kīngitanga was the first real attempt at a pan-Māori organisation, and as such, promoted Māori identity alongside traditional iwi identities. It was also a nationalist movement, forming its own governmental and judicial structures, and with its own emerging Māori school system. It developed from a desire to hold the land and to resist Pākehā hegemony. Initially, this resulted in a 'cold war' between the Government and the Kīngitanga, fought out at public meetings and in the pages of Māori language newspapers.[1]

Disputes over proposed land sales had also been troubling Taranaki in the late 1850s, resulting in feuds and murders. Governor Browne issued a proclamation in 1858 telling Māori that while he did not approve of their feuding, he would not interfere so long as their fighting did not spill over onto settlers' land. The infant colony of New Plymouth was desperately short of land for settlement and pressed the Government to acquire Māori land. When a minor chief, Te Teira Mānuka, offered for sale a prime location at Waitara, Governor Gore Browne was happy to accept, despite the objections of the Te Āti Awa chief Wiremu Kīngi Te Rangitāke. Te Rangitāke had legitimate claims of his own to the land, but objected to the sale because of his *rangatiratanga*, his duty as chief to speak in the best interests of the tribe. The Government was not prepared to accept this, interpreting his actions as a challenge to their sovereignty. When Te Rangitāke established a *pā* on the disputed land in 1860, Imperial troops attacked. Soon other Taranaki tribes, as well as the more militant sections of the Kīngitanga, came to assist Te Āti Awa in their war against the Government. An unstable peace was established the following year and Te Rangitāke's claim upheld, but for many Māori, trust in Pākehā authority had been seriously eroded.

By 1863, tensions had increased between the Kīngitanga and the Government, with both sides fearing that the other intended to attack. However, Taranaki produced the spark for the ensuing wars over land and sovereignty. Taranaki Māori had occupied a Government block of land at Tātaraimaka as security for the disputed Waitara land the Government had not yet returned. Unfortunately Grey, who had returned as Governor, sent troops in to reoccupy Tātaraimaka before restoring Waitara. Hostilities erupted again in Taranaki. Grey, convinced that the war would escalate, issued an ultimatum to the Waikato Māori living south of Auckland which read like a declaration of war, demanding that they submit to the Queen's authority. Before they had time to answer, he sent troops across the Manga-tāwhiri River into the Waikato lands of the Kīngitanga. These troops pushed the Kīngitanga forces out of the fertile Waikato basin into the rugged lands of Ngāti Maniapoto, which became known as the 'King Country'. The Waikato lands, a million acres in all, were confiscated by the Government because of the Kīngitanga's 'rebellion', and settled by Pākehā. This *raupatu* (confiscation of land) was the main issue that divided the Government and the Kīngitanga for many years to come.

The 1860s and early 1870s saw armed resistance to the Government continue in many areas of the North Island south of Auckland. Some, such as continued resistance in the Taranaki region, was a response to the policy of 'creeping confiscation', where the Government would confiscate large areas of land on paper, but only slowly nibble away at pieces when it was convenient. Religious movements, such as Pai Mārire and Ringatū, inspired other resistance (see Chapter 16). Many Māori sought to be neutral in these wars, only becoming involved if hostilities spread into their own lands. Others, pursuing their own tribal agendas, opted to assist the Government forces. By the time Te Kooti Arikirangi Te Tūruki, the last Māori to actively resist the Crown with arms, had evaded capture and gained refuge within the *rohe pōtae* of the Kīngitanga in 1872, Māori realised that they would need to utilise different strategies in challenging Crown sovereignty.

The second phase: 1860s–1940

Māori lost much land through sales to the Government, and in some areas, through confiscation. In 1865, the Government established the Native Land Court, ostensibly to confirm Māori ownership and to individualise holdings. However, for the next 125 years, the Court was particularly effective, as intended, in facilitating the transfer of Māori land into Pākehā hands. Government land purchasers, and later private individuals, often employed unscrupulous tactics, and the legal processes often resulted in huge debts for Māori who were then forced into selling parts of their land. From the establishment of the Land Court until the 1990s, a primary focus of Māori was to stop the ebbing away of their land.[2]

The Government had pushed the Kīngitanga out of the Waikato basin by 1865, forcing more distant supporters to abandon their loyalty to the Māori King. However, an independent Māori state continued to exist in the King Country, bounded by an *aukati* (border) over which Pākehā could not cross uninvited on pain of death and this district remained politically estranged from the Government until 1881. Its slogan was *mana Māori motuhake* (separate Māori authority), a policy it attempted to maintain, with its own tribal structures and its Parliament, the Kauhanganui, even after accommodations had been made with the Government. One of the most influential leaders within the Kīngitanga in the twentieth century was Te Puea Hērangi, a granddaughter of King Tāwhiao. She emerged as a leader during World War I in Tainui's resistance to the conscription of its young men. In the 1920s, she re-established the Kīngitanga's capital at Ngāruawāhia in Waikato, as a focal point for the movement.

Parihaka, a Māori village in Taranaki, emerged as another site of challenge in the late nineteenth century. From the 1870s, under the two prophets, Te Whiti-o-Rongomai and

Religious leader Erueti Te Whiti-o-Rongomai III of Te Āti Awa and Taranaki, who died in 1907

Religious leader Tohu Kākahi (1828–1907) of Te Āti Awa and Taranaki

Tohu Kākahi, Taranaki Māori resisted the continuing confiscation of their land. Rather than resort to military action, the Māori of Parihaka employed land occupations and civil disobedience strategies: ploughing and fencing confiscated land, protest marches, and disruption of surveys. They also wished to limit the effect of the colonising culture, by promoting *tikanga Māori* and removing their children from the Government's schools. Many Māori were arrested for their protest campaigns and were deported to the South Island to endure hard labour. The Government, exasperated at the tactics of this non-violent resistance, invaded Parihaka in 1881, breaking the settlement up. Te Whiti and Tohu were detained for 17 months without trial before being allowed to return to Parihaka. However, the civil disobedience campaigns for justice over the land confiscation resumed and continued into the 1890s. Both men died in 1907.

The teeth of the Native Land Court bit not only those who had fought against the Crown, but also those who had supported the Government's *kāwanatanga*. Many Māori now attempted to redress wrongs through Pākehā legal mechanisms. From 1868, four elected Māori representatives had sat in the New Zealand Parliament. Despite some Māori Members actively striving for justice for Māori within Parliament, their small number, and Parliament's unwillingness to accommodate the Māori language, marginalised them from decision-making up until the twentieth century.[3] Māori also made several attempts to present petitions to Queen Victoria and the British Parliament in the hope that the 'mother country' might step in to right wrongs to Māori. These approaches were passed back to the indifferent New Zealand Government. Māori also used the law courts to seek justice, and were sometimes successful. However, Chief Justice Prendergast's infamous ruling in 1877 that the Treaty of Waitangi was a 'nullity' effectively ruled legal

The town at Parihaka, Taranaki in 1881, founded by Te Whiti and Tohu

claims based on the Treaty out of bounds for the next 100 years. In the mid 1870s, the Repudiation movement of the Ahuriri-Wairarapa region sought to overturn fraudulent land titles through the law courts, but discovered that litigation in Pākehā courts was neither cheap nor sure. It became clear to Māori of the nineteenth century that working within the Pākehā system seldom brought the results they wanted.

Through the 1870s, Māori continued to hold large meetings to discuss political issues. Māori wanted the rights guaranteed to them in the Treaty of Waitangi, and many considered, through Article Two of the Treaty and the Constitution Act 1852, that Māori had a right to self-government. A new pan-Māori movement emerged in the 1880s, *'Te Kotahitanga ki te Tiriti o Waitangi'* (Unity under the Treaty of Waitangi). This movement, led mainly by chiefs of the former pro-government tribes, fought against the ravages of the Native Land Court and for Māori self-determination, seeking to establish a Māori organisation that would exist in parallel with the New Zealand Parliament and other Pākehā structures. The Māori Parliament had widespread support from Māori during the 1890s and even influenced the Pākehā Parliament, for example, in the formulation of the Māori Councils Act 1900. However, it was generally unable to achieve good co-operation with the Kīngitanga in order to present a united Māori voice to the Government. As Māori devoted their energies to implementing the new Māori Councils, the influence of the Kotahitanga movement diminished, despite the Councils' failing to meet Māori aspirations due to continuing governmental control. It was superseded by a new Kotahitanga formed by former Te Aute College students.

The Te Aute Association was made up of well educated, bilingual, deeply religious Māori men who aspired to reinvigorate Māori society. Their most famous member was Sir Āpirana Ngata of Ngāti Porou. By working within the Pākehā system, particularly through Parliament as the Young Maori Party, and by promoting the learning of the English language and other Pākehā practices, they are sometimes accused of promoting assimilation. However, while they did not seek independent Māori political structures, like other Māori they fought for the retention of Māori lands, the material betterment of Māori, and a distinct Māori identity.

Two Māori religious movements emerged in the early twentieth century to challenge the Pākehā assumption of *kāwanatanga*: Ngā Iharaira, the followers of the prophet Rua Kēnana, and the Rātana Church (see Chapter 16). Rua's support came principally from some sectors of the Tūhoe people, all of whom had suffered from the wars and land confiscation of the previous century, and continued to live in poverty. In 1906, Rua established his New Jerusalem in the remote Urewera locality of Maunga-pōhatu, where he sought to remove his followers from European influences as much as possible. This exodus not only disrupted the formal schooling of their children but also affected the flow of available agricultural labour. Rua's movement was essentially pacifist; however, due to a paranoid belief that Rua was a threat to Britain's war efforts, an armed contingent of police attacked Maunga-pōhatu in 1916, killing two Māori men, one of whom was Rua's son. After being imprisoned for a year, Rua returned in 1918 to continue his religious work.

In 1918, Wiremu Tahu-pōtiki Rātana began his religious mission, initially centred on spiritual work and faith. As the self-styled *'Māngai'* (mouthpiece) of God, he established his own church in 1925, attracting Māori adherents from tribes all over New Zealand. Thousands of Māori, known as *mōrehu* (survivors), flocked to the *Māngai*'s base at Rātana Pā near Whanganui. In the late 1920s, Rātana turned to political work, focusing on fulfilling the guarantees of the Treaty of Waitangi by having

15 Mana Māori motuhake

Rātana followers elected to Parliament in the four Māori seats. The first was elected in 1932, and by 1943, with the defeat of Ngata, Rātana MPs held all four 'quarters'. From 1935, the Rātana movement allied itself to the Labour Party, and through that alliance, dominated the Māori parliamentary seats into the 1990s.

Until the 1860s, the Government paid lip service to the Treaty of Waitangi, even when its actions directly contradicted it. Following the wars, and some highly dubious legal decisions, the Treaty effectively lapsed from Pākehā consciousness, until Māori activism forced it back into their view in the last quarter of the twentieth century. However, for Māori, the Treaty never disappeared.

Up until the 1860s, governmental control over Māori was patchy and weak, generally relying on Māori co-operation. Māori, at this time, had sufficient military muscle to seriously trouble the Crown, and some were prepared to use it. However, while Māori could prevail in some encounters, their lack of unity, as well as the extensive resources available to the Government in terms of imperial troops and funds, made ultimate military success unlikely. Māori therefore sought less violent means of challenging colonisation. For some leaders, such as Te Whiti and Tohu, who couched their resistance within a religious framework, this meant removing their followers from Pākehā influence and opposing land loss by non-violent resistance. Others, such as the Kotahitanga Movement, attempted to create parallel political structures for Māori, which could operate alongside Pākehā ones. Some leaders, such as Ngata, worked within Pākehā institutions, notably Parliament. However, the aims of land retention, Māori control of their own affairs, maintaining a distinctive, yet dynamic Māori identity, and the application of the Treaty of Waitangi have remained consistent themes in the Māori relationship with the Crown. Māori, in challenging colonisation and the imposition of *kāwanatanga* whilst pursuing their right of *tino rangatiratanga*, have always attempted to match the right strategy to the conditions that they find themselves in, just as they continue to do today.

Notes

1. The Government published *Te Karere Maori*, a bilingual newspaper, from Auckland at the time. The Kīngitanga produced *Te Hokioi E Rere Atu Na* from 1861 to 1863 at Ngāruawāhia. This was challenged briefly by *Te Pihoihoi Mokemoke*, a newspaper put out by John Gorst, the magistrate at Te Awamutu.
2. The Māori Land Court still exists, but its focus now is to facilitate Māori aspirations regarding their land, rather than the alienation of that land.
3. Māori can now choose to join a Māori roll of electors, or the General roll. The Māori roll did not get representation proportionate to their numbers until 1996 when the MMP electoral system was introduced into New Zealand.

FURTHER READING

Walker, (1990) provides a good introduction to this topic.

Chapter 16

Ngā poropiti me ngā Hāhi
Prophets and the churches *John Stenhouse and Lachy Paterson*

> *Ki a koe, e Maru! Māu e tiaki! (To you, O Maru! It is for you to protect!)*

This saying calls upon Maru, a tribal *atua*, for help. Māori lived in a world where their religious beliefs influenced, and were influenced by, events in daily life. For the missionaries, too, God played an active role in human affairs. Some writers have seen religion as a dying force in Western culture, and marginalised its significance in the history of Aotearoa/New Zealand. This is unhelpful for those wishing to understand Māori history. Furthermore, we must set aside the assumption that religion occupied some kind of separate, private, marginal sphere isolated from Māori social and political life. Most Māori of the nineteenth century did not see the world that way. Neither did the missionaries, nor, indeed, many other Pākehā settlers and officials. For many nineteenth-century New Zealanders, religion, culture and politics interpenetrated and interacted, sometimes explosively. This chapter sets aside a distinction between a 'real' world and a religious world, and instead emphasises interactions and interconnections between these realms. We see virtually all the Māori religious movements discussed below as complex and creative blends of:

- old and new
- tradition and modernity
- ancestral and Biblical worlds
- religion and politics
- protest and hope.

This chapter starts with an overview of some aspects of pre-contact Māori religion, and then looks at how and why Māori embraced Christianity. We examine, in detail, the prophet movements, which in dynamic and creative ways, and often inspired by Old Testament models, pursued Māori religious, political and social goals. The chapter concludes with a brief overview of more recent Māori religious experience.

 ## Pre-contact Māori religion

Unlike a growing group of Enlightenment Westerners, pre-contact Māori saw the physical and spiritual domains as intimately interconnected. No hard and fast boundaries separated natural from supernatural phenomena. The concept of *tapu*, or spiritually grounded restrictions affecting individuals and human activity, regulated Māori life. *Tapu* was a state that came from the *atua*. If carefully observed, it ensured the physical and spiritual well being of Māori people, their society and resources. However, the spiritual elements that Māori had to contend with often posed dangers that manifested themselves in physical form. Māori guarded themselves by observing *tikanga*, that is, by following correct behaviour, and by the careful use of *karakia* and rituals. Māori generally saw ill health, with the exception of wounds suffered in battle, as a failure to observe *tikanga*, a transgression of *tapu*, or *mākutu*. The interconnectedness of spiritual and material realms, and the strict adherence to form in order to maintain spiritual and physical well-being, shaped the ways that Māori later embraced Christianity. Traditional beliefs and practices never simply disappeared with the coming of the Gospel.

Conversion to Christianity

Samuel Marsden and his translator Ruatara jointly preached the first Christian sermon in Aotearoa/New Zealand in 1814, but for well over a decade the early Anglican and Wesleyan missionaries struggled to gain converts. Scholars have identified several reasons why Māori began to turn to the God of the Bible in large numbers from the late 1820s. Some have emphasised the 'fatal impact' of European culture rendering traditional *tikanga* invalid (for example, Wright, 1959: 115–165). Others have stressed the important role played by previously disadvantaged groups such as slaves and younger chiefs using the new religion as a way of gaining influence. Recently, historians have argued that Māori 'converted conversion' by creating distinctively Māori varieties of Christianity, many of which allowed Māori to discard traditional attitudes to warfare that had escalated out of hand with new European weapons (for example, Belich, 1996: 217, 219). No single cause can explain a complex, diverse and erratic process that varied significantly from area to area and over time. It took missionaries over two decades to become established in most Māori communities. Once they embraced Christianity, however, Māori saw it as being an essential element in a package of new *tikanga* by which they could advance into modernity.

Certainly the translation of the New Testament and the appeal of literacy helped Māori Christianity to spread during the 1830s and 1840s. So did improved missionary performance and the work of unofficial Māori missionaries and teachers. Often slaves freed by their convert owners carried the message of the Gospel back to their own tribes well in advance of a Pākehā missionary. Missionary doctrine appealed to many Māori because, like pre-contact religion, it laid out precise guidelines to follow in order to achieve wellbeing. The missionaries could seldom control the new varieties of Māori Christianity that emerged. Many Māori, for example, seeing the Sabbath as an essential Christian *tikanga*, observed it more strictly than some Pākehā.

The great majority of those Māori who embraced Christianity before the 1860s were adherents of three main churches. The Church of England was the most popular, partly because the Church Missionary Society, an Anglican body, had arrived first on the scene in 1814. The Methodists, whose first missionary followed in 1823, took second place. The Roman Catholics led by Bishop Pompallier arrived much later, in 1838, to find Protestantism flourishing. While the British Protestant missionaries co-operated with each other, at least initially, most displayed hostility towards the Roman Catholics, led by a Frenchman, and Māori converts occasionally joined the sectarian fray.

Māori prophets

Alongside these Māori Anglicans, Methodists and Catholics arose a series of remarkable Māori prophet leaders. Reflecting the interconnectedness of the Māori world-view, these mostly mission-educated prophets wove together traditional beliefs and practices with biblical and Christian ones to create distinctive new faiths. Combining the old with the new, tradition with modernity, and spirituality with tough-minded rationality, these movements constituted powerful, effective responses to colonisation. Offering adherents meaning, hope, identity and community, the prophets helped Māori walk through the valley of the shadow of death and into the modern world. The following survey, brief and selective, concentrates on important and illuminating prophets.

1830s and 1840s

In the Bay of Islands in 1833, an area of frequent Māori-Pākehā contact, new diseases to which Māori had no immunity were taking a considerable toll. Papahurihia, a *matakite* (seer) descended from a famous female *tohunga*, attracted many followers he called *Hūrai* (Jews). He criticised the Protestant missionaries working among his people as *kaikōhuru* (treacherous killers), killing Māori by *mākutu*. Papahurihia told his followers that the Protestants' heaven contained 'nothing but books to eat', whereas his contained guns, ships, flour, sugar, sex – and no missionaries. By the time the Northern War erupted in 1845, he had become Hone Heke's chief *tohunga*. Before one battle, he told Heke's people to 'observe all the sacred rites and customs of your ancestors' or to 'pray to the god of the missionaries'. It 'is good,' reflected Papahurihia pragmatically, 'to have more than one god to trust to.'

Te Hura

During the 1850s, many spiritual leaders, worried by the impact of new diseases, offered healing. In Hawke's Bay in 1850, for example, Te Hura, an old woman, received a divine message conveyed through her dead child (a common pre-contact spirit medium) and Moses. Te Hura's call exemplified how naturally, for many Māori, ancestral and Biblical worlds merged. The spirit instructed her to seek out the local Māori Anglican teacher, and to remove the *tapu* of the old gods by washing in hot water. Obeying, Te Hura launched a healing mission. It combined traditional techniques, including a bed of heated stones and steaming herbs, with the new *mana* of Christ. Te Hura prayed over the sick person: 'O Lord O Lord steal away out of this person his stink and rottenness for Jesus Christ's sake Amen.'

Te Ua Haumēne

A decade later, in Taranaki, Te Ua Haumēne founded the Pai Mārire or Hauhau faith, which became one of the most popular and fertile Māori religious movements of the century. War in Taranaki had erupted in 1860, when Governor Gore Browne

16 Ngā poropiti me ngā Hāhi

Te Ua Haumēne of Taranaki, religious leader who established the Pai Mārire, or Hauhau, faith

forced through the sale of the Waitara block over the protests of Wiremu Kīngi Te Rangitāke, a leading Te Āti Awa chief. Hundreds of Māori Christians and a vocal minority of prominent Pākehā Anglicans protested the Government's decision to send in troops against Te Āti Awa peacefully occupying the Waitara.

In this troubled area in 1862, the Archangel Gabriel announced to Te Ua God's special relationship with his Māori people. *Atua Mārire* (the God of Peace) promised to restore his 'forgetful, naked-standing people in the half-standing land'. Te Ua identified Māori with the Old Testament Israelites, suffering in exile in Babylon and longing to return to their Promised Land. Such teachings appealed to a growing group of adherents because they made sense of recent, bitter historical experience, offered a compelling identity as God's people, and, in dark days, hope for a better future. Pai Mārire constituted a faith rooted in the Māori Bible, fully translated by the late 1850s, whose words and world Māori made their own. Te Ua's followers called themselves *Tiu* (Jews),[1] and worshipped on Saturday, the Jewish Sabbath. They erected tall *niu* (flagpoles), like ships' masts, down which hung ropes festooned with flags displaying Pai Mārire religious symbols. Adherents gathered round the *niu* chanting phrases derived from English military language and Catholic and Protestant church services. Gabriel told Te Ua that God was giving His people 'the gift of languages', and teaching them all varieties of religion. Pai Mārire somewhat resembled modern Pentecostal Christianity, not least in rejecting the mainstream churches and their missionaries.

Pai Mārire, a phrase which adherents regularly repeated in prayer, meant 'Goodness and Peace'. This described God's attributes. 'Hauhau' referred to the winds, and to the breath of life, which God gave humans. Old Testament angels, especially Gabriel and Michael, archangels of peace and war respectively, played important roles. In April 1864 Te Ua and a group of followers defended their lands by ambushing a party of soldiers, led by Captain Thomas Lloyd, who were destroying crops in Taranaki. Pai Mārire missionaries took Lloyd's preserved head around the North Island to unite the tribes and announce that God would deliver his people.

Te Ua could not control what such missionaries preached or how hearers responded however, especially when the spread of war rendered large areas of the North Island volatile. The Waikato war of 1863–64, followed by Government confiscation of huge areas of Māori land, encouraged many to join Pai Mārire. By 1865, perhaps a fifth of the Māori population belonged, mostly from across the middle of the North Island. At Ōpōtiki in 1865, Hauhau missionaries Pātara Te Raukatauri and Kereopa Te Rau preached to Whakatōhea, who executed their Anglican missionary, Carl Volkner, for serving as a Government spy. Conflict then spread up the East Coast. In February 1866 Te Ua, who could see in escalating warfare only disaster, surrendered to the Government.

Yet, Pai Mārire had already inspired new religious movements. The second Māori King, re-baptised in 1864 by Te Ua as Tāwhiao, developed a form of Pai Mārire which he called Tariao, signifying the new era of peace he intended to promote. The Kīngitanga, a religious as much as a political movement, took up Te Ua's notion of placing *aukati*, or lines of peace, between Māori and Pākehā, in the Rohe Pōtae – the boundary line that marked off the King Country. Because the 'bloodshed arose from the Pākehā's hands,' Tāwhiao explained, it would 'not be right to bring that blood hither, leave it where it is.' Until 1883, no Pākehā could enter the Rohe Pōtae without permission.

In Taranaki, Tītokowaru of Ngāti Ruanui initially accepted Te Ua's message that fighting must cease. But confiscation made his people's situation hopeless. Tītokowaru fought brilliantly in 1868 and 1869 in south Taranaki to save Ngāti Ruanui lands. After an incident in which he probably violated the strict Pai Mārire prohibition of adultery, however, he lost *tapu*, and his followers melted away.

Te Whiti and Tohu at Parihaka

Te Whiti-o-Rongomai III and Tohu Kakahi, Te Ua's spiritual successors, founded a millennial community, Parihaka, on confiscated land near the mountain Taranaki. 'The wars of the past even unto the present shall not be renewed,' Te Whiti told his followers, who wore white feathers in their hair to show their commitment to peace. In 1869, he announced *'te tau o te takahanga'* ('the year of the trampling underfoot'), beginning the Parihaka campaign to peacefully resist Government attempts to survey and occupy confiscated land. Māori had not rebelled, declared Te Whiti, and therefore the confiscation had no legitimacy. Calling himself Jehovah's 'mouthpiece', and a 'small Christ', Te Whiti told his followers that he exercised authority over the 'ordering of the earth so that all people may see that I am the son of God'.

The Government, unimpressed, began surveying in 1878. In May of 1879, Tohu sent out the first groups of Parihaka men to assert their ownership by ploughing the land. Many were arrested. New groups of ploughmen replaced them (Scott, 1975). Parihaka expanded, as tribes around the country sent representatives. On 5 November 1881, the Government sent 1600 troops to crush Te Whiti's burgeoning Christian kingdom. The soldiers, led by Native Minister John Bryce, though welcomed peacefully, arrested Te Whiti, Tohu, and Tītokowaru, jailed them in New Plymouth for six months, and sent packing 1600 'outsiders'. Te Whiti and Tohu, released after two years, returned to Parihaka in 1883 to rebuild their new Jerusalem (Scott, 1975). A model of Māori Christian modernity, Parihaka boasted wide streets, electricity, running water, a savings bank, a dining hall, and even a billiard hall. It remained a centre of peaceful Māori resistance until its two leaders died in 1907.

In the South Island, the prophet Hipa Te Maihāroa, influenced by Pai Mārire, led a migration of over 100 people to Te Ao Mārama (Ōmārama), to reclaim their ancestral lands. This group, mostly Ngāi Tahu, called themselves Israelites, and rejected the validity of the Government's huge South Island land purchase of 1848. In 1879, however, after local runholders protested, an armed police party ejected them from their promised land.

Te Kooti Arikirangi Te Tūriki

The Ringatū faith founded by Te Kooti Arikirangi Te Tūruki developed largely independently of Pai Mārire. Te Kooti, born into a chiefly lineage of Rongowhakaata *hapū* of Poverty Bay, early developed a reputation as a troublemaker, and in the mid-1860s got caught up in the East Coast wars. Local authorities arrested and sent him, without trial, to Wharekauri in the Chatham Islands. There, '*te Wairua o te Atua*' (the Spirit of God) came to deliver Te Kooti, sick with fever, from imprisonment. The spirit, appearing sometimes in human form, gave him two signs: a *ngārara* (lizard), and a flame that did not burn. On 4 July 1868 Te Kooti and almost 200 men, women and children, mostly Pai Mārire, seized a supply ship and sailed back to the mainland. Arriving back in Poverty Bay on 10 July, they gave thanks for God's deliverance by raising their right hands – Ringatū, the Upraised Hand – which became the name of Te Kooti's new faith.

His forces attacked settlements in the Poverty Bay area, killing or capturing many ordinary Māori and Pākehā, some of them old enemies. Colonial and Māori opponents hunted him remorselessly as the colony, gripped by awe and fear, looked on. Eventually, in 1872, Te Kooti took refuge in the King Country. In 1873, he made peace with the King. Even this remarkably successful warrior-prophet realised that, against overwhelming odds, he could not keep fighting forever.

In 1875, Te Kooti began formulating the rituals and structure of the Ringatū, turning his movement into a church with lasting form and substance. Adherents celebrated the Sabbath on Saturday; and the First of January and the First of July, the first day of the seventh month, as the first two pillars of the faith. *Huamata* (planting rites) and *pure* (harvest rites), introduced in 1879, completed the four pillars of the Ringatū year. Later, the Twelfth of the month, celebrating the safe return of the exiles from Chatham Island, also became a holy day. Te Kooti composed the songs, prayers, hymns, scriptural texts and doctrines of the church, and organised its system of government. Committed to peace from 1873, Te Kooti taught his followers to avoid violence and follow the law to secure their welfare. In 1883, the Government pardoned him.

Te Kooti Arikirangi Te Tūruki of Rongowhakaata, founder of the Ringatū faith, who died in 1893

Rua Kēnana Hepetipa

Before he died in 1893, Te Kooti prophesied that a new prophet, greater than he, would come. In 1905, the Tūhoe prophet Rua Kēnana Hepetipa ascended Maunga-pōhatu, the sacred mountain of the Tūhoe, where he met the Tūhoe ancestress Whaitiri and Christ. The following year he travelled with Tūhoe leaders to Tūranga-nui

(Gisborne) to meet King Edward VII, from whom, it was said, Rua would buy back the country for Māori. After waiting at the wharf for some time, his followers asked Rua why the King had not yet arrived. 'I am the King,' he replied. They followed him, now baptised as *mīhaia* (messiah), back to the promised land of Maunga-pōhatu where, beginning in 1907, they built their new Jerusalem.

Rua's flourishing millennial community, committed to Te Kooti's 'long abiding peace', excited growing hostility during World War I, especially when Rua discouraged his followers from volunteering. On 2 April 1916, an armed police party marched in to arrest him for selling alcohol without a licence. Shots rang out. By the time the firing stopped, two Māori, including one of Rua's sons, lay dead. Tried for sedition, and imprisoned for 'morally resisting arrest', Rua received a sentence whose harshness several members of the jury protested. After returning from prison in 1918, he directed the rebuilding of the community. Rua died in 1937, predicting that, like Christ, he would rise again.

Tahupōtiki Wiremu Rātana

In November 1918, near Whanganui, the Holy Ghost appeared to Tahupōtiki Wiremu Rātana of Taranaki and Ngāti Raukawa. Rātana's aunt, Mere Rikiriki, a faith healer descended from Te Whiti, had predicted this event. The Holy Ghost appointed Rātana

Tahupōtiki, Wiremu Rātana (1879–1939) who founded the Rātana faith and political movement, was of Ngāti Apa and Ngā Rauru. Here, he is seen with his wife, Te Urumanaao Ngapāki. The woman in the centre of the picture (who has been inset later) is Iriaka Te Rio, who in 1925 became a second wife to Rātana and who was a member of Parliament for twenty years from 1949.

'hei Māngai mōku' (my Mouthpiece) and told him to unite the Māori people. The 1918 influenza pandemic, which hit Māori hard, sent thousands, including some Pākehā, flocking to Rātana, who provided faith-healing. Over the following years, Rātana created a new church, to which, by 1926, almost a fifth of the Māori population belonged. Like Te Ua, Te Whiti, and Te Kooti, he called his followers Ngā Mōrehu, the faithful remnant of God's people. Rātana appealed to ordinary, detribalised Māori whose interests he believed tribal chiefs and educated Māori politicians were betraying. A religious moderniser, he also criticised *mākutu* and *tapu*.

Having successfully established a popular new church, Rātana, with Bible in one hand and Treaty of Waitangi in the other, turned to politics. In 1928, he declared his intention to place Rātana men in all four Māori electorates. In 1935, he forged a political alliance with Michael Joseph Savage's Labour Party, which helped secure pensions and improved housing for Māori. The Rātana-Labour alliance helps explain why the great majority of Māori have voted Labour from then on.

The mainstream churches after the wars

The three mainstream churches suffered a decline in Māori membership during the 1860s, especially amongst those who associated the Pākehā missionaries with the colonial oppressor. Some missionaries, particularly the Methodists, did side with the Government, though others, such as Octavius Hadfield, incurred the wrath of settlers for defending Māori and blaming the Government for the wars.

Yet many Māori, particularly from the so-called non-aligned tribes, never left their churches, and, in the 1870s, some of those who had left drifted back. We need to know more about such groups, which are under-researched by comparison with the prophet movements. The Church of England and the Roman Catholic Church remained popular churches for Māori, with many important Māori leaders numbered in their congregations. Sir Āpirana Ngata, for example, a committed Anglican, started his political work through the Te Kotahitanga o Te Aute, a group of young men who had been educated at the Anglican Te Aute College. Dame Whina Cooper, the first head of the Māori Women's Welfare League and a land rights campaigner, was a stalwart of the Catholic Church. Many Māori leaders were educated at Māori boarding schools run by the churches. Such leaders embraced many of the moral values that Pākehā Christians professed, and equipped themselves to engage constructively with modernity and deal with the dominant Pākehā systems. In embracing Christianity, they did not repudiate Māori cultural traditions. Ngata, for example, spearheaded a renaissance of Māori arts and crafts in the early twentieth century.

Sir Āpirana Turupa Ngata (1874–1950) of Ngāti Porou, a scholar and political leader

Modern trends

No one denomination dominates any major *iwi* today. The spread of denominations among Māori tribes often reflects missionary efforts of the past. For example, the relatively high number of Presbyterians among the Tūhoe people (about 15%) reflects the missionary efforts of John Laughton in the Urewera district during Rua's sojourn in jail. By contrast, although Methodism enjoyed early success, and retains a high profile in several *iwi*, today less than 4% of Māori nationwide identify with that church. (Above and following statistics: Statistics NZ, 1998: 107–139).

The mainstream churches faced several challenges during the twentieth century. Just as it had battled against Roman Catholicism in earlier years, the Anglican Church, the first and largest of the missionary faiths, engaged with new Māori faiths, such as Ringatū, Rua's Iharaira, and the Rātana Church. The Māori Anglican Members of the House of Representatives (MHRs), led by Sir James Carroll and Āpirana Ngata, were instrumental in passing the Tohunga Suppression Bill of 1907, which aimed to suppress Rua's prophet movement.

A considerable threat to Māori Anglicanism was the Church of Jesus Christ of Latter Day Saints (the Mormons). Led by American missionaries, it made an impact from the 1880s, partly because it was untainted by complicity in British oppression. The Mormons put more effort into reaching Māori than Pākehā, and the church grew steadily, reaching a high point as Māori migrated to the cities after World War II. However, membership has slipped to less than 5% of Māori today.

Within the mainstream churches, Māori fought hard to make their voices heard, and to ensure that their identity was not swamped by Pākehā majorities. In the nineteenth century, when most Māori spoke *te reo Māori* and lived apart from Pākehā, this had not been a major problem. In the twentieth century, however, Pākehā-dominated dioceses and synods tended to overlook Māori congregational concerns. Although a number of Māori were ordained as Anglican clergy in the nineteenth century, not until 1928 was Frederick Bennett consecrated as first Māori Anglican Bishop, partly as an attempt to stop the loss of Māori Anglicans to the Rātana Church. The first Māori Catholic priest was ordained in 1944, and Max Takuira Mariu was consecrated the first Māori Catholic Bishop in 1988.

Anglicans opened up more fully to Māori voices in 1978, when they allowed the Māori bishopric a semi-autonomous role. In 1992, the Anglican Church divided into three *tikanga*, or cultural streams, for Māori, Pākehā and Pacific Islanders, each an equal partner within the General Synod. The Māori bishopric was divided into five parts, and four more Māori bishops were appointed to assist the Bishop of Aotearoa.

Māori Christians continue to play important roles in social and political debate. In 1998, for example, Presbyterian Māori imposed a *rāhui* to stop a ban on the ordination of homosexuals in the Presbyterian Church. Also in 1998, Māori Anglican clergy and academics helped lead the Hīkoi of Hope, a nation-wide march to protest against poverty and social inequalities. Hīkoi leaders presented to the Prime Minister and Leader of the Opposition A Constitution for our Nation, a discussion document proposing that Government should devolve responsibility for education, health and social welfare spending on Māori to a Māori group with power to legislate.

It is sometimes said that Māori are more 'spiritual' than Pākehā. Certainly twenty-first century New Zealanders are more likely to encounter prayer and other religious rituals at formal Māori occasions than at Pākehā ones. However, census figures show that Māori church membership has declined about as fast as Pākehā membership. Only about 60% of Māori currently identify with a particular church. The proportion of Māori who profess no particular religion is now similar to the general population of Aotearoa/New Zealand. The percentage is significantly higher, almost 40%, amongst Māori who do not know which iwi they belong to, which suggests that the processes of urbanisation, detribalisation and secularisation are linked.

 ## Conclusion

As this chapter has shown, Māori forged dynamic religious movements during the nineteenth and twentieth centuries that helped them survive the tumultuous passage to the modern world. These movements offered adherents meaning, identity, hope and community in days of darkness, as the relentless progress of colonisation threatened to make Māori exiles in their own land. All had political meanings, as government repression and conflict between Māori leaders suggests. They represented creative, intelligent, adaptive responses to the wider, global world opening up to them.

Note

1 A dialectal variation on *Hūrai*.

FURTHER READING

Binney (1996) and Elsmore (1999) are both comprehensive works on the Māori prophets, while Elsmore (1985) and King (1992) give a good introduction to Māori religion and religion in general.

Chapter 17

Te mana o te tangata whenua
Indigenous assertions of sovereignty

Tānia M. Ka'ai

Throughout the world, the usurpation of land by European colonists and the rights of Indigenous peoples to be self-determining, has meant that sovereignty has been of central concern to all colonised people. Since the signing of the Treaty of Waitangi in 1840, Māori, as the *tangata whenua* of Aotearoa/New Zealand, have challenged the rights of the Crown to *tino rangatiratanga* (sovereignty). While Chapter 15 focuses on the nineteenth and early twentieth century challenges to sovereignty by Māori, and Chapter 14 explains the discrepancies between the two interpretations of the Treaty of Waitangi and, specifically, the discordant translations of *tino rangatiratanga* and *kāwanatanga*, this chapter discusses the opposition by Māori, during the mid to latter part of the twentieth century, to the Crown's assumption of *kāwanatanga*.

Contemporary challenges for self-determination have taken many forms, as they did in earlier years. Māori women have been prominent, primarily with achievements in health, child welfare, employment and education, through the Māori Women's Welfare League. The literary medium has been used to advantage, particularly with newsletters and in the field of drama. Some groups have begun as small autonomous units, eventually gaining the support of elders and more established groups. From the 1970s Māori have used the political arena, forming their own political parties. This period also saw the emergence of language advocacy groups and the related Te Kōhanga Reo movement. More latterly, protests have involved land occupations and marches. The Māori traditional art forms have experienced a cultural renaissance and Māori have joined the struggles of Indigenous people world-wide to achieve self-determination.

Māori have challenged the Crown since the signing of the Treaty of Waitangi in 1840 on the issue of sovereignty. This is based on the fact that Māori have never ceded sovereignty to the Crown and that they have been excluded from the physical, economic, political and philosophical development of Aotearoa/New Zealand, even though they are the Indigenous people and a Treaty partner. This can be described as cultural imperialism. Māori assertions of sovereignty have been expressed for at least 160 years and have assumed many different faces from lobbying, making submissions, presenting petitions, mounting deputations, to occupying land under dispute, establishing various movements, organising marches, protests, boycotts, pickets, symbolic acts and demonstrations and establishing political parties. Furthermore, these challenges have been in response to Pākehā attitudes of subjugation whereby they positioned themselves politically to reduce Māori control of the land, fisheries and natural resources, and introduced policies ranging from assimilation to cultural genocide which reduced Māori as the Indigenous people to a powerless minority in their own country.

17 Te mana o te tangata whenua

The following table lists some assertions of sovereignty since the nineteenth century.

Examples of Māori assertions of sovereignty

Churches

Pai Mārire (1864)
Ringatū (1868)
Rātana (1925)

Waitangi Tribunal

Waitangi Tribunal Negotiated Settlements with *iwi* 1985–2002
Ngāti Whātua Settlement
Whakatōhea Treaty Settlement
Muriwhenua Treaty Settlement
Ngāti Awa Treaty Settlement
Tainui Treaty Settlement
Ngāi Tahu Treaty Settlement
Ngāti Ruanui Settlement

Political movements

Kīngitanga (1858)
Kotahitanga (1892)
Māori Council (1962)
Ngā Tamatoa (1970)
He Taua (1979)
Mana Motuhake (1980–2002)
Ngā Kaiwhakapūmau i te reo (1986)
Maranga Mai (1980)

Media

Te Hokioi (1863 & 1968)
Te Wānanga (1874–78)
Te Paki o Matariki (1892–1935)
Te Puke Ki Hikurangi (1897–1913)
Te Tiupiri (1898–1900)
Te Ao Hou (1952–1975)
MOOHR (1952)
Māori Radio (1988)
Māori Television (2002)

Educational initiatives

Te Ātaarangi (1979)
Te Kōhanga Reo (1981)
Wānanga (1982)
Te Kura Kaupapa Māori (1985)

Women's organisations

Māori Women's Welfare League (1951)

Events

Battle of Ōrākau (1865)
Parihaka (1869–1907)
Raglan Golf Course (1970s)
Waitangi Day Protests (1970s to present day)
Māori Land March (1975)
Occupation of Bastion Point (1977)
Occupation of Moutoa Gardens (1995 and 2002)
Chainsaw of the lone pine tree on Maungakiekie (One Tree Hill) (1994)
The Fiscal Envelope (1994–1995)
The Sealords Deal (1993)

People

Hone Heke
Te Wherowhero
Tītokowaru
Te Kooti Arikirangi Te Tūruki
Te Whiti and Tohu
Eva Rickard
Dame Whina Cooper
Joe Hawke
Tame Iti
Sir Robert Mahuta

Chapter 15 provides insights into some of the nineteenth and early twentieth century challenges to sovereignty by Māori. An overview of more recent efforts by Māori during the mid to latter part of the twentieth century will provide a more contemporary understanding of Māori challenges to the Crown's assumption of *kāwanatanga*.

 Māori Women's Welfare League

The Māori Women's Welfare League (Te Rōpū Wāhine Māori Toko i te Ora) was established in 1951 with Whina Cooper (later Dame Whina Cooper) as the Inaugural President. The first national Māori organisation to be formed, it was also the first to provide Māori women with a forum in which their concerns could be brought to a wider audience and placed before the policy-makers of the day (Rogers and Simpson, 1993). The League emerged against a background of thirty years of rural to urban shift and demographic change, World War II, and increasing social challenges for Māori in adapting to a lifestyle largely prescribed by the dominant Pākehā majority. Their concerns included obtaining suitable housing, adapting to a cash economy, coping with declining health and forms of racism (Rogers and Simpson, 1993). The League, together with the Māori Women's Welfare Officers appointed as an outcome of the Social and Economic Advancement Act (1945), was a major force in assisting Māori to make the transition from rural communities to the cities, with a particular focus on Māori women and children in the areas of health, education and welfare. The League is still very active today, promoting leadership amongst Māori women and contributing to the social and economic development of Aotearoa/New Zealand.

Newly elected League President Whina Cooper (later Dame Whina Cooper) addressing the inaugural Māori Women's Welfare League Conference, September 1951

Te Hokioi and MOORH

Te Hokioi and *MOORH* were the names of two separate newsletters that were produced in 1968 by groups of Māori people who shared the common belief in social transformation for Māori by raising the consciousness of Māori people. They were the underground expression of rising political consciousness among urban Māori (Walker, 1990).

Te Hokioi, which took its name from the original Waikato newspaper of Pātara Te Tuhi and King Tāwhiao in 1863, publicised issues such as the plundering of shellfish by commercial divers and the commercial exploitation of *pounamu* in the South Island and related these to Te Tiriti o Waitangi. Similarly, *MOORH*, an acronym for the Māori Organisation on Human Rights, advocated the return of Māori resources held by Pākehā and attacked the education system for denying the use of the Māori language in compulsory sector schools.

Ngā Tamatoa

These newsletters provided a political platform for the emergence of Ngā Tamatoa in 1970, whose members advanced the consciousness-raising process amongst Māori society on issues pertaining to the erosion of Māori rights in Aotearoa/New Zealand. However, their work had a sense of duality about it. They established centres in Auckland and Wellington and quickly initiated programmes to assist Māori in these urban centres to negotiate the transition to this alien and often isolating environment. This included monitoring the courts, providing advice and legal aid to Māori offenders, finding job placements, and taking Māori youth back to rural communities to learn the language and culture in a *marae* context with the support of Māori elders. They also visited Māori elders who had relocated to the cities and set up centres for youth to gather and affirm a sense of identity and pride in being Māori. These initiatives were pastoral in nature and were an expression of *whanaungatanga*.

Hirini Melbourne at a rally about the lack of Māori language on television in the late 1970s, organised by Māori students at The University of Waikato

At the same time they lobbied Government on a number of issues. They presented a petition to the Crown calling for the inclusion of the Māori language in schools and advocated the establishment of a one-year teacher education programme for native speakers of the language. They were the initiators of Māori Language Week, which is still celebrated in places like universities and schools. They also initiated annual protests at the Waitangi Day celebrations. Ngā Tamatoa were largely (but not exclusively) university-educated students. Due in some part to their incapacity to speak Māori, they were motivated to challenge the Government. Having been denied their rights to learn their own language by a monocultural education system made them feel culturally disadvantaged. Termed 'radicals' by the media and Pākehā society, they were considered heroes and heroines by Māori of a younger generation who were inspired by their passion for the rights of the Indigenous people of Aotearoa/New Zealand and their compassion for their elders and community. It was this younger generation of the 1970s who gained from the efforts of Ngā Tamatoa. They were able to learn the language at secondary school and pursue career opportunities that advanced the status and survival of the language.

He Taua

The name He Taua, meaning 'the avengers', was adopted by what was described as a raiding party which, in 1979, confronted students at the Auckland Engineering School who were parodying the *haka* in a culturally offensive manner. For over 20 years, the engineering students had staged a mock war dance as part of the annual

Capping Day festivities. For at least 10 years, Māori students had attempted to have the indecent act stopped, but their efforts were to no avail. However, by 1979 the extent of the cultural insult had become more pronounced, undignified and offensively animated, with the inclusion of sexual gestures and bodily markings made with lipstick depicting caricatures of male genitals and sexist obscenities (Walker, 1990).

The confrontation and use of violence inevitably led to a court case. However, the nature of the incident mobilised sectors of Māori society to support the 14 people of He Taua. This included Māori elders, presidents of the Māori Council, the Māori Women's Welfare League, Māori students from Auckland University and a strong contingent of Māori students from Waikato University who also organised pickets outside the courthouse and police station in Hamilton for the duration of the courtcase in Auckland. The union of both conservative Māori organisations and what was described at the time as 'radical' Māori groups provided a strong statement to the nation of the absolute intolerance of blatant racist acts. This was reflected in the sentencing of eight of the He Taua members by Judge Blackwood, who ruled in favour of periodic detention instead of imprisonment (Walker, 1990). The following 20 years from 1980 to 2000 saw changes that would move Aotearoa/New Zealand as a nation into the post-colonial era.

Māori students and staff from The University of Waikato demonstrate outside the Hamilton Police Station in support of Auckland University Māori students involved in He Taua

Maranga Mai

Maranga Mai was a dramatisation of Māori grievances depicting attitudes to Waitangi Day, the occupation of Bastion Point and land protests at Raglan. It was performed at Māngere College, Auckland, in 1980. The drama challenged the 'we are one people' ideology of a large section of Pākehā society. The media and Government sought to ban the play from being performed in other schools in the South Auckland area, claiming the play incited racial disharmony (Walker, 1990). Attempts to ban the play failed and the *Maranga Mai* group continued to perform around the country undeterred by Pākehā establishment opposition.

The infiltration of mainstream society

Protest activity of the 1970s infiltrated mainstream politics in the 1980s with the resignation of Matiu Rata from the Labour Party in 1979 and the launching of his own party, Mana Motuhake, in 1980. Continued protest activity at the Waitangi Day celebrations took its toll on members of the National Council of Churches, who had become embarrassed at being responsible for blessing a celebration that Māori people saw as an injustice (Walker, 1990). This consciousness-raising was disseminated out into the wider Pākehā society so that by 1982 protest activity at Waitangi Day celebrations included Pākehā activists from organisations such as HART (Halt All Racial Tours) and ACCORD (Auckland Committee on Racism and Discrimination). Sections within Pākehā society seemed to be experiencing their own social and political transformation.

Language initiatives

Te Kōhanga Reo emerged in 1981 as a Māori response to the education of their children and as a contribution to language revitalisation. This was followed by Kura Kaupapa Māori in 1985 and thereafter Wharekura (see Chapter 19). These educational initiatives are admired by Indigenous peoples globally as a model language recovery programme. However, it was not until 1989 that the Education Amendment Act formally recognised Kaupapa Māori schools and Wānanga as educational institutions.

In 1987, largely as a result of the concerted efforts of Huirangi Waikerepuru and Ngā Whakapūmau i te Reo Incorporated Society, the Māori language was made an official language of Aotearoa/New Zealand (Māori Language Act, 1987). As a result, the Māori Language Commission was established. The Te Kōhanga Reo National Trust was also established in the same year.

Symbolic acts and statements

In the 1990s, issues such as the fiscal envelope, and land and fisheries disputes gave rise to further challenges to *kāwanatanga* and the Pākehā establishment. For example, in 1994 Mike Smith expressed opposition to the fiscal envelope in a symbolic act by chainsawing the lone pine tree on Maungakiekie (One Tree Hill) in Auckland. The fiscal envelope debacle was an attempt by the State to settle $18 billion dollars worth of land confiscation with a paltry $1 billion (Walker, 1996). In 1995, Tame Iti also demonstrated his opposition to the fiscal envelope at a consultation *hui* at Te Rere Marae, Ōpōtiki. In a symbolic act, he ascended a stepladder to address the State representatives, who were forced to look up to him as he condemned the State over the fiscal envelope. In the same year Tame Iti argued vehemently with Ian Fraser on national television for the return of 2000 hectares of Tūhoe land which had been confiscated by the State in the mid-nineteenth century.

Another symbolic act demonstrating the expression of Māori sovereignty occurred in 1995 and again in 2002, when the Whanganui peoples occupied Moutoa Gardens, originally a Māori site named Pākaitore. In 1995, Annette Sykes and Mike Smith led a protest at the Asian Development Conference in Auckland to warn off foreign investors, thus challenging the State about the sale of land and state assets to foreigners.

The Waitangi Tribunal and negotiated Treaty settlements with iwi

Since 1985, society in Aotearoa/New Zealand has seen a number of Treaty settlements between the Crown and *iwi*, including Tainui, Ngāi Tahu, Whakatōhea, Muriwhenua, Ngāti Awa and Ngāti Whātua. The claims process is still active and is engaging other *iwi* in the settlement of land and resource grievances with the State. Each of these settlements has involved dynamic tribal leadership from figures such as Joe Hawke (Ngāti Whātua), Sir Tīpene O'Regan (Ngāi Tahu), and the late Sir Robert Māhuta (Tainui).

Cultural renaissance

The revival of cultural pride and prowess amongst many Māori signalises the vitality of *te ao Māori* and its relevance to contemporary society in Aotearoa/New Zealand. The cultural revival includes the rebirth of *taonga pūoro*, led by Hirini Melbourne, and the Aotearoa National Māori Performing Arts Festival, led by Tīmoti Kāretu and others, that attracts over 100 000 people. An increasing number of Māori weavers, carvers and fashion designers profile Māori art works at their very best. *Waka-ama* and *waka-tauā* festivals and regattas are becoming popular *whānau* events where participants demonstrate their physical and mental agility.

The revitalisation of *tā moko* among the younger generation of Māori encompasses a political dimension within a traditional Indigenous art form of beautification. As well as enjoying a reviving tradition, many Māori are wearing *tā moko* as a political statement of cultural integrity.

Contemporary Māori music is also a feature of the cultural renaissance. Themes range through historical and political topics from the sacking of Parihaka and Te Whiti and Tohu's commitment to non-violent resistance, to protest against nuclear arms, to cultural and social issues promoting the significance of the Māori language and other aspects of *te ao Māori*. It is significant that many Māori artists are writing and producing their material in the Māori language, which is itself a strong political statement and an assertion of sovereignty.

Māori Studies departments in universities and Wānanga continue to be bastions for the resurgence of Māori language and culture. Māori people often consider them to be extensions of Kura Kaupapa Māori and Wharekura, that advance key principles such as self-determination and sovereignty related to Te Tiriti o Waitangi. Māori Studies has also emerged over time as a force articulating the legitimisation and validation of Indigenous knowledge forms in the national and international academic world. University Māori Studies departments and Wānanga have a legacy of dynamic Māori leadership from people such as the late Ruka Broughton, Wiremu Parker, Bruce Biggs and Hirini Melbourne and current leaders such as Hirini Moko Mead, Ranginui Walker, Pātu Hohepa, Wharehuia Milroy, Koro Dewes, Sir Hugh Kāwharu and Tīmoti Kāretu. These leaders, and many others have been the 'critic and conscience of our nation', heightening the awareness of Māori issues in society and challenging the Crown about Indigenous people's rights (Mead, 1997). Collectively, they have contributed to the evolving cultural mosaic of society in

Te Urupatu, a Tūhoe protest camp at Ruātoki on the boundary of land confiscated in the nineteenth century

Aotearoa/New Zealand, advancing the voice of Māori people for Māori sovereignty.

Global Indigenous people's rights

> *We declare that Indigenous peoples of the world have the right to self-determination, and in exercising that right must be recognised as the exclusive owners of their culture and intellectual property* (The Mātaatua Declaration on Cultural and Intellectual Property Rights of Indigenous Peoples, 1993).

The assertion of Māori sovereignty also contributes to the struggle by Indigenous peoples globally to achieve self-determination. Most Indigenous peoples throughout the world, and particularly those who have suffered the impact and effects of colonisation, have for the last 30 years argued that they have been denied the right to be Indigenous – a right that embraces the retention of their languages, cultures, traditions and spirituality under the mantle of self-determination. There exists a raft of international charters, conventions and other instruments which recognise the basic human rights of peoples (The Coolangatta Statement 1999). These include:

- the Coolangatta Statement: World Indigenous Peoples' Conference on Education – Hilo, Hawai'i, August 6, 1999
- the Universal Declaration of Human Rights – General Assembly of the United Nations, December 10, 1948
- the International Convenant on Economic, Social, and Cultural Rights – General Assembly of the United Nations, December 16, 1966
- the International Covenant on Civil and Political Rights – General Assembly of the United Nations, December 16, 1966
- the International Convention on the Elimination of All Forms of Racial Discrimination – General Assembly of the United Nations, January 4, 1969
- the Discrimination (Employment and Occupation) Convention – Geneva, June 25, 1958
- the Convention Against Discrimination in Education – Paris, 1960
- the Draft Declaration on the Rights of Indigenous Peoples – United Nations Working group, (latest version: April 2003)
- the Kari-Oca Declaration – Brazil, May 30, 1992
- the Mātaatua Declaration on Cultural and Intellectual Property Rights of Indigenous Peoples – Whakatāne, June 1993.

While these instruments provide some basis for recognising the rights of Indigenous peoples, they are extremely limited in their capacity to protect those rights (The Coolangatta Statement 1999). However, each of these instruments contains a common theme, which argues the rights of Indigenous peoples as citizens in the world. For example, Article 27 of the International Covenant on Civil and Political Rights, 1966 states:

> *In those States in which ethnic, religious or linguistic minorities exist, persons, belonging to such minorities shall not be denied the right, in community with*

> the other members of their group, to enjoy their own culture, and to profess and practice their own religion, and to use their own language.

The Draft Declaration on the Rights of Indigenous Peoples (July, 1993) asserts:

> Indigenous peoples have the right of self-determination. By virtue of that right they freely determine their political status and freely pursue their economic, social and cultural development (Article 3).

The Kari-Oca Declaration entitled 'Indigenous Peoples' Earth Charter (May 1993) states:

> The use of existing Indigenous languages is our right. These languages must be protected. At local, national, and international levels, governments must commit funds to new and existing resources to education and training for Indigenous peoples to achieve their sustainable development, to contribute and to participate in sustainable and equitable development at all levels. Particular attention should be given to Indigenous women, children and youth.

The Coolangatta Statement, 1999, 1.3.1 argues:

> Volumes of studies, research and reports dealing with Indigenous people in non-Indigenous educational systems paint a familiar picture of failure and despair. When measured in non-Indigenous terms, the educational outcomes of Indigenous peoples are still far below that of non-Indigenous peoples. This fact exists not because Indigenous peoples are less intelligent, but because educational theories and practices are developed and controlled by non-Indigenous peoples. Thus, in more recent times, due to the involvement of Indigenous peoples, research shows that failure is that of the system, not of Indigenous people.
>
> In this context the so-called 'dropout rates and failures' of Indigenous peoples within non-Indigenous educational systems must be viewed for what they really are – rejection rates.

It is against this background that Māori assertions of sovereignty (or *rangatiratanga*) can be understood as one of the many challenges by Indigenous peoples in the world seeking the fundamental right to be Indigenous and to live as Indigenous peoples; and not simply exist as images or reflections of the values and cultural practices of non-Indigenous societies.

FURTHER READING

Ranginui Walker (1987, 1990, 1996) has reported on contemporary challenges and his various writings offer the best introduction for events up to 1995.

Chapter 18

Te tāminga o te mātauranga Māori
Colonisation in education

Brendan Hokowhitu

This chapter provides an analysis of State education and its effect on Māori since colonisation. It begins by examining missionary education and the subsequent initiation of State education, followed by discussions on:
- the channelling of Māori into non-academic curricula areas;
- the deficit theories of the 1960s;
- the steps taken towards biculturalism in the 1970s;
- Taha Māori and Tomorrow's Schools.[1]

Essentially, the chapter outlines how State education has historically failed to provide a viable education for Māori. It shows how, initially, colonisers saw the education of Māori in the context of a need to 'civilise' them. Education was also viewed as a way of creating a cultural rupture between one generation of Māori and the next. Later research and commentary by twentieth century historians describes how the State education supplied to Māori up until the 1960s was not of an equal standard to that supplied to Pākehā – rather it was based on curricula that channelled them into non-academic areas and away from access to academic qualifications (and subsequent white-collar employment). Later, the 'failure'[2] of Māori to gain academic qualifications was blamed on Māori parents and the environment of the 'traditional' Māori home. The chapter also shows how, since 1970, State education has offered only diluted versions of *tikanga Māori* in the curricula.

 ## Missionary education

Initially, missionaries and early settlers viewed the civilisation of Māori through education as an evangelical and humanitarian duty. Indeed, policies of control and assimilation through education were justified by the idea that Māori were in a state of 'barbarism' and hence, in need of deliverance through education. In 1808, Samuel Marsden recommended the construction of missionary schools for 'a nation who have derived no advantages hitherto either from commerce or the Arts of Civilisation, and therefore must be in a State of Heathen Darkness and Ignorance' (cited Harvard-Williams, 1961: 115). Missionaries encouraged Māori to adopt European customary, moral and commercial practices, for only a civilised person could hope to be accepted as one of God's flock. Consequently, most missionaries deplored Māori values, attitudes and perceptions and attempted to change Māori views of the world thus interrupting the flow of *tikanga Māori* from one generation to the next. Guided by righteous intent, the first missionaries arrived in 1814 with the goal of replacing Māori cultural institutions with 'civilised' European faculties. The first mission school was established by Thomas Kendall in 1816 at Rangihoua in the Bay of Islands.

Many Māori initially viewed missionary settlements as a means of attaining certain skills (such as literacy) which they felt were necessary to help them deal with Pākehā. Yet Māori resistance to mission schools grew as they became increasingly aware that missionaries taught only a constrictive (i.e. biblical) form of literacy that would not help, but actually hinder their negotiation capabilities with settlers and the emerging Government. Literacy, 'within the constraints applied by missionaries, offered [Māori] little help in dealing with either the settlers or the new government (Smith, 1990:73).

 ## The initiation of State education

Until the mid-1860s missionaries, as they did throughout the world, provided those they sought to 'civilise' with a European style of education. The growing resistance by Māori to what they felt was a constrictive form of education led to debates in Parliament. Most politicians agreed that education was important in the process of civilising Māori. It could have influence over younger Māori, and thus establish a cultural divide between them and the older generation. Parliamentarians who debated the Native Schools Act (1867) clearly feared that Māori who were not educated were more likely to revolt against colonial practices. Major Heaphy, for example, argued that 'any expenditure in [Native Education] would be true economy, as the more the natives were educated the less would be the future expenditure on police and gaols' (cited Harker and McConnochie, 1985: 93). The debates also focused on 'the assimilation of Maori children into European culture and society' (Harker and McConnochie, 1985: 92). Henry Carleton, the Under-secretary of the Native Department, insisted that 'the traditional Maori lifestyle could not be tolerated to continue … things have now come to pass that it was necessary either to exterminate the Natives or to civilise them' (cited in Barrington and Beaglehole, 1974: 102). In

Pupils and teachers of Te Whāiti Native School in the Urewera country, Central North Island, 1911

short, education was seen as an agent of social change for Māori that would benefit the colony. The Native Schools Act (1867) placed the jurisdiction of Māori education under the Department of Native Affairs, and in doing so, replaced mission schools with a national system of secular Māori Village Day-Schools.

The imposition of a British model of education onto Māori was justified by the notion that 'for a people in the position of the Maori race it was a first condition of their progress to put them in the way of learning the language of the inhabitants and government of the colony' (James Crowe Richmond – Minister of Native Affairs; cited in Harker and McConnochie, 1985: 92). In reality this meant that Māori pupils were to be assimilated into an educational system with a policy of encouraging the acceptance of British values while disestablishing the validity of *tikanga Māori*.

Colin McGeorge found that nineteenth-century New Zealand school textbooks commonly outlined differences in race in order to explain the 'growth of the British Empire and New Zealand's unique place in that empire'. He described the classroom history surrounding the New Zealand wars, as a 'travesty of Maori military ability.' Accounts of British victories were either hyperbole or untrue; Māori successes were 'played down as incidents on the way to European victory'. (McGeorge, 1993: 64 and 70). Contrasting the superiority of the British race with other weaker races, such as Māori, was intended to foster imperialistic nationalism in colonies such as New Zealand. British history was the story of a 'long struggle to preserve ancient freedoms and of the clearer and clearer manifestation of the British passion for liberty and justice … weaker races could count themselves lucky to be under British rule' (McGeorge, 1993: 65). Imperialistic rhetoric demonstrated the virtues of being a British colonial subject. Early school journals portrayed a hard-won history based on bloodshed and valour. A perfect example is *The Story of the Union Jack*: 'It is only a small bit of bunting, It is only an old coloured rag. Yet thousands have died for its honour. And shed their best blood for The Flag' (New Zealand Education Department, 1908: 52).

Those who hold power in a society determine what constitutes legitimate knowledge and what makes it superior to or more prestigious than other beliefs. As a result, education authorities based the initial curriculum almost entirely on British instruction. Colonists viewed Māori knowledge as an obstacle to colonisation and the assimilation of Māori. McGeorge (1993) suggests that throughout New Zealand's educational history many Pākehā have resented the inclusion of *tikanga Māori* in the syllabus, finding it 'disconcerting and threatening' (77). Similarly, many *kaumātua* actively resisted the encroachment of Pākehā values: 'the tremendous unequivocal power of the elders, who cling tenaciously to custom and tradition, has been the force opposed to the ready acceptance of European ideas and ideals' (Ball, 1940: 304). Simon (1990) maintains that this resistance led to a strategy of separating 'young Maori from the influence of their elders' (112). In 1899, for instance, a circular was sent to all police commanding officers stating that, 'complaints have reached the government that native tohunga are increasing in number and that they are disturbing the native mind and becoming assertive … take effective steps to bring the offenders to justice' (cited Williams, 2002: 190). Soon after, in 1908, the Tohunga Suppression Act imposed penalties on *tohunga* for imparting their world-view.

It thus became an imperative to invalidate Māori educational philosophies and practices. *Mātauranga Māori* was represented to both Māori and Pākehā as an invalid system of an ancient world that merely supplied insights into the culture of primitive peoples.

The initial State schools proved instrumental in fragmenting Māori because they worked entirely within Western educational frameworks, complete with built-in sets of values and assumptions that cut through the social fabric of Māori society, and teachers who were instructed to be role models of a more civilised way of life. The 'hidden curriculum' in the schooling of Māori attempted to change them to resemble their white brethren. Māori citizenship in an 'egalitarian' State meant subjection to an education system that limited their access to knowledge and ultimately confined many of them to physical labour employment and, consequently, to the lower classes (Hokowhitu, 2002: 82).

Physical labour

Schools influenced the development of strata within the society, serving 'as a social filter, determining the composition of a new middle class, deciding who would enter the white collar professional occupations and who would not' (Fairburn, 1975: 9). As a consequence, Māori communities were to be 'reduced to serving as a reserve army of wage labour for Europeans' (Simon, 1990: 88).

Māori were offered a limited curriculum based upon their perceived natural affiliation with physical skills. Politicians realised that if the dream of a pastoral South Seas Britain was to eventuate, New Zealand required cheap agricultural labour:

> *'Industrial training' clearly was a euphemism for the hard labour of breaking in the land. [Education], while denying Maori children opportunities to gain access to the sort of knowledge they sought and which might assist them in their relations with Pakeha, was preparing them instead for life as agricultural labourers … Maori resistance to this state of affairs … was being rationalised as 'parent apathy'* (Simon, 1990: 76).

Pupils at Whakarewarewa Native School, gathered around the gymnastic apparatus, 1909

18 Te tāminga o te mātauranga Māori

Pupils working in the school gardens at Te Aute College, Hawke's Bay, circa 1913

Essentially, Māori were to receive a 'physical education' that constrained access to the skills and qualifications necessary to compete in the workplace. The provision of free education was underpinned by an egalitarian rhetoric of universal education for all, yet the product of free education was a docile labour force designed to secure the interests of the Pākehā.

Before 1880, the curricula of the Native Schools were mainly based on reading and writing in English and arithmetic. James H. Pope, appointed Inspector of Native Schools, broadened the curriculum to include agricultural, technical, and health instruction. Consecutive Ministers of Education from 1880 deemed the education suitable for Pākehā children as being 'too academic' for Māori. Many Māori parents, however, questioned the level of their children's education: 'I do not think so very much of farming being taught to the children – a Maori can easily teach himself,' said Īhāia Hūtana, 'but there are other trades of which the Pakeha possess a knowledge that I would like to see established' (cited Simon, 1990: 99). However, Māori continued to be portrayed as unintelligent and suited only to physical work.

Nineteenth century educational policy and practice endorsed this image, casting Māori as naturally physical and of limited intelligence. These misrepresentations were perpetuated into the twentieth century, and were continually reinforced as Māori were 'educated' in their roles of agricultural workers, to be employed by Pākehā farmers.

Reverend Butterfield, the headmaster of a Gisborne Māori boarding school, told the Young Māori Party in 1910 that Māori were:

> ... not fitted to the various professions. About 999 out of 1000 could not bear the strain of higher education. In commerce, the Maori could not hope to compete with the Pakeha. In trades the Maoris [sic] were splendid copyists, but not

originators. As carpenters they would cope under a capable instructor but not otherwise. Agriculture was the one calling suitable for Maoris [sic] … It was therefore necessary to teach them the 'nobility of labour' (cited Barrington, 1988: 49).

Thomas Strong, the Director of Education from the late 1920s to the mid-1930s, continued to place limits on Māori access to knowledge. Strong was surprised and disturbed to find that in some schools, Māori were allowed to learn 'the intricacies of numerical calculations'. He warned that educating 'the dark races' and encouraging 'pupils to a stage far beyond their present needs or their possible future needs' was a 'fatal facility' (Strong, 1931: 194).

In 1941, Thomas Fletcher, the Inspector of Native Schools, identified home-making, building, furniture-making, cooking, and child-rearing as the staple curriculum of the newly established Native District Secondary Schools. In so doing, the Department of Education maintained its tradition of designing a curriculum that limited opportunities for Māori. For example, with no School Certificate courses in Native District Secondary Schools, pupils could not gain the qualifications necessary to compete in the broader workplace.

Urbanisation in the mid-twentieth century meant that large numbers of young Māori families relocated to new State-housing zones such as Ōtara and Porirua, with the resulting demise of Native Schools. By 1969, all Māori children were being educated in the general public schools (Simon, 1998: xix). Urbanisation also hastened a progressive change in the Māori boys' curriculum, with a greater emphasis on training for trades. Prior to the 1930s, one of the rationales for training Māori boys to be farmers was so that Māori leaders could remain with their communities. Urbanisation and the developing need for labourers in urban centres debunked the earlier rationale. Māori were increasingly trained in trades for jobs in cities. The search for employment forced many young Māori men and women, and consequently, young Māori families, to leave their *hapū*. Māori were no longer needed as farmers and farmers' wives, rather they were needed as carpenters and carpenters' wives (Ramsay, 1972: 67–71).

 ## Cultural deficit theories

The limited form of education available to Māori until the late 1950s saw them trapped in the lower socio-economic groups: 'It was quite easy to produce an educational elite; that had been done in the 1890s and 1900s. It was far harder to produce a range of educational achievement and an occupational profile that corresponded with those of the Pakeha' (Butterworth, 1973: 14). Māori were culturally different and, in the main, economically different to Pākehā. Education meant assimilation into Pākehā values, attitudes and employment. As a result, Māori often viewed other Māori who achieved educational success as white Māori or 'plastic' Māori. While Pākehā researchers discussed the deprived nature of the Māori home and its impact on educational achievement, many Māori resisted an education that demanded assimilation to the dominant values. Such behaviour occurred despite the corresponding economic ramifications. Māori were in a no-win situation – assimilate or fail. Many chose to hold on to their cultural values and not to assimilate and, as a result, were seen as failures in the Pākehā world.

However, in 1955, 88 years after the enactment of State education, the educational establishment gave Māori a voice for the first time. The Education Department invited a group of Māori leaders to consult with a committee regarding the education of Māori youth. Based on what they had experienced in State education themselves, the group made a number of recommendations that prioritised access to all forms of education for Māori, and an increase of *tikanga Māori* in the curriculum. Unfortunately, most of these suggestions were implemented in a half-hearted way.

Attitudes towards Māori education changed in the 1960s. Whereas previous policy overtly subjugated Māori, Māori 'failure' now began to be viewed as something to define and rectify. The Hunn Report of 1961 considered the integration of *tikanga Māori* into State curricula. Jack Hunn believed the 'Maori problem' would be annulled by integration, defining the official policy of integration as a combination of Māori and Pākehā cultures to form one nation, where Māori culture would remain distinct. However, 'the reality was more like the *kahawai* and the shark analogy. "Let's integrate", said the shark to the *kahawai*. "Have I any choice?"' (Ka'ai-Oldman, 1980: 24). By 'integration' Hunn did not mean the acceptance of *tikanga Māori* as a living vibrant culture, rather the preservation of interesting cultural fossils that might 'keep Maoris happy but which otherwise had little relevance to modern life' (Butterworth, 1973: 15). Hunn defined those features of Māori culture worth conserving as 'the chief relics' (Hunn, 1961: 15).

Hunn's report is also significant because it acknowledged that there was a 'Māori problem' in State education, yet it blamed the State's failure to educate Māori on Māori parents and the 'traditional' Māori home environment. The Report led to a raft of educational research and new policies that shied away from the historical past and hid behind the rhetoric of 'improving the lot of the Maori child' (New Zealand Educational Institute, 1967: 7). The initial response to Hunn's recommendations was the Currie Report of 1962, compiled by the Commission of Education. In this report, Māori education was elevated to an area of concern. The report focused on bridging the gap between Māori and Pākehā students. The blame for the 'statistical blackout'[3] was squarely levelled at poor parenting and parental apathy and thus removed any historical blame from the education system for creating the disparity between Māori and Pākehā. The report stated that:

> *The school has no power to remove the social handicaps under which the Maori pupil frequently labours ... too many live in large families in inadequately sized and even primitive homes, lacking privacy, quiet, and even light for study: too often there is a dearth of books, pictures, educative material generally, to stimulate the growing child ... the Maori custom by which children are so frequently brought up by grand-parents puts a gap between the generations that is not helpful to change ... and even good ability may be frustrated by parental apathy towards education* (The Commission on Education in New Zealand, 1962: 415–418).

Such beliefs led to the 'deficit model' that characterised much of the educational research regarding Māori in the 1960s. Western psychological models of cognitive development claimed 'deficiencies of early childhood experience ... induced growth deficits that interfered progressively with subsequent development and learning' (Simon, 1990: 134). To consolidate the racially based assumptions of deficiency, a plethora of normative intelligence tests were produced, 'designed around the language and cultural capital of the white middle classes' (Smith, 1999: 68). Some researchers defined Māori children as 'retarded' based on Western models of developmental psychology; essentially, they were found to be intellectually un-stimulated based on another culture's criteria of intellectual stimulation. Malcolm Lovegrove (1966: 31–34), for example, concluded that

> Maori and European children from almost comparable home backgrounds performed similarly on tests of scholastic achievement ... the reasons for Maori retardation are more probably attributable to the generally deprived nature of Māori home conditions, [which are not suited] to the complex intellectual processes assessed by tests of intelligence ... compared with the surroundings in which the European child grows, typical Maori homes are less visually and verbally complex, and less consciously organised to provide a variety of experiences which will broaden and enrich the intellectual understandings of their children.

In other words, Lovegrove's analysis argued that Māori children who had been successfully assimilated into Pākehā culture did just as well as Pākehā on Pākehā tests, but non-assimilated Māori children did not. Furthermore, he blamed the retardation of Māori children on the rural and traditional cultural environment, rather than the culturally biased tests. Tragically, as with the Hunn Report, which 'became the touchstone of Government policy for the 1960s and 1970s' (Williams, 2002: 81), Lovegrove's conclusions and findings formed the basis of subsequent research and informed educational policy and practice for several years to come.

In large urban primary schools and secondary schools, the majority of Māori found themselves in low streams based on the standardised intelligence or achievement testing described above. Curricula in lower streams focused primarily on practical rather than intellectual skills; thus Māori still found themselves channelled into manual labour and unable to access high-status knowledge areas. As was the case in the nineteenth century, Māori were taught subjects that denied them access to the type of knowledge needed for entrance into positions of power, while their success in manual training programmes legitimised their placement there. Unlike Pākehā, who enjoyed a normal spread throughout occupational strata, 'nearly 90 per cent of Māori men [were] employed as farmers, foresters, labourers, transport operators, factory workers, or in other skilled and unskilled occupations' (Watson, 1967: 6). The poor statistics were attributed to individual failure rather than the historical failure of the academic system to educate Māori.

Steps toward biculturalism in the 1970s?

In 1970, for only the second time in New Zealand history, Māori were allowed to officially voice their concerns regarding the education of their youth. In stark contrast to the deficit theories of the 1960s, the National Advisory Committee on Māori Education (NACME) attributed the failure of Māori students to a 'lack of recognition of Maori culture in the curriculum'. Moreover, in reaction to normative intelligence testing, the report suggested that 'too many Maori children find themselves in a failure situation by being placed in slow learner groups where they quickly lose interest in schooling' (cited Simon, 1990: 141). The group recommended that classes should comprise 'heterogeneous groups' rather than streams based on intelligence tests.

However, history has shown that State education never seriously considered genuine biculturalism. In the 1970s and beyond, the concept of assimilation has remained the core of education. In the New Zealand Official Yearbook of 1977, the Department of Education demonstrates its devotion to one nation: 'We are, as a nation, committed to a policy of integration: two races, one people …. Any restatement of educational objectives must give full weight to it' (955). It was a timely warning to Māori that State education was prepared to offer only token and diluted versions of Māori culture, and that biculturalism, in its full sense, was not on its agenda. Assimilation of Māori was still the priority.

Taha Māori programmes

An outcome of the reports discussed above was Taha Māori. It was initiated in 1975 to represent those aspects of Māori culture that should be integrated into 'the philosophy, the organisation and the content of the school' (New Zealand Department of Education, 1984: 1). Taha Māori was intended to comprise traditional *tikanga Māori*. It was a first step, but in reality, the culture represented was static and tokenistic. It gave only an air of biculturalism while preserving the tenets of assimilation. This is evident in the Department of Education's list of Māori culture suitable for the school environment:

> *A formal powhiri to visitors to the school, a Maori contribution to school assemblies, school representations at death observances, the careful and accurate pronunciation of Maori names by students and staff, the use of Maori greetings when appropriate, and the use of Maori designs and art forms in the school environment* (New Zealand Department of Education, 1984: 33).

Wary of disrupting the curriculum and of opposition from teachers, the Department of Education required only a very simplistic and basic knowledge of *tikanga Māori*. The result was that Taha Māori was not to be 'too difficult as the objective of the programme was to win friends'; thus, Taha Māori was to be 'invisible,' was 'not to appear as a new subject' and was to merely add a few 'strands to the existing curriculum' (Jenkins and Ka'ai, 1994: 155). Essentially, Taha Māori represented a version of Māori culture so Eurocentric that Māori barely recognised it as their own.

Even so, Taha Māori still met some resistance from teachers. Many teachers based their objections on their desire for a mono-cultural society:

> *I would like to educate New Zealanders and not Maoris and Pakehas … we're living in a European society and I personally believe that if Maoris want their culture retained … it should be the Maori people who are doing it … I don't see why we should learn the Maori language. I've been overseas a lot and it won't serve any purpose to anybody … We've had a terrific lot of comment from European families … Our parents don't think we should be doing this* (cited Simon, 1990: 205).

Such beliefs still reflected early colonial perceptions. Māori culture was seen by some as irrelevant to modern society. Some teachers did, however, view Taha Māori as the first steps to bi-culturalism:

> 'What I would like to happen is [through tikanga Māori] to have the Pakeha children just expect to have a whole generation without this negative feedback we are getting now [so] that these Pakeha children grow up more accepting of other cultures' (cited Simon, 1990: 199).

Labour and Tomorrow's Schools

The 1984 Labour Government introduced a number of economic and political policies based on New Right ideologies that adversely affected the emerging voice of Māori. The tenets of 'user pays' were applied to education.

Brian Picot, an economist originally brought to New Zealand to examine the forestry industry, headed a committee that eventually formed a blueprint for educational developments known as Tomorrow's Schools. The Picot Report recommended a radical devolution of power from the centralised Regional Education Boards to communally administered Boards of Trustees. Elected members accepted legal responsibility for the governance and management of their schools in partnership with their employee, the principal. Unfortunately, Tomorrow's Schools discriminated against minority groups. Those schools that lacked parents with skills in economics or other professions struggled to run their school as a business and, consequently, struggled to compete in the educational market place. Schools in affluent urban areas typically drew on parents with a range of professional skills as Board members. Conversely, parents in poor urban and rural areas often lacked the necessary skills to run their schools commercially.

Tomorrow's Schools implied that local communities would gain more control over the education of their children. For example, the Picot Report suggested that a devolution of power from the state to the community level would benefit Māori because *whānau*, who became elected members of a board, would be given the power to effect change in the education of their children. However, the shift in power associated with Tomorrow's Schools was illusionary. It merely released the Government from full responsibility, and it did 'not guarantee that those disadvantaged [would] be any better off' (Smith, 1991: 11–12). The survival of *tikanga Māori* within State education was transferred in part from the hands of educational policy writers to the hands of the general public. In a country where most people subscribe to the principles of one person/one vote and majority rule, many Māori and some minority groups struggled to find a voice on School Boards.

Conclusion

With the continued success of total immersion initiatives such as Te Kōhanga Reo and Te Kura Kaupapa (see Chapter 19), Māori are seriously questioning the outcomes of State education for their children, and the tokenistic form of Māori cultural inclusion to which it subscribes. In a highly publicised criticism of State education, Māori politician Tāriana Tūria, asked a group of educators 'why Māori should leave their children within an education system that has consistently failed them, and will continue to do so whether bicultural frameworks are in place or not'. Such cynicism appears warranted; most Māori educational researchers regard the current supposedly bicultural initiatives, such as Taha Māori, as disempowering. As has been the case since the inception of State education in Aotearoa/New Zealand, there is a serious discontinuity between what many Māori want in the education of their children and what is currently being provided. In the past, Māori parents wanted an education system that allowed their children to compete on an equal footing with their Pākehā peers. Today Māori parents want an education system that values Māori students by demonstrating that it values their culture.

Māori parents need to be given the power to make decisions that will inform the outcome of their children's education, based on *tikanga Māori*. Given the historical evidence, the likelihood of this happening in New Zealand State education is highly doubtful, for as Audre Lorde states: 'The master's tools will never dismantle the master's house' (cited Smith, 1999: 19).

Notes

1 From the early years of the twentieth century the prohibition of *te reo* by State education aided significantly in the oppression of Māori. However, the banishment of *te reo* in State schools is not covered in this chapter as it is discussed in depth in the chapter that follows.

2 Emphasised here to indicate the author's belief that the education system has failed Māori rather than that Māori have failed in the education system.

3 Crude term for those statistics that demonstrate the impoverishment of Māori.

FURTHER READING

Simon (1998) discusses missionary education and Native Schools; a thorough discussion of the channelling of Māori into physical labour through State education can be found in Barrington (1988); and for the history of State education and Māori see Jenkins and Ka'ai (1994). For further reading on Tomorrow's Schools see Smith (1991).

Chapter 19

Te mana o te reo me ngā tikanga
Power and politics of the language

Tānia M. Ka'ai

Māori have fought for the survival of *te reo Māori*, in response to colonisation, because it is the life-blood of their culture. In 1987 it became an official language of Aotearoa/New Zealand; however, the quest to keep *te reo* a living language has at times been an arduous one. This chapter will look at the highs and lows of that challenge, discussing the difficulties inherent in a society that banned *te reo* from the education system for over 70 years; an education system that also disadvantaged Māori students in other ways. The Pākehā education system focuses on age-specific learning, regardless of ability or readiness; a concept that is alien to the Māori style of learning. Since the early 1980s Māori have responded to this challenge with the establishment of their own system of teaching and learning. This chapter will briefly outline those initiatives demonstrating that education is an ongoing life experience that involves the entire *whānau*, *hapū* and *iwi*. These initiatives have contributed to the revitalisation of the Māori language.

In the 1970s John Rangihau (known affectionately as Te Rangihau), an authority on Māori knowledge for all peoples in Aotearoa/New Zealand and a leader with prophetic insight, developed a model (see Chapter 2) which complemented his nation-wide lectures on *Māoritanga* and bicultural development. It is a widely held view that Te Rangihau, in his powerful delivery of his conceptual model, was a catalyst for social change in New Zealand. Articulate and eloquent in both Māori and English, he commanded respect from Māori and Pākehā across the country. The effect of his work at that time spearheaded huge philosophical shifts in the minds of those who were privileged to hear his message. The effects were twofold. Te Rangihau made the Pākehā aware of the Māori world-view and revolutionised the rights and status of the Indigenous people of New Zealand. Using the model, he made Māori people aware of the value and status of *te reo Māori* and of Māori knowledge, customs and practices. He also engendered a spiritual awakening in young Māori academics of this time to critically analyse and intellectualise the course of events from first contact with Pākehā to the present day (see Figure 19.1). This required an examination of the relationship between the rights and status of Māori people as the Indigenous people of New Zealand, and social, political, and economic trends throughout the history of this country's development.

In his conceptual model, Te Rangihau connects *te reo* to politics, *mauri* and *mana*. This is most significant because it provides some understanding of the passionate response of Māori people to the decline of the Māori language. Te Rangihau argued that without their language, Māori are unlikely to participate effectively in cultural debates and political decision-making on the *marae*. This point relates directly to Māori politics. They are also likely to suffer from a loss of self-esteem and confidence, which relates to *mauri*. The combination of these factors is likely to cause Māori people to experience a huge sense of dislocation and powerlessness in managing their own affairs, which in turn relates to *mana*. The interconnectedness of the conceptual model identifies the key cultural concepts which frame Māori society.

Sir James Hēnare when giving evidence in 1986 to the Waitangi Tribunal relating to the WAI 11 claim lodged about *te reo Māori* said:

> ... the language is the core of our Maori culture and mana. Ko te reo te mauri o te mana Maori (The language is the life force of the mana Maori). If the language dies, as some predict, what do we have left to us? Then, I ask our own people who are we?
>
> 'Language,' according to Oliver Wendell Holmes, 'is a solemn thing, it grows out of life, out of its agonies and its ecstasies, its wants and its weariness. Every language is a temple in which the soul of those who speak it is enshrined.' Therefore, the taonga, our Maori language, as far as our people are concerned, is the very soul of the Maori people. What does it profit a man to gain the whole world but suffer the loss of his own soul? What profit to the Maori if we lose our language and lose our soul? Even if we gain the world. To be mono-lingual, a Japanese once said, is to know only one universe ... (Waikerepuru and Nga Kaiwhakapumau I Te Reo Incorporated Society, 1986: 40–41).

In 1987 the Māori language became an official language (Māori Language Act) in Aotearoa/New Zealand and the Māori Language Commission was established. However, the struggle for its survival is set against a backdrop of colonisation. It is suggested that attitudes to language reflect reaction not to language itself – its aesthetics or its utility – but to the people who speak it (Bell, 1990). Therefore, it follows that Pākehā reaction to the Māori language is a mirror of Pākehā attitudes to the Māori people. Hence, it is such attitudes that have brought the Māori language to the edge of extinction over the last 150 years of Pākehā settlement. The process has been brought about by a culmination of political power and social pressure which has seen significant elements of Māori culture undergo a steady, cumulative deterioration. This is best understood by revisiting the history of education in Aotearoa/New Zealand, as it provides the setting for the revival of Māori language through *kaupapa Māori* initiatives.

Chronology of dates and events	
1816	Formal education began in New Zealand with the opening of the first mission schools by Kendall at Rangihoua in the Bay of Islands. Education provided by missionaries was conveyed in Māori.
1840	The Treaty of Waitangi was signed establishing the concept of partnership between Pākehā and Māori. Māori was the predominant language of Aotearoa/New Zealand at this time.
1847	George Grey introduced the Education Ordinance Act, that is, an assimilation policy.
1850s	The Pākehā population exceeded the Māori population. The Māori language became a minority language in Aotearoa/New Zealand society.

19 Power and politics of the language

1867	The introduction of the Native Schools Act saw the establishment of a new pattern of administration providing for a national system of native schools. Māori people provided the land, and the Government the buildings and teachers. The Act also asserted that English should be the only language used in the education of Māori children, although this was not enforced rigorously until 1900.
1880	James Pope, the Inspector of Schools, drew up a Native School Code. Teachers were expected to have some knowledge of the Māori language, but it was to be used only in the junior classes as an aid to teaching English.
1896	The official census recorded the Māori population as reaching its lowest point of 42 113.
1900	Education authorities took a hard line against the Māori language, which was forbidden in the playground. Corporal punishment was administered to children who disobeyed.
1907	The Tohunga Suppression Act was introduced outlawing *tohunga* practices. This, like the assimilation policy of 1847, had the effect of eroding Māori society.
1913	90% of Māori school children were native speakers of the language.
1930/31	There was a change in direction of educational policy. This was in response to the 1925 Advisory Committee on African Education. The report recommended that education should be adapted to the traditions and mentality of the people and their institutions. From 1931, some schools began incorporating aspects of Māori culture into their programmes but without real commitment. An attempt by the New Zealand Federation of Teachers to have the Māori language introduced into the curriculum was blocked by T. B. Strong, the Director of Education. In Strong's view, 'the natural abandonment of the native tongue involves no loss to the Māori.'
1940s	The 28th Māori Battalion joined the World War II allied forces. As a consequence of this, a generation of male native speakers across a number of *iwi* never returned home. This depleted the numbers of speakers of the language. The Māori urban migration began, leaving rural communities depleted.
1950s	Western influences in the cities began to have an influence on Māori families who, as a consequence, raised their children as predominantly English speakers.
1952	Māori Studies was first taught as a university subject at Auckland University.
1960	The Hunn Report drew attention to the educational disparity between Māori and Pākehā. Only 0.5% of Māori children reached the sixth form as against 3.78% of Pākehā. One of the significant contributions of the report was the rejection of the assimilation policy. Māori-Pākehā relationships were redefined in terms of 'integration'. But minimal attention was given to Hunn's interpretation that integration means to combine, not fuse the Māori and Pākehā elements to form one nation wherein Māori culture remains distinct. Between 1900 and 1960, the number of Māori fluent in the Māori language had decreased from 95% to 25%.
1963	The Currie Report emphasised the need to centralise the notion of Māori educational underachievement, and so began the flood of compensatory education programmes.
1967	The Report on Māori Education reflected a growing awareness of biculturalism. 'It must be remembered that a Māori is both a New Zealander and Māori. S/he has an inalienable right to be both …'
1970	Ngā Tamatoa and the Te Reo Māori Society lobbied for the introduction of Māori language in schools.
1971	The Report of the National Advisory Committee on Māori Education took Māori education off the plateau of the sixties and advanced the concept of bicultural education.
1973	All seven Teachers Colleges had established courses in Māori Studies. Presentation of a Māori language petition to Parliament by Ngā Tamatoa.
1976	123 secondary schools were recorded as teaching Māori language as a curriculum subject.

19 Te mana o te reo me ngā tikanga

1979	The Te Ātaarangi Movement was established as a community initiative to teach Māori language to adults.
1980	The Report of the Advisory Council for Māori Education stated '… impressive as these gains in education appear, deeply entrenched attitudes are not changed overnight … negative attitudes to things Māori remain the legacy from our colonial history of cultural imperialism.' Television New Zealand screened *Koha*, a 30-minute Māori magazine programme. Experiments and pilots in Māori radio broadcasting led to the establishment of Te Upoko o te Ika in Wellington.
1981	The Hui Whakatauira of Māori leaders proposed and established the first Te Kōhanga Reo as a response to the imminence of language death.
1985	The first Kura Kaupapa Māori was established at Hoani Waititi Marae, West Auckland.
1986	The Report of the Waitangi Tribunal on the Te Reo Māori Claim (WAI 11) asserted that *te reo Māori* was a *taonga* guaranteed protection under Article II of Te Tiriti o Waitangi.
1987	The Māori Language Act recognised Māori as an official language. At this time the Māori Language Commission, now called Te Taura Whiri i te Reo Māori, was established.
1989	The Education Amendment Act formally recognised Kura Kaupapa Māori and Wānanga as educational institutions.
1993	Te Māngai Pāho, a Māori broadcasting funding agency was established to promote Māori language and culture through the media. More than 20 *iwi* radio stations began broadcasting throughout the country.
1997	There was a strong push from Māori involved in initiatives to increase the numbers of speakers of *te reo Māori*. The effects amounted to 675 Te Kōhanga Reo, established since 1981, catering to 13 505 children. 54 Kura Kaupapa Māori, established since 1985. Three Wānanga had been established since 1981. Over 32 000 students were recorded as receiving Māori medium education. 55 399 students were recorded as learning the Māori language.
1998	The Government announced funding for a Māori television channel.
2001	The number of Māori speakers had stabilised at around 130 500 people between 1996 and 2001, which constitutes 25% of the Māori population.

Missionaries introduced education to Aotearoa/New Zealand at the beginning of colonisation and *te reo* was the main language of instruction. The signing of the Treaty of Waitangi saw the first changes in Government thinking and this was compounded in the 1850s when the Pākehā population exceeded that of Māori (see page 202). However, it was not until after 1900 with the banning of the Māori language in school playgrounds that the use of the language began to decline, leading to generations of Māori being deprived of one of their cultural *taonga*.

By the mid 1970s, the language was in great danger of becoming extinct as a medium of everyday communication. Fluency was restricted to a small number of speakers, many of them middle-aged and older and residents of rural areas. Fluent te reo speakers were probably outnumbered four to one by predominantly English speaking people of Māori descent. Consequently, the vast majority of Māori youth was growing up with little or no knowledge of the Māori language or of their Māori heritage (Benton, 1987).

The conclusion was obvious – although *te reo* continued to remain an emotive force in the lives of many Māori, and even though it served as an important indicator of

Māoriness, the viability of *te reo Māori* as a language of daily communication was in serious doubt. As a consequence of this dilemma, drastic and innovative steps were taken to arrest the decline of the Māori language to ensure its maintenance and transmission to the youthful generation (see page 204). It is against this background of language decline and language renaissance that one can begin to explain the origin and popularity of Te Kōhanga Reo and Kura Kaupapa Māori, which alerted the Māori population to the necessity of teaching *te reo* to pre-school and school children as a strategy of language survival and in the long term, of success in education. The unforeseen side effects of Te Kōhanga Reo, Kura Kaupapa Māori, and Wharekura (Māori immersion secondary schools) extend to the many young parents who are not only learning *te reo* with their children, but are also becoming politically active as they grapple with the constraints imposed by Pākehā bureaucracy for an equitable distribution of those resources required to attain their goals.

Form IV students during a mathematics lesson at Te Wharekura o Hoani Waititi in West Auckland, 1996

Te Kōhanga Reo, Kura Kaupapa Māori, and Wharekura are characterised by a set of objectives which are couched in a particular Māori ideology and in which a distinctive pedagogy exists for developing the child at both the social and cognitive level.

Te Kōhanga Reo

The primary objective of Te Kōhanga Reo is summed up in the phrase '*kōrero Māori*' (speak Māori). It is one of total commitment with absolutely no compromise. Its intent is to arrest the decline of Māori-speaking people in New Zealand. Children are immersed in an environment where nothing but *te reo* is heard for a significant part of the day. This is based on the principle that the most effective way of increasing the numbers of Māori language speakers is to focus on young learners.

> *Te tīmatanga o te reo, kei ngā ū o te whāea*
>
> The very beginning of language is learnt at the breast.

Another objective is the commitment to *whānau* principles as the bedrock of the educational initiative. The term *whānau* is employed in the sense of a traditional extended family arrangement whereby children are socialised in an environment surrounded by other children and grandparents, relatives and caregivers of all the children. The concept of *whānau* also embodies a cluster of values such as those naturally associated with a family setting. For example, the virtues of *aroha*, *manaaki* and *wairua*. When these concepts are combined, the idea of Te Kōhanga Reo as an early childhood centre, and Kura Kaupapa Māori and Wharekura thereafter as the natural educational progression, is a powerful process which acknowledges the supportive nature of the extended family as opposed to the fragmentation of the nuclear unit. Inherent in this are specific Māori relationships in both management and instructional settings. The structure fosters pedagogical principles such as *whanaungatanga* (children accepting responsibility for each other in the learning process in order that the whole *whānau* progress as a unit); *tuakana-teina* (suggesting the shifting of roles between teacher and learner and the total acceptance of the responsibility attached to the new role), and *mana tangata* (the preservation of a child's self esteem and self worth at all times). This objective is aimed at giving Māori people greater control over their own lives (self-determination) and the ability to plan and organise their own futures within the context of *whānau* and in some instances, *hapū* and *iwi*.

Te Kōhanga Reo as an educational initiative is best described as an example of *Kaupapa Māori* education. There are four significant components of *Kaupapa Māori* education which set it apart from mainstream education in Aotearoa/New Zealand. These components when combined illustrate the *Kaupapa Māori* educational model.

Tamariki enjoying a social occasion at Te Kohanga Reo o Wharehoa, Wellington

Children at the Te Kura o Ōtari, Wellington, at their *noho marae* ('live-in' on a marae), 2002

Kaupapa Māori ideology

This is a philosophical doctrine, incorporating the knowledge, skills, attitudes and values of Māori society that have emanated from a Māori metaphysical base. It informs Māori about the way in which they best develop physically, spiritually, emotionally, socially and intellectually as a people. Central to this is the notion of pedagogy, the way in which we transmit and receive knowledge within a *whānau*, *hapū* and *iwi* context.

Dr Pita Sharples claims that the way Māori people locate the learner begins with the genesis of Māori people from the sky father, Rangi-nui and the earth mother, Papa-tūā-nuku. From these two come all things. The Māori way of teaching this is through *whakapapa*. Descended from the sky father and the earth mother, the whole world is created and manifested, and in genealogical terms the learners find themselves placed at the end of a family tree. Individuals can be traced across and down their family tree. They can relate to any aspect of life or non-life from the butterfly, to the mountains, to the rain, to the sea, to the *pipi* (shellfish), and in fact to all creatures and things in this world. The placement of learners in the world and their personality are two features to which Māori pedagogy, or preferred learning and teaching styles, apply. This is very much the holistic approach to learning and teaching.

Therefore, it follows that pedagogy is culture specific and not age specific, as in western culture. Māori pedagogy is best understood from the following table, which provides a set of key indicators and descriptors.

19 Te mana o te reo me ngā tikanga

Key indicators of Māori pedagogy	
Indicator	Descriptor
There is a fluidity of roles between teacher and learner, which is based on the concept of *ako*.	*Ako* means to learn and teach; *kaiako* means teacher; *akonga* means learner. There is a unified co-operation of learner and teacher in a single enterprise.
Who teaches and when teaching occurs is central to Māori pedagogy as a mechanism of empowerment for the learner.	Children, rather than the teacher, frequently control the teaching sequences. This is strongly encouraged.
Management and instruction of learning occur from the basis of *tikanga Māori*.	*Whanaungatanga*, *tuakana/teina*, *awhi* (foster and cherish), *tautoko* (support), the use of *nē* or *nē rā* as a way of managing social interaction in a non-threatening manner, *mahi tahi* (co-operative learning), etc.
Non-verbal communication is a significant feature of teaching and learning in Māori contexts.	*Whakamā* (unresponsiveness and a withdrawal from communication with others) in all its forms and contexts
All learning is clothed in the medium of *wairua*.	Feelings of *āhua* (semblance or likeness of something within a specific context e.g.: *āhua ngēngē* meaning somewhat tired), *ihi*, *wana*, *tapu*, *noa* and *wehi* are recognised as central to the learner's learning.
The teacher is a facilitator of learning and recognises that each learner will select his/her own pace of learning. This removes artificial demands on learners to perform in a 'one size fits all' mode.	The *mauri* of the learner is constantly preserved. Failure is removed from the learner's environment.
Whānau participation in the classroom is encouraged and valued.	*Whānau*, *hapū*, *iwi* take responsibility for their children's education.
The use of Māori contexts in teaching such as the *wharenui* reinforces the value of the knowledge being imparted to the learner.	This reaffirms the learner's significant place in the Māori world.
Bringing *tohunga* into the classroom also reinforces the value of the knowledge being transmitted.	*Tohunga raranga* (expert in weaving), *tohunga whakairo* (expert in carving), *tohunga tā moko* (expert in tattooing), *tohunga mō ngā mahi a Te Rēhia* (expert in performing arts), *tohunga taonga pūoro* (expert in traditional Māori instruments), *tohunga o te ao Māori* (expert in the Māori world)
Cooperative learning is encouraged so learners learn to interact with one another, share ideas, problem-solve and to promote one anothers' talents.	The attainment of excellence is strongly promoted using images such as a *wharenui* and a *tohunga whakairo* as examples of excellence in the Māori world.
Māori language is the sole medium of instruction.	This ensures accurate transmission, maintenance and preservation of Māori knowledge, ideology and cultural practices.

Source: Adapted from Ka'ai, 1995: 32–33

 ## Te ara poutama

The weaving pattern called *poutama* is symbolic of the 12 levels of thought and the process of holistic development. It is suggested that the horizontal line of the *poutama*

represents the knowledge being transmitted to the learner in the Māori language by the teacher. It is joined at right angles by a vertical line, which represents the *tikanga* associated with that knowledge. Hence the notion that for all knowledge transmitted there is matching *tikanga* which must be grasped by the learner before the learner can progress to the next level of the *poutama*. This supports the notion that learning is developmental. It should be recognised that before a learner can proceed to the next level, it is assumed that they have gleaned the knowledge from the previous level. The process therefore is learner centred. The transmission of knowledge and the assessment of knowledge can occur in Māori contexts. It is contended that the transmission of knowledge and the *tikanga* implicit must occur in the Māori language to ensure accurate transmission is sustained through succeeding generations.

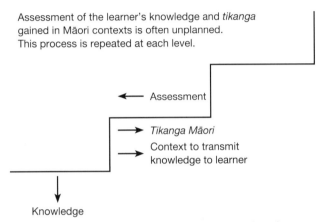

Relationship between the transmission of knowledge, the assessment of knowledge, Māori contexts and *te reo me ngā tikanga Māori*

 ## Tuakiri tangata

Tuakiri tangata refers to the Māori components of the total personality of the Māori learner based on the learner-centred learning process.

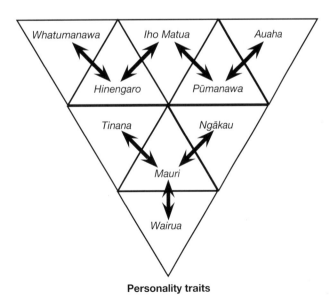

Personality traits

Mauri	The life force of all objects including inanimate objects
Wairua	The spiritual relationships of the learner with the world around them. This includes the various levels of consciousness and the feelings that drive them to certain behaviour.
Iho Matua	The spiritual manifestation of the learner couched in a specific framework. It is the deepest of spiritual relationships that a learner has with people, things and the total environment in which they live.
Tinana	The physical well-being of the learner
Ngākau	The heart of the learner and their ability to feel various emotions
Whatumanawa	Is concerned with processing the deepest of emotions that actually govern the learner's course in life in making decisions about various circumstances or conditions such as love and grief.
Hinengaro	The mental capacity of the learner
Pūmanawa	The learner's potential
Auaha	The creative side of a learner and what they are capable of

Te tātari i te kaupapa

Te tātari i te kaupapa embodies the notion that there is a relationship between theory and practice and that a learner should demonstrate this in the context of their learning. It is suggested that within Māori culture there is a range of opportunities for learners to demonstrate knowledge acquisition. It is on such occasions that rigorous assessment procedures, which are culturally specific to the context, are indeed practised. These occasions are extremely challenging for the learner, who is assessed on their performance in a transient culturally-specific context. The learners are also required to critically assess their own performance. There is an overall expectation that when the opportunity for assessment occurs again, that the learner will improve from the previous occasion.

This notion is captured in the following *tauparapara* (a form of *karakia* before speech-making) from Ngāti Porou:

Tēnei au, tēnei au
Te hōkai nei i ōku tapuwae
Ko te hōkai nuku, ko te hōkai rangi
Ko te hōkai a taku tīpuna a Tāne-nui-a-Rangi
I piki ai ki te Rangi-tūhāhā
Ki te Tihi o Manono
I rokohina atu rā
Ko Io Matua Kore anake
I riro iho ai
Ngā kete o te wānanga
Ko te Kete Tūāuri
Ko te Kete Tūātea
Ko te Kete Aronui
Ka tiritiria, ka poupoua ki Papa-tūā-nuku

> *Papā te whaititiri*
> *Hikohiko te uira*
> *Ka kanapu ki te rangi*
> *I whētuki ki raro rā*
> *Rū ana te whenua e*
> *Ka puta te Ira Tangata*
> *Ki te whaiao, ki te ao mārama*
> *Tihei Mauri Ora.*

This traditional *tauparapara* describes the journey made by Tāne-nui-a-rangi to attain and secure knowledge for Māori people. This knowledge was brought back from the twelfth level of thought, Rangi-tūhāhā, in three separate *kete* (baskets), providing Māori people with the necessary knowledge and skills to survive. The 12 levels of thought begin at the simplest level and progress to the esoteric domain. Implicit is the notion of critical reflection and the challenge of completing a variety of tasks throughout life to further develop and extend one's knowledge base, while still retaining traditional values associated with knowledge, for example, that knowledge belongs to the whole group and that knowledge should be valued and used to benefit others. Also implicit in this *tauparapara* are assessment theories and practices which are derived from the Māori experience and the notion of developmental learning implicit in the well known *tukutuku* pattern called *poutama*.[1]

It is suggested that a learner demonstrates knowledge acquisition in culturally-specific contexts and that the rigorous assessment procedures applied should be based on specific cultural imperatives which could translate into performance criteria. This form of assessment could be described as an integrated approach to standards-based assessment where performance and achievement are measured against a clear set of standards.

> *Ko te reo Māori te iho o te ahurea, arā, ko te mātauranga*
> *me ngā āhuatanga katoa o te ao Māori.*
>
> *The Māori language is the lifeline of our culture of which knowledge*
> *is the cornerstone for a Māori world view* (Ka'ai, 1995: 37).

In the Māori world, *kaumātua* are considered repositories of knowledge. It is reasonable to assume that they have acquired this knowledge over a lifetime of learning and experience. They are recognised as experts or gifted in a myriad of areas such as:

- *te reo Māori*
- *tikanga Māori*
- *whakapapa*
- *waiata*
- *haka*
- tribal history
- fishing
- the production of food

- restoration of *wharenui*
- conservation
- *whakairo*
- *tukutuku*
- *rongoā*
- *karakia*
- *hui*
- protocol
- the role of women and men
- the parenting and education of children
- resource management.

It is accepted that all *kaumātua* have a contribution to make to the life and well-being of a community. It is also accepted that as repositories of this myriad of knowledge, they have a responsibility to ensure the transmission of this knowledge to younger generations to avoid it being lost. It then follows that these people determine:

- to whom this knowledge will be given;
- the process of handing this knowledge over to succeeding generations;
- the timeframe over which this knowledge will be shared;
- the assessment of the candidate being groomed to receive this knowledge and the process of learning it.

Selection is not age-specific. It is based primarily on the demonstration of ability or skill in a particular area. With selection, however, comes responsibility and accountability to be a caretaker of the acquired knowledge and to manage this for the preservation and well-being of the *whānau*, *hapū* and *iwi*.

The proposed *Kaupapa Māori* educational model also reflects the tools of socialisation for the Māori child in Te Kōhanga Reo, Kura Kaupapa Māori and Wharekura. The individual who is socialised in the family context acquires linguistic and social competencies. The family equips the child with expectations about its future through its culture and language (Harker, 1985). Hence, in the Aotearoa/New Zealand context, a middle class Pākehā child acquires a code with which to decipher the messages of the dominant culture which are reproduced in mainstream education. It follows then, that any group other than that whose culture is embodied in the school is disadvantaged. Historically, the reality for Māori children is that there has been a discontinuity between home and school, between the academic knowledge of the school, and the common sense everyday knowledge of the home and community. Mainstream education is not an equaliser because its curriculum, methods and ethos are derived not from the generalised culture of a society, but from the culture of the dominant group within that society.

There are two other aspects of schooling which reflect the knowledge code of a culture in addition to the contents of the curriculum. They are the nature of the way the knowledge is transmitted (pedagogy) and the way that the system measures the success of the transmission (assessment and evaluation) (Harker, 1985).

Differences in cultural perspective such as those outlined above have enormous implications for all aspects of how we approach the tasks of everyday life, not the least of which is the education of succeeding generations. In most Indigenous communities today, it is apparent that aspects of both the Indigenous and western perspectives are present in varying degrees, though neither may be present in a fully cohesive fashion. Furthermore, it is not necessary (nor is it possible) for an outsider to fully comprehend the subtleties and inner workings of another cultural system (even if it is still fully functional) to perform a useful role in the cultural community. What is necessary, however, is a recognition that such differences do exist, an understanding of how these potentially conflicting cultural forces can impact on people's lives, and a willingness to set aside one's own cultural predispositions long enough to convey respect for the validity of others.

Te Kōhanga Reo, Kura Kaupapa Māori and Wharekura are strong statements of Māori people in New Zealand reclaiming power and autonomy in terms of Te Tiriti o Waitangi and *tino rangatiratanga* based on a Māori body of knowledge and Māori ways of doing things. Many Māori are no longer willing to participate in the cultural reproduction of mainstream education in New Zealand. They are engaging in a struggle to change the structure of a society which historically has oppressed them. Furthermore, *Kaupapa Māori* educational initiatives such as Te Kōhanga Reo, Kura Kaupapa Māori and Wharekura have played a critical role over the last two decades in contributing to the establishment of a platform to support a generation of growth and development of the Māori language for the next 25 years. After continual decline for several decades, the numbers of Māori speakers have now stabilised at around 130 500 people between 1996 and 2001 representing 25% of the Māori population (Te Puni Kokiri, 2002: 7).

Note

1   *Tukutuku* is decorative woven lattice work usually found between the *poupou* inside the *wharenui*. *Poutama* is a stepped pattern of *tukutuku* decoration on the walls of the *wharenui*. It is also used in *tāniko* (a form of hand weaving) found on cloaks.

FURTHER READING

Two starting points for the current position of the Māori language are the Waitangi Tribunal Report on Te Reo Maori (1986) and essays in *Dirty Silence* (McGregor and Williams, 1991).

The author of this chapter is grateful to the late Ngoi Pēwhairangi, and Nūnū Kīngi for their personal comments on this topic.

Chapter 20

Ngā tuhituhinga reo Pākehā
Literature in English

Chris Prentice

Māori literature in English offers insight into Māori culture, history and traditions, as well as into the very different contexts in which these exist, interact and undergo transformation in contact with Pākehā and broader international influences. At the same time, it is a literature which has transformed Aotearoa/New Zealand's sense of its cultural identity, and which engages actively with world social and historical events.

Māori literature in English is taken here to refer to published imaginative writing, including poetry, short stories, novels and playscripts. There are points of connection and continuity between Māori oral literature and Māori literature in English: many writers draw on oral traditional forms and narratives, and increasing numbers of writers are writing in both languages. Nevertheless, a brief account of the context for the emergence of Māori literature in English helps to situate this specific and growing body of work.

The editors of *Into the World of Light* (1982) introduce their anthology by pointing out that Māori literature in English has had to struggle for acceptance in the face of both European literary and cultural values, and the lack of a tradition of such Māori literature until the 1950s. The 1940s and 1950s saw massive change in the lives of many Māori people, with an unprecedented migration into towns and cities for work, and an emphasis on education in the Pākehā system as a means of 'getting on in the Pākehā world'. Insistence on English in this education system, along with the dispersal of traditional rural patterns of life and extended family, resulted in the emergence of a generation of young Māori for whom English was their first, and often only language. This was not to be systematically redressed until the 1970s, with the inaugural Māori Language Day in 1972, the establishment of Te Kōhanga Reo in 1981, and the Māori Language Act of 1987 (see Chapter 19).

In the 1950s, Aotearoa/New Zealand's image of itself was of a homogeneous society, although World War II had precipitated a growth in the influence of American culture, especially film, media and consumer culture. Through the 1960s the influence of media increased, and travel became more widely accessible. New Zealanders witnessed and participated in political movements such as decolonisation movements, the American Civil Rights Movement, and the international Women's Liberation movement. At the same time, Māori were becoming aware of the cultural costs of urbanisation and integration into the Pākehā world. The ground was laid for both the 1970s–80s decade of protests, and for what was to become known as the 'Māori Renaissance' of arts and culture. Younger Māori rejected the ideology of assimilation of their parents' era, and rekindled a new pride in their Māori culture and language. Their activism challenged the monocultural national self-image and, bringing biculturalism to the forefront of national consciousness, generated an audience for Māori writing in English among both Pākehā and Māori readers.

The 1970s are generally regarded as the decade that saw the emergence of a Māori literature in English. However, just as there had always been Māori working towards the recognition of Māori political rights and the return of ancestral lands, there had also been earlier Māori writers producing and publishing poetry and fiction in English.

Significant moments in publication of Māori literature in English

Māori writers such as J. C. Sturm published poems and stories in various magazines and literary journals since the 1940s. However, an important early context for publication, the Department of Māori Affairs quarterly *Te Ao Hou*, began in 1952 under the editorship of E. G. Schwimmer. As Lydia Wevers explains, it 'announced itself as "a magazine for Maori people …. [which] should become like a 'marae' on paper"'. At first, the magazine published tribal legends, translated into English, and it continued to publish fiction based on traditional legends. The fifth issue announced a short story competition aimed at fostering Māori writers and sought stories depicting contemporary Māori life. Even if the thematic focus was on the tensions and problems of adapting to new conditions, the editorial emphasis tended to follow the official version of race relations of the 1950s, asserting equal opportunity and mutual goodwill. J. C. Sturm's story, 'For All the Saints' (1955) was the first in a series of stories by Māori writers to be published in *Te Ao Hou*, and it was later one of the first stories by a Māori writer to be published in a collection of New Zealand literature, *New Zealand Short Stories* (vol. 2) in 1966. As more publication outlets became available, questions were raised as to whether writing should be in *te reo* or English, whether it should be addressed to a Māori readership, and whether Māori writers should see themselves as primarily Māori or New Zealand authors. *Te Ao Hou* was succeeded by *Te Kaea*, *Te Maori* and *Tu Tangata*, where such questions continued to be debated (Wevers, 1998).

Publication firsts

- 1964 Hone Tuwhare — *No Ordinary Sun* — Collection of poetry
- 1972 Witi Ihimaera — *Pounamu, Pounamu* — Short stories
- 1973 Witi Ihimaera — *Tangi* — Novel
- 1975 Patricia Grace — *Waiariki* — Short stories (by a woman)
- Heretaunga Pat Baker — *Behind the Tattooed Face* — Historical novel
- 1978 Patricia Grace — *Mutuwhenua* — Novel
- June Mitchell — *Amokura* — Historical novel (by a woman)
- Vernice Wineera Pere — *Mahangi: Pacific Poems* — Collection of poetry (by a woman)

Hone Tūwhare, poet, of Ngā Puhi, Ngāti Kurī and Ngāti Hine

The work of newer and younger writers continued to appear: among the many poets are Āpirana Taylor, whose first collection *Eyes of the Ruru* was published in 1979, and Robert Sullivan, who had been writing since 1986 and who published his first collection, *Jazz Waiata*, in 1990. His later *Star Waka* (1999) and *Captain Cook in the Underworld* (2003) have been greeted with critical acclaim. Keri Hulme had been writing short stories and poetry through the 1970s, but the publication of her novel, *The Bone People* (1983), was a landmark moment in Māori literature in English, winning the Booker Prize in 1985 and perhaps doing more than any previous work to draw out a literary and cultural awareness of Aotearoa/New Zealand literature as the literature of a bicultural nation. Alan Duff's controversial *Once Were Warriors* (1990), its two sequels, *What Becomes of the Broken Hearted?* (1996) and *Jake's Long Shadow* (2002), along with his other works, spoke to a different social, economic and political climate. Phil Kawana's *Dead Jazz Guys* (1996) is set within a contemporary urban street culture of bands, alcohol and drugs.

While the 1970s was the decade associated with the burgeoning of Māori fiction, Māori theatre emerged most strongly in the 1980s. Renée's plays had been performed since the early 1980s, and while they did not focus on Māori characters or specifically Māori situations, her work was listed in the bibliography of Māori plays at the end of the anthology *He Reo Hou* (see McNaughton, 1998). Rena Owen's *Te Awa I Tahuti* appeared in 1987 and 1988 saw Riwia Brown's *Roimata* and John Broughton's first plays, *Te Hara* and *Te Hokinga Mai*. Māori theatre continued to flourish through the 1990s and into the twenty-first century. As well as further works by Renée and John Broughton, including his solo play, *Michael James Manaia* (1991), there were Riwia Brown's *Irirangi Bay* (1996); Āpirana Taylor's *Whaea Kairau* (1995; 1999); Hone Kouka's *Mauri Tu* (1991), *Nga Tangata Toa* (1994) and *Waiora* (1996); Briar Grace-Smith's *Nga Pou Wahine* (1997), *Purapurawhetu* (1999) and *Haruru Mai* (2000); and Witi Ihimaera's *Woman Far Walking* (2000).

 ## Themes and distinctive features

Māori writers have not always focused only on Māori characters or particularly Māori concerns or situations. J. C. Sturm's early stories, Hone Tūwhare's poetry, and the plays of Renée, for example, have dealt with the lives of women and working people, though often as outsiders or isolated figures, marginal to the society they inhabit (Wevers, 1998). More recently, Witi Ihimaera's novel *Nights in the Gardens of Spain* (1995) has a Pākehā protagonist whose homosexuality represents another form of social marginalisation. However, from the time of *Te Ao Hou* and its successors, and especially since the 1970s, Māori literature in English has placed Māori culture, values and experience at the centre of secure and stable patterns of life and intergenerational relationships, as well as within destabilising social and cultural transformation.

 ## Rural and urban life

The early stories and novels of Witi Ihimaera focused on family, community and tribal networks and relationships, often in rural settings. His first novel, *Tangi*, describes rural Māori life, as well as the place of death within life, focusing on the relationship between the young man Tama Mahana and his father. As with many of Ihimaera's works, this setting is framed by a prior departure and return. Tama is already working in Wellington and is called back home to the family land at Waituhi after the death of his father. Ihimaera's stories often depart from, or build towards the event of leaving home and family for the city, for education or for work, and his second collection of stories, *The New Net Goes Fishing* has largely urban settings. While his early work was sometimes accused of being sentimental and 'nostalgic', representing life-worlds that belong to the past, this overlooks the important sense in which for Māori the culture can move forward more securely with a base of knowledge and pride in traditional patterns of community and family identity. Further, such works could serve to recreate a sense of Māori community against the social reality of dispersal through towns and cities.

Hone Tūwhare's poem 'To a Maori Figure Cast in Bronze Outside the Chief Post Office, Auckland' (1972) presents a humorous and yet poignant image of displacement and cultural disempowerment. Presented through the eyes of the statue, '… all hollow inside with longing for the marae on the cliff at Kohimarama', the urban setting of the 1960s and 70s is suggested in references to showing '… the long-hairs how to knock out a tune on the / souped-up guitar', while his own cultural reference-point counters this as he imagines 'my mere quivering, my taiaha held / at the high port'.[1] Complaining, '… Hell, I can't even shoo the pigeons off', the lusty masculine humour struggles against the emasculated position he finds himself in, and the poem casts new dilemmas ('… how the hell can you welcome / the Overseas Dollar, if you can't open your mouth / to poke your tongue out, eh?') within a framework of English colonial history, as '… the ships / come in curling their white moustaches'.

While the later works of Māori writers have become more urban, more explicit about the conditions of work (or unemployment), education and housing (or homelessness and street culture), they have not presented simply bleak depictions of victimisation. Certainly the stories of Grace and Ihimaera, as well as Bruce Stewart's 'Broken Arse' and Alan Duff's *Once Were Warriors*, have shown children looking out for each other as they try to make sense of their often violent world, women isolated in suburbia, men in disheartening jobs or unemployed, young people negotiating the education system, and their parents' expectations (or neglect) of them, and the harsh realities of life as a state ward or a jail inmate. Many works have become more political and optimistic. Patricia Grace's novels *Cousins* and *Baby No-Eyes* narrate not only the difficulties faced by a young people deprived of the language of their elders in the Pākehā education system, or a young Māori woman confronting racism as she seeks accommodation in town, but also young and old women setting about to establish schools for their own young people, Kōhanga Reo, re-establishing the place of the language in the Māori sense of cultural identity.

Language

One impact of the large-scale move into towns and cities after World War II was the decline in Māori spoken as a first language. In the towns, a new generation spoke English as their first language, and Māori was decreasingly spoken at home. Āpirana Taylor's 1979 poem 'Sad Joke on a Marae' gives angry and poignant expression to the sense of cultural alienation that emerged among some young Māori: the speaker is unable to face his ancestors without shame, as all he knows is '*Tihei Mauriora*'. So 'the tekoteko raged/He ripped his tongue from his mouth/and threw it at my feet', and the speaker introduces himself as:

> *Tu the freezing worker*
> *Ngati D. B. is my tribe*
> *The pub is my Marae*
> *My fist is my taiaha*
> *Jail is my home.*

While others battled to regain the Māori language, those Māori writers who worked in English were nevertheless using that language in ways that allowed specifically Māori voices to emerge. Patricia Grace once said,

> *I'm not bilingual, but I am bidialectic, in a way. I mean there are all different sorts of ways of using English; you get different groups of Maori people using English in different ways … I am familiar with the rhythms and intonations of Maori* (cited in Guerin, 1986: 20).

The suggestion of Māori grammatical structure, or more generally the rhythms and metaphorical expressions of oral tradition are found in the opening of her story, 'Toki': 'From the north he came, Toki, in his young day. Ah yes. A boaster this one, Toki the fisherman' (1975: 7), or in the speech of Nanny in 'A Way of Talking': 'At last Nanny got out of her chair and said, "Time for sleeping. The mouths steal the time of the eyes." That's the lovely way she has of talking, Nanny, when she speaks in English' (1975: 1). 'Waimarie' illustrates the hybridised English of an old woman whose speech is shaped through her first language, Māori. At the end though, when she calls the people on to the *marae* at the *tangihanga*, her language, as well as her voice, is transformed: it 'lifted out, weaving amongst the sheddings of light, encompassing the kinsman and his family, bearing them forward' (1987: 13).

A number of Māori writers whose works are primarily in English have incorporated untranslated Māori language into the text, from phrases used in dialogue between characters, to more substantial passages wholly in Māori. Although Keri Hulme's *The Bone People* was published with a glossary of Māori words and phrases, Grace's stories include exchanges of dialogue incorporating Māori, often with a translation built into the exchange itself (an approach used in a lot of plays which incorporate Māori language):

> *E Hika! He aha te moemoea?* called Ben….
>
> What's the dream?
>
> *E tama, he tuna.*
>
> *Ei! Kia tika ra!*
>
> Yeh! A big one this eel. *Ka nui te kaita!*
>
> ('The Dream', 1975: 20–21).

Patricia Grace, writer, of Ngāti Raukawa

Witi Ihimaera's later novels include much longer narrative passages in Māori (see *The Matriarch*, 295–6). Whether the work is fiction, poetry or drama, this creates an even more bicultural textual space, while at the same time posing the question of linguistic territories – zones of inclusion or exclusion, challenge or welcome. These continue to be questions of cultural politics as much as of literary significance.

 ## Traditional narratives

Māori literature in English has underpinned the use of English language, the textual form and the European literary genres, with specifically Māori cultural values, patterns and symbols. Stories with contemporary settings, characters and situations are often revealed to have a basis in traditional narratives. The story of Rangi and Papa-tūā-nuku is evoked in Patricia Grace's story, 'Between Earth and Sky'. A woman about to give birth walks out of her house into the silent early morning landscape of her family farm. Standing on the earth and stretching up to the sky, she feels light, free, able to breathe again as the time approaches for the birth of her child – their separation from each other. After the birth, she celebrates their separation and the world of light in which they can now live, while linking her individual act of giving birth to the continuities of birth, light and life that the traditional narrative embodies. Grace's novel *Potiki* is significantly informed by Māui narratives, as the young boy Tokowaru-i-te-marama is found by the sea, catches a big fish, and is eventually killed as he passes through the doorway of the burning *wharenui*. In *The Matriarch*, Witi Ihimaera interweaves the account of the construction of the sacred *waka*, the Tākitimu, and its voyage from Hawaiki to Aotearoa, with that of the journey of an *ope*, led by the matriarch, to a Wellington *marae* to speak for the land rights of her people. Ihimaera's *The Whale Rider* gives modern significance to the traditional Ngāti Porou story of Paikea's journey to Aotearoa on the back of a whale.

Time

The use of traditional narratives to underpin or interweave with modern stories indicates a specific Māori conception of the structure of time. Grace has explained that 'There's a base in mythology for everything ... for every part of your daily living' (cited in Guerin, 1986: 20), so that myths are not simply stories that belong to the past, but are more like a blueprint for the present and future, relating past, present and future together as inseparable. Māori narratives are often structured in terms of a specific Māori understanding of time. Keri Hulme's *The Bone People* is structured in accordance with a spiral motif that appears in various ways through the narrative. It opens with a description of the three main characters as they are at the end of the story, then circles back to an earlier time to trace their tumultuous lives and relationships until that final resolution which has already framed the story. The reader finishes the work not at a later point in narrative time than it begins, but at a higher level of knowledge and understanding. In other words, it is not simply circular, ending where it began, but spiral, ending on a higher plane. Spirals appear in numerous other forms in the shape of fern fronds, seashells, Kerewin's sculptures, Haimona's music hutches, and more. A Māori sense of time is suggested in a phrase repeated through Witi Ihimaera's *The Dream Swimmer* (1997), which becomes the title of the novel's epilogue: 'Te Torino Whakahaere, Whakamuri'.

 ## Carving and weaving

The forms and patterns of carving and weaving, as well as specific characters who carve and weave – and their relationships to their communities – figure in much Māori literature in English. In the Prologue to Grace's *Potiki*, the carver is an artist who draws out what is already in the wood, and therefore already older than he is: the carver removes the excess wood to release the shape from within. We are told that 'It is as though a child brings about the birth of a parent because that which comes from under the master's hand is older than he is, is already ancient' (1986: 8). The Prologue further links carving to storytelling, as the carvings tell histories, and often represent the skill of great storytellers in fine long swirling tongues, while the people retell the stories of the carvings to each other. Weaving is also related to storytelling in the novel. As well as traditional weaving chants included in the narrative ('And now let there be joining – the dead to the dead, the living to the living. Let the strands fall together' (1986: 28)), women tell stories as they weave. Thus, the community context is important for both weaving, carving and story-telling: 'As the strands worked to and fro, so did our stories ... We sang to and fro, latticing down and along the strips of black, red, white and gold, which had become the strands of life and self' (1986: 144). Ihimaera's *The Dream Swimmer* suggests weaving in the lines which recur through the narrative, '*Hui e, Haumi e, Taiki e*'.

Weaving and storytelling combine as a structural metaphor for most of Patricia Grace's novels: they interweave the stories of a range of narrators, usually members of the same *whānau*, or *whanaunga*, each telling the story from their own perspective, so that the whole is enriched by the qualities of each and the strength of their combination. The stories overlap, cross back and forth in time, and occasionally reach forward to events that have not yet happened, or describe events from the past which have a bearing on the present. In Ihimaera's *The Matriarch*, the education of Tamatea Mahana is represented in terms of the *poutama tukutuku* pattern. Each new level of knowledge and understanding he reaches under the matriarch's tutelage represents a further step on the *poutama*. His play, *Woman Far Walking*, is temporally structured in terms of weaving. Most explicitly, the action and characterisation in Briar Grace-Smith's play *Purapurawhetū* is structured through a weaving motif. One of the settings is the *whare raranga* where a large *tukutuku* panel is being woven, and the different stage spaces – settings of *wharekai* and *urupā* – are signified in the repeated weaving movements of '*puku* up' and '*puku* down' (1999: 30). In his introduction to the playscript, John Huria cites Hirini Melbourne's model for Māori literature in which the *whare whakairo* offers formal devices to the composer, poet or orator, and he suggests that:

> *In Purapurawhetu, the art of raranga is a way of thinking about rangatiratanga, art, values, and traditions when they are met by extraordinary events. The pattern of the tukutuku panel orders the play by paralleling the ohaki, by visually representing to future generations the oral revelation of painful events that occurred some time ago, and by signifying the rightful order of things* (1999: 15).

Marae, wharenui and other cultural spaces

Māori literature in English can create or symbolise specifically Māori cultural spaces, on page and on stage. The development of *marae* theatre is an explicit example of the transformation of a western cultural space into one that has specifically Māori meanings and protocols. In the introduction to *Ta Matou Mangai*, Hone Kouka describes theatre productions that follow strict *tikanga*, with *karanga* and all the elements of *pōhiri*:

> *Lighting is used to encompass all prior to the play proper starting, thus bringing actor and audience together. Some groups get their actors to greet the audience as themselves and some have the welcome in the opening salvos of their performance; the play being the whaikorero, perhaps completed with a waiata. By doing this modern theatre stays true to the protocols of old* (1999: 16–17).

Anthologies have been likened to *marae*, as editors of both *Te Ao Hou* and *Te Ao Marama* offered this analogy. Similarly, some novels have suggested *marae* space, where readers are called into the narrative and the cultural spaces in which it takes place. The *wharenui* has been described in detail, such as in Grace's *Potiki*, where being in the *wharenui* is likened to 'the warmth of the embrace, because the house is a parent, and there was warmth in under the parental backbone, enclosement amongst the patterned ribs' (1986: 88; see also her *Dogside Story* (2001: 268–270)); or in Witi Ihimaera's *The Matriarch*:

> *The house has a head, a backbone, rib-cage and limbs. It is built in the shape of a person and is usually named after an ancestor of the people. The front of the house has at the apex of the gable a large carved head which we call the koruru. Running from the head and along the length of the house is the backbone or tahuhu. Then, as you look at the koruru, you will see the sloping bargeboards like an inverted V, one on either side of the head. These are the arms or the maihi. And within the house are rafters which represent the ribs, So, when you go into the house, you enter into the ancestor, or, if you like, you are taken into the body of the people (1986: 188).*

An important point which arises from these examples is the idea of the novel – the printed book in English – functioning as a pedagogical space, which can sustain the teaching which has traditionally taken place orally and in family or communal contexts.

This represents a form of cultural adaptation that still holds firmly to traditional values. Gran Kura's verandah, in *Baby No-Eyes*, functions in her urban existence in the way that the *marae* would on ancestral land: the space from which family members are farewelled, and where visitors are challenged and welcomed. The value of recreating *marae* space lies in maintaining the presence of, and links to, the ancestors. Intergenerational relationships are central to many Māori works of fiction and drama, particularly those between grandparent and grandchild. The grandparent often represents the link to traditional values, to the history and memory of the *whānau* and the *whenua*, and to the language. However, this figure is not necessarily presented devoid of humour. Ihimaera's story, 'A Game of Cards' includes much laughter and cheating among the old women, and Nanny Flowers, in *The Whale Rider* (1987), is full of lively spirit as well as warmth. Conversely, Artemis, in *The Matriarch*, has drawn much critical debate on account of the dark powers she seems to possess and the uses she makes of them.

Witi Ihimaera, writer, of Te Aitanga-a-Māhaki, Rongowhakaata, Ngāi Tāmanuhiri, Ngāti Porou, Ngāi Tūhoe, Whakatōhea, Te Whānau-a-Apanui and Ngāti Kahungunu

Elders and ancestors

In the novels of both Patricia Grace and Witi Ihimaera, ancestral figures feature in the narrative. In Grace's *Cousins*, Mata returns home for her cousin's *tangihanga*, and having felt alone and dispossessed of family and identity throughout her life, sees the spirits of her mother and ancestors gathered on the verandah to welcome her. In Ihimaera's *The Matriarch*, substantial sections of the novel are concerned with the lives of Tamatea's ancestors, Te Kooti and Wī Pere Halbert. As will be discussed shortly, reference to actual historical figures – and indeed traditional myths, legends and histories as well – raises some specific concerns for Māori writers. Novels which begin with creation, cosmological or *whakapapa* recitations situate the narratives that follow within a Māori world and a Māori world-view. The Prologue to Grace's *Potiki* begins with an invocation of Te Kore, moving towards the stages of Te Pō then Te Ao mārama:

> *From the centre,*
> *From the nothing,*
> *Of not seen,*
> *Of not heard,*
> *There comes*
> *A shifting,*
> *A stirring,*
> *And a creeping forward.*

It concludes with 'Tihe Mauriora', and the story can begin. Ihimaera's *The Matriarch* situates a fuller cosmological account soon after the beginning of the novel, and this moves through a range of mythologies, legends or traditional narratives, including the separation of Rangi and Papa-tūā-nuku, stories of Tāne-mahuta, Hine-ahu-one, Hine-tītama and Hine-nui-te-pō, Māui stories, Kupe's voyage, and the voyage from Hawaiki to Aotearoa. However, Ihimaera's use of these accounts both situates the narrative within the Māori world, and traces the *whakapapa* of the protagonist Tamatea Mahana back to the *atua* and to creation itself.

There are important cosmological and historical implications for characterisation: within the novel, Tamatea's recitation of his *whakapapa* back to the *atua* is regarded as bold and even scandalous, but a further complication emerges when it is remembered that Māori values dictate that only the history of one's own tribe can be told. As a writer, Ihimaera – like other Māori writers – has set his works and drawn his characters from his own ancestral land and heritage. However, Tamatea's name and descent from the captain of the *Tākitimu waka* confers more than individual identity: he embodies his whole *whakapapa* and its *mana*. Towards the end of the novel, then, when he engages in a battle for *mana* and the mantle of family succession with his grandfather's *whāngai* Toroa, who is named after the *rangatira* of the *Mātaatua waka* from which the Tūhoe people trace their descent, it is no longer a battle between two individuals, but between two *iwi*. As Tamatea defeats Toroa, some readers have felt that the *mana* of Tūhoe was insulted in a manner which broke seriously with the protocol that such battles should take place between the contestants on the *marae*, not in the openly circulating space of a published novel.

Māori theatre raises similar questions about characterisation: Hone Kouka's plays carefully remain within Kouka's own Ngāti Porou *iwi* and heritage, and his first play, *Mauri Tu*, which concerns the case of a young man who wishes to have a *marae* rather than court trial, enacts the idea that the individual actor/character (it is important to consider to what extent one is independent of the other, as is taken for granted in Pākehā theatre) is never on stage alone, even in a solo play, but is always accompanied by his ancestors, who speak through him. He stands for his *whakapapa*. He is therefore accountable to his *whakapapa* for his actions. Kouka draws on the convention whereby, 'Taki Tuupuna (identifying chants referring to the Whakapapa – family tree – of the characters), recited during transitions, [serve] as another indicator to the audience of a coming change' (1992: xi). Through the constant presence of the actor's body on stage, all characters are signified, no matter which is 'activated' at any particular moment.

The land

A central theme in the literature has been the special relationship Māori have with ancestral land, the belief that this relationship defines who they are at least as much as their presence defines the land itself. The land is more than the setting for stories. In a possible reference to the story of Rangi and Papa-tūā-nuku and the rain as the tears of grief at their separation, Hone Tūwhare's poem 'Rain' captures something of that mutual definition between the human and the natural world. Having described his knowledge of rain given to him by his senses, the speaker concludes:

> *But if I*
> *should not hear*
> *smell or feel or see*
> *you*
>
> *you would still*
> *define me*
> *disperse me*
> *wash over me*
> *rain*

Tamatea Mahana, in Witi Ihimaera's novel *The Matriarch*, learns to define who he is in relation to the land: for him, the land is 'like a living geography text and history book in one' (1986: 103), and much of the novel concerns his inherited mission to 'save Waituhi', his family land. In a number of fictional works, characters have responsibilities to care for the land, to protect it from developers, to fight for its return to its rightful owners.

In Patricia Grace's story, 'Journey', an old man goes to the city to sort out a subdivision of his land which will allow his family to have their own houses built there after he has passed away. As he travels by train, he notices how 'between the tunnels they were slicing the hills away with big machines.' Although he acknowledges Māori help on the big machines, he ponders:

> *Funny people, these pakehas, had to chop up everything. Couldn't talk to a hill or a tree, these people, couldn't give the trees or the hills a name and make them special and leave them. Couldn't go round, only through* (1980: 55).

As a result, 'the rains'll come and the cuts will bleed for miles and the valleys will drown in blood …. Could find a few bones amongst that lot, too' (1980: 55). Further into town, past the cenotaph, and

> *that's where they'd bulldozed all the bones and put in the new motorway. Resited, he still remembered the newspaper word, all in together. Your leg bone, my arm bone, someone else's bunch of teeth and fingers, someone else's head* (1980: 57).

After an unsuccessful meeting with a bureaucrat where he is reduced to kicking a desk in frustration, the old man journeys home, where he instructs his family that 'When I go you're not to put me in the ground …. Burn me up, I tell you, it's not safe in the ground' (1980: 66). Many of the same concerns – family heritage, unity and sustenance, the well-being of the land itself, sacred sites such as *urupā* – are raised in works by other Māori writers.

Māori perspectives on international and new concerns

Māori literature in English has long presented a perspective on new conditions, and on national and international events and issues. Witi Ihimaera's *The Matriarch* and *The Dream Swimmer* confront accounts of colonial history with the perspectives of Māori as the Indigenous people of this country, revising, supplementing and sometimes totally reversing the received versions of events. International war – its impacts on, and aftermaths for, Māori people – is also an important theme in his later work, *The Uncle's Story*, as it is in Patricia Grace's *Cousins*. *The Uncle's Story* also focuses on issues of resolving Māori and homosexual identity for two characters, family members of different generations. The worlds of the young characters of the stories, novels and plays of Māori writers include Hollywood and television, university education, street life and space invaders. Pita Sharples' poem, 'Te Mihini Atea'/'The Space Invaders', a *waiata-a-ringa* in the manner of the old *waiata-kori*, composed for the group Te Roopu Manutaki and performed in 1983 at the Polynesian Festival in Hastings, shows that poetry also engages with the mixed blessings of the modern world (Wedde and McQueen, 1985: 438, 541). Robert Sullivan's *Star Waka* explores Māori perspectives on modernity and globalisation through a sequence of 100 poems. Patricia Grace's *Dogside Story* is set around celebrations of the dawn of the new millennium.

Perhaps among the most important contemporary concerns engaged with in a Māori novel in English is that of science, medicine and genetic research and engineering raised in Patricia Grace's *Baby No-Eyes*. The novel recounts a hospital's treatment of the body of a baby who died in a car accident, and the concern of a number of characters with the use of Māori and other Indigenous people for scientific research into genetics and genetic engineering. These concerns are linked to questions of damage to and healing of the land, and to the place of *whakapapa* in defining self and land together. People discuss action to ensure 'the bones of our ancestors will not be thieved for medicines … our ancestors will not be used for experimentations … our ancestors' patterns will not be separated from their bones', to prevent Pākehā 'putting a Māori in a sheep or rising a Māori up from a dust' (1998: 185–6). Terms like 'bio-prospecting and bio-piracy' suggest bodies being invaded, stolen and mapped, like land. Although various themes interweave through the novel, this particular narrative strand, based on true incidents from the 1990s, shows how the cultural space of Māori literature in English can indicate the profound significance of Māori perspectives for some of the most fundamental questions of our times.

Note

1 A *mere* is a short flat club.

FURTHER READING

Arvidson (1991), Beatson (1989), Evans (1985), Goldie (1989), Heim (1998), Melbourne (1991), Mita (1984), Pearson (1973), and Simms (1978) discuss a variety of topics that complement this chapter.

Chapter 21

Ngā hekenga hou
Pacific peoples in Aotearoa/New Zealand *Michelle Saisoa'a*

Pacific peoples have made significant contributions to Aotearoa/New Zealand over the past century that have rarely been documented or acknowledged. Unfortunately we tend to focus on present day statistics, where Pacific peoples feature at the lower socio-economic end of the spectrum, and forget the positive contributions and achievements Pacific peoples have made, and continue to make, to Aotearoa/New Zealand.

There has also been an emphasis on political and economic interaction rather than cultural or social, meaning much of the contact has been between Pākehā New Zealanders and the people of the Pacific rather than between Māori and Pacific peoples. Migration has been to the forefront and been the cause of, at times, prolonged and acrimonious disagreements. However, the Pacific population of Aotearoa/New Zealand has continued to grow and flourish, particularly in the fields of sport and entertainment. This chapter will also highlight lesser-known achievements and discuss areas where Pacific peoples have contributed to the developing nation that is Aotearoa/New Zealand today. It will do this by tracing each decade from the pre-1950s to the present, and then highlight specific areas of achievement and concern. While this chapter mentions individuals, we cannot overlook a central feature of Pacific cultures, which is 'community'. When one succeeds, all succeed. When one fails, all feel the pain of that failure. This is what makes our cultures special and is the reason we celebrate our achievements together in this chapter.

There is no officially sanctioned term to describe the group of peoples who have migrated from the Pacific Islands or who identify with the Pacific Islands because of ancestry or heritage. Since 1994, the Ministry of Pacific Island Affairs (MPIA) has used the term 'Pacific peoples'; the plural nature of 'peoples' symbolising the multiplicity of ethnicity, nationality and culture inherent in the term. 'Pacific peoples' is a term used to describe peoples living in Aotearoa/New Zealand. Other terms include Pacific Islander, Pacific Nations person, Polynesian Pacific Islander.

Pacific peoples have been in Aotearoa/New Zealand for more than 100 years. Throughout their history, Pacific peoples have navigated the seas in search of new lands and opportunities. We should not forget that Māori originated from the Pacific and, like them, the newer immigrants have adapted and overcome language difficulties, climatic changes, social transition, cultural changes and many other challenges, while still retaining their cultural values. Aotearoa/New Zealand is now home to over 232 000 Pacific peoples.

Key moments in Aotearoa/New Zealand Pacific relations

Much of the interaction between the Pacific and Aotearoa/New Zealand has resulted from political or economic ventures. During the 1870s New Zealand unsuccessfully tried to get British support for efforts to control a number of Pacific Islands in a federation administered by New Zealand. The prospect of potential profit from island resources led New Zealand to expand its borders into the Pacific. In 1901 New Zealand annexed the Cook Islands and Niue. During World War I men from these Islands and elsewhere in the Pacific volunteered to serve with distinction in New Zealand's army, as part of the Māori Pioneer Battalion. New Zealand took control of the German colony of Western Samoa in 1915 and was given responsibility for it as a League of Nations Mandate from 1920. In 1925 Tokelau also became a New Zealand responsibility. Widespread opposition by Samoans to New Zealand's colonial rule from 1926 led to a promise of reform by the New Zealand Labour Government in 1935.

New Zealand rule in the Pacific was lacklustre and divided. A Minister and administration were responsible for the Cook Islands and Niue, and the Department of External Affairs were responsible for Western Samoa from 1919 (Lal and Fortune, 2000: 608). From 1943 the Department of Island Territories administered all these Pacific dependencies. In the post-war period, New Zealand's Island territories gained independence or self governing status, beginning with Western Samoa in 1962, the Cook Islands in 1964, and Niue in 1974. In 1948 Tokelau became part of New Zealand, and it remains so today.

During this period Pacific migration to Aotearoa/New Zealand began slowly. In 1925 Felix Leavai (Samoa) was one of the first Pacific peoples to be naturalised. Between 1929 and 1938, ten Samoans obtained certificates of naturalisation. In 1926, 988 Pacific peoples lived in Aotearoa/New Zealand. By 1945 the numbers had more than doubled to 2200.

 ## 1950–1960

Following the end of World War II, the migration of Pacific peoples to Aotearoa/New Zealand began to pick up pace. In 1951, there were 3600 Pacific peoples in Aotearoa/New Zealand. These Pacific settlers were pioneers, as there were few support structures for Pacific peoples who wished to live here. After the war, Aotearoa/New Zealand (like other western countries) began the transition from primary agricultural industries to urban-based industrial production. As a result of labour shortages, semi-skilled and unskilled labour was sought from the Pacific. Immigration controls at this early stage were relaxed. Cook Islanders, Tokelauans and Niueans, as New Zealand citizens, entered the country freely (Pearson, 1990). Samoans, Tongans and Fijians also had relatively easy access to Aotearoa/New Zealand. Cook Islanders and Fijians were recruited to work in rural-based primary industries in the 1950s. By the late 1950s, other Pacific peoples (encouraged by family members already living in Aotearoa/New Zealand or recruited directly by individual employers) migrated to work in manufacturing industries in Wellington, Auckland, Tokoroa, Bluff (near Invercargill) and Whangarei (Krishnan, Schoeffel, and Warren, 1994).

1960–1970

A large number of Pacific peoples continued to migrate to Aotearoa/New Zealand despite Western Samoa gaining independence (1962) and the Cook Islands becoming self-governing (1964). In 1966, 26 271 Pacific peoples lived in Aotearoa/New Zealand. At this time Aotearoa/New Zealand was experiencing a boom in the manufacturing industry, and the Pacific population settled in urban, industrial areas such as South Auckland and the Hutt Valley near Wellington, where Pacific workers were employed on manufacturing production lines or in the service sector (Krishnan, Schoeffel and Warren, 1994). New Pacific migrants were assisted in their resettlement by earlier arrivals. In 1966 over-population and a hurricane on the three atolls comprising Tokelau (Atafu, Nukunonu, and Fakaofo) prompted the New Zealand Government to relocate young families in Aotearoa/New Zealand. Over a five-year period, 356 people resettled here (Huntsman and Hooper 1996). Originally many settled in the central North Island around Taupō and Rotorua where forestry work was plentiful. However, general loneliness for familiar faces and the sea caused some of these families to relocate to rapidly growing Tokelau communities in Auckland, the Hutt Valley and Porirua, north of Wellington. By 1966–1967 there were 6968 work-permit holders in Aotearoa/New Zealand from Fiji and 2102 from Samoa (Krishnan, Schoeffel, and Warren, 1994). In 1968 the Departments of Maori Affairs and Island Territories amalgamated to form the Department of Maori and Island Affairs. Its responsibilities were to promote social change amongst Māori and to work with Pacific Island immigrants.

 ## 1970–1980

Fiji gained independence in 1970, and a year later the South Pacific Forum was formed to enable heads of Pacific governments (including New Zealand and Australia) to meet and arrange matters of interest. Between 1973 and 1974, immigration from the Cook Islands, Fiji, Niue, Samoa and Tonga accounted for 6% of migration to New Zealand (Krishnan, Schoeffel, and Warren, 1994). The oil crisis of 1973 and the global economic recession caused an economic decline in Aotearoa/New Zealand, increasing overseas debt and inflation and making industries uncompetitive (Krishnan, Schoeffel, and Warren, 1994). Despite high unemployment levels and a tightening of immigration policies, Pacific peoples continued to be employed in the primary and manufacturing sectors. However, they became a convenient scapegoat for Aotearoa/New Zealand's economic problems. They were labelled 'overstayers' by the conservative National Government in their 1976 election campaigns.[1] This led to the infamous 'dawn raids' executed by police and immigration officials upon Pacific Island homes in search of 'overstayers'. Pacific Island-looking people, including Māori, were arbitrarily stopped on Auckland's streets and asked for documentation, such as passports. Failure to comply led to arrest and detention in police cells.

In 1976, 65 700 Pacific people lived in Aotearoa/New Zealand. A contract labour scheme was introduced for people from Western Samoa, Tonga, Fiji, Tuvalu and Kiribati to work in New Zealand for 11 months (Krishnan, Schoeffel, and Warren, 1994). During this decade, Pacific peoples began to establish mechanisms that would give them a political voice. Pacific advisory councils and associations were established in Auckland and Wellington to represent their views to Government

(Boyd, 1990). In 1975, the Pacific Island responsibilities of the Department of Māori Affairs were transferred to the Ministry of Foreign Affairs. The new Department of Māori Affairs continued to look after the welfare of Pacific people living in New Zealand (Butterworth and Young, 1990).

1980–1990

A Samoan woman, Falema'i Lesa, challenged the immigration policies and took her case to the Privy Council (New Zealand's highest court) in London. In 1982, the Council ruled that the British Nationality and the Status of Aliens Act (1923) and the British Nationality and New Zealand Citizenship Act (1948) conferred New Zealand citizenship on Samoans born in Western Samoa (and their children) prior to 1948. A negotiated treaty between New Zealand and Western Samoa to avoid the possibility of 100 000 Samoans claiming New Zealand citizenship later superseded this decision (Boyd, 1990). For Samoans, this remains a contentious issue evidenced by protests being renewed in March 2003. Between 1985 and 1986 there was a disproportionate number of Pacific people prosecuted as overstayers. Although Pacific peoples represented one third of all overstayers, they made up 86% of prosecutions during 1985 and 1986 (Krishnan, Schoeffel, and Warren, 1994).

The 1980s were a watershed period for Pacific peoples in Aotearoa/New Zealand politics as they began to walk the corridors of power advocating for their communities. In 1984 the Labour Government began consulting Pacific peoples on a range of national policy initiatives. Richard Prebble was appointed the first Minister of Pacific Island Affairs. In 1985 a committee of Pacific church ministers were asked for their views in regard to the development of the New Zealand Bill of Rights. This was followed in 1986 by changes to the immigration legislation and the establishment of the Ministry of Pacific Island Affairs as a department of state. Since 1984 the Ministry had been a unit of the Department of Internal Affairs with the role of providing advice on Pacific matters to the Minister of Pacific Island Affairs. At this time the Minister of Pacific Island Affairs Advisory Council was set up comprising representatives from the main Pacific communities in Aotearoa/New Zealand. In 1985 the Pacific Island Employment Development Scheme was established to develop a viable economic base for Pacific ventures in Aotearoa/New Zealand.

1990–2002

In 1991, 167 073 Pacific peoples lived in Aotearoa/New Zealand. By 2001, the Pacific population in Aotearoa/New Zealand was almost 232 000. Second, third and fourth generation Pacific peoples had multiplied the seeds sown by preceding generations. During the 1990s, Pacific achievers influenced all areas of Aotearoa/New Zealand society, in sport, arts, employment, politics, sport, broadcasting and creative and performing arts.

The first Pacific peoples to stand for national politics were the late Louisa Crawley (Samoa) who stood for Labour and Tetika Dorie Reid (Cook Islands) who stood for National. Although neither was elected, they were both successful in local body elections (Crocombe, 1992). Crawley became Deputy Director of the Ministry of Pacific Island Affairs. A former teacher, she worked to advance the social and economic

These Tongan women are performing either a *tauʻolunga* or a *lakalaka*. The women's costumes determine their rank in Tongan society. The woman in the middle is either a noble or a member of the royal family. A *tauʻolunga* is a dance performed only by females. It originated from the Samoan *taualuga* but it is mixed with elements of the traditional Tongan *ula*. The *tauʻolunga* is a popular dance performed at both formal and informal occasions. It is performed individually or in a group. The *lakalaka* is the most popular dance form in present-day Tonga and can be considered as the national dance. *Lakalaka* are a vehicle of transmitting cultural heritage from generation to generation. Men and women perform *lakalaka*.

conditions of Pacific peoples in AotearoaNew Zealand as a Christchurch City Councillor, and as a founding member and former national president of PACIFICA (Pacific Allied Council Inspires Faith and Ideals Concerning All). In 1993, Taito Phillip Field became New Zealand's first Pacific person to be elected to Parliament. Currently, he is parliamentary under-secretary to the Minister of Pacific Island Affairs and under-secretary to the Ministers of Employment, Justice and Social Services. During this period, other Pacific peoples, especially in Auckland, became active in the National Party, promoting issues in Pacific communities as a counter to the dominance of the Labour Party. In 1996 Anae Arthur Anae was elected National's first Pacific Member of Parliament. In 1999, Mark Gosche (Samoa) became the first Pacific Minister of Pacific Island Affairs. In 2000, Luamanuvao Winnie Laban was elected as the first Pacific woman Member of Parliament. On 3 June 2002, the Prime Minister Helen Clark visited Samoa where she offered a formal apology for the inept and incompetent early administration by New Zealand between 1914 and 1962.

Early church pioneers

Pacific migrants came to Aotearoa/New Zealand with a strong religious faith. The churches began to emerge as a primary support structure that provided spiritual,

Many Pacific peoples belong to a church group. It is a central means of providing an embodiment of Pacific Island knowledge to its members and mirrors life in the villages of the Pacific.

social and economic support to growing communities of Pacific peoples. In Aotearoa/New Zealand the Catholic, Methodist, Presbyterian and Congregational Churches all created opportunities for Pacific members to transmit and maintain their language and cultural values (Tiatia, 1998). In the 1940s the Pacific Islands Congregational Church was founded in Newton, Auckland, to minister to migrants from the Cook Islands, Niue, Samoa and Tokelau. It later spread throughout Auckland, and to forestry towns and other urban centres such as Kawerau, Mangakino, Tokoroa, Porirua, Newtown (Wellington) and Invercargill (Taule`ale`ausumai, 2001). In 1947 the Congregational Union of New Zealand formally accepted responsibility for the Pacific Islands Congregational Church of New Zealand. In 1969 the Congregational Union of New Zealand united with the Presbyterian Church itself. The Cook Islands, Niuean, Samoan and Tokelauan Congregationalists officially became Presbyterian and their name changed to Pacific Islanders' Presbyterian Church (Tiatia, 1998). In the Catholic Church the Samoan and Tongan congregations are each called a 'Community'. Most communities are attached to English-speaking parishes and the needs of Samoans and Tongans are met through Samoan and Tongan Chaplaincies. It was common for migrants from Tongan Protestant churches to join the Methodist church (e.g. in Ponsonby, Auckland) when they first came to Aotearoa/New Zealand. However, some Tongans have chosen to form their own fellowship groups (Tiatia, 1998).

Education

As early as 1903 Pacific students were in Aotearoa/New Zealand. In 1945 Island Scholarship Schemes were established for selected students from New Zealand's island territories to undertake secondary and higher education in New Zealand

(Mara, Foliaki, and Coxon, 1994). A number of distinguished Pacific peoples have been educated here.

1903–1906	Ratu Sir Lala Sukuna (Fiji)	First speaker of the Fijian Legislative Council	Wanganui Collegiate School
1908–1914	Queen Sālote Tūpou III (Tonga)		Diocesan School for Girls, Auckland
1930s	Sir Thomas Davis	Second Premier of the Cook Islands	Kings College, Auckland
1945		Medical degree	University of Otago
1963	Malietoa Tanumafili II	Samoan head of State	St Stephen's College, Wesley College, Auckland.

Source: Adapted from Lal and Fortune, 2000: 282

A milestone for Pacific community development was the establishment of the Pacific Island Educational Resource Centre (PIERC) within the Department of Education in Auckland in 1976, to help Pacific migrants learn English and adapt to life in New Zealand (Mara, Foliaki and Coxon, 1994). PIERC began producing educational resources in the Pacific languages for use from early childhood to tertiary level. These resources are still being used extensively in Aotearoa/New Zealand, and are being promoted in the Pacific. PIERC provided training for Pacific peoples in all Pacific cultures. Currently the centre promotes the importance of family support in Pacific

The making of *tapa* cloth by women is a major art of Samoa, Tonga and Fiji. In Samoa finished *tapa* cloth is known as *siapo*, in Tonga *ngatu*. Samoan and Tongan women have made a conscientious effort to revive and maintain the art of *tapa*. *Siapo* and *ngatu* are given at the formal presentation of gifts to an honoured guest, the investiture of a chief with his title, births, weddings and deaths. They may be worn by high chiefs and orators and by the bride and groom at traditional weddings.

communities, and sustains the languages for Pacific youth. Academic programmes are run within an environment sensitive to the students' cultural needs in order to prepare them for advanced study. The programmes have successfully targeted students who have left secondary school, but lack sufficient qualifications for higher education.

As with Māori society, the maintenance of Pacific languages is critical in Aotearoa/New Zealand for the retention of Pacific cultural identities. It is the most serious challenge facing Pacific communities in Aotearoa/New Zealand (Hunkin-Tuitetufunga, 2001). In 1972, the first Pacific Islands Pre-school was set up. In the 1980s, the growth of Pacific Islands early language groups accelerated, so that by 1993 there were some 350 of them. They were modelled on Kōhanga Reo (see Chapter 19). By 2001, there were 8000 Pacific children enrolled in Early Childhood Education services.

Since the 1970s, the Samoan community has lobbied to have Samoan included in the primary and secondary school curriculum. In 1992, FAGASA (Inc) – the National Samoan Teachers' Organisation – was established to preserve and teach the Samoan language in New Zealand. The Samoan language is now part of the official primary and secondary school curriculum (Hunkin-Tuitetufunga, 2001). Samoan is also taught at two New Zealand universities, with Cook Islands Māori and Tongan also available at the University of Auckland. Pacific Studies is offered as a major subject at the University of Auckland, Victoria University, the University of Canterbury and the University of Otago.

Maintaining Pacific identity through the media

In the 1960s and 1970s, few Pacific peoples worked in mainstream media and Pacific peoples were often portrayed negatively. Political support for a Pacific voice in the media, and community discontent expressed about the negative stories published on Pacific peoples, brought the issue to the fore in the 1970s. One of the first Pacific-oriented radio programmes to be aired was five minutes in duration and piggy-backed on the Māori language segment broadcast on Radio New Zealand. In the late 1970s, the New Zealand Journalists' Training Organisation actively encouraged the involvement of Pacific peoples in the media industry. This was followed in 1986 by the setting up of the Pacific journalism course at the Manukau Technical Institute (Crocombe, 1992).

Pacific announcers began to feature on radio in the 1970s. The early announcers included Samoans and Niueans. These pioneering efforts led to the establishment of the first fully Pacific-owned community radio station in 1995. Radio 531 PI Limited is based in Auckland and broadcasts in nine languages. Other Pacific radio programmes include Samoan Capital Radio (Siufofoga o le Laumua) in Wellington, and a Christian radio station for Tongans and Samoans in Auckland. In 2002, Aotearoa/New Zealand's Pacific communities' first national radio network (Niu FM) broadcasting in Pacific languages began. Niu FM aims to provide Pacific peoples with accurate and current information that reinforces Pacific languages, values and cultures. Radio provides a space for Pacific peoples to discuss issues of interest to them in both English and Pacific languages (Macpherson, 2001).

In the print media, Pacific peoples have also made great strides. There are a growing number of Pacific journalists and writers featuring in mainstream publications, including Sarona Aiono-Iosefa, Tapu Misa, Sandra Kailahi and Martha Samasoni. Current Pacific publications include English and Pacific language magazines and newspapers, such as *Samoana*, the *Cook Island Star*, *Tautua*, and the *Pacific Star*.

Pacific participation in television has developed along similar lines to radio. Again, early Pacific programmes ran alongside Māori programming, with a Pacific viewpoint being shown on an irregular basis. 'See here' (*Titiro Mai*), a five-minute studio show in the 1970s, provided Pacific peoples with a regular presence on TV. In 1987, *Tangata Pasifika* was piloted, paving the way for Pacific presenters and producers. Pacific peoples, like April Bruce, Bernice Mene, Taualeo`o Stephen Stehlin, Ngaire Colely, John Utanga, Osone Okesene, Shimpal Lelisi, Oscar Kightley, Christopher Fa`afoi, Jason Fa`afoi, Frank Bunce and Lisa Taouma are now featuring more prominently in all areas of mainstream and Pacific television. In an age of rapidly changing technology, Pacific peoples are striving to maintain their identity through control of their own media.

Pacific women doing it for themselves

In 1975 PACIFICA was established to give Pacific women opportunities to plan and work for the development of themselves, their families and their communities. PACIFICA initially facilitated information dissemination and provided support amongst Pacific women migrants. PACIFICA has since developed and delivered many initiatives within the education, health, social and welfare sectors.

Sport highlights

Pacific peoples' first introduction to western sports came through British colonisation. They have adapted some sports, like cricket, from a quiet and subdued gentlemanly game by adding a little island flavour *kilikiti* (cricket – island style). *Kilikiti* involves young and old, women and men. The emphasis is on cultural values: group membership, relationships and identity (Te`evale, 2001). The first Pacific Kilikiti festival was held in Christchurch at Hagley Park in 1992. It attracted over 2500 people.

The Pacific Islands Church (PIC) Netball Club was formed by some of Wellington's early Pacific Island immigrants, in order to care for the spiritual and sports needs of their community. The PIC Netball Club is one of New Zealand's oldest, successful, premier clubs, and is a regular national title holder. It is acknowledged as a leading netball nursery in New Zealand, producing players of international calibre who have represented New Zealand, Samoa and the Cook Islands (Lay, 1996).

Since the 1970s, Pacific peoples have made other remarkable sporting achievements and contributions. The following is a representative list (Te`evale, 2001):

- All Black rugby greats: Bryan Williams (1970s Rugby Player of the Decade), Joe Stanley, Michael Jones, Va'aiga Tuigamala, Olo Brown, Frank Bunce, Walter Little, Jonah Lomu, Pita Alatini, Bradley Mika, Carl Hoeft, Tana Umaga, Keven Mealamu, Rodney So'oialo, Doug Howlett and Ma'a Nonu.

- Bernice Mene and Ana No'ovao, former captains of national Silver Ferns netball team
- Beatrice Faumuina, world athletics champion (discus) and 1997 New Zealand Sports Person of the Year
- David Tua and Jimmy Peau achieved international fame in both the amateur and professional ranks of boxing
- Rita Fatialofa, netball and softball player, member of the New Zealand Women's Softball team that won the 'World Crown' in 1982
- Joan Hodge netball, softball player, and the longest serving Silver Fern in the 1980s
- Jeremy Stanley, rugby and softball player at international level.

Social and economic status of Pacific peoples in Aotearoa/New Zealand

Pacific peoples are diverse in culture and language, but share a common migration and history of assimilation in Aotearoa/New Zealand. During the past 60 years the status of Pacific peoples has changed considerably. They have endured the indignity of the 'dawn raids', and an ongoing stereotyping as recently-arrived immigrants. A stereotype such as 'Fresh off the boat', ignorant of life in Western industrialised countries, suggests that Pacific peoples are visitors, not long-term residents, and ignores the fact that the majority of Pacific peoples in New Zealand are born here (Krishnan, Schoeffel, and Warren, 1994).

The social and economic status of Pacific peoples in New Zealand has positive and negative aspects.

Problem areas for Pacific peoples	Positive aspects for Pacific peoples
One of the lowest income levels	Growing number of community-based initiatives and 'By Pacific, for Pacific' service providers[2]
Highest unemployment rate	Pacific youth, culture, arts and fashion gaining greater recognition. Pasifika Festival celebrated its tenth anniversary in 2002
Fewer businesses owned by Pacific people	Growing numbers using entrepreneurial skills
Poor health status	Growing number of distinguished sportspeople
Poor housing	Increasing number of Pacific Members of Parliament
Over-represented in crime statistics	Two Pacific judges appointed 2002
Lower participation and achievement rates in education	Tertiary education providers must be responsive to Pacific people in terms of funding and monitoring
Fewer households own a car or a telephone	The Disability and Pacific Action Plan launched to reduce inequalities between Pacific people and others
Significant loss of Pacific languages	Language taught from early childhood to tertiary level

Conclusion

This chapter gives voice to and validates the experiences of our Pacific communities and their contribution to the society of Aotearoa/New Zealand. Their story is one of courage, sacrifice, love and service. It is a story that echoes the experiences of the first Pacific voyagers to settle in Aotearoa/New Zealand and their struggle to adapt to a new land. Over the years, the negative experiences of Aotearoa/New Zealand's Pacific peoples have given them a greater appreciation of the Māori struggle against the marginalising consequences of colonisation. Māori language and educational programmes have become models for local Pacific communities. The new generations of Aotearoa/New Zealand-born Pacific peoples increasingly recognise the position of Māori as the *tangata whenua*, just as Māori recognise the diverse cultural strengths of their Pacific relations, and seek to forge relationships as Indigenous people with Pacific societies in Aotearoa/New Zealand and wider Oceania.

Notes

1. 'Overstayers' referred to people who lived and worked in New Zealand illegally after the expiration of their immigration permits. Ironically only a third of 'overstayers' were Pacific Islanders, though more than two thirds of those prosecuted were from the Pacific.
2. 'By Pacific, for Pacific' services are Pacific initiatives run by Pacific providers for Pacific peoples in areas such as education, health and employment.

FURTHER READING

Boyd (1990), Lal and Fortune (2000), and Lay (1996) provide good general overviews of this topic. Davidson (1967) writes on the Samoan perspective and Gilson (1980) provides information on the Cook Islands. Statistics are available from Statistics New Zealand (1998 and 2002); Ministry of Pacific Island Affairs publications; and the New Zealand Yearbook (1990).

He papakupu
Glossary

āhua	form, appearance
ariki	paramount chief, high born chief
aroha	love, concern for others, sympathy, charity
aruhe	fernroot
atua	ancestor of on-going influence
aukati	border, boundary marking a prohibited area
haka	posture dances of various types
hākari	feast
hapū	clan
harakeke	flax
he taonga tuku iho	a gift from the ancestors, an inheritance
heke	rafter; migrate
hinengaro	mind
hongi	pressing of noses in greeting
hui	meeting, gathering
ihi	the personal force aroused within a person
iwi	tribe, people
kai	food
kāinga	home, village
kapa haka	Māori performing group
karakia	ritual chant
karanga	call; woman's call onto a *marae*
kaumātua	elder
kawa	protocol, procedure
kāwanatanga	government
kete	basket, kit
kīnaki	relish, embellishment
koha	gift
kōrero	talk, speech, narrative
koruru	carved face on the gable of the meeting house
kōwhaiwhai	painted designs
kuia	female elder, elderly woman
kūmara	sweet potato
maihi	bargeboards
mākutu	inflict physical and psychological harm and even death through spiritual powers
mana	authority, power, influence, prestige, status
mana motuhake	separate power, autonomy
manaaki	care for; show hospitality, empathy
manuhiri	visitors
Māoritanga	Māori culture
marae	space in front of a meeting house, the *marae* and the buildings around it

mātauranga Māori	Māori knowledge
mauri	life principle, life force
Māori	an Indigenous person of Aotearoa/New Zealand
mihi	greeting, speech of greeting
moko	Māori tattoo
mokopuna	grandchild
mōteatea	traditional chant, lament
muka	prepared flax fibre
noa	free from *tapu*
oriori	lullaby, chant about a chiefly child's descent and tribal history
pā	fortified village
paepae	horizontal board; speakers of the *tangata whenua*
Pākehā	a non Māori of European origin
Pākehātanga	Pākehā culture
pepeha	tribal sayings
pōhiri/pōwhiri	rituals of encounter, welcome ceremony on a *marae*
poi	ball on a string used in the performing arts
pounamu	greenstone, nephrite
poupou	carved wall figures; side posts of a meeting house
poutama	ascending steps of a *tukutuku* design
pou tuarongo	centre post at the back wall of a meeting house
pūtōrino	a traditional flute usually made of wood
rāhui	closed season, temporary prohibition on a resource
rangatira	chief
rangatiratanga	right to exercise authority, sovereignty
raranga	weaving, plaiting
ringawera	kitchen workers
rohe	territory, boundary
rūnanga	council, discuss in an assembly
tāhuhu	ridgepole
taiaha	close quarters combat long weapon
tamariki	children
tangata Māori	Māori person
tangata whenua	local people, hosts, people of the land
tangihanga	rites for the dead
tāniko	border for cloaks, etc. made by finger weaving
taonga	treasured item, prized possession
tapu	under the influence of *atua* protection, sacred, prohibited, restricted
tara whānui	wide side of the *wharenui*
tātai	recite genealogies, line of ancestry
taurekareka	war slave
te ao Māori	the Māori world
te Ao-mārama	the world of light
te Korekore/te Kore	the realm of potential being; the void
te pō	the night, the place of departed spirits
te reo Māori	the Māori language
teina/tēina	younger sibling/s of same gender; junior line

tihei mauri ora	the sneeze of life
tikanga Māori	Māori cultural practices
tikanga	plan, protocols, customs
tinana	person's physical reality; body
tino rangatiratanga	self-determination, home rule
tipuna/tupuna	ancestor, grandparent
tīpuna/tūpuna	ancestors, grandparents
tohunga	priest, skilled person; expert
tūāhu	ritual sites of *tohunga* for divination and other mystic rites
tuakana/tuākana	elder sibling/s of the same gender; senior line
tukutuku	ornamental lattice work
tūpāpaku	corpse
tūtūā	commoners
urupā	burial ground
utu	compensation, repayment, reciprocity
waiata	song, chant
waiata aroha	love song
waiata tangi	lament, song of mourning
wahine	woman, wife
wāhine	women, wives
wairua	spiritual life principle; spirit
waka	canoe
wana	a thrilling feeling felt during a performance
wānanga	a tertiary institution that caters to Māori learning needs established under the Education Act 1990; debate, discuss
wehi	a response of awe in reaction to *ihi*
whaikōrero	oratory, speech
whakairo	carving, art
whakanoa	to free from *tapu*
whakapapa	genealogical table
whakataukī	cryptic saying, aphorism, proverb
whakanoa	to free from *tapu*
whānau	extended family
whanaunga	relations
whanaungatanga	kinship network, relationship
whāngai	adopt, adopted child
whare	house, building
wharemate	house of mourning, bereaved family and chief mourners
whare wānanga	house of learning; university
whare whakairo	carved house
wharekai	dining hall
wharenui	large house, meeting house
whatumanawa	seat of emotions
whenua	land, placenta

Te rārangi kaituhi
List of contributors

Pakaariki Harrison is Ngāti Porou. He was the *tohunga whakairo* for a number of *wharenui*, including Whaiora (Ōtara), Mōkau Pūrekireki (Pirongia), Ōtāwhao (Te Awamutu College), Manukau Institute of Technology, Manurewa Marae, Tāne-nui-a-Rangi (Auckland University) and St Stephen's School, Bombay, Auckland. He has exhibited in the UNESCO Buildings in Paris, and in Montana, Ohio, Seattle, Hawai'i, New Caledonia and Beijing. He is the designer of the current New Zealand bank notes and a Te Waka Toi Consultant for Marae and Arts. Pakaariki was awarded an Honorary Doctorate of Literature from the University of Auckland (1991) and a Q.S.O. (2000). He lives at Kennedy's Bay in the Coromandel, and is currently teaching *whakairo* at Te Wānanga o Aotearoa, Te Awamutu.

Janine Hayward teaches in the Department of Political Studies at the University of Otago. She has published on the Waitangi Tribunal, the Treaty and local government, and Māori affairs administration. She teaches New Zealand politics, environmental politics, and Treaty/Indigenous politics. She is currently working on Māori representation in local government.

Rawinia Higgins is from Ngāi Tūhoe and is a Lecturer in Te Tumu, School of Māori, Pacific and Indigenous Studies at the University of Otago. She is currently working on her PhD thesis which is examining the political dimensions behind *moko kauae* amongst Tūhoe from 1920 to the 1950s and current renaissance culture.

Brendan Hokowhitu of Ngāti Pūkenga, teaches in Te Tumu, School of Māori, Pacific and Indigenous Studies at the University of Otago. He has published articles on Māori masculinity, the use of the '*Ka mate*' haka by the All Blacks, Māori and sport, and the history of Māori and State physical education. He teaches courses on critical Western theory, colonisation and Indigenous methodology. He is currently researching the sociological antecedents of Māori male violence.

E. Lorraine Johnston is a Lecturer in Māori language in Te Tumu, the School of Māori, Pacific and Indigenous Studies, at the University of Otago, where she is also completing a PhD. Her research interests include language change, the reversal of language shift, and second language learning and bilingualism. Her PhD topic is syntactic change in Māori language. Lorraine has published in the area of sociolinguistics, and has presented many conference papers related to her research on Māori language.

Tānia M. Ka'ai, the Dean of Te Tumu, the School of Māori, Pacific and Indigenous Studies, is of Te Whānau-a-Ruataupare of Ngāti Porou, Ngāti Wheke of Ngāi Tahu, Hawaiian, Samoan, and Cook Island descent. She holds a Doctor of Philosophy in Māori Education. She has advanced the political status of *te reo Māori* by helping to establish Kōhanga Reo and Kura Kaupapa Māori as educational options for Māori parents in rural communities. Professor Ka'ai specialises in *Kaupapa Māori* research. She has an extensive knowledge of the history of the Māori language and Indigenous epistemology which has been the focus of her writing and research. She is currently working on a celebration of the life of Kumeroa Ngoingoi Pēwhairangi from Te Whānau-a-Ruataupare.

Jane McRae is a Lecturer on Māori oral literature in the Department of Māori Studies at the University of Auckland. She has written on literature in Māori in *The Oxford History of New Zealand Literature* (1991) and on the history of the transition from Māori orality to literacy in *Book & Print in New Zealand* (1997) and *A Book in the Hand* (2000). Her most recent research has been on the Māori-language newspapers, contributing to and jointly editing the book of articles *Rere atu, taku manu! Discovering history, language and politics in the Maori-language newspapers* (2002).

Nathan W. Matthews is from the Ngāti Toki *hapū* of Ngā Puhi. He teaches *te reo Māori* in Te Tumu, the School of Māori, Pacific and Indigenous Studies at the University of Otago. He is currently working on his PhD, which focuses on Catholic Māori Secondary Education.

John C. Moorfield has a Doctor of Literature and is a Professor in Te Tumu, the School of Māori, Pacific and Indigenous Studies at the University of Otago. He taught for eight years in secondary schools and then for twenty-one years in the Department of Māori at the University of Waikato. His major publications are the *Te Whanake* series of four textbooks and associated resources for teaching Māori to adults, which are widely used in tertiary institutions. He has also published on aspects of the Māori language including being co-editor for the first autobiography written in *te reo Māori*, *He Hokinga Mahara* by Hēmi Pōtatau. He is currently collecting data for a dictionary of loanwords used in the Māori-language newspapers.

Erik Olssen retired as Professor of History at the University of Otago in 2002. He has published extensively on New Zealand history, including some 60 articles and several books, including a *History of Otago* (1984) and (with Marcia Stenson) *A Century of Change: New Zealand 1800–1900* (2nd ed., 1997). He currently chairs the Special Committee for the Alexander Turnbull Library and belongs to the Policy Committee for the History Group, the Ministry of Culture and Heritage. He is an Emeritus Professor of the University of Otago and a James Cook Fellow.

Karyn Paringatai is from the Te Whānau-a-Hunaara *hapū* of Ngāti Porou. She is a Teaching Fellow in Te Tumu, the School of Māori, Pacific and Indigenous Studies at the University of Otago where she teaches in the areas of Māori language and Māori performing arts. She is currently working towards her MA on the development of *poi* within Aotearoa/New Zealand and its connections to the Pacific.

Lachy Patterson is currently completing a PhD on the content and impact of the Māori language newspapers from 1855 to 1863. Several publications have surfaced from his research, including two chapters in *Rere Atu, Taku Manu*, a collection of essays on the Māori language newspapers. He has an interest in nineteenth century New Zealand history, especially race relations, as well as *te reo Māori me ōna tikanga*. He is currently employed as a lecturer in the *te ao Māori* programme at the Otago Polytechnic.

Chris Prentice is of English, Scottish and Te Āti Awa descent from Taranaki. She teaches New Zealand and post-colonial literatures in the Department of English at the University of Otago. As well as publishing on literary works by Māori and other Indigenous writers, her research focuses on questions of the politics of cultural difference, from indigenous perspectives, where the post-colonial meets globalisation. This research takes a comparative approach to materials and contexts from Aotearoa-New Zealand, Australia, Canada and Pacific Island nations.

Michael P. J. Reilly first studied *te reo Māori* at Rutherford High School in Te Atatū, Auckland. He graduated with an MA in Māori Studies from Victoria University of Wellington, and a PhD in Pacific Islands History from the Australian National University. Formerly a joint Lecturer in Māori Studies and History at the University of Otago, he is now a Senior Lecturer in Te Tumu, the School of Māori, Pacific and Indigenous Studies. He has written on European ethnographers, such as John White; Māori historical narratives; and the history of Mangaia (The Cook Islands).

Michelle Saisoa'a is of Samoan and Tongan descent. She is a Lecturer in Te Tumu the School of Māori, Pacific and Indigenous Studies. She co-developed a series of Pacific Studies papers in Te Tumu. She is currently completing a PhD titled, 'Sport, Culture, Race and Gender with particular references to Polynesian sportswomen'.

John Stenhouse teaches in the Department of History at the University of Otago. He recently co-edited, and contributed chapters to, *Disseminating Darwinism: The Role of Place, Race, Religion,* and *Gender and God and Government: The New Zealand Experience*. He has published articles on aspects of New Zealand history in various New Zealand and overseas journals. He is currently working on missionary science, looking at interactions between missionaries and indigenous peoples in the cultivation and global dissemination of modern Western sciences.

Kahu Te Kanawa is of the Ngāti Kinohaku *hapū* of Ngāti Maniapoto. She learnt the art of *raranga* from her mother, Diggeress Te Kanawa, and her grandmother, Dr Rangimārie Hetet. Commissioned works by her have included those for the Royal Scottish Museum and the British Museum and she has exhibited and travelled nationally and internationally. In 1998, she graduated with a Postgraduate Diploma in Fine Arts from the University of Auckland. Kahu has lectured, demonstrated and taken workshops throughout Aotearoa/New Zealand and Australia. She is currently a part-time senior lecturer for Unitec in Auckland, where she developed a Certificate and Diploma programme in *Mahi Raranga*.

Jim Williams of Kai Tahu is a Lecturer in Te Tumu, the School of Māori, Pacific and Indigenous Studies, at the University of Otago. His area of research includes traditional Māori ways and Māori environmental management, with particular emphasis on his own *iwi*, Kai Tahu. He is currently working on his PhD, in which he argues a pre-contact environmental ethic in Te Wai Pounamu.

Te rārangi pukapuka
Bibliography

Anderson, Atholl. 1980. Towards an Explanation of Protohistoric Social Organisation and Settlement Patterns Amongst the Southern Ngai Tahu. *New Zealand Journal of Archaeology*, 2: 3–23.

Anderson, Atholl. 1983. *When All the Moa Ovens Grew Cold: Nine Centuries of Changing Fortune for the Southern Maori.* Dunedin: Otago Heritage Books.

Anderson, Atholl. 1991. *Race Against Time: the early Maori-Pakeha families and the development of the mixed-race population in southern New Zealand.* Dunedin: University of Otago.

Anderson, Atholl. 1998. *The Welcome of Strangers: An Ethnohistory of Southern Maori AD 1650–1850.* Dunedin: Otago University Press.

Anderson, Atholl. 2002. A fragile plenty: Pre-European Māori and the New Zealand environment. In Pawson, Eric and Tom Brooking (eds.) *Environmental Histories of New Zealand*, pp. 19–34. Melbourne: Oxford University Press.

Arvidson, K. 1991. Aspects of Contemporary Māori Writing in English. In McGregor, Graham and Mark Williams (eds.) *Dirty Silence: Aspects of Language and Literature in New Zealand*, pp. 117-128. Auckland: Oxford University Press.

Asher, George, and David Naulls. 1987. *Maori Land.* Wellington: New Zealand Planning Council.

Awatere, Arapeta. 1975. Review of *Maori Poetry: the Singing Word*, by Barry Mitcalfe. *The Journal of the Polynesian Society*, 84(4): 510–519.

Ball, D. G. 1940. Maori Education. In Sutherland, I. L. G. (ed.) *The Maori People Today: A General Survey.* Wellington: The New Zealand Institute of International Affairs and the New Zealand Council for Educational Research.

Ballara, Angela. 1990. Hongi Hika. In *The Dictionary of New Zealand Biography: Volume One* 1769–1879, pp. 201–202. Auckland: Bridget Williams Books.

Ballara, Angela. 1991. The Origins of Ngāti Kahungunu. PhD thesis, Victoria University of Wellington.

Ballara, Angela. 1995. Porangahau: The Formation of an Eighteenth-Century Community in Southern Hawke's Bay. *New Zealand Journal of History*, 29(1): 3–18.

Ballara, Angela. 1998. *Iwi: The dynamics of Māori tribal organisation from c. 1769 to c. 1945.* Wellington: Victoria University Press.

Barrington, John. 1998. Learning the 'Dignity of Labour': secondary education policy for Maoris. *New Zealand Journal of Educational Studies*, 23 (1): 45–58.

Barrington, John M., and T. H. Beaglehole. 1974. *Maori Schools in a Changing Society: An Historical Review.* Wellington: New Zealand Council for Educational Research.

Beatson, P. 1989. *The Healing Tongue: Themes in Contemporary Maori Literature.* Studies in New Zealand Art and Society 1. Eds. Dianne Beatson and Peter Beatson. Palmerston North: Sociology department, Massey University.

Beattie, J. Herries. 1918. Traditions and Legends. Collected from the Natives of Murihiku (Southland, New Zealand). *Journal of the Polynesian Society*, 27: 137–161.

Beattie, J. Herries. 1941. *Moriori: the Moriors of the South Island.* Dunedin: Otago Daily Times and Witness Newspapers.

Beattie, J. Herries. 1954. *Our Southernmost Maoris.* Dunedin: Otago Daily Times and Witness Newspapers.

Belich, James. 1996. *Making Peoples: A History of the New Zealanders From Polynesian Settlement to the End of the Nineteenth Century.* Auckland: Allen Lane/Penguin Press.

Bell, A. 1990. The Politics of English in New Zealand. In McGregor, G. and M. Williams (eds.) *Dirty Silence: Aspects of Language & Literature in New Zealand*, pp. 65–76. Auckland: Oxford University Press.

Bellwood, Peter, James J. Fox and Darell Tryon (eds.) 1995. *The Austronesians: Historical and Comparative Perspectives.* Canberra: Australian National University.

Benton, R. 1987. The Māori Language: From the Treaty of Waitangi to the Waitangi Tribunal. In Hirsch, W. (ed.) *Language Revival and Maintenance in New Zealand Today.* Auckland: Office of the Race Relations Conciliator.

Best, Elsdon. 1924. *The Maori.* Vol 1. Wellington: Harry H. Tombs.

Best, Elsdon. 1925. *Games and Pastimes of the Maori.* Wellington: Whitcombe and Tombs Limited.

Best, Elsdon. 1974. *The Maori as He Was.* Wellington: Government Printer.

Best, Elsdon. 1976. *Maori Religion and Mythology, Part 1.* Wellington: Government Printer.

Best, Elsdon. 1995. *Maori Religion and Mythology II*, Wellington: Te Papa Tongarewa, Museum of New Zealand.

Biggs, Bruce. 1961. The Structure of New Zealand Maori. *Anthropological Linguistics*, 111(3): 1–53.

Biggs, Bruce. 1968. The Maori Language Past and Present. In Schwimmer, Erik (ed.) *The Maori People in the nineteen-sixties: a symposium*, pp. 65–84. Auckland: Blackwood and Janet Paul.

Biggs, Bruce. 1989. Towards the Study of Maori Dialects. In Harlow, Ray, and Robin Hooper (eds.) VICAL 1: *Oceanic Languages: Papers from the Fifth International Conference on Austronesian Linguistics*, pp. 61–75. Part I. Auckland: Linguistic Society of New Zealand.

Biggs, Bruce. 1997. *He Whiriwhiringa.* Auckland: Auckland University Press.

Biggs, Bruce and Pei Te Hurinui Jones. 1995. *Nga Iwi o Tainui.* Auckland: Auckland University Press.

Binney, Judith. 1990. Papahurihia, Penetana. In *The Dictionary of New Zealand Biography: Volume One 1769–1879*, pp. 329–330. Auckland: Bridget Williams Books.

Binney, Judith. 1996. Ancestral Voices: Maori Prophet Leaders. In Sinclair, Keith (ed.) *The Oxford Illustrated History of New Zealand*, pp. 153–184. Auckland: Oxford University Press.

Boyd, Mary. 1990. New Zealand and the other Pacific Islands. In Sinclair, Keith (ed.) *The Oxford Illustrated History of New Zealand*, pp. 295–322. Auckland: Oxford University Press.

Brougham, A. E., A. W. Reed, and Tīmoti Kāretu. 1987. *Māori Proverbs.* Auckland: Heinemann Reed.

Broughton, Ruka. 1983. *The Origins of Ngaa Rauru Kiitahi.* Wellington: Department of Maori Affairs.

Buck, Peter, (Te Rangi Hiroa). 1949. *The Coming of the Māori*, Wellington: Whitcombe and Tombs.

Buck, Peter, (Te Rangi Hiroa). 1950. *The Coming of the Māori.* Second edition. Wellington: Whitcombe and Tombs.

Butterworth, G. V. 1973. Highpoint and Hiatus. In Bray, Douglas H. and Clement G. N. Hill (eds.) *Polynesian and Pakeha in New Zealand Education: Volume 1 The Sharing of Cultures*, pp. 7–17. Auckland: Heinemann Educational Books.

Butterworth, G. V and H. R. Young. 1990. *Maori Affairs.* Wellington: GP Books.

Clarke, David L. 1968. *Analytical Archaeology.* Methuen, London.

Colenso, William. 1867. Essay on the Maori Races of New Zealand. *Transactions and Proceedings of the New Zealand Institute.* Vol. 1.

Colenso, William. 2001. *On the Vegetable Food of the Ancient New Zealanders before Cook's Visit.* Christchurch: Kiwi Publishers. Original 1880.

Crocombe, Ron. 1992. *Pacific Neighbours New Zealand's Relations with Other Pacific Islands.* Christchurch: Centre for Pacific Studies University of Canterbury.

Curnow, Jenifer. 1985. Wiremu Maihi Te Rangikaheke: His Life and Work. *Journal of the Polynesian Society*, 94: 97–147.

Dansey, Harry. 1975. A View of Death. In King, Michael (ed.) *Te Ao Hurihuri: The World Moves On*, pp. 105–116. Wellington: Hicks Smith and Sons.

Davidson, Janet. 1984. *The Pre-history of New Zealand.* Auckland: Longman Paul.

Davidson, J.W. 1967. *Samoa mo Samoa the emergence of the Independent State of Western Samoa.* Melbourne: Oxford University Press.

Davis, Te Aue. 1990. *He Korero Pūrākau Mo Ngaa Taunahanahatanga a Ngā Tūpuna.* Wellington: New Zealand Geographic Board.

Dewes, Te Kapunga. 1977. The Case for Oral Arts. In King, Michael (ed.) *Te Ao Hurihuri: The World Moves On*, pp. 46–63. Auckland: Hicks Smith.

Durie, Mason H. 1998. *Te Mana, Te Kāwanatanga.* Auckland: Oxford University Press.

Elsmore, Bronwyn. 1985. *Like Them That Dream: The Maori and the Old Testament.* Tauranga: Moana Press.

Elsmore, Bronwyn. 1999. *Mana from Heaven: A Century of Maori Prophets in New Zealand.* Auckland: Reid Publishing.

Evans, Jeff. 1997. *Ngā Waka o Neherā: The First Voyaging Canoes.* Auckland: Reed Books.

Evans, Jeff. 1998. *The Discovery of Aotearoa.* Auckland: Reed Books.

Evans, M. 1985. Politics and Maori Literature. *Landfall* 153, (39: 1), pp.40-45.

Evison, Harry C. 1993. *Te Wai Pounamu: The Greenstone Island: A History of the Southern Maori during the European Colonization of New Zealand.* Christchurch: Aoraki Press.

Fairburn, Miles. 1975. The Rural Myth and the New Urban Frontier: An Approach to New Zealand Social History, 1870–1940. *New Zealand Journal of History*, 9 (1): 3–21.

Fishman, J. A. 1980. Minority Language Maintenance and the Ethnic Mother Tongue School. *Modern Language Journal*, 64(2): 167–172.

Gilson, Richard. 1980. *The Cook Islands 1820–1950.* Wellington: University of Victoria.

Goldie, T. 1989. *Fear and Temptation: The Image of the Indigene in Canadian, Australian and New Zealand Literatures.* Kingston, Ontario: McGill-Queens University Press.

Grey, Alan. 1994. *Aotearoa and New Zealand: A Historical Geography.* Christchurch: Canterbury University Press.

Grey, George. 1853. *Ko nga Moteatea me nga Hakirara o nga Maori.* Wellington: Robert Stokes.

Grey, George. 1854. *Ko nga Mahinga a nga Tupuna.* London: George Willis.

Grey, George. 1855. *Polynesian Mythology.* London: John Murray.

Grey, George. 1956. *Polynesian Mythology.* Christchurch: Whitcombe and Tombs.

Grey, George. 1971. *Nga Mahi a nga Tupuna.* 4th ed. Edited by H. W. Williams. Wellington: Reed.

Grove, R.N. 1985. Te Whatanui: Traditional Maori Leader. M.A. thesis, Victoria University of Wellington.

Gudgeon, W. E. 1895. The Maori Tribes of the East Coast of New Zealand (Part II). *Journal of the Polynesian Society*, 4: 17–32.

Guerin, Louise. 1986, 15 March. A teller of tales. In Beatson, David (ed.) *NZ Listener*, 20. Wellington: BCNZ.

Hainsworth, David. 1967. Iron Men in Wooden Ships: The Sydney Sealers. *Labour History*, 13.

Hall-Jones, John. 1990. Chaseland, Thomas. In *The Dictionary of New Zealand Biography: Volume One 1769–1879*, p. 80. Auckland: Bridget Williams Books.

Hanson, F. Allan, and Louise Hanson. 1983. *Counterpoint in Maori culture.* London: Routledge and Kegan Paul.

Harawira, Wena. 1997. *Te Kawa o te Marae: A guide for all marae visitors.* Auckland: Reed.

Harker, R. 1985. Schooling & Cultural Reproduction in Political Issues. In *New Zealand Education*. Palmerston North: Dunmore Press.

Harker, R.K. and K. R. M. McConnochie. 1985. *Education as cultural artifact: Studies in Maori and Aboriginal education.* Palmerston North: Dunmore Press.

Harlow, Ray. 1979. Regional Variation in Māori. *New Zealand Journal of Archaeology*, 1: 123–138.

Harlow, Ray. 1991. Contemporary Māori language. In McGregor, Graham, and Mark Williams (eds.) *Dirty Silence: Aspects of Language and Literature in New Zealand*, pp. 29–38. Oxford: Oxford University Press.

Harlow, Ray. 2001. *A Māori Reference Grammar.* Auckland: Longman/Pearson Education New Zealand Ltd.

Harvard-Williams, P. (ed.) 1961. *Marsden and the New Zealand Mission: Sixteen Letters.* Dunedin: University of Otago Press.

Heim, O. 1998. *Writing Along Broken Lines: Violence and Ethnicity in Contemporary New Zealand Literature.* Auckland: Auckland University Press.

Hewitt, D. 1992. Culture, Conflict and Learning Styles: Experience from Teaching Aboriginal Students. Unpublished paper.

Hogan, Helen (ed.) 1994. *Renata's Journey.* Christchurch: Canterbury University Press.

Hokowhitu, Brendan J. 2002. Te Mana Māori – Te Tātari i ngā Kōrero Parau. Ph.D thesis, University of Otago.

Howe, Kerry. 2003. *The Quest for Origins.* Auckland: Penguin.

Huata, Ngāmoni. 2000. *The Rhythm and Life of Poi.* Edited by Te Rita Papesch. Auckland: HarperCollins Publishers.

Hunkin-Tuiletufuga, Galumalemana. 2001. Pasefika Languages and Pasefika Identities: Contemporary and Future Challenges. In Macpherson, Cluny, Paul Spoonley, and Melani Anae (eds.) *Tangata O Te Moana Nui the Evolving Identities of Pacific Peoples in Aotearoa/New Zealand*, pp. 196–211. Palmerston North: Dunmore Press.

Hunn, J. K. 1961. *Report on Department of Maori Affairs: With Statistical Supplement.* Wellington: Government Printer.

Ihimaera, Witi and Long, D. (eds.) 1982. *Into the World of Light: An Anthology of Maori Writing.* Auckland: Heinemann.

Jameson, R. G. 1842. *New Zealand, South Australia, and New South Wales: a record of recent travels in these colonies, with especial reference to emigration and the advantageous employment of labour and capital.* London: Smith, Elder.

Jenkins, Kuni and Tānia Ka'ai. 1994. Maori education: A Cultural Experience and Dilemma for the State – a New Direction for Maori Society. In Coxon, Eve, Kuni Jenkins, James Marshall and Lauran Massey (eds.) *The Politics of Learning and Teaching in Aotearoa – New Zealand*, pp. 148–179. Palmerston North: Dunmore Press.

Johansen, J. Prytz. 1954. *The Maori and his Religion in its Non-Ritualistic Aspects.* Copenhagen: Ejnar Munksgaard.

Jones, Pei Te Hurinui. (comp.) 1995. *Nga iwi o Tainui: The traditional history of the Tainui people: Nga Koorero tuku iho a nga tupuna.* Edited and annotated by Bruce Biggs. Auckland: Auckland University Press.

Kaa, Wiremu and Te Ohorere Kaa. 1996. *Mohi Turei: Āna Tuhinga i Roto i Te Reo Māori.* Wellington: Victoria University Press.

Ka'ai, Tānia M. 1995. Te Tātari i Te Kaupapa. D.Phil. thesis, University of Waikato.

Ka'ai-Oldman, Tānia. 1980. A History of New Zealand Education from a Maori Perspective. In Hirsh, Walter and Raymond Scott (eds.). *Getting It Right.* Auckland: Office of the Race Relations Conciliator.

Karetu, S. 1975. Language and Protocol of the Marae. In King, Michael (ed.) *Te Ao Hurihuri: The World Moves On*, pp. 35–44. Wellington: Hicks Smith and Sons.

Karetu, S. 1978. Kawa in crisis. In King, Michael (ed.) *Tihe Mauri Ora.* New Zealand: Methuen New Zealand.

Kāretu, Tīmoti S. 1991. Te Ngahurutanga: A Decade of Protest, 1980-1990. In McGregor, Graham and Mark Williams (eds.) *Dirty Silence: Aspects of Language and Literature in New Zealand*, pp. 159–177. Auckland: Oxford University Press.

Kāretu, Tīmoti S. 1993. *Haka! Te Tohu o Te Whenua Rangatira: The Dance of a Noble People.* Auckland: Reed.

Kāretu, Tīmoti S. 1996. Ngā Waiata me ngā Haka a Tāua, a te Māori. In Moorfield, John C. *Te Whanake 4: Te Kohure*, pp. 56–70. Hamilton: Te Whare Wānanga o Waikato.

Kāretu, Tīmoti S. 2002. Maori Print Culture: The Newspapers. In Curnow, Jenifer, Ngapare Hopa and Jane McRae (eds.) *Rere atu, taku manu! Discovering history, language and politics in the Maori-language newspapers*, pp. 1–16. Auckland: Auckland University Press.

Kawharu, Merata. 1998. Dimensions of Kaitiakitanga. PhD diss., Oxford University.

Kendall, Thomas. 1815. *A Korao no New Zealand.* Sydney: G. Howe.

King, Michael. 1989. *Moriori: A People Rediscovered.* Auckland: Viking.

King, Michael. 1992. *Moko – Maori Tattooing in the 20th Century*. Auckland: David Bateman.
King, Michael, (ed.) 1992. *Te Ao Hurihuri: Aspects of Maoritanga*. Auckland: Reed Books.
Kirch, Patrick Vinton. 1984. *The Evolution of the Polynesian Chiefdoms*. New York: Cambridge University Press.
Knudtson, Peter and David Suzuki. 1992. *Wisdom of the Elders*. Toronto: Stoddart Publishing.
Knudtson, Peter and David Suzuki. 1992. In Barnhardt, R. Teaching/Learning Across Cultures: Stategies for Success. Unpublished Paper.
Kopua, Mark. 2001. Origins of Ta Moko. On Ta Moko website: http://www.tamoko.org.nz/articles/origins.htm.
Krishnan, Vasantha, Penelope Schoeffel and Julie Warren. 1994. *The Challenge of Change: Pacific Island Communities in New Zealand, 1986–1993*. Wellington: NZ Institute for Social Research & Development.
Kruger, Tamati. 1984. The Qualities of Ihi, Wehi and Wana. In Mead, H. M. *Nga Tikanga Tuku Iho a te Maori: Customary Concepts of the Maori*. Wellington: Department of Māori Studies, Victoria University of Wellington.
Lal, Brij V. and Kate Fortune (eds.) 2000. *The Pacific Islands: an Encyclopaedia*. Honolulu: University of Hawai`i Press.
Lay, Graeme. 1996. *Pacific New Zealand*. Auckland: David Ling.
Lee, Samuel. 1820. *A Grammar and Vocabulary of the Language of New Zealand*. London: Church Missionary Society.
Little, B. 1969. The Sealing and Whaling Industry in Australia Pre-1850. *Australian Economic History Review*, 9: 109-127.
Lovegrove, M.N. 1966. The scholastic achievement of European and Maori children. *New Zealand Journal of Educational Studies*, 1 (1): 15–39.
McGeorge, Colin. 1993. Race, Empire and the Maori in the New Zealand Primary School Curriculum. In Mangan, J. A. (ed.) *The imperial curriculum: Racial images and education in the British colonial experience*, pp. 64–78. London: Routledge.
McGregor, Graham, and Mark Williams (eds.) 1991. *Dirty Silence: Aspects of Language and Literature in New Zealand*. Oxford: Oxford University Press.
McKinnon, Malcolm (ed.) 1997. *New Zealand Historical Atlas*. Auckland: David Bateman.
McLean, Mervyn. 1996. *Maori Music*. Auckland: Auckland University Press.
McLean, Mervyn and Margaret Orbell. 1975. *Traditional Songs of the Maori*. Auckland: A. H. and A. W. Reed.
McLean, Mervyn and Margaret Orbell. 1990. *Traditional Songs of the Maori*. Auckland: Auckland University Press.
McNaughton, H. 1998. Drama. In Sturm, Terry (ed.) *The Oxford History of New Zealand Literature in English*, pp. 321–393. Oxford: Oxford University Press.
Macpherson, Cluny. 2001. One Trunk Sends Out Many Branches: Pacific Cultures and Cultural Identities. In Macpherson, Cluny, Paul Spoonley, and Melani Anae (eds.) *Tangata O Te Moana Nui the Evolving Identities of Pacific Peoples in Aotearoa/New Zealand*, pp. 66–80. Palmerston North: Dunmore Press.
McRae, Jane. 1998. Māori Literature: A Survey. In Sturm, Terry (ed.) *The Oxford History of New Zealand Literature in English*, pp. 1–24. 2nd ed. Auckland: Oxford University Press.
McRae, Jane. 2000. Māori Oral Tradition Meets the Book. In Griffith, Penny, Peter Hughes, and Alan Loney (eds.) *A Book in the Hand*, pp.1–16. Auckland: Auckland University Press.
Mahuika, Api. 1992. Leadership: Inherited and Achieved. In King, Michael (ed.) *Te Ao Hurihuri: Aspects of Maoritanga*, pp. 42–63. Wellington: Reed Books.
Mara, Diane, Lita Foliaki, and Eve Coxon. 1994. Pacific Islands Education. In Coxon, Eve, Kuni Jenkins, James Marshall, and Lauran Massey (eds.) *The Politics of Learning and Teaching in Aotearoa-New Zealand*, pp. 180–214. Palmerston North: Dunmore Press.
Marsden, Maori. 1992. God, Man and Universe: A Maori View. In King, Michael (ed.) *Te Ao Hurihuri: Aspects of Maoritanga*, pp. 117–137. Auckland: Reed Books.
Mead, H. M. 1984. *Te Māori*. Auckland: Heinemann.

Mead, Hirini Moko and Neil Grove. 2001. *Ngā Pēpeha a ngā Tīpuna: The Sayings of the Ancestors.* Wellington: Victoria University Press.
Mead, Sidney. 1968. *The Art of Maori Carving.* Wellington: A. H. and A. W. Reed.
Mead, Sidney. 1969. Imagery, Symbolism and Social Values in Maori Chants. *Journal of the Polynesian Society*, 78: 378–404.
Mead, Sidney. 1984. *Te Māori: Maori Art from New Zealand Collections.* Auckland: Heinemann.
Mead, Sidney. 1986. *Magnificent Te Maori: Te Maori Whakahirahira – he korero whakanui i te Maori.* Auckland: Heinemann.
Mead, Sidney. 1997. *Landmarks, Bridges and Visions: Aspects of Maori culture.* Wellington: Victoria University Press.
Melbourne, Hirini. 1991. Whare Whakairo: Māori 'Literary' Traditions. In McGregor, Graham and Mark Williams (eds.) *Dirty Silence: Aspects of Language and Literature in New Zealand*, pp. 129–41. Auckland: Oxford University Press.
Melbourne, Hirini. 1993. *Toiapiapi.* Wellington: Tīti Tuhiwai.
Melbourne, Hirini. 1994. Nga taonga Pūoro Tawhito a te Maori. In *Te Wharekura 41*, pp. 1–33. Wellington: Learning Media.
Metge, Joan. 1976. *The Maoris of New Zealand Rautahi.* Revised ed. London: Routledge and Kegan Paul.
Metge, Joan. 1995. *New Growth from Old: The Whānau in the Modern World.* Wellington: Victoria University Press.
Ministry of Justice. 2001. *He Hinātore Ki te Ao Māori: A Glimpse into the Māori World.* Wellington.
Mita, M. 1984. Indigenous Literature in a Colonial Society. *The Republican*, 52. pp. 4-7.
Moorfield, John C. 1996. *Te Whanake 4: Te Kōhure.* Kirikiriroa: Te Whare Wānanga o Waikato.
Morton, Harry. 1982. *The Whale's Wake.* Dunedin: University of Otago Press.
Mutu, Margaret. 2002. Barriers to Tangata Whenua Participation in Resource Management. In Kawharu, Merata (ed.) *Whenua: Managing our Resources*, Auckland: Reed Publishing.
New Zealand Department of Education. 1984. *Report on Taha Maori in Schools: Suggestions For Getting Started.* Wellington: New Zealand Government Printer.
New Zealand Education Department. 1908. *The School Journal*, 2, (1).
New Zealand Educational Institute. 1967. *Report and Recommendations on Maori Education.* Wellington: New Zealand Government Printer.
Ngata, Apirana. 1970. *Nga Moteatea.* Part III. Translated by Pei Te Hurinui. Auckland: The Polynesian Society.
Ngata, Apirana. 1974. *Nga Moteatea.* Part I. Auckland: The Polynesian Society.
Ngata, Apirana. 1974. *Nga Moteatea.* Part II. Translated by Pei Te Hurinui. Auckland: The Polynesian Society.
Ngata, Apirana. 1990. *Nga Moteatea.* Part IV. Auckland: The Polynesian Society.
Oliver, Steven. 1990. Te Rauparaha. In *The Dictionary of New Zealand Biography: Volume One 1769–1879*, pp. 504-507. Auckland: Bridget Williams Books.
Oppenheim, Roger S. 1973. *Maori Death Customs.* Wellington: A. H. Reed and A. W. Reed.
Orange, Claudia. 1987. *The Treaty of Waitangi.* Wellington: Allen and Unwin.
Orange, Claudia and Ormond Wilson. 1990. Taiwhanga, Rawiri. In *The Dictionary of New Zealand Biography: Volume One 1769–1879*, pp. 417-418. Auckland: Bridget Williams Books.
Orbell, Margaret. 1978. *Maori Poetry.* Wellington: Victoria University Press.
Orbell, Margaret. 1991. *Waiata. Maori Songs in History.* Auckland: Reed Books.
Orbell, Margaret. 1992. *Traditional Māori Stories.* Auckland: Reed Books.
Orbell, Margaret. 1995. *The Illustrated Encyclopedia of Māori Myth and Legend.* Christchurch: Canterbury University Press.
Orchiston, Rene. 1994. *Harakeke The Rene Orchiston Collection.* Revised edition. Lincoln: Manaaki Whenua.
Papesch, Te Rita Bernadette. 1990. Pupuritia Ngā Purapura i Mahue Mai Rā: Te Waiata-ā-ringa: 1960–1990. M.A. thesis, University of Waikato.
Parr, C. J. 1961. A Missionary Library. Printed Attempts to Instruct the Maori, 1815–1845. *The Journal of the Polynesian Society*, 70(4): 429–450.

Patterson, John. 1992. *Exploring Maori Values.* Palmerston North: Dunmore Press.
Pearson, David. 1990. *A Dream Deferred: The Origins of Ethnic Conflict in New Zealand.* Wellington: Allen and Unwin: Port Nicholson Press.
Pearson, W. 1973. The Maori and Literature. In Curnow, Wystan (ed.) *Essays on New Zealand Literature,* pp. 137-138.. Auckland: Heinemann Educational.
Pewhairangi, Ngoi (comp.) 1985. *Tuini: Her Life and Her Songs.* Gisborne: Te Rau Press.
Pewhairangi, Ngoi. 1992. Foreword to Michael King (ed.) *Te Ao Hurihuri: Aspects of Maoritanga.* Auckland: Reed Books.
Phillis, Eliza Onehou. 2001. *Eruera Manuera.* Wellington: Huia.
Pool, D. Ian. 1977. *The Maori Population of New Zealand 1769–1971.* Auckland: Auckland University Press.
Prickett, Nigel. 2001. *Maori Origins From Asia to Aotearoa.* Auckland: David Bateman.
Prickett, Nigel. 2002. First Settlement Date and Early Rats: an opinion poll. *Archaeology in New Zealand,* 45 (4): 288–292.
Puketapu-Hetet, E. 2000. *Maori Weaving.* Auckland: Longman.
Ramsay, Peter. 1972. Maori Schooling. In Havill, S. J. and D. R. Mitchell (eds.) *Issues in New Zealand Special Education,* pp. 60–76. Auckland: Hodder and Stoughton.
Rangihau, John. 1992. Being Maori. In King, Michael (ed.) *Te Ao Hurihuri: Aspects of Maoritanga,* pp.185–190. Wellington: Reed Books.
Reedy, Anaru (ed.) 1993. *Ngā Kōrero a Mohi Ruatapu.* Christchurch: Canterbury University Press.
Reedy, Anaru (ed.) 1997. *Ngā Kōrero a Pita Kāpiti.* Christchurch: Canterbury University Press.
Report of the Waitangi Tribunal on The Te Reo Maori Claim WAI 11. 1986. Wellington: GP Publications.
Rogers, A. and Simpson, M. 1993. *Te Tīmatanga Tātau Tātau: Early Stories from Founding Members of the Māori Women's Welfare League.* Wellington: Māori Women's Welfare League and Bridget Williams Books.
Salmond, Anne. 1975. *Hui: A Study of Maori Ceremonial Gatherings.* Auckland: Heinemann Reed.
Salmond, Anne. 1976. *Amiria: The Life Story of a Maori Woman.* Auckland: University of Auckland, Department of Anthropology.
Salmond, Anne. 1997. *Between Worlds: Early Exchanges Between Maori and Europeans 1773–1815.* Auckland: Viking.
Savage, John. 1807. *Some account of New Zealand; Particularly the Bay of Islands and surrounding country.* London: W. Wilson.
Scheele, Sue. 1994. *Harakeke: the Renee Orchiston Collection.* Lincoln: Manaaki Whenua Print.
Schrempp, Gregory. 1992. *Magical Arrows: the Maori, the Greeks, and the Folklore of the Universe.* Madison, Wisconsin: The University of Wisconsin Press.
Scott, Dick. 1975. Ask *That Mountain: The Story of Parihaka.* Auckland: Heinemann/Southern Cross.
Shirres, Michael P. 1982. Tapu. *The Journal of the Polynesian Society,* 2 (1): 29-51.
Shirres, Michael P. 1997. *Te Tangata: the human person.* Auckland: Accent Publications.
Simmons, David, R. 1976. *The Great New Zealand Myth.* Wellington: Reed.
Simms, Norman. 1978. Maori Literature in English: An Introduction. *World Literature Today,* 52.
Simon, Judith. 1990. The place of schooling in Maori-Pakeha relations. PhD thesis, University of Auckland.
Simon, Judith. 1998 (ed.). *Ngā Kura Māori: The Native Schools System 1867–1969.* Auckland: Auckland University Press.
Sinclair, Douglas. 1992. Land: Maori View and European Responses. In King, Michael (ed.) 1992 *Te Ao Hurihuri.* Auckland: Reed.
Sissons, Jeffrey, Wiremu Wi Hongi and Pat Hohepa. 1987. *The Puriri Trees are Laughing: A political history of Nga Puhi in the inland Bay of Islands.* Auckland: Polynesian Society.
Sissons, Jeffrey, Wiremu Wi Hongi and Pat Hohepa. 2001. *Ngā Pūriri o Taiamai. A Political History of Ngāpuhi in the Bay of Islands.* Auckland: Reed/Polynesian Society.
Smith, Graham Hingangaroa. 1991. *In Abstentia: Maori Education Policy and Reform.* Monograph

No. 4. Auckland: The University of Auckland Research Unit for Maori Education.

Smith, Linda Tuhiwai. 1999. *Decolonizing Methodologies: Research and Indigenous Peoples*. London: Zed Books; Dunedin: University of Otago Press.

Smith, Norman. 1960. *Maori Land Law*. Wellington: A. H. and A. W. Reed.

Smith, S. Percy. 1898. *Hawaiki: the whence of the Maori*. Wellington: Whitcombe and Tombs.

Smith, S. Percy. 1910. *History and traditions of the Maoris of the West Coast, North Island, New Zealand*. New Plymouth: Polynesian Society.

Spriggs, Matthew. 1984. The Lapita Cultural Complex. *Journal of Pacific History*, 19: 202–233.

Statistics New Zealand. 1998. Te Tari Tatau. 1996. Census of Population and Dwelling, Iwi Volume 1. Wellington: Statistics New Zealand.

Statistics New Zealand. 2002. 2001 Census Snapshot 4: Māori.

Statistics New Zealand Te Tari Tatau. 2002. *Pacific Progress: A Report on the Economic Status of Pacific Peoples in New Zealand*. Wellington: Statistics New Zealand.

Stevens, Emma. 1993. The Kaati Maamoe Hapuu of Mahitahi: A Question of Mana? M.A. thesis, University of Otago.

Strong, T. 1931. The problem of educating the Māori. In Jackson, P.M. (ed.) *Maori and Education: On the Education of Natives in New Zealand and Its Dependencies*. Wellington: Ferguson and Osborn.

Taule`ale`ausumai, Feiloaiga. 2001. New Religions, New Identities: The Changing Contours of Religious Commitment. In Macpherson, Cluny, Paul Spoonley and Melani Anae (eds.) *Tangata O Te Moana Nui the Evolving Identities of Pacific Peoples in Aotearoa/New Zealand*, pp. 181–195. Palmerston North: Dunmore Press.

Tauroa, Hiwi and Pat Tauroa. 1986. *Te Marae – A Guide to Customs and Protocol*. Auckland: Reed.

Te`evale, Tasileta. 2001. We are What We Play: Pacific Peoples, Sport and Identity in Aotearoa. In Macpherson, Cluny, Paul Spoonley, and Melani Anae (eds.) *Tangata O Te Moana Nui the Evolving Identities of Pacific Peoples in Aotearoa/New Zealand*, pp. 212–227. Palmerston North: Dunmore Press.

Te Kanawa, D. 1992. *Weaving a Kakahu*. Wellington: Bridget Williams Books.

Te Puni Kōkiri. 1998. *National Māori Language Survey, 1995*. Wellington.

Te Puni Kōkiri. 2002. *The Health of the Māori Language in 2001*. Wellington.

Te Rangikāheke, Wiremu Maihi. 1992. *The Story of Maui*. Edited with translation and commentary by Agathe Thornton. Christchurch: University of Canterbury Press.

The Commission on Education in New Zealand (Chairman – Sir George Currie) 1962. Report of The Commission on Education in New Zealand. Wellington: R.E. Owen, Government Printer.

Thornton, Agathe. 1987. *Maori Oral Literature as Seen by a Classicist*. Wellington: Huia.

Tiatia, Jemaima. 1998. *Caught Between Cultures: A New Zealand-Born Pacific Island Perspective*. Auckland: Christian Research Association.

Tikao, Teone Taare. 1939. *Tikao Talks*. Wellington: A. H. and A. W. Reed.

Tiramōrehu, Matiaha. 1987. *Te Waiatatanga mai o te Atua: South Island Traditions*. Edited by Manu van Ballekom and Ray Harlow. Christchurch: Department of Maori, University of Canterbury.

WAI 11. 1986. Finding of the Waitangi Tribunal Relating to Te Reo Maori and a Claim Lodged by Huirangi Waikerepuru and Nga Kaiwhakapumau I Te Reo Incorporated Society.

Walker, Ranginui. 1975. Marae: A place to stand. In King, Michael (ed.) *Te Ao Hurihuri: The World Moves On*. Wellington: Hicks Smith and Sons.

Walker, Ranginui. 1987. *Nga Tau Tohetohe: Years of Anger*. Auckland: Penguin Books.

Walker, Ranginui. 1990. *Ka Whawhai Tonu Matou: Struggle Without End*. Auckland: Penguin Books.

Walker, Ranginui. 1992. The Relevance of Maori Myth and Tradition. In King, Michael (ed.) *Te Ao Hurihuri: Aspects of Maoritanga*, pp. 170–182. Auckland: Reed Books.

Walker, Ranginui. 1996. *Ngā Pepa A Ranginui: The Walker Papers*. Auckland: Penguin Books.

Walsh, Allen Crosbie. 1971. *More and More Maoris*. Christchurch: Whitcombe and Tombs.

Ward, Alan. 1986. Alienation Rights in Traditional Maori Society: A Comment. *Journal of the Polynesian Society*, 95: 259–265.

Ward, Alan. 1995. *A Show of Justice: racial 'amalgamation' in nineteenth century New Zealand.* Auckland: Auckland University Press.

Ward, Alan. 1999. *An Unsettled History: Treaty Claims in New Zealand Today.* Wellington: Bridget Williams Books.

Watson, John. 1967. *Horizons of Unknown Power: Some Issues of Maori Schooling.* Wellington: New Zealand Council for Educational Research.

Webster, Steven. 1998. *Patrons of Maori Culture: Power, Theory and Ideology in the Maori Renaissance.* Dunedin: University of Otago Press.

Wedde, Ian and Harvey McQueen (eds.) 1985. *The Penguin Book of New Zealand Verse.* Auckland: Penguin.

Wevers, Lydia. 1998. The Short Story. In Sturm, Terry (ed.) *The Oxford History of New Zealand Literature in English*, pp. 246–320. Oxford: Oxford University Press.

Whatahoro, H. T. 1913, Vol. 1. 1915, Vol. 2. *The Lore of the Whare-wānanga; or Teachings of the Maori College on Religion, Cosmology, and History.* Translated by S. Percy Smith. New Plymouth: the Polynesian Society.

Williams, David V. 2002. *Crown Policy Affecting Maori Knowledge Systems and Cultural Practices.* Wellington: Waitangi Tribunal.

Williams, Herbert W. 1924. *A Bibliography of Printed Maori to 1900, and supplement.* Wellington: Government Printer.

Williams, Herbert W. 1971. *Dictionary of the Maori Language.* 7th ed. Wellington: GP Publications.

Wilson, Ormond. 1985. *From Hongi Hika to Hone Heke: a quarter century of upheaval.* Dunedin: John McIndoe.

Wilson, Ormond. 1990. *Kororareka & Other Essays.* Dunedin: John McIndoe.

Winiata, Maharaia. 1956. Leadership in Pre-European Maori Society. *Journal of the Polynesian Society*, 65(3): 212–31.

Winiata, Maharaia. 1967. *The Changing Role of the Leader in Maori Society: a study in social change and race relations.* Auckland: Blackwood and Janet Paul.

Wright, Harrison M. 1959. *New Zealand 1769–1840: The Early Years of Western Contact.* Cambridge, Mass.: Harvard University Press.

Maps:

Ngā Pou Taunaha o Aotearoa, New Zealand Geographic Board. 1995. *Te Ika a Māui, The Land and its People* circa 1840.

Ngā Pou Taunaha o Aotearoa, New Zealand Geographic Board. 1995. *Te Wai Pounamu, The Land and its People* circa 1840.

Ngā kuputohu
Index

Page numbers in italic indicate illustrations

adoption, 63
ahi-kā, 53, 55
Āhua, 2
Anae, Anae Arthur, 231
ancestors, 26, 51, 54, 63, 64, 117, 119, 222–223
Ao Hou, Te, 215, 217, 221
Aotea (*waka*), 27, 28, 31
Aotearoa National Māori Performing Arts Festival, 187
apakura, 103
ariki, 14, 64, 119
   qualities, 91–92
   roles, 93
   tribal society and, 92–93
   women, 93
aroha, 17
arts, 116–132, 187 – see also performing arts
astronomy, 40
Atamai, 2
atawhai tangata, 92
atua, 1, 13–14, 15, 50, 52, 73, 124 – see also names of individual *atua*
   raranga and, 124–125
   tangihanga and, 85
   whakairo and, 117, 118, 119

Bay of Islands, 42, 140–141, 142–143, 145, 148, 149, 150, 165, 173, 191
Benton, Richard, 43
Best, Elsdon, 9–11
biculturalism, 16, 197–198, 199, 203, 215
bilingualism, 42–43, 46, 48–49
Boyd, 143, 145
broadcasting, 44, 48, 204, 235 – see also television
Broughton, John, 216
Broughton, Ruka, 97, 138
Brown, Riwia, 216
Browne, Thomas Gore, 166, 173
Bruce, Mary (née Atahoe), 145
Buck, Sir Peter (Te Rangi Hīroa), 87, 89, 96
Busby, James, 152, 153, 154, 155
Butterfield, Rev., 194–195

Caddell, James, 145
canoes – see *waka*
Carroll, Sir James, 179
carving – see *whakairo*
Chatham Islands, 32, 176
chiefs – see *ariki*; *rangatira*
children, 62, 63, 70
Christianity, 1, 69, 149, 172–173, 178–180 – see also missionaries; religion
   Pacific peoples, 231–232
Church Missionary Society, 141
class, 67
classical society, 34, 61–67
Colenso, William, 39, 42, 154
Contemporary Māori Arts group, 123
Cook, James, 140, 145
Coolangatta Statement, 188, 189
Cooper, Whina, 96, 178, 183, *183*
Crawley, Louisa, 230–231
creation narratives, 1–12, 50
   creation of humanity, 8–9
   genealogy, 3
   in carvings, 122
   in literature, 219
   myth-messages, 9–12
cultural deficit theories, 195–197
cultural renaissance, 131, 187–188, 214–215
Currie Report, 196, 203
Customary Title, 59

death customs, 17, 43, 73, 77, 85–90, 103
Declaration of Independence (1835), 152, 155, 158
difference, celebration of, 22–23, 24
diseases, European-introduced, 145, 148, 163, 173
Draft Declaration on the Rights of Indigenous Peoples, 188, 189
Duff, Alan, 216, 217

education, 190–200 – see also Kōhanga Reo; Kura Kaupapa; universities; Wānanga; Wharekura
   chronology of dates and events, 202–204
   cultural deficit theories, 195–197
   initiation of state education, 42, 191–193
   Kaupapa Māori ideology, 207–212
   Labour and Tomorrow's Schools, 199
   missionary, 42, 190–191, 203, 204
   Pacific peoples, 232–234
   physical labour, 193–195
   steps towards biculturalism (1970s), 43, 197–198, 203
   Taha Māori programmes, 198–199, 200
   te reo and, 42–43, 44, 46, 48, 49, 201–213
elders (*kaumātua*), 22, 23, 52, 73, 75, 192, 211–212 – see also *kuia*
English language, 42–43, 45, 46, 48
Europeans, early contacts with, 140–150, 151–153

Field, Taito Phillip, 231
fiscal envelope, 186
flax, 40, 108, 123–124, 125–126
Fletcher, Thomas, 195
French interest in Aotearoa, 152, 156

genealogy – see *whakapapa*
Gosche, Mark, 231
Government (*kāwanatanga*), 157–158, 163 – see also Parliament
   challenges to, 163–170
Grace, Patricia, 138, 217–219, *219*, 220–221, 222, 223, 224–226
Grace-Smith, Briar, 216–217, 221
grandparents, 62
'Great Fleet', 26, 27–29, 32
Grey, Sir George, 136, 137, 166, 202

hahunga, 89, 90
haka, 106–108, 184 – see also *kapa haka*
haka pōhiri, 79, 108
haka taparahi, 107
hākari, 17, 89
Hakuturi, 118, 120
hapū, 1, 14, 19, 22, 51, 63–64, 71, 73, 164, 208
   alternative to descriptions of classical Māori, 64–66
   leadership of, 92–93
   modern changes, 69–70, 71
   overlapping interests of *iwi* and, 54
harakeke, 40, 108, 123–124, 125–126
hari, 111–112
Harrison, Pakaariki, 98, *121*
Hauhau (Pai Marire), 70, 131, 166, 173–174
Haumia-tiketike, 4, 5, 50
Hawaiki, 26–27, 31, 39
Hawke, Joe, 187
He Taua, 184–185
Henare, Sir James, 96, 202
Hetet, Rangimārie, 97, 128, 129
Hīkoi of Hope, 179
Hine-hau-one/Hine-ahu-one, 9, 10, 82
Hine-nui-te-pō, 85
Hine-te-iwaiwa, 108, 124
hinengaro, 18, 210
Hobson, William, 152, 153, 154
Hokioi, Te, 42, 183
Hone Heke, 149, 165, 173
hongi, 81–82, 83, 88
Hongi Hika, 142, 143, 144, 146, 148, 149
Horouta, 27
hue, 112
hui, 17, 43, 73, 83, 88
hui-ā-tau, 21
Hulme, Keri, 216, 218, 220
Huna, 124
Hunn Report, 196, 197, 203
hura kōhatu, 90
Huru-kokoti, 143
Hūtana, Īhāia, 194

Iharaira, 169, 179
ihi, 114
Ihimaera, Witi, 138, 216–217, 219, 220, 221–223, *222*, 224, 225
Indigenous peoples, 21, 188–189
infiltration of mainstream society, 185–186
Institute of Māori Arts and Crafts, 123
intermarriage with Europeans, 70, 145–146, 148
Io, 1–3, 11
Io-wahine, 9, 10, 11
Iti, Tame, 186
iwi, 1, 14, 19, 21, 22, 26, 34, 64, 71, 73, 164, 208
   alternative to descriptions of classical Māori, 64–66
   leadership of, 92–93
   modern changes, 69–70, 71
   overlapping interests of *hapū* and, 54

Jones, Pei Te Hurinui, 97, 134, 137

kaea, 111
kai, 19, 52, 82, 91
kāinga, 17, 34, 63, 66
kaioraora, 103, 108
kaitātaki tāne, 111
kaitātaki wahine, 111
kaitiaki, 52, 89, 92
kaitiakitanga, 50, 52, 53, 54
kapa haka, 70, 73, 100, 111, 112
karakia, 1, 55, 77, 83, 89, 134
karanga, 78, 79, 87, 88, 90
Kāretu, Tīmoti, 98, 187
Kari-Oca Declaration, 188, 189
Kāti Māmoe, 33, 52
Kauhanganui (Māori Parliament), 161, 167
kaumātua (elders), 22, 23, 52, 73, 75, 192, 211–212 – see also *kuia*
Kaupapa Māori ideology, 207–213
   key indicators, 208
   te ara poutama, 208–209
   te tātari i te kaupapa, 210–212
   tuakiri tangata, 209–210
kāuta, 76
kawa, 80, 87
Kawana, Phil, 216
kāwanatanga, 157–158, 161 – see also Parliament
   challenges to, 163–170
Kawiti, 165
Kendall, Thomas, 41, 42, 146, 149, 191
kete whakairo, 126
kiekie, 126
Kīngitanga, 42, 160, 161, 165–166, 167
kinship (*whanaungatanga*), 9–10, 18, 24, 61–72, 110, 184 – see also *manaaki*
kiri tuhi, 131
knowledge, constructing, organising and using, 22, 24
kōauau, 113

koha, 81, 88
Kōhanga Reo, 44, 70, 99, 181, 204, 205–206, *206*, 212, 213
Kohimarama conference (1860), 159–160
kōrero, 83, 117, 118, 133
kōrero pūrākau, 41
Kororāreka, 142, *142*, 143, 165
koru, 118
Kotahitanga movement, 70
Kouka, Hone, 216, 221, 223–224
kōwhaiwhai, 41, 75, 124
kuia, 89
kūmara, 31, 34, 40
Kupe tradition, 26–27
kupu whakaari, 80–81
Kura Kaupapa Māori, 44, 70, 186, 187, 204, *207*, 212, 213
Kurahaupō, 27, 31

Laban, Luamanuvao Winnie, 231
Labour Party, 170, 178, 185
lakalaka, 231
land, 22, 23 – see also resources
   alienation of, 56–59
   attitudes to, 50–70
   boundaries, 55–56
   confiscations of, 166, 167, 168, 175, 186
   contemporary concerns, 59
   in literature, 224–225
   Polynesian origins of attitudes to, 51–54
land and resource rights, 50, 52, 53–54, 63, 66
   disputes, 54, 55
   Treaty of Waitangi and, 159
land sales, 165, 166, 167
   pre-1840, 149, 155–156
landscape, 13, 19, 20–21, 22, 23
   ancestors in, 54
Lapita pottery, 36
leadership – see also *ariki*; *rangatira*
   attributes of leaders, 95–96
   contact period, 146–147
   list of leaders, 96–98, 187
Leavai, Felix, 228
Lee, Samuel, 41–42, 149
Lesa, Falemaʻi, 230
life expectancy, 149
literacy, 22, 149, 150
literature, 133–138
   new literature, 137–138
   printing of, 136–137
literature in English, 214–226
   carving and weaving in, 220–221
   elders and ancestors in,

222–224
　land in, 224–225
　language, 218–219
　marae, *wharenui* and cultural spaces in, 221
　perspectives on international and new concerns, 225–225
　significant moments in publication of, 215–216
　rural and urban life, 217–218
　themes and distinctive features, 216–217
　time conception in, 220
　traditional narratives, 219
Lovegrove, Malcolm, 197

mahi kai, 91
mahinga kai, 52
Mahuta, Sir Robert, 187
mākutu, 77, 80, 87
male behaviour, myth-message concerning, 11
mana, 13–14, 15, 17, 22, 50, 55, 131, 201–202
　component of *whakairo*, 117
　leadership based on, 91, 92, 93
mana atua, 14
mana Māori motuhake, 163–170
mana moana, 15
mana motuhake, 15, 131, 165
Mana Motuhake Party, 70, 185
mana tangata, 14, 92, 131
mana whenua, 15, 52, 92
manaaki, 67–68, 92
manaakitanga, 75, 82
manaia, 118, 120
manawa wera, 107
Maniapoto, 94–95
manu ngangahu, 111
manuhiri, 75, 76, 77, 78–79, 80, 81, 82, 83, 88, 90
Māori Councils, 169
Māori Land Court, 56, 64, 69, 70
　– see also Native Land Court
Māori Language Commission, 44, 46, 186, 202
Māori Language Week, 184
Māori Village Day-Schools, 42, 192
Māori Women's Welfare League, 70, 178, 181, 183
Māoritanga, 16, 20, 23, 25, 110
marae, 17, 43, 68, 73–84, 201, 221–222
　committees, 70, 73–74
　speaking rights on, 79–80
　urban, 73, 83–84
　visitors to, 75, 76, 77, 78–79, 80, 81, 82, 83, 88, 90

marae ātea, 73, 76, 77, 78, 79, 83
maramataka, 40
Maranga Mai, 185
Marion du Fresne, 143
marriage, 63, 65
　cross-cultural, 70, 145–146, 148
Marsden, Māori, 1–2, 10, 97
Marsden, Samuel, 143, 144, 190
Mātaatua, 27, 223
Matakore, 95
mate aitu, 87
mate aituā, 87
mate rangatira, 87
mate tauā, 86–87
mate whaiwhaiā, 87
matua, 111
Māui-tikitiki-o-Taranga, 4, 20, 21, 26, 27, 85–86, 124
Maungakiekie, 186
mauri, 2, 13, 18, 26, 50, 80, 117, 201–202, 208, 210
media – see also broadcasting ; newspapers
　maintaining Pacific identity through, 234–235
Melbourne, Hirini, 97, 112, *113*, 134, 138, *184*, 187, 221
migration – see also canoe traditions ; Polynesian migrants
　internal, 33, 69
mihi whakatau, 83
mihimihi, 59, 83, 88
Milroy, Wharehuia, *44*, 98
missionaries, 41, 42, 141, 143, 146, 148, 149, 151, 152, 156, 172–173, 178 – see also Christianity
　education and, 190–191, 203, 204
moa, 34
moko, 129–131
　mythological beginnings, 129
　resurgence, 131, 187
　technology, 130
　tohunga tā moko, 130–131
moko tukupū wānanga, 118
mokopuna, 62
MOORH, 183
Moriori, 32, 147
mōteatea, 80, 87
Moteatea, Nga (Ngata & Jones), 134
Moutoa Gardens, 186
Muriwhenua, 186

narratives, 135–136, 219 – see also creation narratives
National Advisory Committee on Māori Education, 197, 203, 204
National Māori Language Survey, 44, 48
Native Districts, proposed, 160–161
Native Land Court, 167, 168, 169
　– see also Māori Land Court
Native Schools, 42, 191–195, *191*, *193*, 203
navigation, Polynesian, 29–31, 40
newspapers, Māori language, 137, 149, 166
Ngā Puhi, 1, 3, 142, 143, 146, 148–149, 165
Ngā Tamatoa, 184, 203
Ngā Whakapūmau i te Reo Inc., 186
Ngāi Tahu, 33, 52, 54, 142, 144, 146, 147–148, 175, 186
Ngāi Te Atawhiua, 52
Ngāre Raumati, 148
Ngāruawāhia, 167
Ngata, Sir Āpirana, 43, 96, 109, 110, 123, 138, 169, 170, 178, *178*, 179
Ngāti Awa, 186
Ngāti Kahungunu, 1, 3, 26, 56
Ngāti Mutunga, 147
Ngāti Porou, 44, 101, 107, 111, 113, 118–119, 210, 219, 223
Ngāti Rārua, 147–148
Ngāti Toa, 146–147, 164
Ngāti Tūwharetoa, 106
Ngāti Whātua, 186
Ngāwai, Tuīni, 110
ngeri, 107
nguru, 113
noa, 13, 15–16, 17, 22, 76
North Island (Te Ika-a-Māui), 20–21, 55, 57

ōhākī, 86
One Tree Hill, 186
oral literature, 133, 136
oral traditions of the homelands, 31–32
orality, 22
O'Regan, Sir Tīpene, 98, 187
oriori, 41, 105–106
Owen, Rina, 216
owheo, 55

pā, 34, 69
Pacific Island Educational Resource Centre, 233–234
Pacific peoples in Aotearoa, 100, 227–237
　early church pioneers, 231–232

education, 232–234
key moments in Aotearoa
  Pacific relations, 228–231
languages, 234
maintaining identity through
  the media, 234–235
social and economic status, 236
sport highlights, 235–236
women, 235
PACIFICA, 231, 235
pāeke, 80
paepae, 73, 79, 80, 117, 120, *121*
Pai Marire, 70, 131, 166, 173–174, 175
Paikea, 5, 219
pākati, 118
Pākehā-Māori, 143–144
Pākehātanga, 16
Papahurihia, 149, 173
Papa-tūā-nuku, 2, 3–7, 9, 14, 22, 50, 52, 75, 207, 224
pare, 117
pare kawakawa, 88
Parihaka, 167–168, *168*, 175, 187
Parliament
  Kauhanganui, 161, 167
  Māori representation, 168, 170, 178, 179
pātaka, 117, 121
pātere, 108, 109
patu, 109
pedagogy, 207, 208
pepeha, 41, 80
performing arts, 103–115
peruperu, 106, *106*
Pēwhairangi, Kumeroa Ngoingoi, 19, 96, 98–102, *99*, 110, 129
Picot Report, 199
pikopiko, 118
pīngao, 126
place-names, 21, 54
pō mihimihi, 88
pōhiri, 77, 78, 79, 82, 83, 88
poi, 107, 108–109
poi awe, 108
poi āwhiowhio, 112–113, *112*
pōkeka, 107–108
Polynesian migrants – see also canoe traditions
  becoming Māori, 35
  early peoples, 33
  homelands of, 27, 31–32
  internal migration, 33
  phases of occupation, 33–34
  what they brought with them, 31
Pompallier, Bishop, 149, 172
Pope, James H., 194, 203
poroporoaki, 83–84, 88, 89

pōtētē, 111
pounamu, 19, 34, 55, 148
  terms to describe different types, 39–40
poupou, 119–120
prophets, 173–178
prostitution, 145
protests, 161, 184
Proto-Austronesian language, 36, 38
puha, 107
pūkaea, 113
pūkana, 111
Purerehu, 145
pūrerehua, *112*, 113
pūtātara, 113
pūtōrino, 113, *113*
pūwerewere, 118

radio, 44, 204, 234
rāhui, 18, 22, 55, 93
Rakaihautū, 27
rangatira, 14, 15, 53, 55, 64, 68, 69, 86
  moko and, 131
  roles, 93
  tribal society and, 92–93
  women, 93
rangatiratanga, 52, 91–102, 158, 163, 166 – see also *tino rangatiratanga*
Rangihau, John Te Rangiāniwaniwa, 16–17, 23, *23*, 24–25, 96, 201–202
Rangi-nui, 2, 3–7, 14, 50, 75, 118, 120, 207, 224
rank, 66–67
raranga, 123–127, 129, 220–221
  classical period: 1650–1800s, 127–128
  materials and dyes, 125–127
  modern period: 1900–2000, 128–129
  origin of, 124–125
  transitional period: 1800–1900s, 128
Rata, Matiu, 97, 185
Rātana, Tahupōtiki Wiremu, 177–178, *177*
Rātana Church, 70, 169, 178, 179
Rātima, Ākenihi Pātoka Hape, *131*
raupatu, 166, 167, 168, 175, 186
raupō, 108
reciprocity, 24, 68
Reid, Tetika Dorie, 230
religion, 171–180 – see also Christianity; Pai Marire; Rātana Church; Ringatū

Renée, 216
Rereahu, 93–94
resource management, 55
resource rights – see land and resource rights
resources, 34, 35, 50, 51–52
Ringatū, 70, 131, 166, 176
ringawera, 76
Rohe Pōtae, 175
Rongo-mā-tāne, 4, 5, 50, 73, 83
Rua Kēnana Hepetipa, 169–170, 176–177, 179
Ruatara, 144, 172
Rua-te-pupuke, 116
rūnanga, 69, 70
rural communities, 42, 43, 217

Savage, John, 41, 140
schools – see education; Kōhanga Reo; Kura Kaupapa; Wharekura
seafarers, Māori, 144–145
sealing, 141–142
self-determination, 23, 24
Sharples, Pita, 98, 207, 225
Smith, Mike, 186
social change, 19th century, 147–149
social institutions, 13, 17
  – see also *hākari*; *hui*; *marae*; *tangihanga*; *wharekura*
social relationships, 13, 17–18
  – see also *kāinga*; *mana*; *noa*; *rāhui*; *tapu*; *tūrangawaewae*; *utu*; *whakanoa*; *whanaungatanga*
social structure, 14–16, 69–70
songs – see *waiata*
South Island (Te Wai Pounamu), 20, 27, 33, 54, 55, 56, 141, 142
sovereignty
  Crown, 152, 154, 155, 156, 157–158, 159, 163, 164
  Indigenous peoples, 188–189
  Māori, 158, 159, 181–188
spiritual and physical relationships, 13, 18–19 – see also *kai*; *hinengaro*; *mauri*; *tikanga*; *wairua*; *whenua*
spirituality, 22, 23
Stewart, Bruce, 217
Strong, Thomas, 195, 203
Sturm, J.C., 215, 216
Sullivan, Robert, 138, 216, 225
Sykes, Annette, 186

taha kikokiko, 13
Taha Māori educational programmes, 198–199, 200

taha wairua, 13
taharua, 65
tāhuhu, 74–75, 117, 119
taiao, 14
Tainui (tribes), 93, 110, 186
Tainui (waka), 27, 31, 80
Taiwhanga, 150
takahi, 112
takahi whare, 89
take, 50, 52, 53–54 – see also land rights
taki, 78
Tākitimu, 27, 30, 223
Tāne-mahuta, 3–4, 5, 6, 8–9, 10, 11, 14, 50, 82, 85, 108, 118, 120, 124, 126
tangata whenua, 50, 72, 78–79, 80, 81, 82, 83
Tangaroa, 4, 5, 6, 50, 118, 124, 126
tangihanga, 17, 43, 73, 77, 85–90, 103
tāniko, 128
taniwha, 52
taonga pūoro, 112–114, 187
tapu, 13, 15–16, 18, 20, 22, 76, 86, 89, 93
  moko and, 130
  raranga and, 124
  waewae tapu, 78
  whakairo and, 117, 122
Taranaki, war in, 166, 174
Tariao, 175
taro, 40
tātai, 19
tattooing – see *moko*
tauʻolunga, 231
tauparapara, 83, 210–211
taurekareka, 14
tauutuutu, 80
Tāwhiao, 105, 165, 175, 183
Tāwhiri-mātea, 4, 5, 11, 50, 118
Taylor, Āpirana, 216, 218
Te Ao Wairua, 2
Te Arawa (tribe), 26, 39, 80, 107–108, 119
Te Arawa (waka), 27, 28
Te Ataarangi Movement, 70, 204
Te Āti Awa, 33, 166, 174
Te Atua, 2
Te Atua Wera (Papahurihia), 149, 173
Te Aute Association, 169, 178
Te Aute College, 194
Te Haumanu, 112
Te Hauora, 2
Te Hura, 173
Te Ihinga-a-Rangi, 94
Te Ika-a-Māui (North Island), 20–21, 55, 57

Te Kanawa, Kahu, *126, 127*
Te Kapa Haka o Te Tumu, *115*
Te Kooti Arikirangi Te Tūruku, 74, 105, 166, 176, *176*
Te Korekore, 1, 2
Te Kotahitanga ki te Tiriti o Waitangi, 169
Te Kōwhao, 2
Te Maihara-nui, 147
Te Maihāroa, Hipa, 175
Te Mahara, 2
Te Māngai Pāho, 204
Te Morenga, 143, 148
Te Pahi, 143, 145
Te Pēhi Kupe, 147
Te Pō, 2, 5, 7
Te Puea Hērangi, 96, 110, 167
Te Pūoho, 148
Te Rangi Hīroa (Sir Peter Buck), 87, 89, 96
Te Rangikāheke, Wiremu Maihi, 3–5, 11, 91, *92*, 135, 137
Te Rangitāke, Wiremu Kīngi, 166, 174
Te Rauparaha, 55, 146–147, 148, 164
te reo Māori, 13, 22, 23, 36–49, 70, 164, 186, 201–213 – see also literacy
  bilingualism, 42–3, 46, 48–49
  chronology of dates and events, 202–204
  current socio-linguistic situation, 43–44
  literature in English and, 218–219
  origins, 36–8
  lexical expansion in, 44–46, 47
  orthographic development and print, 41–42
  pre-colonial world, 39–41
  regional dialects, 39
Te Roopu Raranga/Whatu o Aotearoa, 128
Te Taura Whiri i te Reo Māori, 44, 46
Te Ture Whenua 1993, 59
Te Ua Haumēne, 173–174, *174*
Te Wā, 2
Te Wai Pounamu (South Island), 20, 27, 33, 54, 55, 56, 141, 142
Te Wānanga, 2
Te Whakaaro, 2
Te Whakataupuka, 142
Te Whatahoro, Hoani, 1–3
Te Whē, 2
Te Wherowhero, Pōtatau, 165
Te Whiti-o-Rongomai, Erueti, 167–168, *167*, 175, 187

teina line, 14, 66, 67, 94–95
television, 44, 48, 99, 100, 204, 235
tikanga Māori, 13, 15, 18, 26, 35, 55, 67, 70, 73, 168, 172
  education and, 192, 196, 198, 199, 200, 208
time, conception of, 21, 24, 220
tinana, 18
tino rangatiratanga, 158, 159, 160, 161, 163, 164, 170, 181–188, 213
Tiramōrehu, Matiaha, 3, 5–7, 8–9, 10, 11
tiwha, 107
toa, 91
Tohu Kākahi, *167*, 168, 175, 187
tohunga, 1, 16, 89, 93, 203, 208
tohunga tā moko, 130–131
Toi, 116
Tokomaru, 27
tono mate, 88
trade with Europeans, 142, 145, 146, 147, 148, 151–152
Treaty of Waitangi, 56, 128, 151–162, *154, 155*, 169, 170
  formulating the document, 153
  ruled a nullity, 168–169
  signing of, 153–156, *155*
  texts and interpretations, 156–160
  today, 160–162
  tribal identity, 23 – see also *pepeha*; *whakapapa*
  collective identity and, 23
tūāhu, 73
tuakana line, 14, 15, 66, 67, 94–95
Tūhoe, 33, 105, 107, 111, 169, 179, 186, 223
Tūhoe Pōtiki, 33
Tuki-tahua, 143
tuku, 54
tukutuku, 41, 75, 124, 126
Tū-mata-uenga, 3, 4, 5, 10, 11, 50, 73, 79, 117, 119
tūpāpaku, 77, 87–89
tupuna, 26, 51, 54, 63, 64, 117, 119, 222–223
tūrangawaewae, 18
Tūrangawaewae Marae, 110
Tūria, Tāriana, 200
tūtū ngārahu, 107
tūtūā, 14
Tūwhare, Hone, 215, 216, *216*, 217, 224
Tūwharetoa, 39

uhi, 130
universities, 187, 203
urban *marae*, 73, 83–84

urban migration, 43, 195, 203, 214, 217–218
Uruao, 27, 33
urupā, 89
utu, 18, 68, 146, 147

venereal diseases, 145, 148
Volkner, Carl, 174–175

waerea, 77
wāhi tapu, 54, 55
wāhine – see women
waiata, 41, 80, 83, 134 – see also *karakia*; *mōteatea*
waiata-ā-ringa, 109–111
waiata aroha, 104, 110
waiata poi, 109
waiata tangi, 103–104, 110
waiata tohutohu, 105
waiata whaiāipo, 104–105
Waikato, war in, 166
Waikerepuru, Huirangi, 186
Wairoa conflict, 164
wairua, 18, 87, 88, 208, 210
Waitaha people, 27, 33, 113
Waitangi Day, 184, 185–186
Waitangi Tribunal, 161, 182, 186–187
   WAI 11 claim, 202, 204
waka, 35, 117, 121
   symbolism, 117
waka kinship groups, 26, 35, 64, 69, 70, 92
waka traditions, 26–35 – see also Polynesian migrants
   deliberate or accidental voyage debate, 29–31
   'Great Fleet', 26, 27–29, 32
   initial migration, 26–27
   landing places, 29
   two-wave theory, 32
wana, 114
wānanga, 119
Wānanga, 44, 186, 187
war, inter-tribal, 55, 65, 69, 143, 146
   manaaki and, 68
   muskets and, 69, 146, 147, 148
wars, land
   1840s, 149, 165, 173
   1860s, 166, 174
weaving – see *raranga*
wehi, 114
wero, 78
Whaanga, Īhaka, 130
whaikōrero, 19, 44, 78, 79–81, 86, 87, 88, 90, 149
whakaeke, 78–79
whakairo, 41, 116–117, 220–221
   elements of, 118–121
   gift from the ancestors, 121–123
   modern, 123
   rectilinear influence, 119
whakanoa, 17, 76, 82, 86, 88, 89
whakapapa, 13,14, 15, 16, 19, 27, 29, 61, 81, 124, 133, 136, 207
   connection to land by, 50, 51–54
   in literature, 222–224
   moko and, 131
   poi, 108
   South Island Māori, 33
   waiata and, 134
   whakairo and, 117, 119
whakatauāki, 41, 76
whakataukī, 41, 76, 80, 119
whakatautau, 111
Whakatōhea, 186
whakatū waewae, 107
whaling, 140–141, *141*, 142, 143, *143*, 144, 145, 147
whānau, 22, 50, 61–63, 71, 73, 208
   modern changes, 70, 71
   usages of, 61–62
whānau pani, 87–88, 89, 90
whanaungatanga (kinship), 9–10, 18, 24, 61–72, 110, 184 – see also *manaaki*
whāngai, 63
wharariki, 125
whare karakia, 73
whare tipuna, 73, 74–75, 80
   names for, 74
whare tūroro, 86, 89
whare wānanga, 116
wharekai, 73, 76, 83
Wharekura, 17, 44, 70, 186, *205*, 212, 213
wharemate, 77, 103
wharenui, 77, 79, 117, 121, 123, 208, 221–222
wharepaku, 73
wharepuni, 34, 76
Whatahoro, 9, 10
whenua, 19, 50, 54, 59 – see also land
whētero, 111–112
White, John, 137
Williams, Henry, 153, 154, 155, 156, 158, 159
wiri, 111
women
   conflicts over, 55, 65
   intimate relationships with Europeans, 145–146
   marae speaking rights and, 79–80
   myth-message concerning, 10–11
Pacific peoples, 235
relationship with the land, 22
seafarers, 145
trained for warfare, 109
Woon, Rev., 42
world-view, 13, 19–24, 133
   key indicators to understanding, 23–24

Yates, William, 42
Young Māori Party, 169, 194